SLAYING
THE TIGER

A YEAR INSIDE THE ROPES
ON THE NEW PGA TOUR

SHANE RYAN

Published in the United States by Ballantine Books, an imprint of Random House, a division of Penguin Random House LLC, New York.

BALLANTINE BOOKS and the HOUSE colophon are registered trademarks of Penguin Random House LLC.

Library of Congress Cataloging-in-Publication Data
Ryan, Shane.
Slaying the Tiger : a year inside the ropes on the new PGA tour / Shane Ryan.
pages cm
ISBN 978-0-553-39066-7
eBook ISBN 978-0-553-39067-4
1. Golf—Tournaments—United States—Anecdotes.   2. PGA Tour (Association)—Anecdotes.   3. Golfers—United States—Anecdotes.
4. Ryan, Shane—Anecdotes.   I. Title.
GV970.R92 2015
796.352'640973—dc23   2015010411

Printed in the United States of America on acid-free paper

www.ballantinebooks.com

2 4 6 8 9 7 5 3 1

First Edition

Book design by Susan Turner

TO EMILY

CONTENTS

SEPTEMBER   *A Final Push*

OCTOBER AND EVERYTHING AFTER

INTRODUCTION

My year on the PGA Tour began on Georgia's barrier islands, in November of 2013, at the Sea Island Golf Club—a course built on the salt marshes near an old antebellum plantation, full of stately live oaks and Spanish moss. There, I watched twenty-eight-year-old Chris Kirk navigate a tense Sunday to win the McGladrey Classic. The man he beat on the final hole, forty-one-year-old Briny Baird, held the bittersweet distinction of leading the PGA Tour career money list among players who had never won an event, and that day likely represented his last real chance to hold a trophy.

At the time, Kirk's victory gave me a sense of optimism for this book. I had a theory: The 2014 season, which began in the fall, would bring a generational shift in professional golf. The old stars—including Tiger Woods—would fade, and a new class would emerge. It would be a year, I thought, that would change the face of the sport. Watching an up-and-comer like Kirk beat a veteran like Baird seemed like a positive sign: I was onto something.

Of course, that hope existed beside fear: What if the old guard made a glorious last stand? What if Tiger won two majors, Phil Mickelson and Jim Furyk won the others, and Ernie Els won the Players Championship and the FedEx Cup? The whole project would be ruined, and I'd look back at Kirk's victory in Georgia with bitterness—a sunny day in a year of rain.

Over the next year, I embarked on a journey that took me to thirty tournaments, including all four majors and the Ryder Cup. I drove when I could—up and down the beautiful Pacific Coast highway in California, over the Colorado River and into Arizona's stark Sonoran Desert, through congested Florida resort towns, from rust-belt Ohio to sweltering Kentucky, across the deep south from Augusta to Hilton Head to the sand hills of North Carolina, west through the primordial Louisiana bayous, and into the heart of Texas—and flew when I couldn't, to Liverpool and finally to Scotland, where golf was born and the season concluded.

Throughout my travels, I made it my goal to learn—to *really* learn—everything I could about the rising generation. Writers and broadcasters have made a habit of treating golf like a religion, complete with sacred grounds and mythical heroes. They may be right about the sport's beauty and history, but I knew from the start that they were wrong about the people. Professional golfers are human beings, with all the vulnerabilities and flaws that come with the title. I knew that what happened to them on the course—successes and failures alike—was a result of who they were *off* the course. I needed to know where they came from, what motivated them, and how they behaved when the red light of the TV cameras went black.

This book is a subjective account of what I saw that year—journalism mixed with opinion. Everything you will read is colored by my personal experience, and if that style offends you—as it seems, at times, to have offended the sport's traditionalists—at least you can consider yourself warned.

As for those young golfers, I found them to be as diverse and interesting as you'd expect from a group of men on the threshold of greatness. Some of them fascinated me, some amused me, and a few were little more than overgrown children. Discerning their true natures was often difficult, because rich athletes today travel with entourages designed to protect them from people like me. I began to feel like a spy, infiltrating layers of agents and coaches and caddies, hoping to smuggle a bit of truth. Where I found that truth, I've presented it without garnish; I never wanted to make a hero or a demon out of anyone, only to be honest.

By midsummer, one anxiety disappeared for good. My theory

about the rise of the young stars had come true—they were winning in droves, from the small tournaments to the majors. With a speed and urgency that I wouldn't have imagined in my most hopeful hours, they began to claim the sport as their own.

With each success, they struck a blow against the icon that had dominated golf for two decades, and whose legend threatened to overshadow it for two more. With each victory, and each rebel yell, they were slaying the Tiger.

"Often people say, what is it that makes a champion? It's an accumulation of many things. Talent? It's something more than talent. It just doesn't happen. It's hard work. It's a work ethic, it's a big sacrifice. Patience is a big thing. You've got to have great nerves. It's a puzzle, with many little things in it. . . .

The other thing is if we all knew, everybody would be a champion. There's something called 'it' that nobody yet has been able to describe."

—GARY PLAYER

NOVEMBER 11, 2013

The Mysterious Frenchman

1

ANTALYA, TURKEY

Victor's Sunday

Victor Dubuisson opened his eyes on that November morning in Antalya, Turkey—more than a thousand miles southeast of his childhood home in France, but on the coast of the same Mediterranean Sea—hoping for a career-changing victory. He rose in obscurity, ignorant of the season that awaited him—how he'd be shoved onto the biggest stages, paired with giants, and asked not just to walk alongside them, but to *win*. Ignorant, too, of how the next twenty-four hours would foreshadow the coming year, when a talented generation that had grown sick of waiting drove the sport madly into its new era.

Only the most intense American golf junkies had ever heard his name, and even they couldn't predict what his day would hold. The anonymous Frenchman, holding the first fifty-four-hole lead of his career—a significant five-shot advantage—was up against the likes of Ian Poulter, Justin Rose, and his idol: the man who had supposedly inspired his love of golf in 1997 with one of the most historic wins in the history of the sport; the man who became golf's foremost icon, and the high tide on which golf had soared for more than a decade; the one who cast a shadow over the game, even when he was hobbled, even when he was absent; the man who would be chasing the young Frenchman on the final day—Tiger Woods.

. . .

I didn't know Victor yet, and I couldn't guess how his story would come to fascinate me in 2014. To call the quiet Frenchman inscrutable would be underselling the point—the man was a sphinx, and arranging the puzzle pieces of his life would prove to be a huge challenge. Information of any kind was hard to come by, and on the rare occasions when an interesting nugget slipped through the cracks, you couldn't trust it. Every quote, and every biographical detail, only deepened the mystery.

A French journalist, for instance, warned me that he liked to exaggerate, and I should have heeded those words when I sat down to hear Dubuisson speak later that season. At Donald Trump's Doral, Florida, resort, the twenty-three-year-old—with his shoulder-length hair, scruffy goatee, and sleepy eyes—told a room full of reporters that he had more or less finished school by age ten, and spent all his time at the golf course. When a puzzled journalist asked about his parents, he said they weren't around, and then refused to elaborate.

The story shocked us, and if I had paused to really consider the information, it might have triggered my bullshit detector. After all, he came from France—still, at last check, a participating member of the modern world, and not a place where a ten-year-old vagabond can quit school, live alone, and devote himself to the lonely pursuit of golf. But my skepticism failed me, and I jotted the words in my notebook, happy for a precious sliver of biographical detail.

At that point, I still believed that any golfer not named Tiger Woods was a boring country club kid with no personality. I wasn't alone. This is a persistent image, and it's even cultivated by the people in charge. Golf doesn't *need* to be cool. The game's keepers want the faintest hint of the reckless and rash to attract new fans, but not so much that it costs them the old ones. Caution is paramount.

Considering this, you can't blame me for assuming that the players themselves followed the same formula: offbeat in superficial ways, maybe, but safe and boring in all the ones that matter.

I was wrong. The truth is that professional golf, which exacts a greater psychological toll than any other sport, attracts a motley crew of neurotics. The human landscape of the PGA Tour is strewn with egomaniacs, obsessive-compulsives, manic-depressives, ADHD cases, narcissists, and zealots.

The question is, how did they get this way? Were the players *always* screwy, and did their afflictions prepare them perfectly for a sport that rewards a certain amount of mental imbalance? Or were they promising youths with bright futures who had their brains twisted into strange shapes by the prolonged tortures of an unrelenting game?

Whatever the case, I believed Dubuisson's latchkey tale, and so did everyone else. It was odd, yes, but nobody questioned its essential truth. Honesty is at the core of golf's image, and who could believe this blushing Frenchman was anything other than scrupulously honest? Anyone who saw him perform in front of a microphone—painfully shy, mumbling every answer, eyes fixed on the floor—would know he was incapable of fabricating even the faintest show of *enthusiasm*, much less an entire childhood. Clearly, young Victor was not trying to mythologize himself; he just wanted to get the hell off the stage. Why would he say something so provocative about his youth, and then refuse to elaborate, unless it was the truth?

What I didn't know—what would take a year to discover—was that when it came to Victor Dubuisson, simple explanations failed. He had his honest moments, but he could also distort and dissemble with the best of them, and the glare of the spotlight made him react in strange ways. He loved and hated this new attention all at once, and the more famous he grew, the more the balance tilted toward hate. I saw the early stages of this when I asked him what he liked to do for fun.

"Like any young men do, I go to cinema," he said. The barest hint of a smile, secretive and tight, had crept onto his face. "I don't know."

"What's your favorite movie?" I asked.

"I don't know," he repeated, and the smile tightened.

I smiled back, wondering if we had just shared some inside joke. I couldn't quite understand. It would be months before I learned that when Victor smiled, there was nothing friendly about it. It was a sign of fear—of a bashful kid who senses someone probing into a private life he desperately doesn't want to share. What seemed to me like an innocuous question, an icebreaker about movies, was to him a declaration of war. His smile was half defiance—*"how dare you ask me a personal question!"*—and half plea—*"why won't you leave me alone?"* It was the smile of someone who had been cornered.

I didn't put it all together until another French journalist, who had been tolerated by Dubuisson after good rounds and scorned after bad ones, laid it out for me.

"You saw Victor smiling at you?" he asked. I nodded. "It means he doesn't like you."

A truer picture of Dubuisson would take months to emerge, but in the meantime, we printed what we thought we knew: Eccentric Young French Golf Hermit Quit School at Age Ten, Lived Alone, Hates Media, Especially French, May Be a Deranged Paranoiac. In the golf world, that passed for a salacious story.

Even if he wasn't a household name, Dubuisson's résumé pegged him as a future star in Europe. Since turning pro in 2010 after reaching the number 1 amateur ranking in the world, he had managed twelve top-ten finishes on the European Tour. In the midst of this rapid ascent, he set the course record at St. Andrews, the most famous track in the world, with a 62, and by November 2013 he had earned more than one million Euros in a season. His résumé grew, and all he lacked was a win.

As he approached the putting green before his final round in Turkey on that fall morning in 2013—Dubuisson walks with a slow, duck-footed shuffle—he saw his idols spread out before him: Tiger, Rose, Stenson, Poulter. He already knew this was the biggest day of his career, but their presence hammered the point home.

The nerves hit hard on the first tee, but beneath it all were the seeds of confidence. His game had been sharp all week, and his lead was huge. With a good round—hell, even a decent round—nobody could catch him. As he prepared for his opening drive, he hoped simply that the first few holes would pass with no mistakes.

. . .

Nine holes later, he had yet to make a birdie. That was the bad news. The *worse* news was that his playing partner, Poulter, had made three of them to reach -19, and Justin Rose had made four, plus an eagle, to climb up to the same score. Tiger Woods had made three of his own, but a bogey kept him at -17, while Jamie Donaldson lurked at -16.

The *good* news was that Dubuisson had not made a bogey either, and his overnight lead had kept him two shots clear of the field at -21. Not the ideal start he'd envisioned, but he was heading into the back nine with a lead.

A driver at the tenth, a short par 4, ended up in a bunker near the green, and though his angle wasn't great, he nearly holed his wedge. A short putt gave him his first birdie of the day, and a bit of relief. But the field kept coming. Poulter birdied 11 to cut the lead to two, and when he bogeyed 12 to give it back, Rose was ready with a birdie of his own on 13 to reach -20. Jamie Donaldson, meanwhile, had taken flight on the back nine, with four birdies propelling him to -19, three behind the leader.

The dreaded moment finally came to pass on the par-3 14th. After missing the green with his tee shot, Dubuisson discovered his ball in an awful lie, from which he had no recourse but to hack out to fifteen feet. As he was preparing to putt, a roar came from somewhere ahead. Victor didn't know it, but Jamie Donaldson's tee shot on the 16th had just gone in the hole. The ace sent the Welshman to -21. When Dubuisson's par putt sailed past the hole a moment later, forcing him to settle for bogey, he had officially blown his cushion.

Before he could catch his breath, Justin Rose birdied the 16th, and the three golfers now stood knotted at -21. Four holes remained.

Losing the big lead had a paradoxical effect on Dubuisson—it calmed him down. The burden he'd carried all day was gone; now he could just *play*.

His second life began on the 15th hole, a 337-yard par 4. After watching Poulter hit a drive to the front of the green, he pulled his own driver and launched a long, straight bomb of his own. It showed tremendous nerve at a critical time, and with his next shot, a chip that stopped three feet from the cup, he displayed the pinpoint short game that would make him famous later that year. He knocked in his birdie putt, and followed that by stiffing an iron into the par-3 16th, leaving himself ten feet for another birdie. He two-putted for par, though, and after his drive on the 17th, Jamie Donaldson finished his round with yet another birdie, tying for the lead at -22 with a brilliant Sunday 63.

With two holes left, Tiger and Poulter had faded, and Justin Rose finished with a bogey. Donaldson was the last opponent standing, and Dubuisson needed just a single birdie for his first win—or, alternatively, just one bogey for a devastating loss. He hit his approach on 17 to about thirty-five feet, which seemed to take him out of birdie range—even the best putters in the game don't sink more than 10 percent of their putts from outside twenty-five feet.

As the putt ran toward the hole, he could tell the speed was perfect. He felt like he'd pulled it a shade left, but as it ran closer and closer, it broke slowly back to the right. Dubuisson watched the putt track, and at the final moment, it curled one last inch, caught the outside lip of the cup, and dropped. He pumped his fist downward, frantically like he was punching an invisible tabletop.

"Seventeen was the big one," he told me later, "as you can probably tell by my reaction! I laugh at that when I watch it again but it was a really massive moment."

In truth, the reaction was far more muted than most players would allow themselves with even less at stake. For the shy Frenchman, though, it passed for jubilation.

He took this energy to the 18th hole, a shot ahead of Donaldson and needing only a par for his win.

He managed to keep his first two shots in play on his final hole, leaving himself a short pitch to the flag. Par was almost a guarantee at that point, but standing over his third shot, he felt more nervous than he ever had in his career. It was easy, yes, but easy just meant there was so much to lose.

He backed off the ball, took two short practice swings, settled his body, and took aim. The ball rose lightly over the edge of a greenside bunker, landed on the green, and trickled toward the pin. By the time it stopped, he had left himself a two-putt that even the most anxious professional golfer couldn't screw up.

He wouldn't need the second stroke—he holed the birdie to win by two. Dubuisson removed his black Titleist visor, shook hands with Poulter, wiped his brow, and then fled in terror as three friends raced onto the green to douse him with champagne.

Over the next year, Dubuisson would leave his indelible mark on the game, intriguing and baffling and impressing us along the way. For now, he simply conducted his television interviews with that enigmatic style—a raised eyebrow, a Gallic shrug—the look of a man who would be happy to conceal his mystery forever.

What none of us knew, as 2013 wound to a close, was that he was in the vanguard of a movement that would come to transform the sport. Soon there would be others like Victor, young and fearless, waging war on their idols. Many of them were under thirty, and those that weren't, like Bubba Watson and Sergio Garcia, belonged in spirit to the electric, eccentric successive generation. To a man, they embodied the passion that Tiger Woods had introduced to golf almost twenty years before.

Which was no accident—Tiger was their example, and the man they looked up to as children. He was bigger, badder, and meaner than his opponents, and he inspired a class of players who molded themselves in his image.

When I spoke with Jim Furyk at the Masters, he told me that he actually tried to *hide* the fact that he played golf in his high school days.

"It was a nerdy, goofy sport to play, and a lot of the kids that weren't athletic played golf," he said. "I was embarrassed by it."

What Tiger did, on an international scale, was to make golf exciting for a new generation. He brought power and style to the sport, and he dazzled the kids who watched him in his prime. Those kids grew up, and they followed his lead. The moment Tiger won his first green jacket, he had anointed his successors—the same children who would one day compete on the same battleground, but with the crucial advantage of youth.

In early 2014, Tiger's aging body got the better of him, and peers like Phil Mickelson were too battered to pick up the slack. In the vacuum, the balance of power shifted to the young. It spawned a year of evolution, and the season's defining moments of brilliance and infamy belonged to players like Rory McIlroy and Rickie Fowler, Jordan Spieth and Martin Kaymer, Patrick Reed and Bubba Watson, Dustin Johnson and Jason Day.

Golf's most exciting season since Tiger's prime was imminent, and it was presaged on that November Sunday with a victory by an elusive Frenchman on the Mediterranean coast.

FEBRUARY

The West Coast Swing

2

PACIFIC PALISADES, CALIFORNIA

The Two Bubbas; Riviera and the Rise of the Second Wave

> *"I just have to rejoice. That's what this whole year is about, trying to rejoice . . . I can think of a quote from Bible. I think it's Philippians 4:11 that says, 'I'm not in need. I'm content with my circumstances.'"*
>
> —BUBBA WATSON, January 30, 2014,
> after an opening round 64 at the Phoenix Open

Heading into the final round of the 2014 Phoenix Open, on Super Bowl Sunday, Bubba Watson held a tenuous lead on Kevin Stadler. He had not won a tournament in almost two years, and he badly wanted to break his slump. Bubba is a complicated man, though, and the only safe bet was that February 2 would be a complicated day. It ended for him with a missed par putt on the 18th hole, and Stadler left Phoenix with his first professional victory. Bubba's drought continued, and the Tour moved on to Pebble Beach, where Jimmy Walker won his third event of the season along the cliffs of the Monterey Peninsula. Walker's surprising domination—before the 2014 season, the thirty-five-year-old had never won on Tour—propelled him to the top of the FedEx Cup standings as the players headed south, to the Riviera Country Club outside Los Angeles.

"When you get the first win, media says 'where's your second win?' When you get your first major, where's your second? When you get your first major, where's your next win? So it's a never-ending story, and the one thing nobody ever talks about, they never put on your tombstone how many wins and losses you have on Tour. If you look at me, I'm a loser my whole life. I've only had like five wins and lost like four hundred times."

—BUBBA

The smell of eucalyptus—fresh mint and honey, sharpest when the wind blows off the Pacific—hung in the air at Riviera Country Club, emanating from the tops of the massive trees that tower over palms, magnolias, and the ashy, gnarled sycamores. It's a stimulating scent, something to inhale as you hike up and down the hills on the lovely course in the Santa Monica Canyon, just a stone's throw from the ocean.

Here, you're treated to certain architectural novelties, like the bunker built smack in the middle of the sixth green, or the 10th hole, with its narrow, sand-protected green, making it the most confounding drivable par 4 on Tour. Everywhere, players fight the wind, the hills, and the steep, stone-faced barranca winding through the fairways. The journey ends on the 18th in a blind, uphill tee shot and a tricky approach into the green, where embankments form a natural amphitheater, sloping up to the massive Spanish Revival clubhouse with its seashell-white stucco walls and clay tile roof.

Bubba Watson puzzled over the course during the first two days of the Northern Trust Open, finishing Friday at -1 and positioning himself in the middle of the pack. Then he came out firing like a howitzer on Saturday, posting a 64 to fight his way into the penultimate group for the final round. Ahead of him, William McGirt (-12), Charlie Beljan (-10), and George McNeill (-10) had very little experience winning PGA Tour events, and it showed—the best any of them would shoot on Sunday was a 70. On a clear day with wind gusts rarely topping out above 10 mph, that was never going to be good enough.

The stumbling leaders opened the door to a charge from below, and Bubba took the reins, sinking two sixteen-foot putts and a thirty-three-footer on the way to posting a front nine 30. He was nine holes from finally securing that slippery title, but as badly as he wanted to win, there were others—many others—who would be rooting for a collapse.

Anti-Bubba sentiment has been around as long as Bubba himself, but until 2014, it had largely simmered below the surface. There are very few outlaws in golf, and the players enjoy certain protections from the media, especially on the television side. Fans take their cue from the broadcasts, and have followed suit in fabricating saints from the raw material of mere athletes. It takes a lot to lose this security blanket—to stand exposed before a press that typically goes out of its way to accommodate.

To truly understand Bubba's trajectory over the years, we have to jump ahead in time, past Riviera, to late 2014 and the PGA Championship. That's where it happened—the moment when the tide finally turned, and a friendly press turned hostile.

During Tuesday's practice round, the PGA of America decided to resurrect the long-drive contest that had been a tournament staple back in the fifties and sixties. The organizers set up a digital scoreboard on the par-5 10th tee, and from the start, the contest was a huge success with players and fans. Padraig Harrington took a running start into his swing, *Happy Gilmore* style. Phil Mickelson, Keegan Bradley, and Rickie Fowler, playing together, hammed it up with the crowd. Rory McIlroy hadn't even planned to play number 10, but came over after his front nine to hit a drive for the fans . . . and when it went out of bounds, he hit another for the hell of it. All in all, it was a harmless exhibition, and a bit of fun for anyone with a practice round ticket and the fortitude to endure Kentucky's stultifying late-summer humidity.

You might have thought Bubba would enjoy the spectacle more

than most. He can hit the ball a mile—he's led the Tour in driving distance several times—and he famously encouraged fans at the 2012 Ryder Cup in Medinah to cheer *during* his swing, so that he was surrounded by a delirious wall of noise as he teed off. Bubba relished the attention, and though he later claimed the stunt was meant only to "grow the game," the ego was hard to deny.

The long-drive contest was another attempt to grow the game, but when Bubba arrived on the 10th tee, he didn't feel so charitable.

"This is fucking ridiculous," he muttered, cursing at the PGA staff assembled around the hole. He said that he'd be hitting a driver every other day, but not today.

After playing partner Chesson Hadley teed off, he barely had time to pick up his tee and step aside as Bubba raced up and hit a lazy 3-iron. Before the announcer even finished saying the words "Bubba Watson," the ball was in the air and he was striding angrily down the fairway.

Later, I asked two of the kids manning the tent on the 10th tee to name their favorite player. They debated between Mickelson, Bradley, and Fowler. There was no hesitation when I asked for their least favorite.

"Bubba," they said in unison.

"He's an asshole," added the first.

"Not wanting to do it is one thing," said his friend. "But be a man about it."

Afterward, he offered no explanation except that he was trying to "learn" the course—as though asking him to hit one driver on a hole where he would almost always hit driver anyway was an unforgivable imposition on his process. He went on to insist that he didn't care what people thought of him, and he was only concerned about how he looked in the eyes of God.[1]

The story becomes even stranger when you consider that the prize

---

[1] An interesting statement, considering he had removed all Internet browsers from his phone earlier that year because he couldn't handle reading anything negative about himself.

for winning the event was twenty-five thousand dollars to the charity of the winner's choice. Bubba uses charity and religion as his sword and shield; why wouldn't he jump at the chance to win free money for the cause of his choice?

As the week went on, Bubba's outlook did not improve. On Friday, as a light rain fell throughout the morning and his game suffered, he resorted to temper tantrums on the course. He began his round on the back nine, and by the 16th hole, he was already whining as Rory McIlroy waxed him.

"I can't play golf, man," he said to his caddie Ted Scott, one of the most respected bagmen in the game. "I got nothing."

The language took a turn for the worse on the 18th, when he moaned about his poor play. "It doesn't matter what I do, man. It doesn't matter. It's fucking horseshit."

After the turn, he threw a club, then blamed it all on the weather. "Water on the clubface, bro," he barked to Scott. "Water on the club-face. I've got no chance."

He had managed to survive the fallout from the long-drive contest, but this was the final straw—the response, both from media and fans, was instantaneous. Bubba refused to come out for his post-round interview, but Golf Channel's Jason Sobel waited him out for an hour and a half. Sobel's reward was a handful of halfhearted quotes, and he proceeded to lambaste him in that day's column. Dave Kindred followed suit at *Golf Digest,* ratcheting up the sarcasm:

> "He had to play with raindrops on his driver's face. We all know that is Satan's work, for surely the prince of darkness diverted the raindrops from all other players and caused them to settle only on Bubba's sticks. Raindrops everywhere, all morning, beginning at 6 o'clock and falling even through Bubba's tee time at 8:35. For hours, raindrops kept falling on Bubba's haircut, causing, methinks, reverberations in the vast empty spaces beneath."

The blogs were even less kind, and Twitter was blowing up with fans spouting anti-Watson rhetoric, spearheaded by two hashtags that proved devastatingly effective. The first, #YearOfRejoicing, referenced the philosophy he had been repeating all season, a reminder to himself to be grateful for the millionaire's life he was leading. As an instrument of blunt irony, these words worked beautifully when paired with a quote such as "water on the clubface, bro!" The second hashtag, #Pray-ForTedScott, referred to his caddie, and needed no further explanation.

Bubba made a token apology on Twitter later that day, and had his PR-crafted contrition act ready for the Barclays tournament two weeks later. The entire fiasco, though, left a larger question unresolved:

Who the hell *is* this guy?

There are two Bubbas, and they exist side by side, engaged in an endless power struggle.

The first Bubba is the good ol' boy with a wild streak—a free-swinging maverick with a fearless approach to the game. This is the image he presents to the public, and taken at face value, it's a welcome antidote to golf's stuffy atmosphere. He looks like a young Randy Quaid, speaks with the choppy, self-assured cadence of George W. Bush, and swings like he's trying to come out of his shoes. He'll often refer to himself in the third person—*"Well, if you ever heard about Bubba Watson's career, you know that I'm in trouble a lot"*—and he has one of the sport's great shit-eating grins. Even his name—*Bubba,* strong and southern, folksy and historical, and loads of fun for a gallery to shout—lends him the aura of a people's champion.

He relentlessly promotes his own altruism, and at times, it's almost possible to believe it. When Ping ran a campaign to raise money for the Phoenix Children's Hospital, Bubba made up the $110,000 shortfall at the end. He once gave thirty-five thousand dollars to his high school and choked up as he spoke to the students about his own academic troubles. He donates to adopting families, and sick kids, and earthquake victims, often bringing his sponsors on board to increase the payout. And while you might raise an eyebrow at just how *public* the entire process can be—he's not the only golfer to be charitable, but he gets far more PR mileage out of it than anyone else—the fact remains that he's giving.

Then there's the beginning of his relationship with Angie Ball, his future wife. They spent their first date at a golf course—she didn't know Bubba played, and you can imagine how much he enjoyed her shock when he launched his first drive. Afterward, sitting in the car, she told him that she couldn't bear children. Bubba told her it was okay, and that he wanted to adopt.

These are the rare times when it's possible to see his Christian beliefs in action, and it's why his entourage will defend him so forcefully, even in the difficult moments.

"I think when Bubba Watson gets too serious about golf or life, that's when you see a different side of him," said Webb Simpson, a fellow Christian on Tour and one of Bubba's biggest defenders. "Bubba's love language is giving you a hard time, so if he's giving you a hard time, it means he likes you."

America saw the "good" version of Bubba in 2012, when he found himself stuck in the pine straw on the second hole of a Sunday playoff at the Masters. Blocked out by trees, he had no angle to the green, and so he invented his own—a physics-defying snap hook with a fifty-two-degree gap wedge that sailed toward the far side of the fairway before making a boomerang sweep to the right and, incredibly, settling on the green ten feet from the pin.

Dressed all in white, his long hair trailing out the back of his visor, he emerged from the trees looking like golf's true messiah. The crowd roared one word in unison—"Bubba!"—and reached out to touch him as he glided past. When Louis Oosthuizen failed to get up-and-down from the front of the green, Bubba two-putted to win the green jacket. It's no exaggeration to call his approach one of the most memorable shots in golf history, and whatever else happens in Watson's career, he leaves behind a memory that will last as long as people play the sport.

What's more, it was the perfect consummation of "Bubba Golf," a sui generis style that is both reckless and awe-inspiring. In the moments *before* that shot, CBS's Nick Faldo summed up his chaotic magic when he said that Bubba was "rewriting the instructional book every time he hits a shot."

In preaching the virtues of that approach, Bubba is his own best promoter.

"My whole game is built on me playing golf, me manufacturing something," he said. "If you watch, sometimes you'll see me slice my driver fifty yards to just get into play. Sometimes you'll see me bomb away and put it in the rough to have an easier shot at the green. All I'm trying to do is score. I don't care how I do it. There's no pictures on scorecards."

Bubba Golf is an explosive, edge-of-your-seat show that produces triumph and tragedy in almost equal measure. It rises from the un-apologetic individuality of its practitioner, and would be impossible for anyone else to duplicate. And while it's unfathomable that another golfer could even *imagine* the shot he pulled off at Augusta, much less execute it, it's equally impossible to imagine Bubba winning his first major in any manner that could be called routine. This is a man who operates at many speeds, but "average" is not one of them.

"I've never had a dream go this far, so I can't really say it's a dream come true," he told the TV cameras at Augusta, showing the sense of poetry and drama that would come to define his public persona. He broke down in tears as he hugged his mother and thought of his son, Caleb, the one-month-old boy he and his wife Angie had adopted two weeks earlier. At age thirty-three, he was a new father and a major champion. He looked to be armed with a new outlook, and it seemed like his career trajectory could only sail higher. He had us in the palm of his hand.

The second Bubba is the one that took this affection—you might even call it love—and systematically spoiled it.

In 2013, Bubba couldn't find the winning touch. He managed a couple of top-tens, but failed to make the right shots at the critical mo-ment. Coming into the Travelers Championship in late June—on the same course, River Highlands, where he won his first tournament—he was running out of time to capitalize on the momentum from the previous year. The Connecticut course suited him, though, and with just three holes to play on Sunday, he held a one-shot lead on the field.

On the tee at the 171-yard par-3 16th, he was stymied by the wind and stuck between clubs. He consulted with Ted Scott, who convinced him that he should use a 9-iron instead of the 8-iron. Bubba listened, and whether a fugitive gust of wind rose from nowhere or the club was simply wrong, the ball hit the front of the bank and rolled backward into the water.

Bubba turned to Scott with a look of indignation. "Water," he said, biting off his words. "It's in the *water*. That *club*." The two proceeded to the drop zone, where Bubba took a penalty and hit his third shot over the green. "You're telling me that's the yardage?" he asked Scott. He turned away in disgust. Moments later, when he missed his putt for double bogey, he looked back at Scott and whined, "There's just no reason for me to show up."

The CBS cameras caught everything, and the incident became infamous; the video had more than one million views on YouTube before it was removed. On the broadcast, David Feherty summed up the collective reaction: "Now, wait a minute . . . hey, *you* hit it, bud!"

Watson took a triple bogey on the hole, and lost the tournament. Later, when pgatour.com's Brian Wacker asked him about the exchange with Scott, he blew up.

"Don't try to make me look bad," Bubba said. "You always do. Don't. Don't. We're not talking anymore."

The incident painted Bubba in an unflattering light, and it was not an isolated embarrassment. In 2011, he traveled to Europe to play in the French Open near Paris. He missed the cut with back-to-back rounds of 74, but it was his conduct off the course that provided the real fireworks, and led to exchanges like this one:

Q. I heard you went to Paris yesterday?

BUBBA WATSON: Yeah, yesterday.

Q. Did you like—what did you see?

BUBBA WATSON: I don't know the names of all the things, the big tower, Eiffel Tower, an arch, whatever that—I rode around in a circle. And then what's that—it starts with an L, Louvre, something like that. One of those.

Ignorance is one thing, but Bubba also managed to distinguish himself in France as a temperamental prima donna. He wouldn't accept any interview requests with foreign outlets, demanded his own courtesy car when someone had the audacity to suggest he share with a European golfer, complained about the lack of ropes keeping the gallery at bay, and howled about the fans with their cameras and phones.

He was the caricature of an ugly American, and fellow pro Stuart Appleby called him out on Twitter, writing, "I'm not perfect all the time, but it is not acceptable to come to another tour and more than once show a lack of respect."

The cherry on top of Bubba's international diplomacy sundae came when he told reporters that he would probably never return to Europe—except for the British Open, because it was a major.

So the long-drive outburst at Valhalla was just the latest of Bubba's greatest hits, and it wasn't even a surprise. Earlier that week, before any of it happened, Doug Ferguson at the AP had mused that although Bubba was a 33 to 1 shot to win the tournament, he "could get much better odds on annoying someone."

But we haven't answered the question: Who is he?

For as much as he craves attention, Bubba Watson is loath to reveal his past. Karen Crouse of *The New York Times* is one of the few writers to earn unfettered access. In an excellent story called "Growing up Bubba," she details how his father, Gerry (Bubba's first name is also Gerry), a Green Beret who served in Vietnam, first took his son to a driving range in the panhandle town of Bagdad, Florida. The boy was six, and it was there that he began playing with a sawed-off 9-iron. Gerry was his only teacher and, according to Bubba, he's never had a formal lesson.

Scott Michaux of the *Augusta Chronicle* unearthed another telling detail—Bubba's father wanted him to play baseball, but to nobody's surprise, Bubba was an irritable teammate who expected perfection from everybody else. He would become angry when they failed, and he once yelled at a coach whose son made four errors in a game.

Golf was a no-brainer: He could rely on, and blame, only himself. (Though, as we've seen, he does manage to get creative within those limitations.) His inventive hook-and-slice style developed in part because he spent his days whacking away at Wiffle balls—bending them in every direction—and in part because of the varied terrain and tight fairways of Pensacola golf courses, which demanded creative thinking.

On the Golf Channel's interview show *Feherty,* Bubba opened up about his father's struggles adjusting to civilian life when he returned from Vietnam. He spoke in his usual clipped style, arms crossed, leaving off pronouns and keeping the narrative tight. Even so, he couldn't hide his emotion.

"They lived on Pensacola Beach," he told Feherty. "It was before beach property was really a thing to have so he was the man around the beach. Went to jail a few times—we just won't say the number—but been to jail a few times for fighting. Just not knowing how to deal with it, a lot of guys don't know how to deal with stuff, because that's what they were trained to do . . . when I was born my mom said 'no more.' . . . so he straightened up and changed and just was a hard worker and just kinda left that life."

The more you learn about Bubba, the more you understand that Gerry was the dominant influence in his life. Even Bubba's emergence as a flamboyant loner came straight from the old man, who wore colorful handkerchiefs to work and inspired his son's bright clothes and equipment.

Chris Haack, the future coach at the University of Georgia, was working with the American Junior Golf Association (AJGA) when Bubba first burst onto the junior golf scene, and had a front row seat to one of the most singular players he'd ever come across. "He wore these canary yellow knickers or hot pink shorts," Haack remembered. "He stood out—he was just kind of the guy who had attention drawn to him, and I think he also liked the attention, and wanted to be recognized."

He never changed. In 2011, an AP story by Doug Ferguson listed the ways he sought the spotlight—how he inserted a pink draft into his driver when he made the PGA Tour, how he always made sure people were watching when he drove on the practice range, and how he campaigned on Twitter to be on the Ellen DeGeneres show. "And then he would try to explain that he only plays golf for the love of the game, not to get any attention," Ferguson wrote.

The article came too early to mention Bubba's purchase of the *General Lee* car from *The Dukes of Hazzard,* or the various goofy YouTube videos he made with friends, or his 1.3 million Twitter followers, but the idea comes across—Bubba is an attention hound, right down to his driver cover, which is a miniature shirtless Bubba doll in overalls.

In Michaux's *Augusta Chronicle* profile, there's an old photo of Bubba wearing a typical childhood-era outfit: two-tone golf shoes, long white socks, red knickers made for him by his grandmother, a white-collared shirt with an American flag pattern, and a white Panama-style hat with a blue, star-spangled band.

"Everything he hit was a big rope hook," said Stephen Hamblin, executive director of the AJGA and someone who watched Bubba play from an early age. "He introduced a cut later on, but oh God, he hooked everything."

The flair for the dramatic, too, was present in its nascent stages. Hamblin can vividly recall a moment from the 1996 Canon Cup, a co-ed east vs. west junior match play competition held in Jackson Hole, Wyoming, when Bubba was teamed with Shauna Estes (now the head women's golf coach at Arkansas) in the alternate shot session on the second day of competition.

"It's the last match," Hamblin told me. "Everyone else is done, all the kids are up by the green, and they're on 18. It's a par-4 dogleg left, and there's a creek that runs in front of the green, all the way around the left and all around the back. And the green kinda slopes, kinda right to left into the creek. Pin front left.

"Shauna's got this long sweeping downhill putt, going to break a ton. She gets too cute with it, leaves it about eighteen feet short. So Bubba's got this putt, it's eighteen feet and it probably *breaks* six feet. So he's got his back to the kids, because he's left-handed, and they're all over here sitting down on the edge of the green. Everybody—kids, coaches, parents. And if he makes this, they win the match for the east. So he gets over this putt, and the *second* the putter touches the ball, he turns around, puts his arms up in the air, and walks to his teammates. He's not even *looking* at it. He's not! Everyone's still watching, and he's holding his hands up. And the ball goes in!

"The hair stood up on the back of my neck. And of course, everyone went crazy. I saw that and went, 'This guy's a totally different cat.' I couldn't believe it, I hadn't seen anything like it in my life. I went, 'He *can't* be that good. That's total bullshit.' Well, he's that good."

Haack may have the best perspective on Bubba, having watched him from childhood to college. But even he can't explain what contrary spirit sometimes takes hold of the former Bulldog. His theory hinges on the idea that despite Bubba's attempts at presenting a cavalier face to the world, deep down he feels intense pressure. He still hasn't fully learned to cope, and when something goes wrong, he succumbs more quickly than others to the natural inclination to blame anybody but himself.

This defensiveness seems to stem from insecurity. He was always a poor student, which was a constant source of self-doubt, as was his lower-middle-class upbringing and the contrast it presented with the wealthy kids of the junior golf world. Then, too, he must have felt like an oddball for his strange swing—a reckless creation compared to the mechanical precision he saw in others.

He compensated in different ways. When things went well, he embraced his difference and let it swell his self-image. When things went poorly, he looked for somebody else to blame.

"I would be willing to bet you that deep down he regrets he did that," said Haack, of the long-drive contest at Valhalla. "But at that particular moment, there was something there that struck him wrong, and he was just going to do totally the opposite of what everyone wanted him to do."

When Bubba came to Athens after a stint in junior college to improve his grades, he found a trailer where he could live cheaply near campus. He played well for Haack his junior season, won a tournament, and was voted a preseason All-American the next year. But if there's one constant among those who remember Bubba's childhood, it's doubt—doubt that he could ever conquer his own attitude, doubt that he could ever thrive even on a college level.

As if fulfilling those lowered expectations, Bubba had a falling-out with Haack that may have been begun when he went for a par-5 green in two at the NCAA championships against the coach's orders. That's only a rumor, but Bubba sat out the next year and watched all five playing teammates, including Erik Compton, become All-Americans.

After leaving Georgia without a degree (he would later reconcile with Haack and earn his diploma in 2008), Bubba toiled on the minor tours for years before finally earning his way onto the PGA Tour in 2006. He had proved everyone wrong, and once he made it, he never looked back.

The one thing he *couldn't* do at the PGA level, and had never done on the Nationwide Tour, was win. His nerves, which he had generally overcome against everyone's predictions, still hindered him when a tournament was on the line. At age thirty-one, he didn't have a single PGA Tour win to his credit. His attitude on the course soured, and he became so negative that Ted Scott threatened to quit. It was a bold move—Scott had a lot to lose. But the process was becoming miserable for everyone, especially Bubba, and a change was in order.

Bubba listened. He worked on staying calm and positive, and it paid dividends when he won the Travelers Championship in 2010. He wept then, and spoke about his father, who was suffering from the throat cancer that would take his life less than four months later. He and Scott would put considerable effort into converting Gerry to Christianity in his last days, and though the old Green Beret was resistant, the turning point came when Scott wrote him a letter explaining how much it would mean for Bubba to be able to see his father in heaven.

He nearly won his first major that August at the PGA Championship after Dustin Johnson grounded his club in a disguised hazard, costing himself a chance at the Wannamaker trophy. Bubba finished in a tie for the lead, but lost in a playoff to Martin Kaymer.

After two more wins in 2011, he arrived at Augusta National the following April, not knowing that his life was about to change.

Even after winning the green jacket, his behavior remained frosty to outsiders. And to Bubba Watson, almost *everyone* is an outsider. That includes the other Georgia Bulldogs on Tour, five of whom won tournaments in 2014. Their relationship with Bubba is strained to the point of antipathy. When I asked Brian Harman if Bubba was connected to the other Georgia alums, he could only laugh.

"He's *not,* man," he said, shaking his head. "He's just not. It's unfortunate, because we all come from the same Georgia family. At one point, Bubba and Haacker had their differences, they just had a little bit of a falling-out."

Harman held out hope for a true reconciliation, but Brendon Todd was less diplomatic. After he won the Byron Nelson in May, a reporter had asked him whether he received any congratulations from Bubba, and his response—Todd is as considerate and unpretentious a person as you'll find on Tour—was uncharacteristically terse. "No, I'm not close with Bubba," he said. "I don't expect to hear from him."

"Bubba's never been friendly with the Georgia players, and none of us really have a good relationship with him," he told me later. "I don't know what the reason is. It definitely seems like he has his group out here and he sticks to that group and he doesn't really socialize with other people."

Todd's early career was filled with heartbreak and doubt, and in his first season, when he struggled and eventually failed to keep his Tour card, he thought it would be helpful to have a high-profile player like Bubba, a fellow Bulldog, as a friend. He was disappointed when he tried to approach and introduce himself, though—the only response was a cold blow-off. It was the same in 2012, after Bubba won the Masters and Todd attempted to congratulate him on the range—nothing doing.

Todd decided to give him another chance this year. He had just won the Byron Nelson, and he approached Bubba on the range at the Memorial in Ohio. Again, he congratulated him on his season, hoping he might get a kind word in return.

"Thanks," said Bubba, barely looking at Todd as he walked away.

"I played with him for the first time at the Greenbrier in July for two days," Todd told me. "He was fine to play with in the sense that we both played our games. I got the sense that he wanted to be buddies, but the feeling I had gotten from the previous five years was so much the opposite. I just couldn't." Todd let a small smile creep onto his face. "I was just there to do my work and listen to him complain."

Todd may be one of the few Bulldogs who will express his disdain on the record, but it's a feeling that's shared, and that comes out in unprotected moments. When, after his best season ever, Georgia alum Chris Kirk failed to make the Ryder Cup as a captain's pick, his former teammate Kevin Kisner sent a consolation tweet.

"Don't worry @ChrisKirk," it said. "They would probably just pair you with bubba."

Like many of his peers, Todd believes that Bubba hides behind his Christianity without truly putting its tenets into practice. When things get tough for Bubba, retreating to the Bible has become a sort of reflex. At the PGA Championship, when he was asked whether he cared what people thought of him, he was ready with his standard defense.

"Truthfully, no. Because the way I'm trying to live my life, read the Bible, follow the Bible . . . no matter what I do, no matter if I win every single tournament, half the world is going to love me and half the world is going to hate me no matter what. You can't impress everybody and you can't make everybody happy."

It was classic Bubba—reverting to religion, scolding anyone who questioned him, and placing himself above those with the temerity to criticize a man of God. All of which leads to a familiar question: Does he practice what he preaches?

Later in the summer, I spoke with Stephen Bunn, vice president of the College Golf Fellowship, a group that also collaborates with the PGA Tour Fellowship to run weekly Christian Bible study sessions at each Tour stop—sessions at which Watson is a regular. In the course of a long conversation about his beliefs and his mission in golf—since 1998, Bunn has played a key role in growing the organization, to the point that they now receive over a million dollars per year in donations—I asked if the attendance at the Bible sessions had grown in the past decade. He hesitated a moment.

"People can be prohibited from coming to something because of who's there," he said, speaking carefully. "They'll know that in that group there are going to be both moral guys and immoral guys, and there's going to be guys who might have a stench of Christian body odor. I can't think of one, I'm just saying. . . ."

Bunn was too diplomatic to mention anyone by name, but it's hard not to think that one of the players poisoning the well is Watson. There's an aggression and a sense of superiority to his faith. You can see it in the way he sends Bible verses to friends, or casts them at the media like a fire-and-brimstone preacher in his pulpit. Bubba isn't just a Christian; Bubba is special. Bubba is the *best* Christian.

As you might imagine, my attempts to engage him went poorly. A select few journalists are able to gain his trust with time and persistence, but I was new to the Tour and didn't have that luxury. As much as Bubba is generally disinclined to speak with established media, he was even less eager to open up to someone he didn't know.

Still, I had to try. After laying what I thought was a decent foundation at press conferences in the first half of the year, I made my first one-on-one approach at the Travelers Championship in late June. He had just finished his Wednesday pro-am[2], and I waited inside the roped-off putting green while he made his way down up the hill past the 18th hole, signing autographs for fans. He looked irritated, and when he finished he gave his playing partners a signed ball before issuing a terse goodbye. Free from the crowds, he walked toward me, and already I had the sense that my timing was poor. Unfortunately, I was committed.

"Bubba," I began, but the words were barely out of my mouth before he snapped.

"I can't talk right now!"

I had seen this type of reaction before, and I would become more familiar with it as the season wore on—his face flushes, he becomes tense, and he recoils in a defensive posture, as though you've just insulted his mother or asked to borrow money. I had been rejected by other golfers so many times that it practically became a pastime, but this was the first time the situation felt truly hostile—like I had cornered a panicked animal. Maybe I should have walked away, but I didn't.

"Well," I continued, ashamed at how meek my voice sounded, "I just wanted to introduce myself."

"You've done it," he barked, moving past me. "You've introduced yourself."

I had an idea, though, something I thought might appeal to his ego, and his sense of his own humble origins.

"I'm writing a book about the Tour," I offered, "and I think the story of your childhood and where you came from hasn't really been told."

---

[2] Each Wednesday at regular events, the Tour stages a pro-am featuring fifty or so of the best players in that week's field. Those are the pros. The amateurs are the wealthy business people in the area who want to shell out big bucks to play a round with a "real" golfer. They'll usually pay around ten thousand dollars for the privilege, but it fluctuates. At the Deutsche Bank in Massachusetts, I overheard a participant tell his friends how he had negotiated the fifteen-thousand-dollar pro-am price down to ten thousand, only to be asked later to donate five thousand dollars to the Tiger Woods Foundation.

He flashed me a suspicious look. "You're writing a book about my childhood?"

"No, it's about the PGA Tour," I tried to clarify, "but you're a big part of that this year."

Thinking we were now in a legitimate conversation, I took two steps toward him on the practice green.

"We're practicing now!" he yelled, and then Ted Scott, the man he publicly humiliates once or twice a year, jumped in front of me like a secret service agent shielding the president from a pistol-toting lunatic.

"We're practicing!" Scott echoed.

I trudged away, thoroughly beaten and humiliated.

I made my second effort two months later, at the WGC-Bridgestone, and that attempt somehow felt even *more* doomed. Again, I found him on a practice day, and this time I made sure he had finished his work on the putting green before I approached. Again, I got the flushed face and the frantic eyes when I brought up the idea of a short interview.

"I'm not going to do that," he yelled, bristling once more with that surprising anger. I wondered if I had murdered a family member of his in a past life. "I've got offers to write my own book," he said. "Why would I give it to you?"

I considered the logic of this, and found the argument fair—though I wished he could get past the idea that I was writing an *entire book* about him. I didn't want a repeat of our last confrontation, and had by this point fulfilled my own sense of obligation—I hadn't succumbed to cowardice and avoided him completely, as I desperately wanted to do—and so I prepared to leave. Unfortunately, we were going in the same direction.

"I'm going to do it for myself!" he barked. He must have realized he'd forgotten to mention Christianity or charity, and so he turned back for a parting shot: "And my charities!"

His agents were no more enthused about a formal interview than their superstar, so I soon gave up the fight. I had to settle for asking him questions at press conferences, which, to his credit, he always answered in interesting ways. There is an undeniable charisma to the man, and there are times when his natural energy and charm shine through. In those moments, you catch yourself liking him—at least until he screws it up again, which is never long in coming.

Those were the two Bubbas who walked the back nine at Riviera that Sunday in February, dividing the golf world as they sought to end a two-year drought.

Jason Allred and Brian Harman had made an early run as the leaders fell, and they lurked two shots behind Bubba as the back nine began.

For Allred, whose biggest claim to fame was winning the U.S. Junior Amateur all the way back in 1997, this proximity to an actual tournament was uncharted territory. The skinny journeyman with the toothy smile had earned his place in the tournament through Monday qualifying, and nearly set a Riviera course record with a 64 on Friday. The timing couldn't have been better for the thirty-three-year-old; with his third child on the way, and a golf career that had been mostly lackluster since he lost his PGA Tour card for the second time in 2008. Outside of Q-School, he hadn't even *played* a PGA Tour event since the 2010 U.S. Open, and he needed a good result.

He also managed to capture the media's attention with his attitude off the course—gracious, emotional, and brimming with gratitude for this unexpected chance. He gave me the shock of my life on Sunday's back nine when he actually approached me behind the tee box on no. 11. He remembered me from Saturday's press conferences, and as I tried to keep my jaw from hitting the dirt, he said hello and shook my hand. I've seen some strange things on the golf course, but a golfer approaching a media member *during a competitive round* is by far the most unnatural. I hesitated before accepting his handshake, sure that I was violating at least thirty Tour protocols.

It was impossible not to like Allred—he cried in sheer joy after Saturday's round, and it didn't surprise me at all when Jill Painter of the New York *Daily News* wrote about the contrast between him and Bubba:

Bubba Watson—his friend and playing partner—was angry at his caddie because of an errant shot. Watson loudly exclaimed "Wrong club!" three times and kicked the club. . . .

[Allred] simply walked down the fairway smiling and chatting up the standard bearer the whole way.

"Oh yeah, Keith!" Allred said later. "He was great. He was high-fiving me the whole round."

Allred played bogey-free golf on Sunday, but couldn't quite muster the birdies he needed to win. Even so, his third-place finish earned him more money—$386,000—than he had won in his entire career. More important, the great finish spread his story, opened the door to sponsor exemptions, and gave him a fighting chance to earn enough money and FedEx Cup points—as one of the Tour's non-members—to secure a card for 2015.

Harman gave it a run, too, but he hit the same back nine cold streak, making seven straight pars to end his round. The closest anyone came to challenging Bubba was Dustin Johnson, whose 66 was the second-best round of the day. He finished with par to take the clubhouse lead at -13, and when he threw his ball into the crowd, a fat man dove in front of a kid to make the catch. He stood up and smiled, very proud of himself for just an instant, before a torrent of angry shouts rang down from the hillsides.

Ahead by a stroke, Bubba had a chance to close it out on the 17th, but came up a few inches shy on a twenty-eight-foot birdie putt. That left him the blind tee shot on 18—realistically, the only thing standing between him and the end of the winless slump that dated back to Augusta. Poised over his ball, he gave a final look up the hill, swung the pink club, and ripped his drive 315 yards—dead straight.

"Nice shot!" Allred gushed, genuinely happy.

Bubba barely nodded as he trekked up the hill. With 166 yards left, he hit his approach to 14 feet, and, with his quintessential flair for the dramatic, canned the birdie putt and set off a raucous eruption on the hills. He gave a little jab and soaked it all in. That night, his wife Angie told him he needed a better fist pump, but that was his only mistake. With the final birdie, he had posted a 64 to blow away the field. The drought was over.

After the presser, as Bubba signed the flags a Tour rep slid in front of him, he talked about shooting 14-under on the weekend.

"I could've pouted," he said, "but I manned up."

"Does that imply you've pouted in the past?" someone asked.

"You gotta pout," he said, in one of those comic moments of self-awareness that almost redeems him. "We think the world's going to end."

Harman, a fiery competitor who had yet to break through and win on the PGA Tour, still had some leftover anger in the media room. When a reporter asked whether it impressed him that Bubba had won without playing "spectacular," Harman gave the inquisitor an incredulous look.

"You don't watch a lot of golf if you don't think *that* was spectacular."

When I think of Bubba now, after a year in his orbit, two thoughts return. The first is that despite discovering the nuances and the complexities beneath the surface, my gut instinct remains the same—he's a hypocrite and a prickly narcissist whose occasional flashes of humanity tend to be self-serving.

The second thought, though, is that I'm thrilled he plays professional golf, and I hope he sticks around for years. Everything he does, from the sacred to the profane, makes the entire sport more exciting. "Did you see what Bubba did?" are words I heard again and again in 2014, and each time, I knew I was in for a good story.

Everybody has a quintessential Bubba moment that they never forget, and mine came on Tuesday at the PGA Championship, after his strange performance at the long-drive competition. A few of us caught Bubba by the doorway of the press tent, and the short story he told highlights everything that matters about Bubba—the hypocrisy, the aspiration, the self-righteousness mixed with a total lack of self-awareness, and, yes, the reservoirs of generosity brimming somewhere beneath the surface.

"Last night I sent Teddy and three other guys a verse," he told us. "James 1:22. I was doing a little study at the house . . . and it says, 'Don't merely listen to the word, and so deceive yourselves. Do what it says.'"

Looking back, you could divide the 2014 season into four distinct waves. The Jimmy Walker Wave had begun in the autumn and crested with his third win at Pebble Beach. Now it had petered out, and conditions were ripe for something new—a second variation on the theme.

The man from Bagdad, Florida, was waiting. The Bubba Wave began to form in Phoenix, rose up to full, intimidating height at Riviera, and was now rolling eastward, looking for somewhere to break.

3

TUCSON, ARIZONA

Jason Day and the Never-Ending Mountain;
The Match Play Championship

The Tour moved away from dense Los Angeles, to the south and east, across the Colorado River and back into Arizona's Sonoran Desert. Everywhere you looked, the earth was hard and dry, and only the stony Tortolita Mountains punctuated the endless thorny flatlands. The landscape here is a study in progressive shades of brown, from tan to raw umber, with fleeting glimpses of color from the occasional wild-flower. The rattlesnakes are still asleep in February, but it's easy to imagine them lurking in the crevices around the desert floor—blending in with the cacti and the agave plants that look like upside-down pine-apples shoved into the baked soil—waiting for a golfer to take one wrong step. . . .

What green exists in this barren patch of desert is muted, beaten into drab olive by the relentless sun. The languid spirit of the desert lingers until the moment you step onto a golf course. There, the bright, verdant fairways will trigger a state of ecological shock as you wrangle with the obvious question: *Wait a minute . . . where did they get the water?*[3]

---

[3] It turns out they use an irrigation system that takes advantage of reclaimed "effluent water," which is a euphemism for partially purified waste water from sewage works or factories. Every time you flush a toilet in Phoenix or Tucson, you're supporting the PGA Tour.

On these courses, the sand traps and rough are easy enough to manufacture—just let the desert have its way with the land, as it's done for centuries. Any spot that doesn't receive a steady supply of water becomes "waste area"—a dismissive term that ignores the land's stark beauty. In late winter, the yellow sunflower-like blooms of the brittlebush and the red flowers of the chuparosa serve as a bright contrast to the plants that will draw blood—the saguaro cacti and the beavertail and the jumping cholla.

This was the end of the West Coast swing, and Marana was hosting its very last Accenture Match Play Championship. It wasn't a fond farewell—the company was bolting, the players hated the course, and the tournament's future was a big mystery. A dull sense of duty pervaded: Let's get this over with, and move on to greener pastures.

The Match Play Championship had been in Marana at the clumsily named "Golf Club at Dove Mountain" since 2009. At 7,849 yards, the Jack Nicklaus–designed course was the longest in PGA Tour history, but it wasn't the length that drove the players crazy—it was the greens. The extreme slopes earned harsh critique from the likes of Tiger Woods, Phil Mickelson, and Geoff Ogilvy, and the course's response—to make them very slow, in order to take away some of the downhill speed—made the uphill putts unreadable. A total overhaul in 2010 failed to resolve these issues, and the world's top players began finding excuses to stay home.

The situation reached a low point in 2014, when Woods, Mickelson, and Adam Scott all dropped out of the field. For a World Golf Championship event, with sixty-four players competing in a single elimination bracket, this was a disaster. A WGC was supposed to attract the strongest field in golf, but the game's three biggest stars—and the first-, second-, and fourth-ranked golfers in the world—were no-shows. Woods and Mickelson stayed mum, but Scott admitted that if the event had been held at a different course, he'd be more inclined to make the scene. The Tour wouldn't officially drop the axe on Dove Mountain for several months, but this sealed its fate.

The format, too, was headed for the scrap heap. The beauty of the single elimination bracket was the pure excitement of the opening rounds. Unlike the NCAA basketball tournament, where no 16-seed has ever beaten a 1-seed, total chaos ruled in the Match Play. As of 2013, 1-seeds had a first-round winning percentage just over 70 percent, and 2-seeds were even lower at 60 percent. Upsets abounded, and the unpredictability made Wednesday (the Match Play is a five-day event) the most exciting opening round on the PGA Tour calendar.

The problem came in the messy aftermath. While it's thrilling to see Tiger Woods and Rory McIlroy fall to no-names on Wednesday, it can make for some very unexciting weekend action. This is not always true—past finals have included Woods, McIlroy, Henrik Stenson, Ian Poulter, Martin Kaymer, and Hunter Mahan. But a handful of duds had sneaked into the mix, such as 2002's Kevin Sutherland vs. Scott McCarron battle, or the lackluster duel between Jeff Maggert and Andrew Magee in 1999. The entire tournament was a calculated risk, and a boring weekend made for unhappy TV executives. The best Wednesday in golf, it turns out, isn't worth the price of the worst Sunday.

The confluence of events made 2014 the end of an era in three ways—sponsor, venue, and format. Cadillac took over as the title sponsor for 2015, the Match Play moved to TPC Harding Park in San Francisco, and a new round-robin stage grouped the golfers into sixteen groups of four players each, ensuring that even if a marquee star like Rory laid an egg, he'd be guaranteed three rounds before packing his bags when the elimination portion began on Saturday.

Match play also produces complicated feelings among pros. Some of them, like the savage god of match play himself, Ian Poulter, love the one-on-one competition. Others, like Phil Mickelson, who held a career 23-21-3 singles record in match play and hadn't played the Accenture event since 2011, tend to underperform. The detractors do have one good point—it can be quite unfair. As McIlroy pointed out before the event began, it's possible for a player to shoot 65 and still lose, while another might shoot 74 and win. Consistency is less important—a 10 on a hole is no worse than a 4, if your opponent makes 3—and in a single elimination event, the best player isn't always rewarded. This is no different from the NCAA basketball tournament, or the NFL playoffs, but golfers aren't used to it, and some of them bristle at the injustice.

As the players convened early in the week, a black cloud of death loomed over Dove Mountain, and all indications were that the Accenture Match Play would limp off into an ignominious sunset. From there, the players would make tracks for Florida, trying to forget this odd little footnote in Tour history.

Instead, against all odds, the lame-duck tournament raged against the dying of the light. The week began with no further dropouts, the tournament retained a few shreds of deathbed dignity, and the hated Dove Mountain produced some of the year's most exciting golf.

The surprises came fast and furious on Wednesday, beginning with Rickie Fowler, one of the Tour's poster boys. Fowler was best known, at that moment, for his signature outfit—the orange Puma jumpsuit, complete with flat-brimmed hat. His sponsors and handlers had carefully crafted a modified skate-punk image for him, and the fans ate it up. At every tournament, you'd find a few kids dressed head-to-toe in Fowler orange, and, more worryingly, at least one grown man. In its attempts to market to a younger audience, the PGA Tour found a perfect subject in Fowler, and they promoted him relentlessly.

This rubbed some players the wrong way. At a Saturday press conference a month later at Bay Hill, Matt Every referred to a group of "fakers" on Tour, and added, "Just because you wear stupid clothes doesn't mean you have style. It means you wear dumb clothes." Later, he expanded on the thought to me, making it clear that he didn't blame certain players for taking advantage of good marketing, but that they "may get a little too much attention because of it, and the Tour definitely promotes who they want to promote."

If the critique was directed at least partly at Fowler, it made sense; he was doing well, especially for a twenty-five-year-old, but not *spectacularly* well. He'd won once, in a playoff against Rory McIlroy at the Wells Fargo Championship in 2012, but there was no question that his golf celebrity came more from his clothes than his results.

The impression that Fowler was a complacent dilettante, on the other hand—golf's answer to Anna Kournikova—didn't hold water.

He worked as hard as anyone, and late in 2013, he teamed up with legendary swing coach Butch Harmon in an attempt to jump-start his career. It was slow going—Harmon's changes weren't easy to implement—and coming into Tucson, his results lagged behind the effort. Which made it something of a shock when he eagled the 13th hole on Wednesday to go 3-up on Ian Poulter.[4]

On paper, a struggling Fowler had no chance against the Ryder Cup legend. Not only had Poulter won the Match Play in 2010, and made the semifinals in 2013, but he was also known as one of the most intimidating golfers in the game. In 2012, he had endured insult after insult from the American fans at the Medinah Ryder Cup to strike a huge blow for Europe on Saturday night when he finished with five straight birdies to keep his team's deficit from spiraling out of control. On Sunday, he beat Webb Simpson in singles, helping to set the tone for the greatest comeback in Ryder Cup history—a devastating loss for the Americans on their own soil. And he did it all with a vicious energy, expressed in angry roars and bugged eyes and clenched fists. In contrast to the genteel manners of many golfers, Poulter never tries to disguise the very personal conflict at the heart of match play.

He clawed a hole back on no. 14 with a birdie, stalking off as Fowler missed his own birdie putt—Poulter is a devout practitioner of that classic match play gambit—but two pars on 15, a long par 4, kept Fowler 2-up with three holes left. Poulter needed to strike quickly on the par-3 16th, but a solid chip by Fowler forced the Englishman to sink a long birdie putt. Just as he took his putter back, a baby in the stands began to cry. Poulter's putt sailed well wide, and his face froze

---

[4] Unlike stroke play, match play golf is measured by holes. Winning a hole by shooting a better score means a player is 1-up, and his opponent is 1-down. If the opponent wins the next hole, the match goes back to "all square." It ends when one player is up by more holes than remain to be played, and that's how the victory is noted. For example, if a player goes up by four holes after the 15th hole, with just three holes left, the match ends with a "4&3" win. In the Ryder Cup, matches can be "halved," with each side getting a half point, but at the Accenture, tied matches go to extra holes until somebody wins.

into a cold rage. He slammed his putter in his bag and marched to the 17th hole.

"Goddamn fucking asshole," he hissed. I couldn't be sure he was talking about the baby, but I also couldn't rule it out. One hole later, Fowler had a 2&1 win, and Poulter's face was strung tighter than a violin wire.

Fowler reacted serenely to the win—he had expected his game to come together at some point, he'd been swinging the club well, and so forth. It seemed that he should be doing cartwheels, considering the size of the scalp he'd just taken, but Fowler's equanimity is legendary—he wasn't about to break character. And maybe he could sense big things coming; we didn't understand, as he may have, what sort of tournament, and what sort of year, he was about to have.

Elsewhere on the first day, Victor Dubuisson made quick work of Kevin Streelman, winning 5&4 on the 14th hole, and an Australian golfer named Jason Day played a bogey-free round to beat Thorbjorn Olesen 2-up.

―――――

"Somebody once said about certain golfers that they're afraid to win. When they have their good weeks, and a chance to get into the top five, a chance to win, there's something in their head that says, 'I'm not supposed to do this. I'm not good enough for this. I don't deserve this.'"

—Doug Ferguson, *Associated Press*

If you think of golf as a haven for the spoiled and rich, Jason Day is the hardscrabble kid who crashed the gates.

The twenty-six-year-old Day came into the Match Play Championship ranked number 11 in the world—by any measure, one of the best young golfers in the game. Among players in their twenties, you could argue that he was second in merit only to Rory McIlroy. He had the sport by the short hairs, and he was becoming an icon in his home country. There was only one blot on his résumé, but it was glaring—he'd won just a single event on Tour.

That's an abnormally low total for a player who spent more than three years ranked inside the world's top forty, and almost a year inside the top ten. Day is young, and his legacy is decades from rounding into final form, but for a golfer of such proven skill to have held a trophy just once . . . it hinted at deeper issues. Compare him, for instance, to McIlroy, a year younger but with more than a dozen titles to his name. Or Dustin Johnson, who had his own troubles with closing a tournament, but still had four wins before his twenty-seventh birthday. Or, climbing down from those dizzying heights, take Patrick Reed, or Harris English, or Keegan Bradley, all of whom had multiple wins early in their careers despite résumés and career earnings that paled in comparison to Day's. As the young Aussie would be the first to admit, part of it is growth. Part is learning *how* to win.

During one interview at the Accenture, Day listened as the topic inevitably arose. Why couldn't he finish the job?

"I think I finally realized," Day began, before hesitating as he looked out from the podium. "I think at the start of my career—"

He paused to collect himself.

"I'm going to be honest here," he finally said. "I came from a very poor family. So it wasn't winning that was on my mind when I first came out on the PGA Tour. It was money.

"I wanted to play for money, because I'd never had it before."

Day was born in Beaudesert, a town nestled in the southeast corner of Queensland, about sixty miles south of Brisbane and forty miles west of Australia's Pacific coast. Beaudesert has grown in the past three decades, but in 1987 it held about three thousand people. The name means "beautiful desert," a euphemism that disguises a mean landscape—one that terrorized early settlers who attempted to cultivate cotton or raise sheep, making them vulnerable to droughts and devastating floods from the nearby Logan and Albert Rivers.

Alvin Day, a native Australian, and his wife, Dening, who was born in the Philippines, met through letters, and never even saw each other in person before Alvin made the trip for the wedding. Back in Australia, they had two daughters and a son named Jason. Alvin worked on the kill floor of a meatworks, and Dening worked in the office, and together they struggled against the poverty that was forever encroaching.

Jason remembers his first house as an "old, broken-down home" on Dunsinane Street. The Days never had money to buy new toys, so the whole clan, including Jason's sisters Yanna and Kim, would sometimes visit the town dump ("the rubbish kip," as Day calls it) to forage. On one trip, Alvin found an old three-wood somebody else had trashed. He had been a decent tennis player in his day, but a toy was a toy, and so he brought it home to his son. Jason was three then, and he took to the club immediately, using it to smash whatever object was handy. The first thing he hit was a tennis ball, and the family legend has it that Alvin declared, on the spot, that his son would be a champion some day.

Day's obsessive nature was evident early, when he would toddle around in his backyard, fixated on the club. He lacked the strength to hit the balls over the fence, so he'd simply whack them from one end of the lot to the other, retrieve them, and start over again.

This went on until he was six years old, and finally met the minimum age requirements at the Beaudesert Golf Club. He started out playing six holes at a time, and sometimes his dad would drive him to local youth tournaments on Saturdays. At that point, he was using a mixed bag of clubs that included a 1.5 wood and anything he or Alvin could find on the cheap. Before long, recognizing his son's skill, Alvin went to a pawnshop to raise some cash. He bought Jason a set of second-hand Aussie PowerBilt 2000 clubs, and if his son wasn't addicted yet, that sealed the matter.

Shortly after Jason began playing at a real course, Alvin found a new job at a meatworks in the city of Rockhampton, just off Queensland's Capricorn coast, and relocated the family seven hours north. The move didn't improve their financial lot—that year, Jason and his two sisters bought their school clothes at the St. Vincent de

Paul Society, where they stuffed five-dollar bags with all the clothes they could fit. His new classmates teased him about his shabby wardrobe, called him a "refugee" and, because he was the only student with Asian blood in the school, asked him if he had just come off the boat.

But the move did change his access to golf. In Rockhampton, eight-year-old Jason would race home from school every day at three p.m. and wait for his next-door neighbor, a high schooler. Together, they'd set off for Capricorn Country Club, a course that has now expanded to fifteen holes and was even shorter then. The words "country club" inspire thoughts of well-manicured lawns and exclusive social milieus in America, but at the Capricorn, the name was quite simply a nod to the fact that it was plunked down in the middle of the bush. A club, sort of, and very much in the country.

It cost the Days only one hundred dollars to buy Jason a yearlong membership, which included unlimited golf. As long as you had enough balls and the daylight didn't run out, nobody would bother you. When the balls became scarce, Day would head for the lake on the first hole and dive in, fishing them from the floor. Golfers played through, hitting over their heads, and when Day came up for air, he sometimes found half a dozen leeches attached to his back. But he'd also have enough balls to continue.

Junior golfers in Australia are measured by grades, from d-grade to a-grade, and Day began working his way up the ladder rapidly. Before long, he was b-grade, which allowed him to play eighteen holes. The families at Capricorn would hire a bus and send their kids out at four a.m. for the long drive to each weekend's junior event, and Jason began to win. He gained a reputation, and his addiction grew.

It got harder before it got easier. When Day was eleven years old, his father began experiencing chronic stomach pains. Doctors dismissed it at first, but the pain persisted. Less than a month after he first had it checked, Alvin was diagnosed with stomach cancer. He died four months later.

By his own reckoning, Day went off the rails. He was only twelve, but he began drinking, staying out late, and getting in fights at school. His father had been the one to facilitate his golf game, from that first 3-wood to the pawnshop to the day he built Jason a putting green at the family home in Rockhampton, but his role had gone deeper than that.

"My dad was the strict one in the family," Day said. "My mom was always the one that, after we got the belt, she would hug us and tell us it was okay. My dad . . . I remember saying "shut up" one time, and he belted the crap out of me. But that's just how it was. I mean, he kept me in line. And as soon as he passed away, you know, we all got out of line."

Because Day is friendly, and far more open than your average golfer, I felt okay asking him what he remembered when he thought about this father.

"I *can't* remember him," he said. "I can't remember. It's just like I've blocked most of my childhood. I can't really think of anything. . . . You have little windows, and then you've got these little memories in each window, but it's pictures. Just pictures of my memories."

Had he blocked it out on purpose, or was this just a matter of memory fading with time? It wasn't a new question for him; his wife, Ellie, has suggested that he visit a psychologist to see if anything might open up. But it's not something he thinks about until he's asked, and in truth his relationship with his father is more complex than he sometimes lets on. He admitted to *Sports Illustrated*'s Alan Shipnuck that Alvin was an alcoholic and, depending on the interview, Day either credits his dad for giving him the focus he needed to pursue a professional career, or implies that he felt a pressure that could almost be crushing.

After Alvin's death, the family unit began to break down. One of his sisters ran away from home for three years, and Day's drinking got worse. Young as he was, he became an alcoholic. He brawled in school, and became sullen. His mother knew he had potential as a golfer, and she made a desperate choice. By taking a second mortgage on her home and enlisting help from one of Jason's uncles, she sent her son to Kooralbyn International, an independent boarding school known for producing top-tier athletes like track star and gold medalist Cathy Freeman, and the golfer to whom Day would always be compared, Adam Scott.[5]

Day remembers the loneliness of the trip south, when he was dumped without ceremony and left to fend for himself. His new school was in the middle of nowhere—some of the students had been sent by parents who wanted to get rid of them, and others were promising athletes hoping to turn professional. The culture, and the lack of surrounding temptations, made it easy for him to stop drinking and focus.

But the change wasn't immediate. On one of his first days, a Kooralbyn golf coach approached Day while he was on the range. He suggested that Day should work on his short game, and Day said he'd rather play the par-3 course. The coach insisted, but since his father's death, Day didn't listen to anyone. His stubbornness, and his issues with authority, quickly turned the exchange into a shouting argument. He and the coach raised their voices until they were swearing at each other, and Day stormed off to the par-3 course—he was going to do what *he* wanted, authority be damned.

One thing you quickly learn when speaking with Day, though, is that his life is defined by moments of personal reckoning. This was the most important of them all.

---

[5] It's worth noting that certain details of Day's biography tend to change or evolve from year to year, from story to story—particularly the parts that relate to his father's death, and his move to Kooralbyn. In 2011, *USA Today*'s Steve DiMeglio wrote that his mother had taken a second mortgage on her home to send him to school, and this detail also appeared in other stories at the time . . . either because other writers had read DiMeglio's version, or because Day repeated the detail in other interviews. On the day I interviewed him, at Concession Golf Club in Florida, he simply said that his mother borrowed money from an uncle to pay for school. *Sports Illustrated*'s Alan Shipnuck and Karen Crouse of *The New York Times*, who interviewed him the same day for the same type of story, wrote that she sold the house outright. These discrepancies can probably be ascribed to the ambiguity with which Day views his own childhood, and the extent to which trauma erased many of the details . . . or at least clouded them in his memory.

"I just thought, man, that wasn't a good thing to do," he said. "I mean, my family's trying to sacrifice so much to get me to come here. I should just kind of listen to him and see what he has to say. And from there, I went back and apologized."

The coach's name was Colin Swatton, and he was impressed by Day's atonement. After that day, he became a sorely needed father figure for Day. They stuck together through Kooralbyn, and when Day was ready to head for America, Col was by his side as coach and caddie. He's still on the bag today, and he probably will be for a very long time.

The Kooralbyn International School closed in 2002, and he and his class moved forty miles north to Hills International College in Jimboomba. Day, now fourteen, borrowed a book about Tiger Woods from his roommate. In the back pages, he read Woods's detailed results from age thirteen onward. What he saw was alarming—where Woods was shooting 68s and 66s, Day was stuck at 74 and 72.

"I kept saying to myself, why is he shooting those scores? Why is he so much better than me?"

He realized what Swatton had been trying to impart from the beginning—he needed to work on his short game. He also needed to work harder in general, and to channel the inherent obsessive nature that would let him focus on golf and golf alone. Day knew he had it in him somewhere. It had been present from age three, when he wouldn't let go of his rotting 3-wood, and it was the secret urge that drove almost every golfer who has ever made it big. Where others would get bored, or distracted, the future pro can spend hours on the range and the putting green, alone if necessary.

The realization change Day's life. He would wake up every morning at five—there's no daylight savings in Queensland, so the sun would be waiting for him—and practice until eight thirty. After sneaking in a half-hour breakfast, he'd be in school from nine until one, take a thirty-minute lunch, and go at it again until six p.m. Then dinner, then homework, and then it was out to the night range, where he'd hit under the lights until fatigue overcame him.

Each day, and each week, he'd use the book to track his progress against Tiger Woods. Other players at Hills would try to keep up with his extreme schedule, but it was rare for any of them to last more than a week before the allure of sleep trumped their own lesser obsessions.

Day's breakout came in 2004, at age sixteen, when all facets of his game seemed to cohere at once. When it clicked, it clicked fast. He won the Queensland Junior tournament, the touring Junior, the South Australian Junior, the Australian Junior, the New Zealand u-19s. Then it was home to the Queensland Amateur, where he competed against players of all ages and became the youngest winner in 104 years.

The results were enough to get him to America, and Torrey Pines, for the World Junior. There, he faced a group of the best fifteen- to seventeen-year-olds around the world on an incredibly difficult course. Only three players managed to shoot under par. At -7, Day bested them all. A year later, he finished as top amateur at the Australian Masters and the Australian Open, tournaments won by Robert Allenby. The last amateur event he ever played was the Australian Masters of the Amateurs in January 2006. He won with a gross score of 281.

Day had spent a painful childhood dreaming of the big money, and the hardest part of his life was about to end. The sponsors with the fat checks had seen plenty. Day, just eighteen years old, turned pro and signed a deal with TaylorMade and Adidas. From the moment he put his name to that first contract, he would never be poor again.

"I thought winning was going to come easy," Day told me, "because I'm like, 'Oh, everything's so natural.'"

Maybe that was the product of his short memory. Nothing had come easy before, but the success of the last two years must have seemed simple. Everything was progressing in a straight line. Day got sponsor exemptions into seven tournaments on the PGA Tour—his first chance to play with the big boys—and he and his team were optimistic (or naive) enough to hope he could earn his Tour card for 2007 with a series of spectacular results.

It wasn't a disaster—Day made five of seven cuts, and earned almost $200,000—but it wasn't nearly good enough.

Day knew how close he'd come, and that gave him hope through the disappointment. In 2007, he started his Nationwide Tour career in Australia, finishing thirty-first at the Jacob's Creek Open. He followed that up the next weekend with a tie for sixth in New Zealand. The money from those two finishes wasn't huge, but it was enough to return to America in April.

That spring, he learned his first lesson in media relations that year, when he told an Australian paper that his goal was to eventually wrench the number 1 spot in the world from Tiger's grasp.

"I'm sure I can take him down," he said, and the fallout was huge. The context he gave later in the quote didn't matter—he gained a reputation for brashness, and for putting the cart ahead of the horse.

Two years earlier, visiting Twinsburg, Ohio, as an amateur, Day walked into Mavis Winkle's Irish Pub with Col Swatton, who was meeting a friend for a drink. That was the first time Day laid eyes on a server named Ellie Harvey. She was nineteen, two years older, a girl from Ohio farm country who attended Paul Mitchell Beauty School by day. Day's behavior that day was proof that he wasn't *actually* brash—he was too shy to approach her, but he returned to Mavis Winkle's every afternoon with Swatton in tow. After they left town, Day used Swatton again to get her phone number. He began texting her in 2006, and though Ellie mostly blew him off, he wasn't deterred.

Now he was back in America as a professional. Within a week of his return, the Nationwide Tour brought him to the Legend Financial Group Classic in Highland Heights, just twenty miles north of Twinsburg. He and Ellie "ran into each other" again that week at Mavis Winkle's, and Day convinced her that he owed her a dinner. She knew nothing about golf, but she ended up watching him play that weekend, and it turned out to be a case of perfect timing—with a score of -16, Day won his first professional event, taking home a cool $94,500 and becoming the youngest player to win an event on any of the PGA's three major tours.

The next week, they had their first date at an Applebee's in Columbus. His career, and his romantic life, were off and running. He finished fifth on that Nationwide Tour that year to earn his PGA Tour card for 2008, and he and Ellie married a year later. Col Swatton was his best man.

At that point, the central question of Day's life changed from "how do you *become* great?" to "how do you *stay* great?"

Players find it difficult to describe the difference between simple excellence and actually winning tournaments. They recognize that at the highest level, the separation is mostly mental, but putting the concept into words is much more difficult. Most players grasp for the answer without success, but Day, eloquent as ever, gave the best explanation I've heard.

"You get to a point where it's that fight or flight," he told me. "Everyone has it—that point where you're like, 'Oh, I'm out of my comfort zone. I want to pull back a little bit.' And that's where you start making bogeys, and once you make a couple bogeys, then you're like, 'Ahhh, okay, now I'm back between fifth and tenth, back in my normal range.'"

It's unusual for a player to admit that there's comfort in losing, but you see it all the time, especially in majors—that tug that brings a front-runner back to the pack when he finds himself isolated at the top. First place can be terrifying, and in the critical moment, some players feel a pressing, subconscious need to escape the stress. The heartbreak comes later.

"What you have to do when you're in the fight or flight moment," Day said, "and you're out of your comfort zone and you have a chance to win—you have to be like, 'Screw it, gotta punch through it, let's go and do it.' And when you do, it's the most rewarding because you actually got *past* that barrier. And once you get to that uncomfortable stage a lot, you know exactly what you need to do, then it becomes easier to win."

Day got his big win at the Byron Nelson Classic in 2010, and entered the top ten of the world rankings after finishing at both the 2011 Masters and U.S. Open. The most acutely he's ever felt the pressure, though, came at the 2013 Masters.

Day and Adam Scott are inevitably lumped together as Australians at the very top of the game, but in some ways, they're opposites. Where Day, with a thin goatee framing his wide, friendly face, looks eminently approachable, Scott is so good-looking that he seems remote, even intimidating. Where Day is gregarious and a good storyteller, Scott is shy and intensely private. Where Day came to the sport from the most unlikely background, Scott is the son of well-off golf enthusiasts, and enjoyed a more traditional path to the top.

Despite the differences, they share a trajectory that goes beyond their Kooralbyn roots. In 2012, Scott led the British Open by four shots with four holes to play before a nightmare stretch of bogeys allowed Ernie Els to steal the Claret Jug by a single stroke. The collapse invited comparisons to Greg Norman, and though Scott did his best to hide his pain, it was no secret that the loss left him devastated. Was he just another Australian with immense skill who couldn't handle the pressure of a major championship?

Then came Augusta, 2013. Late into Sunday's final round, it looked like the younger Aussie would beat Scott to the punch. Day had shot up the world rankings, but his nagging problem had blossomed into a curse—in three years of excellent golf since his win at the Byron Nelson, he had never won a tournament. On its own, the stat was a little staggering; how could someone that good, who performed so consistently, *never* win? It became a talking point whenever Day's name was mentioned: great player, humble guy, couldn't close.

Ever honest, Day admitted that he had been a little distracted in 2012 by the birth of his son, Dash, and that it was tough to watch a player like Rory McIlroy receive all the "next big thing" accolades when Day felt that he was just as good. As his focus wavered, his team had to stage another intervention. "Work harder," they told him.

He did, and he rushed back up the world rankings in early 2013. It all led to Sunday at Augusta, where Day made birdies on 13, 14, and 15, and led the tournament with just three holes left. It wasn't quite the runaway lead Scott had enjoyed at the British, but the parallels were clear. He had a chance not just to *win*, but to win the biggest damn tournament of them all. It would put every question to rest, and it would do so emphatically.

The reason Day can explain the stress of winning, though, is because he's faced it so often on the biggest stage. It met him head-to-head that Sunday, and Day couldn't push through. Bogeys on 16 and 17 dropped him back to -7—away from that terrifying, lonely place atop the leaderboard—and when Adam Scott and Angel Cabrera each birdied no. 18, he was relegated to third.

He admitted in the post-round interview that the pressure got to him, and in 2014, he elaborated. "When I walked up to the sixteenth tee, my whole body froze," he said. "It seized up like never before."

Even in defeat, Day hoped an Australian would win. He got his wish minutes later when Scott sank a fifteen-foot birdie putt to win his country's first Masters.

It hasn't been easy for Day to move beyond the money. Ellie teases him for being a cheapskate, but he can't help it—sometimes, he told me, he'll visit his online bank account simply to gaze at the numbers, still shocked by what life has given him. And still wondering, deep down, if it will all be taken away.

As the millions piled up and Day's game continued to improve, he forced himself to ask a new question—"How do I become *so* great that I win tournaments?"

Day is a fierce match play competitor, and he had marked the Accenture as his best chance of the season to break the winning drought. He was suited to one-on-one golf, and he had already earned a reputation as a master at the head game. He's known for making his opponents putt everything out (some consider it rude not to concede the short "gimme" putts), and he doesn't care who it pisses off. Russell Henley was one of his victims in 2013—Day could sense his anger when he forced him to hole a series of short ones—though it nearly backfired when the Georgia native birdied the 18th to force extra holes before losing in 19. He did the same to Paul Casey in 2011, making him sink an eighteen-inch putt the likes of which Casey probably hadn't missed in two decades.

"I knew he was going to hole it," Day said afterward. "But it's not about that hole, it's about the future holes coming on. So if I can make him a little angry, if I can, you know, get him out of his game plan and force him to make silly decisions out there, you know, that's obviously part of the mind games that you play."

In 2014, his winless streak spilled into its fourth year, accruing the worst kind of psychological momentum, and he knew he had to make a move in Arizona. On Thursday, he almost took an early dive when he fell 3-down to Billy Horschel—a Florida native and one of the few American golfers who shares a modest economic background—and faced an uphill battle just to survive the round of 32. With a chance to go 4-up on the 10th green, Horschel three-putted, and Day capitalized on the mistake by winning 11 and 12 to shave the deficit to a single hole. The match raged on to the 22nd hole, when a final birdie by Day sent him through to the round of 16.

Fowler, the face of the Tour's youth movement, defied the odds to slay a second titan in Jimmy Walker, and the most anticipated match of the second round, between Harris English and Rory McIlroy, lived up to its billing as the Northern Irishman fell late.

While English basked in the glow of victory, Rory dealt with life as an icon. As he walked off toward the waiting SUVs, a group of preteen girls waited outside the ropes. They screamed his name as he passed by, like they were auditioning to play extras in a film about the Beatles. He flipped them a ball without looking over, and the girl who caught it began crying hysterically. Her family laughed at her, and she laughed at herself, too. But she couldn't stop crying.

• • •

On Friday, in the Sweet 16, neither Victor Dubuisson nor Bubba Watson played especially well. Dubuisson took a two-hole lead early, held on to the edge throughout the front nine, and increased his lead to 3-up with just four holes to play. Of the six holes he won on the day, five of them came on pars as Bubba bogeyed his way around the course. The Northern Trust champion finally woke up on 15, and fought back to 1-down with a hole to play. He could do no better than par, though, and the inscrutable Dubuisson was on to the Elite Eight.

Jordan Spieth, just twenty years old, was a machine without pause, dispatching Matt Kuchar 2-up. Jason Day beat one South African, George Coetzee, for the honor of facing another, Louis Oosthuizen. As for Rickie Fowler, his week wasn't getting any easier. After Poulter and Walker, he drew Sergio Garcia, another of Europe's Ryder Cup studs. Undeterred, Fowler caught fire on the back nine for a 1-up victory.

Graeme McDowell had come back from the dead in each of the first two rounds, but on Friday, facing his old Ryder Cup rival Hunter Mahan, he looked to be in fatal trouble. Down two with two to play, Mahan had him on the ropes. Cosmic justice was in the air—the Accenture didn't mean as much as the critical Ryder Cup match Mahan had lost to McDowell after a flubbed chip in 2010, which led to the American breaking down in tears at the press conference—but considering their history, the match surely meant more to him. Maybe it was the memory that made him tighten up no. 17, or maybe it was just a bad shot, but he bogeyed, keeping McDowell in the match. On 18, Mahan put his approach forty feet away and got in safely for a par. The onus was on McDowell, who had stuck his iron into the green, and needed a birdie from five feet to send the match to extra holes. He hit it, pumped his fist once, and strode off to the first tee.

From there, the match progressed like a nightmare for Mahan, and three holes later, McDowell put him out of his misery with a 14-footer for birdie. Mahan did his best to take it in stride as McDowell dropped his putter and brought his hands to his face in a combination of fatigue and disbelief. Hunter's eyes were dead. He had lost to his chief tormentor again, and after shedding his sunglasses and Ping hat to shake hands, he re-donned the disguise and walked to the black SUV waiting to take him away. Through the tinted windows, as the vehicle pulled away, you could see him staring out, obscured in his pain.

Eight players returned on Saturday, all of them fighting for a chance at the semifinals. It began poorly for Jordan Spieth, and it ended that way, too. After missing a par putt on the 16th hole, he took off his hat and conceded the match to Ernie Els. As he walked off the green, Spieth turned to look back at Els, who was taking his par putt just for practice. It lipped out, and Spieth turned away, disgusted.

"I *knew* he was going to fucking miss," he said.

A Sirius radio reporter asked if he had time for a quick interview, but Spieth disappeared into the SUV.

"I was a little mental midget out there," he told the media later. "Actually kind of embarrassing, looking back. I was dropping clubs and kind of just whining to Michael [Greller, his caddie], and you just can't do that."

It's difficult to dig beneath Spieth's surface sometimes, considering his immense skill at presenting himself as a mature adult, but the two keys to figuring him out as a golfer were both on display in the quarterfinal loss to Els—his impressive maturity, and a self-defeating petulance when things got tough. In 2014, the twenty-one-year-old's season would be defined by these dueling impulses.

For Day, it was never much of a battle in the first quarterfinal match, as Louis Oosthuizen fell 3-down early, giving Day an easy win and a trip to the semifinals for the third straight year.

Rickie Fowler took a day off from his bright colors, and came into his match against Jim Furyk wearing all black. Since Monday, he had spent his afternoons hiking up the hills behind his hotel. He went alone the first day, climbing twenty minutes to the top and enjoying the view, and on Tuesday he brought his sister and mother. His communion with nature was paying off, and he took an early 3-up lead over Furyk. The veteran fought back and survived to the 18th hole, but his approach came up short and rolled down into the desert valley. His whole body hinged forward at the waist as he realized what he'd just cost himself. Fowler hit safely onto the upper tier, and needing a great shot, Furyk tried to be too perfect. He came up short yet again. As the ball rolled back to him, a fan yelled out, "Always easier the second time, Jim!" Fowler two-putted for an easy win.

McDowell actually took a lead before the 18th hole for the first time all week in his match against Dubuisson, but the Frenchman fought back, and a seesaw battle ensued. On the 9th, Dubuisson pitched out from the rough left of the pin, and landed his ball perfectly on the fringe to dampen the speed. It was a brilliant shot before it ever went into the hole, and if anyone was paying attention, they might have begun to suspect what he had in store for Sunday. He pumped his fist like a man who had never done it before—like someone nervously shaking a pair of dice—and came into the 18th with a 1-up advantage.

Against McDowell, after the three matches he had just won, a late lead seemed almost like a curse, and when Dubuisson missed the green on his approach, it looked like the Northern Irishman might slither away again. But a fan encouraged Dubuisson with a very American exhortation—"Come on, Pepe!"—and his short-game magic saved him. A brilliant chip up stopped a foot from the green for a conceded par, and he had done what nobody else could do—he closed the un-closeable McDowell.

If Dubuisson felt any joy, he disguised it well in the press room, where he was distant, detached, and nearly sullen. This would soon come to seem normal, but for an American media that was largely meeting Victor for the first time, the mystery deepened.

And then there were four.

On Sunday morning, the Saguaro cacti on the foothills of the Tortolitas looked like solemn crosses marking the graves of an ancient race. Fowler brought some color to the scene, ditching his funereal black outfit for a pair of checkered orange-and-white pants and a hat with a screeching orange puma diving across the front. Day took the fight to him early in their semifinal match, going 3-up after eight, and again after 11, but nobody had been able to tighten the noose on Fowler yet. True to form, he won 12 and 13 to dig back.

But that was the point when his fight ran out. A bogey at 15 gave Day a 2-up advantage with three to play, and on the par-3 16th, Fowler needed a straightforward three-footer for par to extend the match. It was the kind of pressure putt he had been sinking with ease all week, but this time it lipped out on the left, and his run was over.

In the other semifinal, the early sense in the media room was that Dubuisson had finally come to the end of his Cinderella week. Like the cartoon coyote whose feet still churn even after he's run off the cliff, the French phenom was no longer on solid ground. When he went 3-down to Els at the start of his match, it looked like he would finally plummet.

Once again, we had misjudged him. He gathered himself from holes 5 to 7, and then went on a rampage, making birdies on three of the next four holes to surge to a 1-up lead. On the par-3 16, 1-down and thirty-two feet away off the tee, Els banged home a birdie putt to square the match yet again. After a half on 17, Dubuisson was rock solid again on 18, and Els blinked first. The lumbering South African missed his par putt and conceded Dubuisson's short effort, ending the match.

As the cameras converged on Dubuisson, he spoke so quietly that everyone in the press room leaned in to hear. He didn't sleep well the night before, he said. As he stood in the cluster, his clothes bedecked with odd, unheard-of sponsors—J. Lindeberg (clothing), Audemars Piguet (luxury watches), Robertet (a "fragrance and flavor house"), and something called Exelia, the purpose or origins of which I refuse to spend any more time attempting to uncover—he seemed to retreat without moving an inch.

The semifinals and finals are each played on the final Sunday, which meant Dubuisson and Day were sent right back out in the cool afternoon to decide the champion. Again, Day was red-hot at the start. He established another 3-up lead, and made spectacular birdies at 11 and 15 to arrive at 17 2-up with just two holes to play. Needing two wins to force extra holes as the sun began to set in Tucson, the unsinkable Dubuisson delivered. He birdied 17 and made a par on 18 that Day failed to match. In a tournament full of high drama, there was no way the final match could have ended in anything but sudden death. On they went, into the fading light.

The win had been tantalizingly close for Day, and he felt that familiar urge beckoning—*enough is enough. Back down.* The discomfort of being in the lead had haunted him at the end of the first eighteen holes, and now he had to shake himself loose. He managed to steel his resolve and submerge the negative thoughts, and on the first playoff hole it looked like he had the tournament won when Dubuisson nuked his seven-iron approach over the green.

The ball came to rest at the base of a jumping cholla, stuck among the needles, covered by sharp branches and seemingly inaccessible. The lie was miserable—smart money said that any attempt would result in five to seven branches of prickly cholla embedded in his upper body, and zero balls on the green. The Frenchman had run out of options, though, and knew he had to try. Without much prepararation, he took a sudden swing and smashed a branch off the cholla, hitting a television cable in his follow-through. Miraculously, the ball jumped off the desert floor, bounced onto the green, and rolled to within five feet.

Jim Nantz, on CBS, hadn't even finished speculating about whether he might take an unplayable lie. He interrupted himself as he watched the result: "Oh my goodness!"

"That's it, I've seen it all," said David Feherty. "I mean, if Arnold Palmer rode by on a scooter . . ."

To Day's disbelief, Dubuisson had set himself up for par. He made the putt, and the match continued. If that great escape felt karmically unjust, imagine Day's state of mind when it happened *again* on the very next hole. This time, Dubuisson's approach nestled beneath a yellow-flowered brittlebush. Again, the lie looked totally unplayable. And again, Dubuisson took an awkward sideways stance and smashed his club at the plant. The ball shot out over the hard desert floor, cleared the corner of the black stadium risers, and landed with perfect speed just off the putting surface. Somehow, against the laws of physics and logic, it rolled onto the green and settled about eight feet from the hole.

"This is absolutely bizarre," said Nantz.

"I give up," offered Feherty.

After that, there was no question about whether he'd make the putt. He had desert voodoo magic in his hands. Another par, another extension. More disbelief from Day, this time caught on TV—his mouth hanging open, an incredulous smile on his face. He later put words to the expression: "Why won't this guy go away?"

Twitter blew up, with the likes of Graeme McDowell, Jason Dufner, Gary Player, and Tom Watson expressing their astonishment. Much was made of the fact that the name "Dubuisson" loosely translates to "of the bush." Javier Ballesteros, son of legendary Spanish golfer Seve, put the thoughts of many into words when he wrote, "It doesn't matter who wins, Victor Dubuisson is my new hero! #magic."

"Haven't seen short-game magic like that since Seve," added Rory McIlroy.

John Peterson put it this way: "There is no tweet that can justify how nasty those 2 up and downs were."

When Day described how it felt to watch Dubuisson hit those incredible escape shots from the desert, his answer doubled as a metaphor for his life.

"It was just like you'd turn the mountain and you'd see more mountain," he said. "And like, God dang, you'd come to the part every time where you just felt like you just couldn't go anymore. But I'm like, no. I'm going to push until I can't push. If I need to play thirty-six more holes, if I need to come back Monday, if I need to come back Tuesday—I don't care how long it's going to take. I'm going to win, and I'm not going to stop."

The next two holes were both halved, which brought them back to no. 15, the drivable par four. Both took out their drivers—the time for laying up had come and gone. Dubuisson hit first, landing his tee shot in the rough to the right of the green. Day did the same. Crucially, though, he kept it close enough to have a reasonable pitch from the rough. He stopped it close to the hole, leaving himself a birdie attempt. Dubuisson's own pitch, from the deeper grass, got nowhere close; his short-game Santeria had finally run out. His long try went begging, and when Day knocked his birdie home, the odyssey was over.

In the hectic aftermath, Feherty grabbed Dubuisson to conduct a post-match interview. He seemed to be expecting some type of enthusiasm, but the Frenchman was totally, unrepentantly, and incorrigibly himself. He muttered his way through a few questions, mentioned that he hit some terrible shots, and seemed ambivalent about his incredible desert escapes. Feherty, who is just as funny as he seems on TV, can usually coax blood from a stone. With Victor, though, he'd met his match. The interview was a dud, and when the camera stopped rolling and Dubuisson had walked away, Feherty shook his head and sighed.

"Shoot me now," he said, to nobody in particular. "Shoot. Me. Now."

Day had no such inhibitions. It had taken him almost four years, but he was a winner again, and he did it by surviving the greatest duel—and the last—in Accenture Match Play history. At that moment, every dream was in reach.

MARCH

One Month in Florida

4

PALM BEACH GARDENS, FLORIDA

Russell Henley, Rory McIlory, and the Moving Needle;
The Honda Classic

"This game . . . seems like the harder I try, the harder it is."
—RUSSELL HENLEY

With the onset of spring, the Tour leaves the West Coast. Gone are the jaw-dropping ocean vistas of Pebble Beach, the electric hustle of Los Angeles, and the violent beauty of the desert. In their place, we get the Florida swing—a monthlong trek, from Palm Beach Gardens to Miami to Tampa to Orlando, through a state without a soul. Somewhere in this mess, I became convinced, was the exact spot where the American dream turned into a nightmare.

Traveling across the country almost always gave me a deeper appreciation for the spirit and diversity of my native land, but in Florida I found an exception. This was our national heart of darkness—a crowded, endless stretch of homogenous highways and homogenous homes blurring together in a feverish hallucination of stucco and palm trees, broken up by chain restaurants and box stores. Without knowing it, I had embarked on a depressing journey that felt claustrophobic from the very start. The entire month was an extended vision of uniformity and tacky commerce run amok. Soon, a creeping sort of ennui had me in its grips, and I had vague thoughts of driving to the Everglades and renting an airboat and a swamp-side villa just to clear my head. God knows what would happen to me there, but at least if a fifteen-foot gator had me in its jaws, I'd feel something other than this bleak Florida dread.

Paradoxically, though, I began to love the golf more than ever—it was the only escape. So I was present on the first day of March, when, after a third-round 68 at the Honda Classic, Russell Henley sat between two potted plants on a plush chair in the makeshift interview room at the PGA National Resort & Spa and fielded questions about Rory McIlroy.

Henley, twenty-four and still a minor figure on Tour, was running up against a harsh reality that defines the vast majority of golf coverage in America. There are very few players who "move the needle"—an insidious piece of media jargon describing how certain content can drive traffic to a website, sell newspapers or magazines, or otherwise produce profit. Since golf is a niche sport, the only players who truly move the needle are icons—such as Tiger, Rory, and Phil—or buffoons, like John Daly.

It doesn't take a genius to see how this becomes a vicious cycle—if you tell casual fans only about Tiger, Rory, and Phil, they'll only *know*—and care—about Tiger, Rory, and Phil.

Resistance is futile. It's the nature of the business of golf that mainstream outlets—by which I mean media giants that cover a broad selection of sports and aren't golf-centric—will sacrifice depth of coverage in order to generate traffic by churning out content on the select group of needle-movers. It's nobody's fault; the writers get their mandates from the editors, who get their mandates from data, which dictates the happiness of the advertisers, which determines the bottom line. Jobs are at stake, and making an ethical stand is a poor career move. More than ever before, writers can be replaced, but traffic cannot.

In this case, the questions about Rory were justified. Henley would enter the final round in second place, trailing the Next Tiger Woods by two strokes, and a close look at the Georgia alum gave you the distinct impression that he would be the helpless victim of a brutal ass-kicking in less than twenty-four hours.

At first glance, Henley emits that cloying country club vibe—blond hair worn in the thick, side-swept style known as the "southern swoop" or "Bama bangs," and a cocky grin that makes him look like the evil rich kid in an eighties teen movie. Watch him for longer than a minute, though, and that impression slips away as you start to notice two other quirks. First, his eyes—they default to a wide, awestruck stare, so that he looks like a child meeting his hero for the first time—or, as his college coach Chris Haack put it, "like a deer in headlights." Second, his mouth, which hangs in a slack-jawed, insensible state, and combines with the shell-shocked eyes to give him the air of a mental patient who has just wandered into Times Square at rush hour.

Henley is another Georgia boy—an all-state basketball player from Macon. He started golf late, but he became a surprising star at Georgia. With Chris Haack by his side, he went 5-0 over two years in NCAA match play golf, capping off his career with a win over Augusta State's Henrik Norlander in the national championship match.

As his presser wound to a close, a clamor rose outside the room as the crowds began to yell. You could hear the word "Rory!" floating up from the cacophony, and suddenly the mob had purpose. Just then, as if the scene had been choreographed specifically to terrify Henley, the sound of bagpipes pierced the din.

The real explanation was innocent—Rory was next up with the press—but from inside, it felt like Henley was a pretender to the throne, waiting with trepidation as the true king arrived with his army at the castle gates.

Then again, nobody knew exactly what to expect from Rory, either. He had solidified his status as the greatest young player in the game by winning two majors before his twenty-fourth birthday, but 2013 hadn't been exceptionally kind to the boy wonder. Entering the season, the heir apparent no longer looked like the wunderkind of popular imagination. By his high standards, his last year had been a bit of a disaster, and critics harped on the so-called distractions. A sponsorship change from Titleist to Nike in November 2012, along with a pending lawsuit, had seemingly screwed up a very good thing.

The Honda was just his second American event of 2014 after the Match Play, where he'd been eliminated on Friday, and it was America's first real chance to see the new and improved Rory.

"I'm currently in a little bit of a rebuilding phase, in a way," he told us. "I feel like I'm much more experienced, I'm much wiser sitting here at twenty-four."

He also thought back to the 2011 Masters, which stood as the chief disappointment of his young career. After holding a four-shot lead heading into the final round, he closed with a disastrous 80 to drop all the way to 15th. Since then, he had never lost a 54-hole lead, and that was no coincidence—he'd learned not to play cautious and merely hope for a win, but to aggressively pursue it even from the top.

For Henley, already trailing by two strokes, the situation looked untenable. He left the interview room, just one night's sleep away from what became the strangest final round of the season.

If anyone expected Henley to make a move, they were keeping it to themselves. At PGA National, with its endless expanse of palm trees and water hazards, the final round went according to script for eight holes—Rory adhered to his "make them come to you" mind-set, and after a few birdies and bogeys for both, they were right back where they started heading to the ninth hole, -12 and -10.

At that point, I noticed something odd—beyond a short greeting on the first tee, the two players hadn't spoken to each other once. It was my first experience with Rory's subtle, intimidating style, and it took almost nine holes before I noticed. Even now, after watching Rory for an entire season, I can't tell if anything he does is intentional, or just the unconscious dominance of a superstar. He speaks only when it suits him, he rarely bothers to watch an opponent's shot, and when he does turn his focus to another human, he has a way of looking *through* them.

Everything is internal with Rory—he twists his mouth up on one side when he walks, lips pressed tight, as though he's literally suppressing whatever judgment is on his mind, zipping it all up and letting you guess what he might be thinking. And while everyone is aware of *his* presence, he seems to be unaware of anyone else's. Even the way he walks gives an ambiguous impression—his head bobs up and down, like he's nodding at everyone he passes, and his upper torso barely moves, so that if you watched him from the waist up, you might think he was riding a horse.

You can sense greatness in him, but it's not the aggressive superiority of Tiger Woods or the wild, reckless talent of Phil Mickelson. Instead, it's a self-contained, quiet belief that resonates with unshakable confidence. It conveys a single message to his opponents: You will react to *me*.

It's very different off the course, where Rory is friendly, sharp, and quick to smile. The transformation he undergoes is strange to behold, and can be very uncomfortable to face in a competitive environment.

Rory's ascension to his former glory was still a few months away. His play became shaky almost out of nowhere on the seventh hole, and a bad chip on the ninth dropped him to one-over for the day. At that point, phones around me began to buzz, and the other media members who had been following the final group suddenly sprinted away in a mass exodus. Word spread rapidly in a series of urgent whispers—Tiger had withdrawn! Back spasms! Thirteenth hole! In a flash, I was alone with the two men most likely to win the golf tournament—the latest, greatest instance of move-the-needle journalism.

Henley had climbed within a shot, but a penalty on 10 cost him a stroke, and a hole later, a scoreboard told us that Ryan Palmer and Russell Knox had improved to -10. When Rory hit his drive in the rough on 12 and missed his long par attempt, he had accomplished the direct opposite of his goal—he had come back to the field.

A photographer hit him with a rapid-burst shot on 13, a staccato sound that annoyed Rory—"Really?!" he yelled. Henley's terrific approach to 11 feet led to a birdie that brought him to -9, just one shot away. We passed the modest fairway homes on 14, and after a mediocre approach, Henley sunk a thirty-seven-foot chip shot. He pumped his fist, and now there was a four-way tie for the lead.

The cheers of "Go Dawgs!" came flying at Henley wherever he walked, and now they were louder than usual as he stood over his tee shot on the 15th, a 179-yard par-3. It was the start of a series of three holes known as the "Bear Trap"—named after Jack Nicklaus himself, who had redesigned the course in 1990. The murderous troika is narrow all the way, with water lining the right side of each hole, and the ubiquitous wind wreaking extra havoc. A statue of a bear on his hind legs greets you as you walk up to the 15th hole, along with a plaque featuring a quote from Nicklaus: "It should be won or lost right here."

Hopped up on adrenaline from his chip-in and smelling blood, Henley went right at the flag. The shot faded badly, and he didn't even have to watch it land—he'd found the water. He failed to get up and down from the drop area, and the resulting double bogey looked like the end of his tournament.

But the weirdness had just begun. On 16, Rory's drive flew way left into a fairway bunker. With 192 yards to the hole, he left the ball out right, and it, too, found a home in the bright blue water. Like Henley, Rory couldn't get up and down from his drop, and after having the tournament in his grasp, he was back down to -8.

Russell Knox had double-bogeyed 14, relegating him to a -8 finish, and now Ryan Palmer had the lead at -9. When Henley made par on 17 and Rory bogeyed—"Put it in the drink, Rory!" someone had shouted, to general boos and a few guffaws—all Palmer had to do was par the 18th. He made a bit of a mess of the hole, but still gave himself five feet for his par . . . and missed.

That left one group on the course. Henley found his brother Adam in the gallery between holes, high-fived him, and asked, "Having fun yet?" He'd been drinking water compulsively in the humidity all day, and he chugged another bottle while he waited to tee off. The clouds were low, the breeze whipped the palms behind he green, and in the lake to the right, four fountains spewed geysers around a Honda car that seemed to float on the water's surface.

Rory bombed his drive into the right fairway, leaving himself 236 yards to the hole, and Henley gave himself an even better angle on the left side. The 18th hole bends hard to the right by the green, even as the water encroaches into the turn. It meant that Rory would have to fly his shot almost entirely over water, and a couple of bunkers, to land the green. Henley had a much better angle, but his second shot stayed left, and wound up landing in a woman's merchandise bag among the gallery. Rory stepped up next, and delivered what looked, at the time, like the shot of the tournament—a spectacular 5-wood that flew over everything and stopped on a dime, eleven feet from the hole.

Henley barely got this third shot onto the green, and was lucky to escape with par after a solid fifty-seven-foot lag putt. The crowd's attention turned to the icon; somehow, despite disasters on 16 and 17, Rory's shot had given him an unlikely eagle putt to win the tournament.

He missed—it just wasn't his day. The tap-in for birdie completed an ugly round of 74, but he still held a share of the lead at -8. When Rory walked through the tunnel leading away from 18, they passed the tournament trophy, a giant ceremonial car key, and his fiancée, Caroline Wozniacki, decked out in yoga pants—"Good to see you," "Good to see *you*." Girls all around screamed his name, but he didn't look up. Henley, unnoticed, slipped off to use the bathroom, but not before shooting a wide-eyed stare at Wozniacki.

With darkness settling in on Palm Beach Gardens, four players— Rory, Henley, Knox, and Palmer—headed to the 18th tee for a playoff. The sloppy play continued. Rory found the back bunker on his approach and chipped over the green with his third shot, while Knox hit a rough lag putt and Palmer missed his birdie. Henley, the only player on the green in two, lagged his eagle putt to three feet, tipped his visor to his brother, and knocked in the birdie to win the tournament.

Henley's win was the ultimate proof of the old adage—you don't have to be perfect to win on the PGA Tour. Afterward, he stood with just a handful of journalists and friends at the scoring tent, while Rory commanded a huge audience on the other side of the path, his pale Irish face glowing in the bright lights.

Even in defeat, and even in doubt, Rory maintained his aura. He resonated in a way that you could feel. And even in triumph, Henley seemed somehow diminished by comparison. When the winner walked away, I wondered if that essential fact could ever change. One day, I thought, as I watched him go, maybe you'll move that needle, too. If they ever let you.

5

THE VILLAIN

Patrick Reed

I f you were on the lookout for a tournament that could serve as a catchall metaphor for the Changing of the Guard—how Tiger gave way to Tiger's Children, and how the generation he inspired is mercilessly ushering him out of the game while he fights a losing battle against time and karma—then the place to be in 2014 was the WGC-Cadillac Championship, where sixty-nine of the best players in golf came to do battle at Trump National Doral's redesigned Blue Monster course. They made up one of the toughest fields of the season, all of which was pure satisfaction to the Gray Monster himself: Donald Trump, the tournament host.

On that Sunday, in the second-to-last group, you could watch Tiger tee up on number one, three shots off the lead and fixing to prowl like the old days. Red shirt, black pants, slim and fierce. And if you looked to his right, to the putting green about thirty yards away, you'd see Jason Dufner stop everything to watch the spectacle unfold. It's hard to ignore Tiger anywhere, but Sundays find him at his most essential, striding like a Colossus down the fairways he's owned for the better part of twenty years, trailing an afterglow of awestruck spectators. He commands an energy unlike anything the sport has ever seen or may ever see again, and he carries himself like a man born to the role. The announcer on the first tee puts an added emphasis on the name, the people erupt, and the noise settles into reverie as he addresses the ball. All eyes are on him.

With one exception. Look past Dufner, farther down on that same putting green, and dig the chunky kid wearing headphones—they're blaring "Radioactive" by Imagine Dragons—hunched over his ball, facing defiantly away from the icon. He's wearing the red-and-black combo, too, as he's done since age ten, in homage to the man on the tee. You'd guess that the moment might be too big for the kid; that he'd wilt in the presence of his hero. But that's only if you didn't know Patrick Reed.

———

Q: Do you think the media's making you out to be a villain?
REED: Yeah. For sure.

Patrick Reed: Twenty-four years old, built like Babe Ruth—short, heavy, with a barrel-chested frame that makes you think "stocky" and "power-ful" rather than "fat"—quick to anger, even by pro golf standards, and a born winner.

Those are the descriptions that come to mind when you study Reed's résumé and watch him on the course. He recently became just the fourth player in the last two decades to win four times on the PGA Tour before his twenty-fifth birthday. The other three are Tiger Woods, Rory McIlroy, and Sergio Garcia—names that demonstrate the lofty company he keeps.

With Reed, though, success is never simple. There has always been something a little off-key brewing beneath the surface of his story—a swirl of rumors dating back to his college days, when he lasted a year at Georgia before transferring to Augusta State and eventually facing his former school for the national championship.

The more Reed won on Tour, the more inevitable it became that his complicated history would return to haunt him. Finally, after the big-gest win of his career at the Cadillac Championship last March, *ESPN's*

Ian O'Connor dragged some of the skeletons from the closet in a Masters-week story called "Patrick Reed's Turbulent Rise." O'Connor's research, spanning courthouses and coaches and parents and former college and high school teammates, lifted the veil, at least slightly, on Reed's youth. The story made it clear that his peers had never really liked him, especially at the college level. A new picture of Reed emerged: brash, arrogant, abrasive, unapologetic, driven. He turned potential friends against him, and he never seemed to care about the consequences—at least not enough to change.

In terms of the nitty-gritty details, O'Connor couldn't quite pierce the wall of silence put up by the very same people who seemed to despise Reed. A citation in an Athens courthouse revealed that Reed had been arrested for intoxication his freshman season, but if that was the standard for a villain, half of the country would be doomed. The reason why Georgia coach Chris Haack had kicked Reed off the team remained a mystery, as did the ensuing troubles at Augusta State, which head coach Josh Gregory and Reed's former teammates kept close to the vest.

It was clear that the ESPN story had struck only a glancing blow—there was more here than a drunken night. As another media member put it to me, "That was as close as anyone ever got, and they didn't get that close."

From the start of my travels in a year on Tour, I found Reed to be one of the most compelling young golfers on the scene, and I tried to arrange an interview with him as early as January. He proved an elusive figure, even with a cooperative agent, but I finally sat down with him and Justine—his wife and former caddie, who had just given birth to their first child—at the Greenbrier Classic in West Virginia in early July. I held off on his college years as long as I could, but eventually I broached the topic. It led to an awkward exchange:

ME: Did you read Ian O'Connor's article?
PATRICK: No.

ME: I mean, a lot of people want to know—
PATRICK: I talked to him about it.
ME: You did talk to him?
PATRICK: I think so, yeah.
JUSTINE: Yeah, I read it.
PATRICK: Yeah. Yeah no, it was at . . .
JUSTINE: You read it.
PATRICK: We were at Augusta, huh? He talked to me before he wrote it.
ME: But you didn't read it?
JUSTINE: I think he read it.
PATRICK: I think so, I don't know. There's so many articles . . . it's so hard . . .
JUSTINE: There's so many stories. But I do recall that story.

From Reed's body language after I said O'Connor's name, I sensed that he knew exactly what I was talking about. I didn't blame him for his reticence—it's not incumbent upon Tour players to provide unfavorable information about themselves. Total honesty can have a detrimental effect, and there was no reason for Reed to do my work for me.

But I *was* curious to see his reaction to O'Connor's story, and the fact that he had feigned ignorance until his wife essentially called him out was telling—it had hit home, and it was something he worried about. Before moving on, I brought up the idea that when you *really* looked at the story, there was nothing too damning beyond the kind of alcohol infraction experienced by hordes of college students every year—including myself.

ME: But see, the interesting thing for me was . . . I mean, I'm someone who got arrested in college for shooting off a fire extinguisher. It feels like everyone I know does, so it felt like whatever he wrote wasn't *everything*. It was like, "Oh, that's it?"
JUSTINE: It was everything.
PATRICK: No, the article he wrote was everything. I mean, it's . . .
JUSTINE: There's nothing else out there.

Those responses came quickly, and reminded me of an old trope: The cop standing in front of a grisly car wreck, saying, "Move along, nothing to see here!"

Patrick Reed was almost literally born with a golf club in his hands. His father, Bill, worked as a medical sales rep, and he came to realize over the course of his business career that his bosses mysteriously formed strong bonds with employees who could break 80. With his wife Jeannette, a stay-at-home mom, Bill began to learn the game, and when Patrick was born they placed a set of plastic clubs in his crib.

The Reeds belonged to the Dominion Country Club in San Antonio, and Bill and Patrick first played in a father-son tournament when the boy was three. Patrick caught his first glimpse of Tiger Woods at a pro-am when he was six years old, and though he couldn't fight his way through the masses to get an autograph, a fascination was born—he idolized the consummate winner.

Despite his age, Reed became addicted to the sensation of a great shot—those blissful moments when you couldn't even feel the ball come off the face. He improved rapidly, began competing in youth tournaments, and even appeared on Saturday morning children's TV programs to show off his skills.

After a few years in Pittsburgh, the Reeds moved back to San Antonio, where Patrick would race home from school on weekdays to squeeze in a few holes. Even at a young age, he brought an unusual focus to the sport, right down to the smallest details. When he was ten, he stopped wearing shorts on the golf course because he saw that the pros had to wear pants. At his junior tournaments, in the brutal heat of midsummer, he'd be the only kid in khakis.

Reed began to dominate the youth golf circuit in Texas, and his father placed him in higher age brackets. He had a few friends, but his dedication to golf, and the fact that the family kept moving while Bill climbed the corporate ladder, made him a natural loner.

His obsession with golf deepened. His parents took him to junior tournaments both locally and across the country, and with the con-

stant travel, Reed soon learned to adapt to new circumstances. He also
spent a lot of his childhood sick—the frequent changes in climate and
temperature meant a never-ending litany of colds and sinus infections.

Two of Patrick's dominant personality traits emerged early, and both
worried his parents. The first was his incredible capacity for rage. He
expected so much of himself that when he went into a slump, he'd
transform into a sullen powder keg of frustration and anger, to the
point that his parents wondered whether he truly enjoyed the sport.
Reed always insisted he was fine, but the explosions painted a different
picture.

The other problem was his outward shows of confidence, which
crossed over into a cocky, arrogant tone too often for Bill's liking. He
knew his son's success somewhat depended on this self-assurance, but
when Patrick introduced himself to strangers by saying things like,
"I'm Patrick Reed, and I'll kick the shit out of you at golf anytime you
want," Bill also knew he had a problem. The issue was that Patrick's
obsession was all-consuming—he had no other interests, and though it
made him one of the best juniors in the country, it also meant that his
self-worth was entirely wrapped up in the game. Combined with a
natural arrogance and a snarly demeanor, he had a knack for bad first
impressions.

But what was the solution? The difficulty, according to his parents,
was that while they tried to keep him humble, everyone around them
was telling Patrick how great he was. The constant praise made it difficult to regulate his behavior outside the home. They worried about
burnout, but those fears never came to pass. They watched as other
top-ranked junior golfers dropped out or peaked too early while Patrick surpassed them all.

By the time he was fourteen, he was traveling on his own to AJGA
tournaments and other major junior events, staying within the network
of host families wherever he went. In those homes, meeting strangers,
he mastered the language of grown-ups. Later, his coach Josh Gregory
would laugh at the fact that despite all the troubles, you could always

put Reed in a room full of adults and he'd be totally at ease, and totally charming.[6]

In eighth grade, Reed and Cody Gribble committed to the University of Texas and head coach John Fields, creating a bit of a stir. Though it had become common in big-time sports, they were the first golfers to declare at such an early age. Bill and Jeannette didn't know if it was a smart move, but once again, Patrick's will proved indomitable. The family had moved to Baton Rouge a year earlier, though, and by the time Reed entered high school, the commitment had already softened considerably.

University Laboratory School, a prep high school on LSU's campus, is generally reserved for the progeny of wealthy Louisianans— senators, governors, rich executives, athletes. The Reeds had no delusions about applying to send Patrick there, but word came through the grapevine that maybe, yes, he *should* apply. Chuck Winstead, the LSU golf coach, knew about Patrick, who had just won the junior British Open in Liverpool, and though it was never made explicit, the Reeds came to understand that by getting Patrick into the school, the LSU golf program hoped to get a leg up in the recruiting process.

In order to apply, they needed two letters of recommendation, and they knew nobody of any importance in Louisiana. Not to worry— they were told that this, too, had been settled. The application went in, Patrick was accepted, and it wasn't until later that the Reeds learned about the letters. One came from a former basketball player, they told me, and the other came from Nick Saban, the football coach who would go on to win the national title at LSU that season—neither of whom they knew, and neither of whom knew Patrick.

At U-High, as it was called, Reed had access to excellent college golf facilities. It was also where he met Kris Karain, a fellow student

---

[6] Incidentally, I found the same to be true—the angry tyrant I had watched on the course, and the rowdy troublemaker I'd imagined, were never in evidence in a one-on-one setting. I enjoyed my time in West Virginia with him and Justine more than most of my interviews with Tour players, and I thought of him as a good storyteller with more charisma than I'd expected.

who became a good friend. The Karains turned out to play an important part in Patrick's life—he later met Kris's older sister, Justine, who was in school at LSU and Our Lady of the Lake College working on a dual degree (nursing and health administration). In time, she became his wife and caddie, and when she became pregnant in 2013, a third Karain—her younger brother Kessler—took over on Patrick's bag.

Reed won two state titles in Baton Rouge, and in O'Connor's *ESPN* story, one of his teammates illustrates his demeanor:

> "If you ever challenged him at something, he answered it every single time," [Darren] Bahnsen said. "In one practice round I hit a drive down the middle, about 275 yards, and felt good about it. Patrick said, 'Man, that's a good drive,' and then he got down on two knees and hit his ball 10 yards past me. From his knees."

Success followed success, and during a chance visit to Athens, Georgia, on the way home from a summer tournament, the Georgia coaches used the opportunity to show him the school facilities and make their pitch. Reed fell in love. A few weeks later, he reversed his commitment to Texas, ignored LSU completely, and pledged his college years to Georgia.

Again, Reed's parents faced a conundrum—would they make him honor his commitment to impart a lesson about keeping promises, or would they allow him to pursue the college life he wanted? In the end, they let Patrick determine his own path. John Fields was more than a little upset in Austin, but there was nothing he could do.

Reed won the Louisiana state championship as a junior, and since he already had enough credits to play Division 1 golf, Chris Haack encouraged him to come to school a year early. The class above Reed was full of unknown quantities, and Haack thought he might need Patrick sooner than expected.

As it turned out, those unknown quantities were Russell Henley, Harris English, and Hudson Swafford, all of whom panned out in a big way. It was too late for Reed to reverse course, though, and when he finally came to Georgia, he found himself as a cog in a stacked roster that included the three super sophomores and senior star Brian Harman.

Haack had a rule that any player who made the semifinals of the U.S. amateur in the summer wouldn't have to qualify for the first college tournament in the fall. When Reed advanced to the final weekend, losing to Danny Lee in the semis, he was exempt for the start of his college career. This, along with his penchant for boasting, isolated the seventeen-year-old Reed when he arrived on campus. The fact that he knocked out a veteran whenever he qualified for a tournament didn't help—Reed wasn't the kind of kid who was equipped to handle the delicate situation with the requisite tact. If anything, it was reminiscent of another Georgia player who ran afoul of his teammates and coach in a year with an unusual amount of talent. Like Bubba Watson, Reed quickly drifted outside the Bulldogs' tight inner circle.

When he explained to me what went wrong in his freshman season, Reed chalked it up to being overwhelmed by the sheer amount of *people* in such a small area, leading him to seek out a more comfortable environment.

The full story, however, shines a light on a golfer who veered completely out of control in his one year at Georgia. If arrogance were the only issue, he might have merely remained an irksome presence. It wasn't, he didn't, and the situation grew much worse.

Long after I spoke with Reed in West Virginia, I contacted multiple sources close to the Georgia program. What they told me was startling: Reed's teammates that season didn't just hate him—they actually suspected him of cheating during a qualifying event.

When I presented these accusations in an article before this book was published, Reed appeared on the Golf Channel and stated that he had never been suspended for cheating (which, for the record, I never wrote). He claimed he had a sworn statement from Chris Haack affirming his position. Two days later, the journalist Stephanie Wei reported that the sworn statement from Haack was quite short, and simply said that while Patrick Reed was at UGA, Haack "was not aware of any allegations of cheating" against Reed, and that such allegations "played no role" in Reed's dismissal from the UGA golf team. However, in Wei's report, Haack confirmed that he *had* heard of these allegations after Reed left Georgia. "It seems as though Reed's lawyers are attempting to play a game of semantics," Wei wrote, "and hoping that the public will misconstrue Haack learning later as Haack never learning at all—which is not the case."

It also turned out that the arrest for intoxication—when Reed was found drunk at two-thirty a.m. on campus—was only the first of two alcohol violations. The second came during the week of a Georgia football game. That day, Reed and a friend had loaded up on alcohol before leaving for the game.[7] Later that night, near Atlanta, he was arrested again on a second alcohol charge.

This time, the Reeds hired a lawyer, and were able to keep word from reaching the team after a judge threw out the case. By February, though, Chris Haack found out, and he scheduled a meeting with Patrick. According to the sources, Reed came in for the meeting with his mother Jeannette. When Haack brought up the second arrest, Jeannette reacted with surprise:

"We thought no one knew," she said.

At that point, sources say, Haack realized there had been a cover-up, and he couldn't trust anything that came from Reed or anybody else in the family. Haack's discovery that Reed had kept his second alcohol violation a secret was the straw that broke the camel's back. Haack began the process of severing ties between Reed and the golf team. Reed kept his access to all facilities for the rest of the academic year, along with academic tutoring, but in terms of Georgia golf, the relationship was over. It was understood that Reed would transfer for his sophomore season.

* * *

[7] To Bill and Jeannette, the drinking was a new side of Reed—he had never had much of a social life at all in high school, and though he had the odd girlfriend here and there, drinking was never part of his agenda. Their theory today is that Patrick was trying to fit in on a college campus where he felt desperately alone.

The choice came down to Florida, Wake Forest, and Augusta State, and considering that his parents now lived in Augusta, he didn't brood over the decision for long. Head coach Josh Gregory sold him on the idea that he'd already tried the big schools, and it was time to see how he'd function in a smaller environment. Reed could see the wisdom in that, so he chose to spend the next two years at Augusta State, living at home the second year.

Gregory's program was an interesting anomaly in the sport—golf was the school's only Division 1 program, and the college itself had none of the allure of the surrounding SEC and ACC universities. Augusta State lacked their huge student populations, top-level football programs, and sprawling campuses. When Reed was in high school, Gregory didn't even bother recruiting him; as he told me, "Augusta State doesn't get the Patrick Reeds of the world."

Recruiting against schools like Georgia and Georgia Tech was a pipe dream—no student would visit both places and come away with an urgent desire to make Augusta his college home. Instead, Gregory would look for mid-level talents in the southeast that had some of the competitive drive he coveted—guys he could mold into great players. He also recruited internationally, where the reputation of his competitors didn't carry quite as much weight. And, when fate dealt him a lucky hand, he'd take the odd castoff; the stud like Reed who, for whatever reason, couldn't cut it at his original school.

Gregory had been a lifelong underdog himself, a college golfer under Hank Haney at SMU who never won a tournament, and he knew almost from the minute he turned pro that he lacked the mental game to succeed. When he looked around at his friends who were thriving at the highest levels, he saw players who believed they were twice as good as they actually were. Gregory was the opposite—he never thought he was half as good as he really was—and the sport made him miserable. But the analytical brain that spoiled his playing career made him an ideal coach. He knew exactly what to look for, and he became an expert not only at finding diamonds in the rough, but training them to take down the high-profile stars who had overshadowed them their entire lives.

Even for Gregory, Reed represented a new challenge entirely. He understood that he needed a player of Reed's caliber to put a very good Augusta State team over the top, and he also knew that Reed wasn't squeaky-clean. But he had no idea how bad things would get, and how fast. Once again, Reed made a terrible first impression, angering his teammates and making life difficult for his coach. He talked too much about himself, refused to listen to advice, and came off as someone with deep insecurities who was trying to project an infallible image.

When I asked Gregory what form Reed's behavior took, he described a player who was so intent on proving that he was the best golfer—motivated by an intense fear of failure—that he couldn't turn it off and have normal social interactions with his teammates. Even though adults liked him, he had a one-track mind around people his own age, and his relationships with golfers became antagonistic and tense. He would openly tell his teammates that he was better than they were, that he was going to beat them, and so forth. They didn't enjoy having him around, and Reed could sense their dislike. It hurt him, and it exacerbated his need to prove his value on the golf course—to identify completely with the idea of Patrick Reed the golfer. The self-defeating cycle perpetuated itself, driving an enormous wedge between Reed and the rest of the team.

On one memorable night—one of the few times he hung out with his teammates in a social setting—sources say he became so belligerent toward one of his teammates that the situation grew violent. He also got suspended at the start of the season for reasons that long remained shrouded in mystery, kept secret by golf's omertà.

The news *did* reach the Georgia golf community, and the cause of the suspension—confirmed by multiple sources—didn't surprise those who knew him back in Athens: accusations by teammates that he had shaved strokes in two qualifying events.

Reed has denied these allegations, and in his Golf Channel appearance he referenced a second sworn statement his lawyers had obtained from Josh Gregory to back him up. The statement that Gregory provided to Reed's lawyers stated that Reed's suspension stemmed from a "scoring error" and asserted that Gregory had "no evidence that [Reed] ever cheated." The statement from Gregory also mentioned that the relationship between Reed and his teammates was "very strained at this time."

After Reed's Golf Channel denial, Stephanie Wei and Steve Eubanks contacted former teammates of Reed's, and they elaborated on the events leading to Reed's suspension from the Augusta team. According to them, Reed turned in incorrect scores in two straight qualifying rounds, which Reed's teammates took as a clear sign of cheating. Reed's teammates confronted him in a team meeting, where he became aggressive and denied shaving strokes on purpose. Gregory sat the team down down a second time without Reed present, and they voted unanimously to kick Reed off the team. According to Wei, Gregory initially assented, but later changed his mind and reduced the penalty to a two-match suspension. The players briefly considered sitting out as a protest, but finally accepted Gregory's decision.

The suspension cost him the first two tournaments of the season, and Gregory told him that unless he grew up, and grew up quickly, he'd never make it either in college or on the PGA Tour. Gregory also placed a phone call to Haack, angry at just how difficult his player had proven to be, and Reed's teammates held several meetings that year deciding what to do about the black sheep. In addition, a source close to the scene told me that Reed would have tense phone conversations with his father after events he didn't win, and that these often became accusatory and angry, devolving into intense shouting matches before Reed hung up. The exact nature of the relationship wasn't well known, but the sense among the team was that Bill was unreasonably tough on his son.

There were never any official findings at either school regarding these claims. Nonetheless, allegations of cheating dogged Reed during his early career at both schools. It's tempting now to paint a story of redemption—a path upward from the darkest hours. But with Reed, there was never a seismic personality shift in college. In 2011, he stopped hanging out with his teammates off the golf course completely. He was slightly more cordial with his teammates, but when I asked multiple sources whether this meant they actually *liked* him, the response was unanimous: hell no.

In fact, something odd began to take shape with those Augusta State teams. Where most coaches preach team chemistry, what developed between Reed and his teammates was the opposite. They so despised each other that the environment became abnormally competitive—particularly between Reed and Henrik Norlander, two alpha dogs who wanted to beat each other so badly that they played with a desperate intensity even in practice rounds. It's not the textbook way to build a team, much less one that any coach would recommend, but for Augusta State, it created a hard edge among the players that served them well in NCAA match play. The idea of being intimidated by some unknown opponent was laughable—they had to deal with Patrick Reed every day.

Everyone I spoke with agreed on one thing—if it wasn't for Josh Gregory's guidance and belief in Reed, he would have gone off the rails and been out of NCAA golf within a matter of months. The fact that he showed any improvement, or at least kept himself out of trouble, was due entirely to the standard Gregory set, and the artful way he dealt with a player who didn't respond well to authority.

Still, his teammates' attitude never changed. Before the last round of his college career, in the national championship against Harris English, a group of Reed's Augusta State teammates approached English—one of the most well-liked, easygoing players in the sport—with an emphatic message: They wanted to win a national title, but they hoped English would whip Patrick Reed.

The trouble was, *nobody* whipped Patrick Reed, especially in match play. In a one-on-one situation, he could escape his head completely and focus on beating a single opponent. During his sophomore season, after riding out the suspension, Reed proved that he was a valuable addition to the team, quickly forming a strong 1-2 attack with Norlander.

In June, at the NCAA Championships at the Honors Course in Ooltewah, Tennessee, the Jaguars shot well enough to secure the sixth position after the three stroke-play rounds ended. A year earlier, the championship format had changed; it used to be a stroke-play event from start to finish, but now the top eight teams after the medal rounds would face off in a match play bracket. That meant Augusta State, the 6-seed, would face Georgia Tech, the 3-seed, with five players from each team squaring off in a best-of-five contest.

Reed drew Chesson Hadley that day, the Yellow Jacket who would go on to become PGA Tour Rookie of the Year in 2014. Neither player ever established more than a one-hole lead, but coming down the 18th hole, Reed, who had proven his match play chops at the U.S. amateur the summer before he came to Georgia, was 1-up. They needed his win, as Tech led 2-1 in matches completed. Hadley's approach was medio-cre, landing more than thirty feet from the pin, and Reed, sensing blood, put his twelve feet away. Barring a miracle, a two-putt would win. Incredibly, though, Hadley holed his long birdie attempt. The pressure was squarely on Reed, and he responded, sinking his own birdie and letting out a primal shout when it fell.

Henrik Norlander won the deciding match on the 18th hole, and Augusta State pulled off the upset to advance to the semifinals. There, they handled the Florida State Seminoles, with Reed winning again, and it was on to the championship, where they'd face their stiffest chal-lenge yet in top-ranked Oklahoma State. The Cowboys featured future pros like Morgan Hoffmann, Kevin Tway, and Peter Uihlein—son of Wally Uihlein, CEO of the Acushnet Company and the man who runs Footjoy and Titleist, which makes him one of the most powerful peo-ple in golf.

Uihlein is as close as anyone comes to golf royalty, and Reed, with his combative nature and the giant chip on his shoulder, seemed to take a special pleasure in playing against him. They drew each other that day, and after Uihlein took the first hole, Reed won the next three. That led to the seventh hole, where Uihlein conceded a short par putt to Reed, and Reed refused to return the favor when Uihlein's birdie attempt rolled up next to the hole. Uihlein, annoyed, missed the near-gimme. The annoyance turned to rage as he swatted the ball into a water hazard, and Reed, now 4-up, knew he'd won the mental game.

He coasted from there, and the match ended 4&2 in Reed's favor. Henrik Norlander and Mitch Krywulycz came through in their matches, and Augusta State's motley crew of underdogs had its first national title.

Afterward, Reed approached Gregory with tears in his eyes and thanked him for sticking by his side. He knew how close he'd been to losing his second team in two years, and how it would have poisoned him for every other college program. He had nearly sabotaged himself out of both a national title and the stable foundation he desperately needed before launching his professional career. Only Gregory's forbearance had saved him.

The 2011 national championship was held in Karsten Creek, Oklahoma State's home course. When the hosts won their quarterfinal match and Augusta State—now the 7-seed—topped Georgia Tech for the second straight year, a revenge narrative took shape. The bitter Oklahoma State players had made comments the year before to the effect that the best team had lost, and they were eager for another crack at the upstarts who had left a sour taste in their mouths.

Thousands of Oklahoma State fans lined the course for the semifinal. Josh Gregory compared the atmosphere to a Ryder Cup—the fans erupted when one of their players hit an approach to thirty feet, yet stayed completely silent if an Augusta State player stuck one inside five feet. Gregory walked with Henrik Norlander during his match against Kevin Tway, and they were on their way to the 13th tee when he decided to stir the pot.

"Tough crowd out here today," he said loudly, giving Norlander a fist bump.

"Shut up, asshole," came the response from a voice in the crowd.

Gregory loved it, and the atmosphere was right up Reed's alley as well. He was set to go last in the running order, and he knew the match could come down to him, which was just fine—he wanted the pressure on his shoulders. When the draw came out, and he saw that he'd be facing Peter Uihlein for the second straight year, he thought, "Even better."[8]

Uihlein was now the reigning U.S. Amateur champion, and had played in the Masters in April—a rare honor for a college student—but the accolades only seemed to stoke the flames of Reed's competitive fire. Uihlein, from the start, never had a chance.

Reed birdied six of the first eleven holes, and as he walked up the 10th, Uihlein looked at him with something like disbelief.

"Every time I play you, it's like I run into a buzz saw," he said. "You just cut me down."

Reed won the match by the gaudy score of 8&7—he had faced the top amateur in the world, and the player *The Wall Street Journal* had called "the next great champion" just two months earlier, and humiliated him on his home course.

Norlander won again, and in a dramatic final match that went extra holes, the team had to rely on their fifth golfer, Carter Newman. "He was probably the most nervous guy out of all of us," Reed told me, adding that when he realized their hopes depended on Newman, his first thought was "Oh, *no*." But Newman salvaged a victory, and

---

[8] After telling me how happy he was when he realized who his opponent would be, Reed was quick to add that Uihlein was his "good friend"—a typical verbal maneuver for Reed, and one which I might even have believed if he didn't keep using it in reference to certain golfers, such as Harris English, who I knew definitively were not his friends.

  Later in the year, when I told Henrik Stenson that Reed had included him in the "good friends" list, he laughed, and responded with his unique brand of dry Swedish humor.

  "I wouldn't say that we go way back," he deadpanned. "I played one practice round with him at Wells Fargo a couple years ago. And . . . well, it's nice if he thinks that everyone he knows a little bit is one of his friends. That's obviously a way to look at it. But if I'm going to express myself politically, I guess he's an interesting character."

  Later, when I asked why he kept to himself on the range, I got a truer version from Justine: "Really, he has few good friends out here, but he's not worried about being the most popular guy." I looked to Reed, who nodded. "She basically nailed it."

sent Augusta State to the championship round for the second straight year.

Waiting for them, on the other side of the bracket, were the Georgia Bulldogs.

Gregory worried that Reed would be too amped up for his match, considering the circumstances, and he tried to emphasize that focusing on the opponent wouldn't help. It had limited effect—Reed wanted the win worse than he ever had before, and nothing Gregory could say would calm him down.

Reed's teammates delivered their message of support to Harris English, and the match was on. This time, Reed fished his wish—Russell Henley beat Norlander, Hudson Swafford lost, and the teams split the other two matches, leaving Reed and English as the last men on the course. Their point would decide the national championship.

"If you were to go back in history and ask Harris if there's one match that he wanted to win," Chris Haack told me later, "that was the match. Not only did it mean winning the national championship, which was ultimately what we all wanted, but just a lot of the . . . oh, gosh, I don't know, the way that things always transpired with Patrick . . . it just wasn't a very . . ."

Here he trailed off, before concluding, "I want to take the high road here."

Reed held a 1-up lead early, and though English squared the match before the turn, Reed won the 10th and 13th holes to go 2-up. He held the same lead heading into the 17th, and needed only a half to win the match. Neither player hit a great drive, but when English hit his approach into the water, the match was down to its dying embers. Reed made a mess of the hole, but still left himself with two putts from six feet to win. His first crawled up to the cup, and the second was conceded.

Just like that, Reed had finished off the greatest two-year underdog act in college golf history. Josh Gregory and Augusta State had won back-to-back national championships, and they did it in style, beating two of the sport's biggest juggernauts.

For Reed, it was the end of a short but brilliant college career, and the cherry on top of a 6-0 match play record at the NCAA championships. He kept his emotions in check—deep down, he knew Haack wasn't wrong to let him go, and as badly as he wanted to win, there was a bittersweet feeling knowing his college career was over.

To the Georgia players and coaches, though—and even to some of Reed's teammates—the win represented the opposite of a fairy-tale ending. Reed and English had deserved different fates in their final match, they thought, and everything about it felt deeply unfair. One of O'Connor's sources, in the *ESPN* story, called it "the death of karma."

———

Q. Do you ever feel guilty, like your wife is kind of tiny and she's carrying your big bag?

PATRICK REED: No, not really, due to the fact the first time we ever carried it, it was 106, humid and sunny, and once the 18th was done [she] was like, 'All right, I'm ready for some more,' and I was almost done. I could barely move. So I don't feel sorry for her. She should feel sorry for me.

That same night, Reed was in a car, driving from Oklahoma City to Memphis, where he had a sponsor's exemption at the FedEx St. Jude Classic. In the span of a day, he opted out of his senior year and turned professional. He proposed to Justine in January, and his new fiancée told him that she'd like to try caddying. Her endurance on that first blistering day in Houston—Reed loaded up the bag with extra water bottles and rain gear to make it as tough as possible—sealed the deal.

In 2012, they decided to use sponsor exemptions on the PGA Tour where they could, and to compete in the one-day Monday tournament qualifiers, where non-exempt, non-Tour golfers can fight for a spot in the field. From April to August, their lives took on a hectic rhythm—drive to the Monday qualifier, play in the tournament if they succeeded, make the cut, finish up on Sunday, and drive like hell to the next Monday qualifier. They endured more than a few sleepless nights as they raced across America, hellbent and exhausted.

His record on the year was remarkable—he went six-for-eight on those Mondays, twice making birdies on the 18th to qualify on the number, and got a handful of sponsor exemptions to boot. He made seven of twelve cuts on the season, and earned just over $300,000. A nice start, but as in 2011, it wasn't nearly enough to earn his Tour card for 2013.

Instead, he took his second crack at Q-School, and this time he qualified for the final stage—six rounds in La Quinta, California, for the last time ever. Only the top twenty-five plus ties advanced, and after the second round, when Reed shot a 75, he was below 130th place and ready to throw in the towel. He had checked out, and he knew his failure meant another year in limbo, without a PGA Tour card. The thought is enough to devastate even the toughest golfer, but when he told Justine, she refused to let him quit.

"It's another Monday," she told him, and that would become a rallying cry whenever Reed needed to muster a single great round. He strung together a series of 67s and 68s, and he made the cut in 22nd place. The unbelievable comeback was complete, and he had his card. Later that month, he and Justine were married.

. . .

At the Wyndham Championship in Greensboro, North Carolina, the next August, Reed found himself holding the first 54-hole lead of his PGA Tour career. He caught fire on Sunday, shooting a 66, but ahead of him, Jordan Spieth did one better with a 65. That left the two tied after 72 holes, and they headed to the 18th tee for a playoff.

If Reed vs. English had been a good vs. evil story for some of the players involved, Reed vs. Spieth wasn't far off. Where Reed, still largely unknown on the Tour, had a rough reputation, Spieth, who had just turned twenty, was a poster boy for all that golf was supposed to represent. He was clean-cut, respectful, well-spoken, and professional—a fantasy of what an athlete should be. He was already a winner, too—he'd holed out to make a playoff at the John Deere Classic, and survived five playoff holes to beat Zach Johnson and David Hearn.

The two were like fire and water, which may be why they would go on to form such a strong team at the Ryder Cup a year later. After Spieth survived the first playoff hole with a miracle recovery, they moved on to the second playoff hole—the par-4 10th. This time, the roles were reversed—Spieth bombed a 3-wood into the fairway, and Reed went right, barely staying in bounds. It was so close to the white stakes that a volunteer signaled out-of-bounds—effectively ending the tournament—and Reed pulled his hat down low so nobody could see his face. In the midst of this low, four other volunteers ran out to the fairway and gave the safe signal—the first volunteer had made a mistake.

Spieth put him under the gun yet again with a beautiful approach that left him twelve feet for birdie. Worse, Reed's drive had stopped under a hanging tree branch, off the fairway and even off the rough, resting on an uphill lie in a bed of dirt next to a clump of bushes. He tried to move two TV cables away from his ball, and nearly tripped over his bag as he moved them backward.

The situation was impossible, but Spieth's excellent second shot left just one option—a low screamer through the trees, dead straight with a three-quarter 7-iron that he measured at 163 yards. With the ball well above his feet, Reed felt like he was playing tee-ball again, and he knew if he hit the full 8-iron he needed, the ball would fly left. Even clubbing up, the shot wasn't exactly inviting, since a fairway bunker and plenty of rough obstructed him from getting much roll, forcing him to carry the shot all the way to the uphill green. Reed also hated straight lines—he saw curves whenever he envisioned a shot, but the trees wouldn't allow for a draw.

He punched the ball out with almost no follow-through, and it took off low and climbing. The improbable shot cleared the crest of the hill by a foot, and landed six feet from the pin. It was the feeling from childhood all over again—the ball coming off the clubface like a dream, barely felt, going exactly where he wanted it to go. Spieth gave him a thumbs-up from across the fairway, and later called it one of the most unbelievable shots he'd ever seen.

Spieth was up first with his birdie attempt, and he over-read the break by a half inch at most. Reed had the easier putt, shorter and straighter and uphill, and he hunched over, struck the ball, and watched it break toward the left edge of the hole. When it dropped, he was a PGA Tour champion.

"I'm hoping one day he'll come out and have the honesty to talk about his past. It would really be a great cleansing process for him, but I don't know if he'll ever do that. I wish he would, because unfortunately he's going to always get questions about his past. Always questions about what happened at Georgia, what happened at Augusta State, what happened with his parents. I wish he would get it off his chest at some point in life, because I think it would help him become a better person."

—Josh Gregory

It's hard to know whether a troubled athlete ever truly changes, and the ubiquity of high-paid experts dedicated to crafting their player's image casts a cynical light on the concept of personal growth. Which changes are sincere, goes the unanswerable question, and which are mere PR window-dressing and stagecraft, designed to lure a gullible writer?

"He has a big heart," said Bill Reed. "It's hard for him to show it in certain circumstances, because he needs to be on guard. He's so driven, and to him he thinks it's a sign of weakness. And you have to understand, too, he's still only twenty-four years old, and he's been in the adult world a lot sooner than children his age should be and need to be."

Brian Harman put it more bluntly.

"You have to remember that he was seventeen years old," he said, of Reed's freshman year at Georgia. "We all do a lot of stupid shit when we're seventeen."

• • •

Reed became estranged from his family after graduating from Augusta State and leaving home in 2011—an estrangement that has lasted to the present. Neither his mother or father were invited to his wedding in December 2012, and contextual clues indicate that the relationship worsened from there.

When the *Augusta Chronicle,* ignorant of the longstanding rift, ran a tame video interview with Bill, Jeannette, and Patrick's younger sister Hannah after his win at the Wyndham Championship, sources told me that the Legacy Agency, which represented Reed at the time, requested that the video be taken down. The matter died when the *Chronicle* refused to capitulate, but the gesture shows how strained the relationship must be.

For their part, the Reeds didn't want to speak on the record about the divide—"As a parent, no matter how much pain you're going through, our philosophy on it is we're never going to throw one of our own children under the bus," Bill said. "No matter how much our children hurt us, I'm not going to hang them out to dry in a national setting."—but Bill is on Twitter, with a profile picture showing father and son at a golf tournament, and a tweet from December 2012—on Patrick's wedding day—seems to make a pointed statement about his relationship with his son: "You can love someone with all your heart but there is no promise they are going to love you back. The ladies in my life are best!"

His mother, Jeannette, also has a social media presence, and her Twitter feed is dense with vague messages that hint at a relationship gone sour, and alternate between bitterness, sadness, and the hope of reconciliation. The latest instance came in December, when she wrote, "One would imagine the pure joy of Christmas past would touch a person's heart in some way #miracle #hope."

One message in particular seems to be a reference to Justine: "There are doers, givers & takers in the world. You do & give it your all out of love & support, the takers step in & take what is not theirs."

Bill Reed put the subtlety aside in 2015 when he became angry that Patrick didn't reach out on Hannah's birthday.

"Very sad and heartbreaking at #PatrickReed did not wish his little sister happy birthday God has a plan wish we could see it," he wrote, and both Jeannette and Hannah responded in kind.

In 2015, Alan Shipnuck ran a piece for *Sports Illustrated* alleging that Justine had gone so far as to have police officers throw Bill and Jeannette out of the tournament at the U.S. Open in Pinehurst when she spotted them watching Patrick. On December 19, 2012, Hannah Reed tweeted "It's the devil's birthday todaaay #hopeyouhavefun." The devil, in this case, was Justine.

But the full scope of family relations is too complex to be untangled from a few words on social media. For now, it's enough to say that Patrick Reed is fighting a battle on two fronts. On the golf course, he's winning in style, and may be the toughest young American in a generation loaded with talent. Off the course, he's been painted into a corner by a complicated past and the questionable choices of the present.

These were the conflicting lives he brought to Doral that Sunday, when he stood on the putting green with a three-shot lead, ignoring Tiger Woods.

6

DORAL, FLORIDA

The Cadillac Championship; Tiger and the Top-Five Kid

Q. The red shirt, I know your previous two wins you wore a red shirt. Do you always wear a red shirt in the final round?
PATRICK REED: I do.
Q. Why is that?
PATRICK REED: Well, the best player ever to live when I was growing up wore black pants, a red shirt.

Doral is a charmless, monotonous lump of a city that blends in my memory with the rest of Florida, but Donald Trump's Blue Monster course isn't half bad. It's a difficult track, with lots of water and a wide diversity of trees—bischofias, java plums, oaks, strangler figs with their veiny, intertwined trunks, and palms everywhere—and as you make your way down the attractive fairways, you can almost forget that you're in the middle of a suburban hellscape.

As it happened, Tiger had bigger problems that afternoon than his unwanted protégé—he could barely cope with himself.

Off the first tee, Tiger yanked his drive to the right and took out an unsuspecting German tourist with a direct hit to the head. You could hear the cries ahead, and by the time I hustled up to the scene of the carnage, he was an awful bloody mess—his white shirt stained red, bloody rags littering the ground around him, and no medic in sight. He was curled up on himself, and Tiger walked over and pretended to be sympathetic as he counted the moments until he could continue his round and let actual trained professionals do their job. "I'm sorry about that," he said, shades still on, as the man rocked back and forth in a daze. Tiger gave him a signed glove and moved on.

It sounds convenient to say this now, but I swear I could feel Tiger's power ebbing with each hole. After his Sunday withdrawal a week earlier, the chinks in his armor had grown suddenly visible, widening with alarming speed until you looked at him and could see only vulnerability. He wasn't alone. There were other signs of generational change, too—on Friday, Phil Mickelson made three straight double bogeys, and after the round, when Golf Channel's Jason Sobel asked him when he'd last had a stretch that bad, he snapped back with, "Four hours ago." Even Jim Furyk, the ageless wonder, had opened with 78-77-75 to fade to the bottom of the leaderboard.

I knew I had to stay with Tiger, at least for nine holes, to watch this bizarre scene play out. It didn't take long—on the third, his drive hooked left, back into the gallery, and hit another spectator just below his jaw. Unlike the bleeding German, this victim—maybe twenty years old, American, male—couldn't have been more pleased at the new throbbing bump on the side of his neck. Tiger, who by now was running perilously low on gloves, signed another and gave it away. "Can I get a pic?" the kid asked, but that was more than Tiger was willing to abide. He stalked away from the gallery, his round going to shit, and promptly smashed his next shot into the water.

It got worse from there, although he managed to spare his fans any more violence. He re-aggravated his back injury while hitting out of a bunker on six, suffered spasms throughout the rest of his round, and limped in with a 78, falling to 25th place. He left Doral that day and spent the next weeks trying to rest and get ready for the Masters. Gradually, though, the pain from the nerve impingement got worse—he experienced shooting sensations down his leg, as well as numbness in the extremities, and in the end it was difficult to even get out of bed.

Tiger is a stubborn man, but even he realized that this back problem wasn't going away. He was left with no choice—he opted for a microdisectomy on the last day of March. It was the same surgery Graham DeLaet, a much younger man, had undergone in 2011. DeLaet didn't start hitting balls for four months, and it took him a year to fully recover. Woods, on the other hand, couldn't make himself wait three months before he was playing competitive rounds, and he paid the price for his haste—the rest of his year was a disaster, and cast serious doubt as to whether he could ever return to his previous form.

Tiger would be back, and maybe one day he'll rediscover his greatness, but that Sunday at Trump National, it felt like we were watching the final act of a legend.

While Tiger was waging war on the spectators, German and American alike, Reed got off to a hot Sunday start with three early birdies. On the third and fourth holes, he made putts of twenty-three and nineteen feet to take a six-shot lead on the field—Dufner and Mahan were fading almost as fast as Tiger, and would each finish with a 76—and proceeded to make nine straight pars to take a commanding lead into 14.

Elsewhere on the course, as his rivals plummeted, there weren't many players putting up red numbers. Jamie Donaldson had stumbled early, which left Bubba Watson within threatening distance at -1. Soon the gap would tighten, just as it had at the Humana. Bubba stuck his tee shot on the par-3 15th to nine feet and sunk the birdie, and then opted to go over the water on the par-4 16th, landing in a greenside bunker and getting up and down for another birdie. He made par on the last two holes to finish with a 68—the second-best round of the day, after Jonas Blixt's 66—and took the clubhouse lead. Two groups ahead of Reed, Donaldson quickly got his act together, with lethal approach irons on 10, 14, and 17 that produced birdies. With a hole left, he improved to -4 for the tournament.

The tournament was still Reed's to lose, but he found the rough off the tee on 14—not a thick rough, necessarily, but clumpy and irregular—missed the green from there, and took bogey when he couldn't get up and down. That left him at -5, and his situation began to look tenuous when he landed his iron in a greenside bunker on the par-3 15th. From forty-four feet away, holding on to a slim lead, he pulled off one of his best efforts of the day, a soft bunker shot that nearly found the hole for birdie. He tapped in for par, and couldn't help but smile at himself. He slapped five with the kids near the ropes as he walked to 16, where he decided to play cautious on the dangerous par 4. Instead of taking the water route like Bubba, he laid up on the right side. The "safe" option wasn't much safer, though, because of the narrow fairway, and his tee shot found yet another bunker. Now in full scrambling mode, staving off bogey after bogey, he got up and down from twenty-two feet for another par.

Inside a glassed-in viewing area overlooking the 16th green and 17th tee, you could hear the sound of blaring salsa music. Most of the spectators drank cocktails and socialized without paying attention to the action outside—Miami sports fandom in a nutshell. At the entrance to this VIP area, desperate lonely men could get their photos taken with two beautiful, busty women in white dresses who would fake a toothy smile while Miller Lite girls in tight shirts offered free gift certificates. This kind of blatant selling of sex isn't typical at professional golf events—they're too proper for that kind of thing—and it was in these deft touches that you could see the tacky, invisible hand of Donald Trump.

Wearing a white dress of her own—the maternity style—Justine followed Patrick outside the ropes. She was due with their first child in late May, and her younger brother Kessler was on the bag. They'd put him through a caddie boot camp in December—a "grueling month," he told me—and it had paid dividends already with the Humana win. Now, as they stepped up on 17, a look at the scoreboard revealed that Donaldson had made birdie on the hole and closed to within a shot.

Reed took out driver on the long par-4 and missed the fairway for the fifth straight hole, and wound up in the bunker for the fifth time on the back nine. Only a day before, he had called his fairway sand game a weakness, but this time he managed to find the green with his second shot. His aim now was to two-putt from fifty-four feet and pray that Donaldson didn't birdie the 18th—a realistic prayer, seeing as how it was one of the toughest holes on the course. Once again, facing a tough par save, he manufactured a special shot; his lag traveled fifty-three feet and stopped less than a foot from the hole for another easy par.

On the 18th tee, Reed peered into the distance at the green. The Blue Monster's final test is also its signature hole. A 471-yard par-4, it bends to the left, curving around a lake. The fairway is narrow and dotted by palmettos, and anyone who takes a risk by using a driver off the tee brings the water into play on the left, and fairway bunkers on the right. Those who *don't* take a risk, though, can end up with an impossibly long approach to the green, which veers to the left at a harsher angle than the rest of the hole, so that there's a water risk in the front and the left . . . not to mention the spitefully narrow bottleneck landing area ahead of the green, and the greenside bunkers on the right.

Reed needed to know where he stood, and the groans and cheers ahead made it unclear exactly what Donaldson was enduring on the green. The fans around him speculated blindly, with the kind of assurance that only the totally clueless can muster. Everything from birdie to double bogey was mentioned, until the man holding the boom mic for NBC received word—Donaldson had bogeyed.

Reed now held a two-shot lead with nobody left on the course to trouble him, and he shifted his mind-set accordingly—it was time to play for bogey. A 3-iron landed safely in the right rough, just where he was aiming, far away from the water. From there, he laid up to the right side of the fairway, seventy-six yards away and with a dry approach angle. A cautious wedge to the back left pin placement came up thirty-two feet short—his only iffy shot—and a good lag left him a foot and a half for the bogey and the win. He polished off the putt, looked up, and raised a fist. He had secured the third, and biggest, win of his career.

"Not since Ian Poulter declared a few years ago that Tiger Woods would soon be his only rival has a player caused such a stir as the American Patrick Reed."

—*The Daily Mail,*
in a story called "Meet the Yanks' Answer to Ian Poulter"

In the immediate wake of his victory, after receiving homage from the big shots who descended on the 18th green—Donald and Ivanka Trump and all the well-coiffed Trump children, Jeb Bush, PGA Tour Commissioner Tim Finchem—Reed stood with NBC's Steve Sands and made a comment on live television that would forever change his relationship with the media.

In an interview that ran on NBC the day before, Reed mentioned that he considered himself a top-five player. It didn't produce much of a reaction, and the real clamor—including the comment that would follow Reed around all year—didn't start until Sands brought it up again as Reed basked in the glow of victory.

"I've worked so hard," he said. "I've won a lot in my junior career, did great things in (my) amateur career, was 6-0 in match play in NCAAs, won NCAAs two years in a row, got third individually one year, and now I have three wins out here on the PGA Tour.

"I just don't see a lot of guys that have done that, besides Tiger Woods, of course, and, you know, the other legends of the game. It's just one of those things, I believe in myself and—especially with how hard I've worked—I'm one of the top-five players in the world."

I was minding my own business in the press center when the words that would live in infamy came blaring out of the big-screen TV at the front of the room. In truth, I hadn't been paying attention, as I was already inured to the dull, superficial sound bites television interviews usually produce. I might have missed the whole thing completely if I hadn't heard the subsequent uproar from the reporters all around me.

What the hell was going on? They couldn't believe the audacity, and some of them couldn't stomach it, either.

"I don't even want to go *listen* to the tosser!" huffed an Australian reporter to my right, threatening to boycott his upcoming press conference in a move that would surely have devastated Reed.

With the win, Reed moved up to the 20th spot in the world, and clearly had a decent argument to make about the top-five business, having won three times since the previous August. The claim wasn't *that* crazy—it wasn't like Bubba claiming to be one of the world's top-five Christians—but, in a pattern that had dogged him for most of his life, the way he delivered the words rubbed everyone the wrong way.

When he made his way to the interview room, the best question came from Doug Ferguson.

"If you consider yourself top-five," he began, "who are the other four? Who else do you consider there?"

Ferguson had brilliantly put Reed on the spot, and he fumbled his way to naming *five* other golfers—Woods, Adam Scott, Phil Mickelson, Graeme McDowell, and Dustin Johnson. But as much as I enjoyed the verbal sparring, the capital-M Media cared little for the logistics of Reed's bold proclamation. They needed grist for the mill, and Reed's brashness worked perfectly.

Reed maintained publicly that none of it fazed him, and he had a good defense prepared by the time the next tournament rolled around—it was simply a statement of self-belief, and an aspiration for future accomplishments, and so on—but when I spoke with him and Justine in July, they admitted they were surprised by how it had spun out of control.

"They amped it up," Justine said. "They need a villain, in a sense, and that's sad that they do that to what he said. Because at the end of the day he just believes in something, and yes, he *does* want to be a top-five player in the world."

Both emphasized to me that none of the actual players cared about what he said. If anything, they found it funny, and Henrik Stenson even teased Patrick on the range, judging each shot he hit by whether it qualified as a top-five effort or not. Matt Every defended him two weeks later at Bay Hill, though he found fault with the way Reed had listed his résumé. As for the media, Patrick told me that they'd never really know him—myself included.

If that had been true before, it was especially true after Doral. Whatever trust had been built up collapsed like a house of cards. To Reed, the media became just like everyone else who had failed to understand him, and who had isolated him along his path to the PGA Tour. And if that was the way it had to be, then okay. He had his loyal inner circle now—Justine, Kessler, Janet (the Karain matriarch), his agents and swing coach, and soon a new daughter who would be raised on Tour. He was a millionaire with a brand-new David Yurman bracelet, and his ascent up the world rankings proved that his system worked. He didn't need acceptance; he *never* needed it. The media, and anyone else who didn't believe in him, could go to hell.

He withdrew further into the shadows; the wagons circled tighter. In a culture that loathes gray area, Reed had been typecast before his twenty-fifth birthday. He was golf's remorseless villain, and stood as a rare exception to the old proverb—not everybody, it seems, loves a winner.

7

ORLANDO, FLORIDA

Bay Hill, or Matt Every Is Sweating

"You remember in high school, you'd have those assemblies where some kind of professional athlete came in, and he'd tell you to always have a backup plan? 'Only .02 percent of you guys are going to go pro in your sport.'

I remember sitting in there and just thinking, 'Fuck this guy.' If you have a backup plan, guess what? That's what you're going to be doing."

—Matt Every

It had been my plan to stay in Florida for the entire month, with a brief hiatus in Austin, Texas, to unwind at the South-by-Southwest festival, but after having my spirit crushed in Doral, it became clear early in the Bay Hill week, driving through the gaudy wreckage of American civilization known as Orlando, Florida, that I was danger-ously close to a complete nervous breakdown. This could be life or death, or so I thought in my nervous state.

I tried to stick it out . . . I sat through a press conference with Ar-nold Palmer, suffered through an antagonistic and ultimately boring interview with Keegan Bradley, and drove around looking for decent food, or at least a parking spot, in the strip malls. But after skipping the action on Thursday to watch the first round of the NCAA Tournament, it became imperative that I drive home to North Carolina immediately. I made a break for it on Saturday morning, and when I was accosted by a raving madwoman at a McDonald's near the Disney World exit—clearly, another victim of her environment—I knew I'd made the right choice.

Unfortunately, this also meant I missed seeing the final round at Bay Hill in person, where Adam Scott, within a whisper of the world number 1 spot, looked to be a certain winner. But there was something strange happening in Florida that month, and if Russell Henley could erase a two-shot deficit on Rory McIlroy despite shooting two-over on Sunday, there was hope for the chasers at Bay Hill.

As it happened, the leaders were in for another rocky start. Bradley double-bogeyed the second and bogeyed the third to seemingly take himself out of contention, but Scott didn't fare much better, with three bogeys of his own by the seventh hole.

While they continued to falter on the back nine, a winless Tour player named Matt Every pumped the gas, making three birdies in four holes to grab the lead away and put himself five shots ahead of Bradley and two ahead of Scott at -15. With five holes remaining, Every had overcome a significant deficit and put himself in prime position. If he could play par golf the rest of the way, he'd walk off with his first win.

When I sat down with Every at a shaded table outside the Colonial clubhouse in late May, it didn't take long before he cemented his reputation as the most outspoken professional golfer in the universe. We had met just once before, and didn't speak for more than five minutes. Clearly, my status as a stranger—and one armed with a tape recorder—didn't faze him. Within minutes, he was boasting, complaining, joking, and opining about golf and himself—his two favorite subjects—with a startling amount of insight and intelligence. I liked him immediately.

If you can take this onslaught in stride, it quickly becomes clear that the recurring criticism of Every—his arrogance—was off base. He *does* carry himself with a certain amount of swagger, and has a smile that verges on smug, but there's not much self-importance or superiority to him—far less anyway, than you get from your average golfer. The world is interesting to Every, and he makes himself vulnerable to outside elements. He wouldn't like the word I'm about to use, and you wouldn't know it by his bulldog build—five foot eleven and solid, with a head like a cinder block—but the truth is that he's sensitive, albeit in the most combative way possible.

Every, then thirty, has been kicked around the Tour, mocked by fans and media, and targeted for his past, but unlike the vast majority of American golfers, he never tries to hide his emotions or retreat into a cocoon.

Instead, he's the kind of guy that lets you drop the usual journalist-athlete code of conduct. I never felt the need to be deferential to him, as so many athletes' egos require, and I never got the sense he was bullshitting me. For a brief moment, and for the first and only time in a year on Tour, I even considered the possibility that he and I, in a different universe, might actually overcome the wide gulf separating our lifestyles and—I can't believe I'm saying it—be friends.

Then again, some of the things he told me are too good to waste on a friendship. We had barely sat down, for instance, before he began complaining about another journalist.

"He's done it before," he said intently. "He's picking me out to be a villain because I'm an easy target."

The subject was Geoff Shackelford, a blogger who covers the sport with an irreverent tone. But since this is golf we're talking about, with all its claims to propriety, Shackelford toes the line, choosing his victims strategically in order not to offend anyone with real influence. For him, Every made a perfect target—here was a player with no power.

Earlier that month, Every caused a minor stir when he complained about the state of TPC Sawgrass. He called it "the worst-conditioned course in Jacksonville" and compared the greens unfavorably to "Miami munis." (This rant later earned him a "talking-to" from Tour officials.) However, he also took pains to blame himself for his 76-77-CUT performance, leaving the conditions out of it. Shackelford ignored that last part, and suggested that Every was merely making excuses for himself.

"And why is his opinion so fucking important?" Every continued, still chafing at the perceived dishonesty two weeks later. "I told you I don't like Geoff Shackelford, and you can write that in your book." He lowered his head inches from my tape recorder, speaking slowly and loudly for emphasis: "Fuck you, Geoff."

"That will go in the book," I promised.

This approach continued throughout the interview. When I asked him if he felt "lucky" in the general sense, and then clarified that I didn't mean "lucky" in the way that outsiders use it—as in, oh, he's so *lucky* to be a professional golfer—it set him off on a tangent.

"I'm glad you said that, because it pisses me off when people write, 'Oh, that guy, I can't believe he'd say something like that, he should be privileged to play on the PGA Tour!'" he said. "Like I got fucking picked out of a lottery. I mean, I've worked my *ass* off to be here. It's not like they handed me this spot, you know?"

That set us on the path of how golfers behave on the course, and why it's so difficult for spectators to understand their anger.

"It's a job," he said. "And you see people say, 'Everyone looks so miserable while they're playing.' Well, the highs are really high out here and the lows are really low. I mean, you're not making any money when you're down, and it feels like you're going to be down your whole life. It's like you honestly *do not know* when you're going to play good again."

And since the lows are more frequent, that's what fans will see almost every time.

Matthew King Every grew up on the water in Daytona Beach, the son of Kelly, a construction worker who had tried professional golf, and Penny, a secretary at a lawyer's office. He started golfing at age six, and he grew up playing at the Riviera Country Club in Ormond Beach, a public course owned by a friend of the family where he could play for a song.

From the time he was very young, Every loved golf because there were fewer politics involved in who would make a team, or who succeeded, than the other sports. Still, there were things that frustrated him. The Everys were middle-class, and Every bristled at the cost of the premiere junior tournaments. Kelly went on to own a construction company in Matt's high school years, but the recession hit the business, as well as family real estate investments, hard.

"If you step back and look at these kids grinding out there," he told me, "it means nothing. It means *nothing*. You don't want to peak when you're fifteen. That's terrible. I think that's what happened to James Vargas at Florida [a teammate of Every's]. He was a world-beater when he was a kid, he was a stud, and then he got to college and it was like, 'Where's your room to improve?' "[9]

When Every couldn't golf, he'd shoot hoops on the strip of concrete outside his house, playing so long that eventually his father put lights out for him. The sport was his first love, and until age twelve, he was convinced he would play for the Orlando Magic, following in the footsteps of heroes like Scott Skiles, Dennis Scott, and Nick Anderson. Then high school came around, and while most of his friends went to Seabreeze High, Every was off to Mainland High in Daytona, where he suddenly found himself in a very different demographic. Playing with the brothers, Every barely made his freshman basketball team, and wasn't nearly good enough to start. He couldn't lie to himself, and when the school switched the golf season to overlap with basketball, the choice was easy—golf or bust.

He improved enough in the next two years to start getting letters

---

[9] That distaste for unearned plaudits persists today. He didn't want to speak on the record about the aspects of Tour promotion that bothered him, but he gave Jordan Spieth as a counterexample.

"It's awesome he's getting the attention he is, because there's no sideshow about him. He does have his moments where the camera might catch him whining, but whatever, he's twenty years old, and my point is, he's not wearing stupid clothes to get noticed. I feel like some guys out here—and it's not their fault—they're taking advantage of it, and they get a little too much attention."

from smaller colleges, but his heart was set on being a Florida Gator. Buddy Alexander, the head coach, liked him, but not enough to give him a scholarship.

"Matt likes to tell people that he's a walk-on," Alexander said, "but that's not true. I *did* have to tell Matt that I was out of money, and he decided, 'I don't care.' His comment was, 'I'm not North Florida material. I'm coming to UF.' And if you know Matt, you're chuckling because you know exactly how it sounds coming out of his mouth."

Every came in a little bit anonymous—"fucking terrible," in his own words—but his improvement during his freshman year turned heads. Alexander considered red-shirting him in the fall, but by the spring, he had done so well that the coach, who loved his confidence, took a calculated risk and made Every the team's number 5 player for the postseason. From there, he finished top-ten individually in the SEC Championship, top-20 in NCAA regionals, and, most surprisingly, 12th at the national championships. By the end, Every was calling himself "the greatest number-five man in college golf history."

Every went on to become first-team All-American three years in a row, and won the Ben Hogan Award as the nation's top college golfer in 2006. He discovered that entering a slump wasn't the worst outcome in the world, and that he could sometimes break out of it with the power of positive thought—or, as he put it, lying to yourself and then believing it.

He also gained a reputation as a "cocky" golfer and an outspoken nonconformist. At the 2005 U.S. Open, he told reporters that he was equal to, if not better than, the other players in the field, and after playing the Walker Cup later that summer, he let the *Orlando Sentinel* know that he hated the U.K. because there was "nothing to do, nothing to eat," and that even the French fries were terrible.

Socially, Every spent most of his free time with his girlfriend, Danielle, who he married in 2009. Drinking held little appeal; he had worked at a seafood restaurant in high school, and the smell of stale beer that confronted him each time he took the trash out was enough to put him off the suds. ("I would party in other ways," he told me.) Nor were academics a priority, a truth he doesn't go out of his way to hide.

"People asked, 'What do you want your major to be when you go to college?'" he remembered. "It's like, psssh, whatever has the least amount of math. I don't care. I'm not going to use it. My major was commercial recreation. I don't even know what I could do with that."

"Man, I hate it when you see a Tour player interviewed and he has absolutely nothing to say," Every said. "All that, 'One shot at a time, staying in the moment, playing my own game.'
    "How boring is that? Blah, blah, blah."

Every, a two-time NCAA All-American, is an endearing, animated mix of combustible quotes, edgy enthusiasm and occasionally smug obnoxiousness."

                                  —Orlando Sentinel, 2005

It didn't take long after graduation for Every to find out how meaningless his Hogan Award would be in the professional ranks. He missed Q-School after graduation, and didn't make the PGA Tour until 2010. He also missed six weeks in his rookie season when he broke his finger playing a game called "burnout" that involved him and his caddie pegging a football at each other. That was a minor setback compared to what came next. Just two weeks after his return, at the John Deere Classic, Every made a mistake that would come to define his golfing life—or at least how he was perceived by the media and fans—for years.

At the Isle Casino Hotel, in Bettendorf, Iowa—just across the Mississippi River from the TPC Deere Run course in Illinois, where the tournament is held—Every stepped off an elevator and wandered into a room where his caddie and two others were smoking marijuana. According to Every, he was only in there for a few minutes when hotel security burst through the door, tipped off by someone who had smelled the telltale odor that seeped through the door.

"I probably could have gotten out of that situation if I did things a little differently," said Every, "but it doesn't fucking matter now."

The four of them didn't move, and Every maintains that the security guards violated their rights and didn't go to great lengths to mention that they weren't actual police officers. They pulled the culprits one by one into the bathroom, extracted confessions, and finally turned them over to the real cops, who booked and arrested them.

"I don't know if they just have a hard-on, or they feel like they're saving the world, or what," Every said.

The PGA Tour makes a policy of not commenting on its suspensions—a fact that would come into play later in 2014—but Every's PR company revealed in August that he'd been hit with three months for "conduct unbecoming a professional." He came back in time for the final tournament of the season, but he failed to keep his Tour card, and was back on the Nationwide Tour for 2012—a brutal demotion, subtracting a zero from his average paycheck.

He fought back, finishing 18th on the money list and regaining his Tour card within a year. Every still thinks winning that fight was his greatest professional accomplishment, and one that validated his status as a "real golfer"—the kind who deserved to be on the PGA Tour.

The arrest and suspension dogged him long after he fought back to the big leagues. Every has no problem with marijuana, but he doesn't identify as a stoner, and it bothers him that the people who know his name tend to associate him with drugs.

"There's so much more to me than that," he said, "but that's just the way it's going to be, man. You hear stuff all the time in galleries. Mostly conversations, but you'll get a guy who will yell out '420!' or something, and I don't think it's a fair representation of me. And now that Twitter's out there, everyone thinks they're a comedian. Even the media, some guys will put the dumbest shit out there. Like if it's foggy out, they'll write, 'Oh, Matt Every must be playing this week.'"

It would have been easy for Every to kowtow to the conservative faction and claim that he was a changed man, that drugs were Satan's work, and that he had recognized the error of his ways and reformed himself in the image of a law-abiding family man. Instead, he scoffed at the punishment and refused to hand anyone—especially the media—the easy redemption story.

"No, I still hang out with the same people," he told reporters at the 2012 Sony Open, his first tournament back on Tour. "I have great friends, man. If one of my friends likes to smoke marijuana every now and then, I'm not going to say, well, you can't be my friend anymore. Honestly, man, I know more people who smoke marijuana than who don't smoke marijuana. I know that's probably not the politically correct thing to say, but it's the truth."

After the second round that week, a 64, he sat down with the Golf Channel's Kelly Tilghman. After some chitchat about golf and snorkeling, Tilghman got down to business and unleashed what stands as the most awkward segue in television history.

"I look back at this island," she said, turning to a mass of stones and palm trees in the water behind her, "and it kind of reminds me of that TV show *Lost*, which you say is one of your favorites."

"Oh yeah, I love that show."

"And I know that the word 'lost' might also be a fitting word to describe the state of your mind and game about two years ago," Tilghman continued, in all her ham-fisted glory, "when you were arrested on drug charges and suspended by the PGA Tour. That must have been a difficult experience for you. Take us back to that time and what it was like."

Every stared at her for a moment, grinned uncomfortably, and sank even lower in his chair. His eyes were mostly hidden by the shadow from the brim of his Bridgestone cap.

"Uhhh. . . ." He said. "It was all right. I mean, I just got three months off."

The interview devolved from there. Every told her that he wasn't doing anything wrong, that he's the same person with the same friends, and that worse things happen all the time on Tour. Tilghman, not content to settle for anything less than the trite, made-for-TV coming-of-age story she'd envisioned when she asked the question, followed up, wanting to know what Every had "learned."

When I reminded him of this moment, Every had only one regret. "What have you learned from that?" he asked rhetorically. "Put a towel under the door. I should have said that."

This, it seemed, was Every's curse. He was doomed to be misunderstood by everyone; either you thought he was a chronic pothead who wandered around in a drug-induced stupor, or you wanted to pigeonhole him as a reformed criminal who had emerged from the depths of depravity to resurrect his life and career. The truth—that he'd been a bit stupid and a bit unlucky, wasn't palatable. And he knew that the only thing that could truly put his arrest in the rearview mirror was winning.

On a positive note, he'd finally found a good ADD drug after experimenting for a couple years (he wouldn't tell me what it was), and it made a huge difference for him on the course. His game rounded into shape, and after four top tens to start his best season to date, he came into Sunday's round at the Arnold Palmer Invitational in third place, trailing Adam Scott by four strokes and Keegan Bradley by three. By the 14th hole, he was poised to beat them both.

On the final day of the Florida swing, Scott made Every's task a little easier by closing with bogeys at 14 and 17 to stumble in with a 76. Bradley, though, wasn't finished. He had emerged as one of the flukiest major winners of all time when he survived a disastrous triple bogey on the 15th hole at the 2011 PGA Championship, so he knew as well as anyone that his ugly stretches at Bay Hill were not necessarily a death sentence. Just like he had at the PGA, he birdied 16 and 17, reaching -12.

Which still wouldn't have been anywhere near Every, or at least the version of Every that would finish with birdies and pars. But that's when the nerves hit him, and the focus he'd maintained all round began to slip. On 16, he stood up on his tiptoes as he swung his driver, launching the tee shot into the right rough. When he attempted to hack out to the fairway, he hit the trunk of a small tree and watched the ball ricochet backward. He now had a choice to make—go for the green, even though he was still obstructed, or hack out of the rough into the fairway and try to get up and down for par.

The NBC cameras closed in on Every as he listened to Derek Mason's advice. "If we just put this right in the fucking end of the fairway, we're gonna fucking get up and down 75 percent of the time," the caddie said. Gary Koch apologized to the audience, but said he agreed with Mason. So did Every. He didn't get up-and-down, though, and the bogey brought him to -14.

On the par-3 17th tee, he was a twitchy, sweaty mess. He looked so uncomfortable that Johnny Miller wondered aloud if he could perform at all. His tee shot didn't do much to assuage those fears, landing in a bunker fifty feet from the hole. On the brink of disaster, he pulled out a brilliant shot from the sand and saved his par. On 18, needing only another par to secure his win, he hit his approach over the water a touch too far and into the deep grass. He walked up the fairway with a stupefied smile, hit a perfect chip, and watched it trickle to the hole.

When it stopped, he had five feet left for par. He'd been lucky to avoid that tricky distance all day—he'd missed a few twelve-to-fifteen-footers, but nobody expected him to make those, and he knew missing shorter putts might have killed his confidence. Now he'd have to face it head-on, with a chance to lock up his first win on Tour. The vague pressure he'd felt all day escalated into a throbbing, full-body hum. He knew exactly where he stood, and he wanted badly to make the putt so he could celebrate on the green. Framed by the water, with Arnold Palmer looking on, he hunched over the ball.

"The only way I can describe it is, it's like someone is chasing you," he said, looking back on the round. "Like they're running you down, and you're running as fast as you can. And you can't look back to see where they're at. You just keep running. That's the feeling."

He ran the putt three feet past the hole.

"I don't know if I've ever seen emotions so raw on a guy trying to get it done for the first time," said Dan Hicks, on the NBC broadcast.

When he made the comebacker for bogey, his lead was down to one shot over Bradley, who was now playing the 18th. Every moved off to the scoring trailer, where they had a small TV, and he watched Bradley on the final hole. His drive was good, but his approach was just average, leaving him thirty feet for the birdie he'd need to force a playoff. Every began pacing back and forth in the scoring area, glancing back at the television as Bradley read the putt, lined it up, and sent it toward the hole.

He had barely made contact when Every heard a loud groan from the 18th hole, and the sound of his wife and parents cheering just outside the tent. Watching on delay, he saw the ball run by on the left, and he knew that after ninety-three starts on the PGA Tour, he was finally a winner.

The Golf Channel's Steve Sands grabbed him for the reaction interview, and Every was already crying. "It's hard," he said, his voice cracking. "It's tough, man. You just never know if it's going to happen. You get there so many times . . . I kept telling myself maybe it was going to be somewhere special. I still can't believe I won."

The cocky facade, the way he grimaced and sighed and groaned, the bluster and the brio . . . it all shattered in the startling face of the dream.

It didn't take long for the pieces to reassemble—Every couldn't stop being himself for very long.

When *Golfweek*'s Jim McCabe wrote an article taking him to task for skipping the ensuing events in order to prepare for Augusta, Every found the writer's phone number and called to confront him. At Augusta, he arrived too early and over-practiced, stumbling to a 77-78 cut. By the time we spoke at the Colonial, he was using the two-year exemption he'd gained from winning to make swing adjustments.

I saw him next at the British Open, and though he was upset because he "putted like shit," his trademark confidence hadn't wavered. "Dude, my game is coming along pretty good," he said. "Like, the end of the year is going to be *good*. I'm excited."

After that prediction, he played seventeen more rounds in the 2014 season. He broke 70 only three times, missed a couple of cuts along the way, and hit rock bottom when he shot an 86 in the third round of the Deutsche Bank Championship.

None of which, really, felt surprising. Matt Every's golf career was a delirious roller-coaster ride long before Bay Hill; why would the simple fact of winning change anything?

His win came with more than just $1.1 million and a two-year exemption. It also earned him a spot in the tournament that every pro—sane and crazy alike—covets with the deepest part of their being. Every season, toward the beginning of March, they begin dreaming of America's most famous course, and their eyes look ahead, past Florida and Texas, to the promised land hidden in the heart of Augusta, Georgia.

APRIL

The Holy Land

8

THE MASTERS

Jordan Spieth, the Great White Hope

The skeleton of Augusta, Georgia's, former glory can be seen in the old buildings lining Broad Street and spread throughout the downtown historic district on the south side of the Savannah River— the cotton exchange in its Queen Anne grandeur, the red brick Italianate homes, the Greek revival columns of the old medical college. The ghost of a thriving, vibrant Southern city is everywhere, and it gives you an immediate sense of nostalgia for the time before urban decay set in during the 1970s, and back even further, when the city was a cotton powerhouse.

Today, despite a revitalization effort, there's a decrepit feeling to the downtown, and once you leave the old part of the city, it gets worse. If you ever visit Augusta and are expecting to enter a pastoral paradise, as I was in April, be advised that this won't happen until the exact moment you turn off Washington Road and enter the grounds of Augusta National. This is not mighty Atlanta, quaint Athens, or elegant Savannah; it's the part of Georgia that got left behind.

The Augusta National Golf Club is set apart from the city, as it has been from the very start. You may be able to see a water tower from certain parts of the course, but otherwise you're safe from the modern realities, surrounded by the tall loblolly pines that usher you along the verdant fairways—steeper than they appear on television—through one of America's most beautiful golf courses.

In the week leading up to the 2014 Masters, Fuzzy Zoeller was on everyone's mind. In 1979, in his first Masters appearance, he won the green jacket. No Masters rookie has won it since. Augusta National is a course that rewards experience in a thousand subtle ways, and the Masters generates the kind of pressure that can crush a newcomer—or, hell, a veteran. But the concept of a 2014 youth movement had taken root, and considering the class of first-timers at Augusta—Spieth, Reed, English, DeLaet, Dubuisson, Horschel, Kirk, Stadler, Every, Walker, and the young Swede Jonas Blixt, among others—it seemed like the twenty-five-year rookie drought might end.

Two small items made news as Masters week got under way: Adam Scott was serving Moreton Bay Bugs—a kind of small lobster you find in the oceans of Australia—at the champions dinner, and the famous Eisenhower tree on the 17th hole was irretrievably damaged in a February ice storm, and had been euthanized.

The biggest story, though, was the absence of Tiger Woods. Most players who held a press conference between Monday and Wednesday had to field at least one question about him, and what I learned from their answers was: Tiger Woods is a famous golfer, Tiger Woods was not playing that week, and the fans seem to be interested in Tiger Woods. In terms of the Masters, the fact that he wouldn't play was either basically unimportant, a minor disappointment, or a total disaster that would ruin the whole week.

The gentlemen who operate Augusta National don't allow journalists inside the ropes, and if we want to follow the players, we have to do it like every other civilian, in the midst of a dense gallery. I tried it out on Thursday, but I'd grown spoiled by easy access. After a fruitless hour fighting for a glimpse of a player, I'd had enough. I gravitated back to the flash area near the clubhouse, and waited as the Masters rookies came through, collecting their reports on the toughest maiden voyage in golf.

Matt Every was annoyed when a rules official put him on the clock after he asked for a ruling that took longer than it should have, and made seven bogeys en route to a +5 start. I asked if he gave himself any allowance since it was his first competitive round at Augusta, and he looked disgusted with the idea.

"I'm not a hack," he said. "I'm not here just for fun."

Harris English had played ten rounds at Augusta in the past, but he was still shocked by the speed of the greens Thursday, and the nerves didn't help either. He scrambled well, but that only saved him from complete disaster, and he signed for a 74.

Patrick Reed stayed in red numbers for most of his round, but bogeyed the last two holes to finish +1. He stormed by the reporters, refusing to talk, and when a few caught up with him in the locker room, he told them he "hit it like shit all day."

Many of the players talked about the pin placements, which were unusually difficult for a Thursday. When Graeme McDowell first saw the sheet with all the locations, he laughed. "They're not easing us into it, are they?"

Spieth, who beat most of his fellow rookies with a 1-under, played with Rory McIlroy and Reed, and he noticed how Rory took angles that looked strange on certain holes, but ended up being perfect. On 17, for example, Reed made a mistake by hitting the ball on the downslope of the green, while Spieth hit what looked like a perfect approach that came to rest on the upper ridge, leaving him a short but difficult putt. Rory, on the other hand, hit a wedge that landed fifteen feet left of the hole—a place neither Reed or Spieth would have thought to look—and had the easiest putt of the three.

All of them were learning what it felt like to be thrust into the unique cauldron of Augusta National. The Masters is arguably golf's most prestigious tournament, but it's also the only major played on the same course year after year. You can't really accumulate experience at any other major, because the courses won't repeat for another five to ten years, if ever. Only Augusta rewards repeat visitors, and the course itself is so strange and difficult that there's no good way to prepare if you've never been.

Every had given it his best shot, arriving the previous Friday to get some extra rounds, but he still missed the cut, and felt disgusted with himself.

"I felt so prepared going into this week, and I couldn't have been less prepared," he said. "I usually just fucking show up on Tuesday and do my thing, and this was just me being an idiot and thinking that if I do a little extra, it's actually going to matter. It doesn't. The course in the practice rounds was nothing like it was during the tournament."

Every's observation was shared by many—Augusta has the unique ability to completely transform in the space of a day, drying out and cranking up the speed on the fairways and greens. Derek Ernst, another rookie, put the problem of Augusta succinctly after he missed the cut with a 76-76. "I don't know how you practice for it," he said. "There's nowhere I know of that's like this."

Nor can anyone give you advice. "It's like parenthood," said Hunter Mahan, a veteran of seven Masters and one child. "I could tell you all about it, but nothing's going to prepare you for what's coming."

In Thursday's swirling winds, Bill Haas took a first-round lead at 4-under, with the past two champions, Bubba Watson and Adam Scott, lurking a shot back. Three rookies finished at -2, and two of them, Jimmy Walker and Kevin Stadler, were recent winners on Tour. The other, Jonas Blixt, was just a few days shy of his thirtieth birthday, and playing in his third major championship ever.

On Friday, the Masters officials decided to move the media into an improvised cattle pen near the clubhouse, packing us in where a collection of sneering Pinkertons could zap us with cattle prods if we leaned too far over the ropes or tried to escape. Several local media members, unaccustomed to the aggressive nature of golf reporting, were suffocated to death during high-volume interviews.

Or at least those were the rumors I tried to spread when I saw our new accommodations. Outside the pen, under the famous "big oak tree," the scene was far more elegant. Caroline Wozniacki wandered around with bright pink hair and a long skirt, looking extraterrestrial and beautiful, and the American tennis star John Isner, towering above everyone, chatted with friends and fans.

Graham DeLaet had received a congratulatory letter from the premier of Saskatchewan in his locker, and he recovered from his opening round collapse to shoot 72, still missing the cut but leaving with his dignity intact. Harris English also failed to make the weekend, but was friendly and positive after his round, and felt that he'd learned something crucial. Matt Every was less enthused with his +11, but his message was similar: With the unpredictability of the wind, and the tricky pin placements, and the extreme slopes, there's no substitute for experience. Patrick Reed came in with a 79, and when a Masters official asked him to stop by and speak with local media in the town where he had won two college championships, he simply said, "Nope," beckoned for Justine, and was gone.

Billy Horschel, who played with Tom Watson the first two rounds, focused on keeping his anger in check around the Ryder Cup captain in case he needed a pick later in the season. He made the cut by a stroke, but Watson advised him to let his game "mature." Chris Kirk rallied with a 72 to sneak under the cut line; Steven Bowditch did the same. Kevin Stadler and Jimmy Walker were two of the only Masters rookies to finish under par for the first thirty-six holes, but above them, tied at -3, were the best of the new class: Jordan Spieth and Jonas Blixt.

Beginning on the back nine, Bubba Watson had laid waste to the course. With five birdies in a row starting on the 12th hole, he rocketed up from -3 to -8, and though he faded to -7 with a bogey on 18, he had taken complete command of the tournament. He led John Senden by three shots, and a pack that included Spieth, Blixt, and defending champ Adam Scott by four. With the confidence from the Northern Trust win, and his triumph at the 2012 Masters, it was clearly his tournament to lose.

He was in fine fettle at his post-round press conference, bantering with the media in his usual borderline aggressive way. "How many green jackets you got?" he asked one reporter, in a discussion about the stress he had endured after winning his first.

"I hit nine-iron the last two days, flew it 186 yesterday on sixteen . . . I guess it's all right," he boasted, when someone asked him about his athleticism. He was in his element, needing just one more great round to make Sunday a cakewalk.

Instead, on Saturday, he came back to the field, making three bogeys in four holes on the front nine and finishing at -5.

That afternoon, I set up shop at Amen Corner, the famous three-hole stretch beginning at no. 11, the 505-yard par-4 with a pond guarding the left side of the green. After making the long approach to the most difficult hole on the course, players move to the par-3 12th, with its short but perilous 155-yard tee shot over Rae's Creek—named after an early settler who operated a grist mill—onto a narrow green framed by bunkers and azaleas. The green on 12 is like a sanctuary, where no fans are allowed. When players leave the tee and cross Hogan's Bridge, they are isolated . . . a last lonely moment before the pressure cooker of the finishing stretch.

The par-5 13th completes the evil troika, forcing players to hit a draw off the tee to position themselves for the approach. Alternatively, you can cut the corner, go as the crow flies, and hit over the trees and the creek tributary on the left, but only a crazy person would even attempt it. A crazy person like, say, Bubba Watson.

But that was all to come. On Saturday, I watched the leaders pass through 11 and 12. I saw Fred Couples, who always rises to the top of the Masters leaderboard on Friday, make Saturday's first birdie on the 11th—there would be only two all day—and react to the standing ovation with the preternatural cool that seems to be his birthright. Kuchar bogeyed the hole, but caught fire afterward, reaching -5 before making bogey on 18. Spieth overshot his mark on the approach to 11, and the green was so infernally fast that his chip rolled twenty-five feet past the hole, forcing him to two-putt for a bogey and sink to -3. Jonas Blixt reached -5 before the 11th knocked him down a peg, too, and Amen Corner bit him again on 13, taking another bogey for its massive trophy case. Bubba came through with pars after his shaky front nine, and managed to make just one bogey on the back nine and survive the day with a 75.

As I hustled back to the big oak and the cattle pen, results trickled in from the final holes. Adam Scott had survived Amen Corner, but tanked the rest of his round, finishing with a 76 that all but ensured he wouldn't defend his green jacket.

Blixt and Kuchar had each finished at -4, tied for second, while Rickie Fowler closed fast with a 67 to reach -3. At the top of the leaderboard, though, two men were tied at -5. The first was Bubba Watson, which wasn't unexpected. The second was Jordan Spieth, who would tee off in the last group on Sunday at the Masters at the tender age of twenty.

Q: When did he commit to Texas? Was it his senior in high school?
A: It was his junior year. Feb. 6, 2010, which was a Saturday, and he called at 2:30 pm in the afternoon. But who's counting?
　　—Exchange with JOHN FIELDS, golf coach, University of Texas

Jason Day, keen observer that he is, was the first to spot the pattern. After his Monday press conference at Augusta, as a group of reporters milled around the podium, he joked that anybody who watched the Golf Channel on a regular basis might start to believe there was an emerging young golfer with a long, cumbersome name: "twenty-year-old Jordan Spieth."

There's truth in every jest, and Spieth's story can't be separated from his youth. On the other hand, the fact that he's young and plays golf with enormous skill only begins to explain the collective fascination. What really gets us, fans and media alike, is the *maturity*. He speaks with the wisdom and perspective of someone with fifty years of experience, and he never seems to deviate. By all rights, he should come off like a pretender, like a kid playing a part, but everything about his behavior feels sincere. *That's* what differentiates him from the other child stars.

Words like "composure" and "polish" follow him around like faithful pets, but even they don't tell the whole story. Spieth's maturity is so atypical that you catch yourself looking around for a puppet master, or at least a few strings. Is he a flawless golfing Frankenstein created in a lab run by PR officials? Or just a marketer's Superman, programmed to say and do the right thing at each moment?

You can count on him to say "*Mr.* Palmer" and "*Mr.* Nicklaus" when talking about the legends of the game, and in those rare moments when he lets his on-course emotions stray from the script—as he did in his match against Ernie Els at the Accenture—he issues an immediate apology. He's the straight-laced, All-American boy, and if you think it's all an act and that *surely* he's got to break character eventually, well . . . don't hold your breath.

In many ways, he's the savior the golf establishment has been waiting two decades to find. The concept of golf as a "gentlemen's game" was always ridiculous, but Tiger put the kibosh on the antiquated notion for good. He fist-pumped, he roared, he intimidated, he swore; he eventually got caught committing adultery on a scale that would have made JFK blush. Everything the man did was inflated—pundits loved to censure him, the Tour loved to fine him, the players loved to hate him, but deep down Tiger never cared. He didn't have to.

But where was the great white hope? Sure, golf had its share of drab country club clones—an army of them, really—but where was their king? Where was the young gun with the rosy cheeks and the respectful demeanor who could rise to Tiger's dizzying heights? Where was the kid with the 1950s charm who never said too much? Who had a pleasingly tame sense of humor, and never offended anybody? Who was smart, but strictly of the establishment? Who was a nice Christian that went to Bible study, but didn't mention it in every interview? Where was the kid who could remind everyone how great golf had been before Tiger teamed up with Nike to corrupt the whole scene?

Golf's retrogressive element had a fantasy. They fetishized the mythical upright citizen. They longed for the kid who could make their nostalgia tangible and grow into a gentleman superstar.

You can imagine their delight when the dream came true. Jordan Spieth was the redeemer.

It wasn't easy to get a private moment with Spieth. He didn't necessarily object, but he didn't seem particularly enthused about the idea. The first time I approached him, after an early round at Riviera in February, he was chatting with a friend outside the clubhouse as a mass of kids screamed his name and demanded autographs. He was moving down the line, and I waited for him at the end.

"Are you going to go practice?" the friend asked.

"No. I'm going back to the hotel to sit on my ass," Spieth replied, with an air of fatigue.

Behind him, his caddie Michael Greller, a former sixth-grade teacher, stood talking near Spieth's bag. I noticed the putter cover—it was emblazoned with dollar signs and the words "Cash is King." When I looked up, Spieth was gone—the first artful vanishing act I would witness, executed whenever he sensed a journalist lurking nearby.

That commenced an odyssey, lasting months, that involved negotiating with agents, asking personal questions in large press conferences, and generally trying to read everything I could about him, including old transcripts and two thorough profiles—one by *Golf Digest*'s Jim Moriarty and one by *Sports Illustrated*'s Alan Shipnuck.

Finally, at the Congressional in June, I found him on the driving range with his agent. I waited for an off moment, and made my last-ditch approach.

"I had an idea," I said, after handshakes. (In the golf world, each encounter starts with a handshake, even if you see the person every day, and there's no way around it.) "I get the feeling some guys don't love the pro-ams," I continued, "so I was thinking maybe I could join you on the back nine and walk a few holes, and then I wouldn't bother you the rest of the year."

It was a laughable gambit: All his agent had to do was continue saying no, easy for him, and I was operating from a position of no power.

"Let me just say," said Spieth, "I thoroughly enjoy the pro-ams, no matter what the other guys say."

That was the great white hope in action. I wanted to tell him he didn't have to lay it on so thick with me, but looking at him, I realized he was totally sincere. This, I thought, is why the keepers of the game love him so much—the crazy bastard actually means it.

The next day I showed up at the tenth hole with my tape recorder. There—after more handshakes—Spieth told me we'd be chatting for only one hole, because he didn't want to take time away from his pro-am partners, and he had a friend coming to carry his bag the rest of the way.

Bad news, I thought, but what the hell. So for thirteen minutes and thirty seconds I fired questions at him, trying to prioritize and get a year's worth of work done in a single hole. When he finished putting out on the tenth green, I shadowed him while he signed flags for the kids lining the ropes. "I'd love to do pictures right after, guys," he said, and when he spotted a man holding a camera, he politely warned him to keep it out of the way.

I kept walking with him to the tee, trying to squeeze every last second out of our one and only private encounter. Finally, after answering one final question, he turned to me and shook my hand. "I appreciate it, man," he said. His intent was clear, just as it had been with the kids—he's learned the veteran's trick of delivering negative messages with a positive turn of phrase. Although I was disappointed that our time had been cut short, there was another part of me that felt grateful. Of all the ways I'd been told to fuck off over the course of the year—and there were many—this was by far the nicest.

On the 11th, when Beck missed an 8-footer to halve the hole, Spieth's dad, Shawn, said to no one in particular, "The door's open now, buddy."

—USGA's KEN KLAVON, in a recap of
the 2008 U.S. Amateur semifinals

Spieth is the oldest child of Shawn and Chris, former college athletes—baseball at Lehigh for Shawn, basketball at nearby Moravian for Chris—and high school sweethearts from tiny Hellertown, Pennsylvania, in the Lehigh Valley. Part of Jordan's maturity can be chalked up to the hard-earned perspective that prevails in his family—Chris's mother suffered a brain aneurysm when she was only four, which split up the family until the father could reunite them. When Jordan's younger sister, Ellie, was born, she had neurological problems that threatened her life, and Jordan grew up volunteering at her school for special-needs children. The pain of real life was never an abstraction for Spieth, and even if his parents hadn't emphasized humility, circumstances would never have allowed his ego to spiral out of control.

Spieth grew up in north Dallas, where Shawn—"a man's man" with "incredible intensity," per Spieth's college coach John Fields—worked in various business ventures, from Alcoa to Sprint to a social media startup. His mother quit her job at Neiman Marcus to raise the three children before taking administrative work at Jordan's schools when the kids grew up. The Spieths were middle class all the way, with a modest home that they built up over the years. Jordan's bedroom was small, and stuffed with trophies.

As a kid, Spieth told me, his personality contained equal parts of his mom and dad, and he inherited an extreme competitiveness from both. They gave him a plastic set of golf clubs when he was very young, and when the family went to the beaches of North Carolina for family reunions in the summer, his grandfather would make him a new club. He had a plastic basketball rim and baseball equipment, too—Spieth worried aloud that he was coming off like a spoiled kid when he listed off his gear—and he loved playing outdoors.

Baseball was his game in the early years, and he became a strong lefty pitcher (though he golfs right-handed) who made traveling all-star teams. Like many golfers I spoke to, though, he didn't like the loss of control in team sports. Unlike most golfers, he explained the flip side of that coin—when the team won, he didn't like sharing the joy. On the links, the glory was his alone.

He started golfing around age eight at Brookhaven Country Club, staying from morning to sunset. He'd play with older kids, which kept his competitive instincts sharp. His parents didn't push him, but his father asked him to set goals at every level, and Spieth hit most of them. When he turned twelve, he shot a 63 at a tournament in Waco, and that's when he began to believe he could play golf for a living.

That year, he started working with Cameron McCormick, a respected swing coach who still works with him today. Spieth began playing AJGA events, and his first title came in 2007, where he defeated Justin Thomas at Walnut Creek in a match that would have echoes in his college career. At age sixteen, he earned an exemption into the Byron Nelson Classic, his first PGA Tour event. Nobody expected Spieth to actually compete, with the exception of Spieth himself. In a feat that's almost too amazing for hyperbole, he made the cut and finished sixteenth.

When he played an AJGA event shortly after, there was such a demand from the media to speak with the budding star that Stephen Hamblin took the rare step of organizing a press day for him. He'd done it just once before, and that was for Tiger Woods. When Spieth took the stage, Hamblin still remembers the self-assurance as he told the media that he felt ready to compete on the PGA Tour. If the journalists thought they were getting a wide-eyed kid who had just fluked his way into a once-in-a-lifetime moment, they were shocked by the composure of the young man onstage. For many, it was the first indication of the preternatural maturity that would come to define Spieth's public persona. His confidence never came off as arrogant, and his politeness felt genuine. Already, somehow, he was the complete package.

A fierce recruiting battle ensued between Texas, Oklahoma State, Stanford, USC, and UCLA. John Fields, the Texas coach, first saw Spieth when he was eleven years old at a junior event in Ardmore, Oklahoma, and he became enthralled. He made it a point to watch him play whenever he could, and when he traveled to Trump National for the 2009 U.S. Junior Amateur, he was approached on the course by Donald Trump himself. Trump was already campaigning to hold a U.S. Open or PGA Championship at one of his courses, and during their conversation, Fields told him with no uncertainty that fifteen-year-old Jordan Spieth was going to win the event.

"How can you tell me that, with so much golf left?" Trump asked, but Fields knew. And he was right—Spieth won the medal play portion, and blazed his way through the match play rounds to capture the biggest tournament of his career. Trump sent Fields a note calling him "the predictor," and two years later, Spieth became the second player in history to win the event twice. The first—you'll notice a pattern here—was Tiger Woods.

Fields got the big call when he came back from a vacation in Hawaii. "I'm not going to beat around the bush," Spieth said. "I'm coming to Texas. I'm coming to help you win national championships."

Spieth missed the first event of Texas's season his freshman year—he was busy going 2-0-1 at the Walker Cup—but he was back for the Jerry Pate event in Alabama, where he lost a final round lead. At the very next tournament, at Muirfield Village, two bogeys and a double on the last three holes cost him another win.

When he returned to Texas, one of the first people he saw was Chuck Cook, an Austin-based instructor known as "The Wizard" who has worked with Tom Kite and Payne Stewart, and counts Jason Dufner, Keegan Bradley, and Luke Donald as students. Cook was in his late sixties then, but he hadn't lost his no-nonsense approach or his love for needling the players. It sometimes got to the point, Fields told me, that Cook's barbs went over the edge. When he saw Spieth in a hallway at the golf academy, he stopped and gave him a long look.

"Hey, Jordan," he said. "Just how big a lead do you need before you can *win* a golf tournament?"

Spieth managed to put a good face on and take it in stride, but inside, Fields said, he was steaming. The next tournament was at Isleworth, and this time Spieth had his foot on the gas the whole time. When he won in a runaway, he couldn't wait to return to Texas to find Cook.

"What do you think about *that*?" he asked. "Was that good enough?"

Fields witnessed Spieth's competitive instincts sharpen throughout the year. In one practice match against junior Cody Gribble—who, unlike Patrick Reed, had stuck to his eighth-grade Texas commitment—

the teammates came up the 18th green so angry at each other that Fields was genuinely worried that they might fight. Gribble poured in a fifteen-footer on the last green and pointed defiantly at Spieth, but the freshman answered by sinking a ten-foot birdie of his own to win the match.

"If they hadn't been in different carts, they might have gone at it right there," said Fields. Minutes later, they were best friends again, but there had been no mistaking Spieth's fire in the heat of battle.

He went on to win four tournaments that year, and the Longhorns entered the national championships at Riviera as the number 1 seed. In the second of three stroke play rounds, Spieth collapsed on the back nine, and his teammates didn't fare much better. Heading into the third and final day, they were ranked thirteenth, and in serious danger of missing the eight-team match play round. But Spieth rallied to shoot a 69 on the final day, and Texas finished in third place, safely inside the cutoff.

The Longhorns coasted to the finals, where Alabama waited. At number 1 singles, Spieth would face fellow freshman Justin Thomas—the same player he had topped at an AJGA event five years earlier, and whom he had been competing against for most of his life. Thomas won NCAA freshman of the year *and* player of the year that season, edging Spieth out for both awards, but Spieth was confident. "I've got a great feeling about this," he told Fields. "I always play well against Justin. I think I can get him."

By the 15th hole, Spieth had established a two-up lead. He took out his 4-iron for the approach on the long par 4, and the shot looked great off the club. He knew if he could land it in the middle of the green, the slope would guide it toward the hole. The ball touched down in the perfect spot, and began tracking. It moved like a well-struck putt, breaking left to right and gaining speed. Thirty feet later, it dropped in the hole for an eagle two.

Thomas stared at him across the fairway in disbelief.

"Nice *fucking* shot," he said.

Spieth won the match on the next hole, and Texas won the national championship. Another promise delivered.

That summer, Spieth finished as low amateur at the U.S. Open, and made another cut at the John Deere Classic in July. The fact that he was succeeding on Tour without necessarily having his "A-Game," often on strange courses, gave him the confirmation he needed—it was time to turn pro.

That plan took an early hit when he failed to make it to the final stage of Q-School, and was left with no status for either tour. He found his way into two Web.com events in early 2013, finishing top ten in both, and was just a few thousand dollars short of full status when he got word that he was in the next week's PGA Tour field in Puerto Rico with a sponsor's exemption. John Peterson, a fellow pro, told him he'd be crazy to leave the Web.com circuit at such an important time. Spieth ignored the advice and flew to Puerto Rico, where he finished in a tie for second. A brilliant career had been launched.

From there, he took the Tour by storm, notching four more top-ten finishes before arriving at the John Deere Classic in mid-July. Three straight 65s, and an incredible forty-four-foot hole-out from the bunker on the 18th hole on Sunday—"the luckiest shot of my life," he said later—put him into a playoff with David Hearn and Zach Johnson. It took five holes to decide, but a final par sealed the deal for Spieth—he had actually *won*. At nineteen, he became the youngest tournament winner in eighty-two years.

The momentum carried him through the year. He turned twenty, two weeks later, and nearly secured his second win that August before Reed beat him in a playoff. He took Rookie of the Year honors at season's end, and was selected by Fred Couples for the President's Cup team, which America won thanks in part to his 2-1 record in pairs with Steve Stricker.

The great white hope had arrived, and he was good.

———————

"Spieth (rhymes with teeth) has always been an old soul. He was raised in Dallas to be a Texas gentleman—sir and ma'am were built into his vocabulary, and community service was stressed through school and church."

—ALAN SHIPNUCK, *Sports Illustrated*

"Lacking neither confidence nor grace, 20-year-old Jordan Spieth is a young head with an old soul . . . Off the course the word universally chosen by his peers to describe him was 'mature.'"

—Jim Moriarty, *Golf Digest*

"You can't talk about Spieth without mentioning his almost unexplainable maturity . . . I said early on that whatever his parents were feeding him should be bottled and sold to an entire generation of kids from this 'look at me' generation."

—Jeff Skinner, *Links Life Golf*

"Jordan Spieth is one mature 20-year-old. A faultless performance in front of the press."

—Sky Sports Twitter

"He speaks as if he has neither time nor interest in being 20. He sits straight. He looks questioners in the eye. He doesn't stammer or stumble. He doesn't raise his voice or lower it. Despite 82-degree heat Saturday, he appears to have no interest in sweating."

—Tom Sorensen, *Raleigh News & Observer*

For all I know, the hype could be true. The tricky part about understanding Spieth is that off the course, he's never going to give anything away. He's too smart and too canny, and he knows he's got a good thing going. But I don't believe the image is an act—if it is, he deserves an Oscar.

You won't find many golfers who can keep their composure at all times, and still avoid the boring patter of lesser personalities. Spieth's handlers keep him close, scanning for any sign of subversive elements, but the vigilance is unnecessary. He isn't stupid, and he's not going to embarrass himself by telling an off-color joke, or spitting out a string of curses on national television, or hopping from bed to bed with escorts who will one day destroy his reputation. He just stands before the hordes of journalists, left hand on his waist, elbow jutting out, making smart observations and tame jokes. As a writer, you'll get enough information to write your story, and no more. More than any young golfer I've met, he obeys his own limits, and he knows when to disappear. If he's that good at managing his brand at age twenty, he'll only become more efficient with time.

One thing Spieth rarely talks about is the immense pressure that comes with being the young face of golf. When I asked him at Doral if it got old answering the same questions about his youth, and whether it created interference in his head since he has to behave like he's a savvy veteran on the course, he brushed it aside and extolled the virtues of his youth.

When we spoke at Congressional, though, he opened up about the saviorlike expectations heaped on his shoulders. "I mean, when Tiger's out," Spieth said, "people are asking, 'Are you going to take over the game?' It's just ridiculous. First of all, yeah, Tiger's done for our sport what maybe he and Arnie and Jack and only a couple of people have ever done. And I'd love to have that happen someday, but that's not going to happen by people telling me that it needs to be me."

He pointed out that he still had a year to win his first major to match Tiger's pace, and when I offered that he must have a good filter in order to exist in this maelstrom of expectations, he told me that he'd had to learn to ignore comments on his articles or the replies to his Twitter posts.

"People just say stuff with no backing to it," he said, "with no experience whatsoever. They say stuff just to say stuff, because they feel like they need to barge in on something. And typically I would get bothered by that, but I'm learning to block it out."

This was the most open I would see Spieth all year, and it made me wish we had more time to talk. As our interview came to an end, I asked him how someone in his place avoids becoming cynical about the fans, the media, even the game.

"I don't think I'm cynical, but it's hard to answer questions about the future," he said.

And then he shook my hand, and we were done.

"I think it's very tough to describe a person like this, because everybody says the same thing. He's mature, he's doing great . . . but for me it's more impressive the way he talks to you. The words that he's using, it's not the normal stuff that—it's not over-exaggerating, it's very true. Something like this [is] very rare for someone who is that young."

—MARTIN KAYMER

The endless, breathless soliloquizing about his maturity can become tiresome, but it exists for a reason—the effect is like watching a six-year-old child prodigy solve complex math problems in his head. It happens so often that you know it's not a fluke or a trick, and yet it never stops feeling slightly unnatural. And like any other exceptional quality, Spieth's maturity has become marketable.

Anyone who wants to get beyond the *image* of Jordan Spieth has to watch him on the golf course. His personality bears a resemblance to Derek Jeter, in the sense that he makes himself into a blank slate onto which you can project your own hopes and desires—hence the hagiographies. Unlike Jeter, though, he wasn't born with ice water running through his veins—with the pressure on, you can finally start to see the first cracks in the facade.

Crunch time is where Spieth finally emerges from his shell. He keeps up a constant monologue with himself, criticism mixed with advice, as though there's a second, neutral Spieth looking down on the one playing golf. His game can be spectacular, but when the nerves hit, he appears vulnerable. At these times, and these times alone, the famous maturity looks less like a solid fact and more like a work in progress.

In time—even in a short time—he may become a consummate winner with piles of major championships to his name. His past argues for the trajectory—he lost his first youth tournament, and U.S. amateur, and college event, all under pressure, before winning. If and when that day comes, the entity known as Jordan Spieth will present a united front to the public. His transformation into myth will be complete, and the idea of anyone outside his inner circle "knowing" him, even a little, will be laughable.

In 2014, we still had those rare Sundays; those afternoons when he finds himself in the terrifying glare of contention. There, for the briefest moment, the image shatters, and the rest of us can peer through the cracks and look into the competitive psyche of golf's child star.

Spieth wanted to leave Augusta as quickly as possible as the sun went down on Saturday, so the print and TV media combined into one horde as he spoke about his patience, and how he had worked hard to curb his aggressive tendencies through fifty-four holes. While other rookies succumbed to the tricks and traps of the course, Spieth played it safe, used what knowledge he had—some of it from Carl Jackson, Ben Crenshaw's caddy—and made a few putts to give himself a legitimate shot at what would surely be the most famous Masters victory since Tiger in '97. He nearly slipped at one point, almost calling Crenshaw by his first name before correcting himself with the usual honorific. Later, at the press conference, he was asked whether he'd call Bubba "Mr. Watson," and he laughed. "Yeah," he said, "just because it will mess with him."

As for Bubba, the snappy tendencies that typically manifested after a bad day were somewhat tempered by the circumstances—whatever else had happened, he was heading into the final round tied with the lead. When told that Spieth joked about calling him "Mr. Watson," he joked back, saying he'd be hitting it past him all day—a classic Bubba joke, the purpose of which was mainly to bolster his ego. He told us he planned to sleep late, drink lots of water, play with his son in the morning, and suffer through Sunday's nerves the best he could.

Considering that Bubba had a coin-flip possibility of imploding at some point the next day, it began to seem like Spieth might actually have a shot. Couples, the '92 champ, spoke for nearly everyone when he praised Bubba's young challenger, who he had captained in the President's Cup. He did, however, add one major caveat. "Tomorrow, obviously, is going to be a really, really hard day to try to win this."

If anything could faze the seemingly unshakable Spieth, it was the final round pressure at Augusta. When the last rays disappeared behind the magnolias, a question hung over the grounds: In the blinding light of an Augusta Sunday, could twenty-year-old Jordan Spieth keep his head?

After a night that was understandably a bit restless, Spieth walked out the locker room door and onto the driving range at 1:32, almost exactly seventy minutes before his tee time. Dressed in a light green shirt and blue pants with a white Under Armour hat, he walked alone to the putting green—past Justin Rose and Lee Westwood and John Senden and Miguel Angel Jimenez and Thomas Bjorn and Kevin Stadler—applauded all the way by the excited patrons sitting in the stands. He met Ted Scott on the green, and when Michael Greller joined them moments later, Scott teased his friend and fellow caddy for letting Spieth come out alone. Bubba appeared moments later to his own round of applause, and he and Spieth shook hands. With hundreds looking on, they chatted, and they tried to ignore the massive nerves they'd face in an hour.

"We're at 2:20, right?" Greller asked Watson and Scott, purposefully getting the 2:40 tee time wrong.

"Same as you," said Scott.

"Why'd you tell him an *earlier* time?" Spieth asked, recognizing a joke gone awry.

"Oh, right," said Greller. "It's 3:20."

Spieth and Watson spoke about Jeff Knox, the amateur "marker" the club used to make up an odd-numbered field, who had played with and beaten Rory McIlroy a day before. Spieth twirled his putter like a baton, and Bubba laughed the nerves away.

When they moved back to the range, only Matt Kuchar and Jonas Blixt remained. Bubba was particularly chatty, talking to the caddies, Kuchar, Spieth, and anyone else who would listen. Blixt stayed by himself, looking like the classic European also-ran that seems to appear in the final groups at Augusta every year, but never wins (José Mariah Olazabal was the last European to win the Masters, in 1999). Spieth and Watson faced each other, hitting iron shots at a flag in the distance. A camera on a crane hovered near them, and when Blixt and Kuchar left, they were alone. Their shots soared past the pine trees, onto the Bermuda grass fairway. In the background the bulbous Augusta water tower marked the end of this strange anachronistic golf oasis and the beginning of a very real, very unglamorous American city.

The magnitude of what awaited them both hung over the scene. When Jordan left to go hit shots from the bunker onto the practice green, Bubba took out the pink driver that would make or break his day. At 2:22, he walked down the cement path, ignoring the hands reaching out to him, his face taking on that taut, red complexion that lets you know the butterflies are churning. He sat in the front seat of the cart that would drive him to the first tee, quiet at last. Spieth left a moment later, slapping five with the kids and smiling as he drove off.

The biggest round of his life began with an erratic kind of luck. Off the first tee, Spieth released his right hand off the club—a universally bad sign—and the ball flew toward the trees on the left-hand side of the fairway. He recovered with a terrific punch shot that trickled onto the green, but on the second hole, the first par 5, his hand came off the 3-wood again, and the ball hit a pine tree on the left. Again, he saved himself from disaster, this time aided by the luck of the bounce. He laid up, hit a sand wedge to fifteen feet, and curled in a beautiful birdie. Bubba, meanwhile, found bunkers off both tees and had to scramble for pars.

Up ahead, Matt Kuchar briefly tied Spieth for the lead on the third hole with his second straight birdie, but his history was one of toil and strife on major Sundays. Nobody quite believed he could muster a real run, and the sense that he would fade came true almost immediately, with a four-putt double bogey on the fourth hole that dropped him to -4. Jonas Blixt, trying to tame his nerves, was a par machine for the first six holes, and ended the front nine right where he began, at -4.

Rickie Fowler got off to a quick start with a birdie, but a bogey on no. 2 put him at -3, which was as high as he'd get the rest of the day. It became clear that there would be no magic runs from the bottom of the leaderboard. The sun beat down on Augusta National, and the players realized they were in the midst of a grind.

In the final group, the crushing pressure reached Bubba first. After annihilating a drive almost to the third green, 350 yards away, he opted to play an odd little bump-and-run shot that didn't suit the terrain at all. The ball ran over the slick green, and the pitch back was almost as treacherous—Bubba's third shot barely made it up the hill, leaving a long par putt that he missed. When Spieth's approach tailed left toward the hole and left him an easy two-putt for par, the twenty-year-old held a solo lead at the Masters.

The long par-3 fourth clocks in at 243 yards, and Spieth hit his third wayward tee shot of the afternoon, leaving it in the front bunker. Bubba responded with a pinpoint iron that stopped six feet from the hole, and it looked like he'd gain at least a stroke back, if not more. Facing a difficult second shot, Spieth stood in an ocean of sand, hoping to get it close enough for a realistic par chance. He blasted out, and the ball left his club like a heat-seeking missile. Spieth marched to the left, watching it track, and stared in disbelief when it dropped in the hole. He raised both arms in triumph—a birdie from the bunker.

Facing a three-shot deficit, Bubba's own birdie effort now looked a bit less comfortable. He stepped up and holed it under pressure, and at -5, he now stood alone in second place. With the rest of the challengers grappling just to make pars, the final group had the feel of a match play duel. They laughed on the way to the fifth tee, trying to ignore the tension. Spieth had the honors, and he sent yet another tee shot careening to the left. "Oh, Jordan, come on, not *again*!" he hissed to himself. "Hit softly . . . no, softly!" It headed toward a fairway bunker, and Bubba blasted his drive into the right rough.

Both had started wild as hell, but there was a sense that although luck had favored Spieth early on, chaos and entropy were the province of Bubba. At some level, they were already playing on his turf. The twenty-year-old would need to level off, and soon.

Spieth got lucky again when his drive came up short of the bunker. His approach wasn't so lucky, skidding past the green and into the sand. He left himself a sweeping par putt that broke too far left, and when Bubba salvaged a par, Spieth's lead had dwindled to one. On the short par-3 sixth, Spieth had a long discussion about the wind with Greller—"Are you sure it's not hurting right this second? It's swirling . . ."—and stuck his iron to three feet. Bubba nodded at him, stiffly, and marched down the fairway. Facing a slippery right-to-left twelve-footer for birdie, he gave it a delicate little tap and watched it follow a perfect line and drop. Spieth canned his short birdie in response, and they joked to each other about how "easy" the par 3s were playing.

The Masters rookie split the fairway with a driver on seven, and seemed to be in a full groove—the nerves had settled, both hands remained on the club, and he was ready to do battle over the next two hours and change. He stuck his approach, landing the ball short and watching it track uphill toward the flag. It left him a twelve-footer for birdie, moving slightly back to the left and slower than usual. He read it like a textbook, and drained it to reach -8. Bubba ended up in another bunker and used the backstop to spin his birdie attempt to three feet, but all he could do was save par.

Spieth opted to leave his driver in the bag on the long par-5 eighth, and the move paid off when he found the fairway again. Despite some dodgy swings, he was -3 for the day and leading the Masters by two strokes.

It had played out like a fantasy, and at that moment, before Bubba stepped up to the tee, Spieth had the world in his hands. Golf rarely gets this perfect, and dreams are rarely realized so early in life . . . ten and a half more holes of this, and he'd be in the clouds.

He should have taken a snapshot, at that divine instant, because the cold reality of Masters Sunday was about to deliver a savage body blow.

Bubba, playing with the kind of productive rage only he can muster, bombed a drive that carried the bunkers 310 yards down the fairway.

With 232 remaining to the hole, he ran his approach safely over the green. Spieth laid up to the right, and after aiming his third shot at the inside of the scoreboard beyond the green, he was shocked when the ball landed and checked, refusing to roll out to the hole. Bubba nearly holed his eagle chip, and Spieth, still fearing the speed of the greens, struck a weak birdie putt. He left himself just a few feet for par, but it was long enough to make him nervous.

He missed. Around the green, the fans groaned, but the truth was that he had been lucky not to tally a bogey this long. When Bubba drained his short birdie, Spieth had suffered the dreaded two-shot swing. The lead vanished that quickly, and both players now stood at -7 heading into the final hole on the front side.

Now with the honors, Bubba stepped up to the ninth tee infused with energy, and crushed a driver down the middle. Spieth stayed in the fairway, too, but wound up forty yards behind his opponent. On his approach, he failed to get the ball past the false front, and the CBS announcers were quick to mention Greg Norman making the same mistake in the midst of his Sunday collapse against Nick Faldo back in '86. Bubba, feeding off the momentum, knocked his approach to eleven feet, and hit a bending right-to-left putt that snaked into the back of the hole for birdie. Spieth's chip ran up to four feet—a good effort, especially under the circumstances—but his par putt hit the hole on the right and caromed around the edge before dying a feckless death on the grass. More groans, and more grimaces from Spieth.

It was another two-shot swing. Spieth would enter the back nine at -6, one-under for the day but feeling like he had just lost everything. Meanwhile, at -8, Bubba had a death grip on the tournament yet again.

Before the round began, Michael Greller overheard a fan tell a friend that when Bubba drove it straight, he was so long that he started with a three-shot advantage on the field. He knew it was true, and he knew on the first tee that they needed to pounce early.

And they had. But Bubba had reacted with incredible resolve, pouring in four birdies to stem the charge and reassert control when it looked like Spieth's momentum might bury him. Already, it had been the toughest performance of his career, and one look at Spieth told you all you needed to know about his mental state. He was deflated, and whether he admitted it to himself or not, the tournament was lost.

On the CBS broadcast, Nick Faldo summed up the situation with a classic bit of English understatement: "This is a significant moment, isn't it?"

The decisive blows came on the back nine in the form of two very different shots.

The first happened on the 12th tee, when Spieth sized up the short par 3 in the heart of Amen Corner. In his book *No Limits,* Ian Poulter called this hole "one of the most volatile holes in the sport," and compared it to "taking a penalty in a football match and looking at a goal that is only three feet by three feet." The green offers a landing area of less than ten yards, and the wind is impossible to judge—even the flag on the 11th green can be deceptive.

With the grandstands rising behind him, on the biggest stage of his life, Spieth pulled a 9-iron. Greller implored him to aim for the right side of the bunker, at a television tower, where a mistake wouldn't hurt him too severely. Spieth didn't believe the swirling wind was truly blowing at him, though. He felt the hole was actually playing *downwind,* and that if he hit his 9-iron perfectly on the safe line, it would fly into the back bunker and put him in a pickle.

As he stood over the ball, he convinced himself the wind was, at the very least, dead. He made the last-minute choice to play a fade, trying to work the ball at the hole. Up in the blue heights where the ball soared, though, the wind was indeed gusting toward the tee. It held up the little white orb just enough, and when it landed on the fringe in front of the green, it rolled back, slowly but inevitably, into Rae's Creek. That's where Spieth lost the tournament.

The coup de grâce came from Bubba on the 13th tee. Instead of bothering with a draw onto the fairway, he decided that Sunday at the Masters would be a good time to bash a driver over the trees and cut off some distance. It was an audacious move even in an ordinary round, and borderline insane considering the situation, but it nearly worked to perfection. The ball grazed a tree somewhere along the way, but it was only a glancing blow—it came through the pines and dropped in the fairway. In the media room, a collective gasp echoed off the walls. Nobody had ever seen anything like it, including the writers who had been around for decades. The incredible risk produced an incredible reward—Bubba left himself a mere sand wedge into the green, at which point birdie on the par 5 was a formality.

Seeing that, Spieth knew he was licked—they were playing a different game.

The rest of the round played out with a heavy sense of fate. Bubba hit drive after drive into the fairway, inexorable and straight, and Spieth couldn't get the birdies to fall. Blixt fought back to -5 and a tie for second place, but Fowler and Kuchar couldn't muster even a remote challenge.

As the back nine wore on, Spieth's lower body was out of sync with his torso, and his hand came off the club over and over. He began muttering to himself, and crouching defensively after bad shots. Only a strong short game kept him from total collapse, but that didn't include the putter—which, at times, he looked like he wanted to throw.

"Dangit, Jordan, God!" he hissed, when his 8-iron on 16 missed the magic spot that would let the ball trickle all the way to the hole. "Come on!" he moaned after a bad drive on the next tee. As he walked up 17, caught up in the emotion of the moment, he turned to Greller. "I've worked my whole life for this. . . ." he said. He let the sentence trail off. Greller reminded him that there would be many more, but Spieth wasn't in the mood for perspective.

That afternoon, America had its first glimpse at Spieth's tendency to let negative emotions overwhelm him. The problem isn't anger, but self-pity—a weaker emotion that encourages its victims to give up. Before the year was over, I would watch it reduce Spieth to rubble twice more. Like Sergio Garcia, it transformed his whole affect, and changed the thrust of his game. Unlike Sergio, it never felt like Spieth was doomed to repeat the mistakes across the decades.

. . .

The cameras captured a beautiful image on the 18th tee, after Bubba hit a 3-wood into the fairway. He posed, silhouetted against the late-afternoon sun still burning through the clouds, with the towering pines behind him. Here, in the full blaze of his greatness, you could forget everything else and appreciate his sheer, unmistakable brilliance.

After his approach from the fairway, he spun his iron emphatically, soaked in the adulation on his way to the green, two-putted for par, and sobbed onto Ted Scott's shoulder. The boy from Bagdad, Florida, had won his second Masters by three strokes over Spieth and Blixt.

In front of the cameras, Jordan held his head high and Bubba was up to his usual bluster—"a guy named Bubba from a small town," he marveled, infused with wonder at himself and his victory.

The mystery of the final round, in the end, could be summed up in the fickle virtuosity of the erratic lefty who slipped on the second green jacket of his career. In the most unpredictable moments, under over-whelming pressure, he can summon a terrific resilience that goes against all the thin-skinned blunders that dog him on his bad days. He stands massive on his favorite stage, swinging the mighty pink driver in audacious arcs—*obliterating* the poor ball—and sending it just where he wants. The two Bubbas congeal into one as the fear and insecurity disappear, and the genius that emerges, in that transcendent moment, is far greater than the sum of its parts.

9

A FEW THOUGHTS
ON AUGUSTA NATIONAL

---

*"Gentlemanliness had been the very basis of the tournament
founder's life and of his golf; Cliff, the keen assistant, picked up
on the boss's strict standards of behavior, his love of honor. Roberts amplified Jones. Together, they made a fetish out of monitoring the behavior of everyone in or near their tournament."*
—CURT SAMPSON, *The Masters: Golf, Money,
and Power in Augusta, Georgia*

Some people buy into the mythos of Augusta, and you may be one.
So, fair warning: If you prefer to believe that walking those holy
fairways will induce a state of golf nirvana, or that the Masters is a
noble-minded fairy tale come to life, you may want to skip this section.
And for God's sake don't come within a thousand feet of Curt Sampson's excellent history of Cliff Roberts, Bobby Jones, and the origins of
the sport's most famous tournament.

On the other hand, if your bullshit detector hasn't quite run out of
batteries, consider a second argument: There's something deeply disturbing and anti-democratic about the whole operation, and the club

represents almost everything that's archaic and exclusive about golf. Sampson's book is a great starting point if you want to learn the truth, and the best endorsement came from Augusta National itself, whose members privately accused him of multiple factual errors without being able to identify one.

Make no mistake—the men in green jackets know what they're doing, and they do it well. The Masters became the most prestigious major with remarkable speed, despite being the youngest of them all. Horton Smith won the first "Augusta National Invitational" in 1934, eighteen years after the founding of the PGA Championship, thirty-nine years after the inaugural U.S. Open, and seventy-four years after Willie Park Sr. beat Old Tom Morris by two strokes in the 1860 British Open.

So how did the new kid on the block gain such status? Bobby Jones, for one. He was America's first golfing icon, and any endeavor to which he attached his name was bound to come with a certain cachet. The course didn't hurt, either—designed by Alister Mackenzie on a former indigo plantation, the layout and landscape were beautiful from the start.

But the real star of the show was always Clifford Roberts, the Augusta National co-founder and, by every account, the brains of the operation. Roberts came from Iowa, and he had a rotten early life—his mother killed herself with a shotgun blast when Cliff was nineteen, and his father stepped in front of a train, possibly on purpose, eight years later. Roberts rarely spoke about these rough beginnings, so it's impossible to guess what effect it had on his psyche. Whatever the damage, he was a man of considerable talents. He made money hand over fist—after profiting hugely in Texas land sales, he became an investment banker at the Reynolds Company in New York. He could market the hell out of anything, and he could ingratiate himself with powerful men like Bobby Jones and Dwight Eisenhower. That, more than anything, may have been the source of Roberts's great power—his ability to flatter influential icons in just the right way.

The two of them, Roberts and Jones, made a perfect pair—Jones the noble face of the enterprise, Roberts the vital, tireless heartbeat, ceaselessly operating behind the scenes. He's the one who secured the initial investments, and who planned the tournament to fall after baseball's spring training ended in Florida, thus allowing the New York reporters to stop by on their way home, where he treated them like royalty in exchange for glowing coverage. He's also the one who fostered an atmosphere of exclusivity even in the financially unstable days when they had to turn to the city of Augusta to bail them out by purchasing unused tickets.

Roberts invented the "Masters" name, which Bobby Jones never liked. He even managed to get legendary figures like Grantland Rice to do his dirty work for him—in one of the original club meetings, Rice proposed that Jones and Roberts be allowed to run the whole operation without interference, which set up the dictatorship that would last forty years.

He was also a mean, petty racist with a paranoid streak so wide it would make Joseph Stalin blush. It's easy to chalk up the initial racism at Augusta National to the mores of the American Southeast at the time, but the fact is that by and large, the majority of founding members were Roberts's people—businessmen from the northeast. They're the ones who brought in local black boys on weekend nights, blindfolded them, and had them beat the shit out of one another inside the confines of a boxing ring. They're the ones who sat around smoking cigars and drinking cocktails, cheering the carnage. They're the ones who kept blacks, Jews, and women from joining the fun.

When Bobby Jones began to wither away with a neurological disease called syringomyelia, Roberts stepped into the power vacuum and made the tyranny absolute. He ran off employees he didn't like, bullied members and guests, extended and withdrew invitations on a whim. He even cooked up an excuse to kick a golfer named Frank Stranahan out of a tournament for reasons that have never been confirmed, but were rumored to stem from Stranahan's involvement with a woman Roberts fancied for himself. He also vowed to keep blacks out of the Masters except as subservient caddies—a promise he kept until 1976, when Lee Elder finally broke the Augusta color barrier decades after it had been demolished in most other walks of life.

Just a year after this unthinkable breach, eighty-three years old and suffering from cancer, Roberts made his way to the par-3 course, settled on the banks of Ike's Pond, and blew his brains out with a .38 revolver.

"I wish I'd been there when he committed suicide. I would have rolled the son of a bitch into the water."
—FRANK STRANAHAN, to *Sports Illustrated*, April 6, 1998

The ghostly shadow of this strange man hangs over Augusta still. The Masters has come into the modern age slowly and reluctantly at every step, illustrated most famously when they decided to run the tournament commercial free in 2003 rather than cave to protesters and allow a woman to join the club. (It wasn't until 2012 when Condi Rice and a South Carolina businesswoman named Darla Moore accepted membership.) They never welcomed television with open arms in the first place, as any viewer who remembers the frustrating days when you could only watch the back nine can attest.

Even today, there's a distressing amount of paranoia and obsessive control evident in the people who run Augusta. Like most golf fans, I grew up watching and loving the Masters, even in my youngest days when "normal" golf bored me to death. I finagled a credential in 2014 after months of begging, and I expected to be overcome by emotion and goose bumps when I first stepped onto the hallowed grounds.

Instead, the entire experience felt like tiptoeing through a minefield, and it started long before I crossed the border into Georgia. Numerous reporters gave me warnings in the days leading up—don't you dare take your cell phone on the course, or they'll kick you out, since the Masters is the one tournament that doesn't allow journalists to carry phones outside the media center. Don't get caught running anywhere on the course, or you're gone. Don't write anything controversial, because they read everything, and you'll never be invited back. Make sure you personally thank the key officials before the tournament begins, or your rudeness will be noted. Et cetera, et cetera.

The Pinkerton presence, too, is very real. Steve Elling wrote about these hired thugs, spiritual descendants of union busters and corporate henchmen, for CBS in 2011, noting that they "take their jobs as seriously as TSA agents screening incoming passengers from Baghdad." Elling was run down and nearly evicted from the premises for the crime of ducking under a rope near a putting green to cross a forbidden expanse of five feet—the Pinkerton finally got to him one hundred yards later and made him walk, like a child, back to the spot where he had misbehaved. Elling had no choice but to comply—his press credential was at stake.

Elling also made waves when he had the gall to interrupt Billy Payne, the Augusta chairman, when he dodged questions about why the club wouldn't admit a female member. The exchange was tense, but it never devolved into shouting or profanity. So Elling was surprised when he got a phone call shortly after from his boss, whose first words were: *"What did you do?"*

The complaints went from Augusta to CBS quickly, and rolled downhill until they landed back on Elling's head. The message was clear—stop rocking the boat.

"Those Augusta guys play dirty, man," Elling told me. "I had the audacity to demand he answer a question, and stop being evasive, and they went and complained to my boss. What a bunch of fucking . . ."

Elling was let go by CBS shortly after, and though he doesn't believe it had anything to do with the Augusta debacle, he doesn't know for sure, and never will.

"They just make up the rules on the fly," said Elling. "If you ask them why, it's like you're ten years old and asking your dad 'Why can't I watch that TV show?' And your dad says, 'Because I said so.' I'm sorry, man, that's not good enough for me! You cannot put enough Grey Poupon on your shit sandwich to get me to eat it without complaint."

When I finally arrived, things got even stranger. I strolled around the course on Wednesday with a media member who I'm sure would prefer to remain anonymous, and he stopped me on the back nine.

"Look down," he said. "You see any pinecones?"

I thought it would be easy—the loblolly pines were everywhere, and so was the pine straw—but I couldn't spot even a single pinecone. What I *did* see were black men in white jumpsuits, one assigned to each acre, tasked with scooping up any piece of litter—which, at Augusta, apparently includes pinecones—the minute it hit the ground. It was a site, I imagined, that would have delighted Roberts.

"Now look around," my friend said again. "Find a squirrel."

I couldn't find a squirrel. Nobody seems to have any explanation for this, besides the questionable theory that squirrels prefer softwood trees and Augusta doesn't let softwoods like the native sweetgum grow on the grounds.

"Now look up," he said, obviously having performed this patter before. "Notice any birds?"

At this point, I felt a low rumble of panic in my stomach. How the hell do you keep *birds* out? Some kind of electric sonar sky fence that scrambles their brains? Or do you pay locals to come shoot them en masse in late March?

(When I called Curt Sampson, he had a different explanation for the missing animals: "They couldn't get a membership.")

I began to consider all the other ways Augusta tampers with the environment—the dyed blue water, the way they ice the azaleas in a warm year to make sure they don't bloom before the television cameras arrive, the piped-in birdsong CBS has used to atone for the lack of actual flying creatures. Even the minor details reek of fanaticism . . . the green sandwich wrappers, specially designed so the rogue escapees can't be seen standing out against the green grass on TV . . . the tape that goes over the Coca-Cola logos at the concession stand in a move that is more about Augusta's tremendous ego than any true anti-commercial instincts, since Bobby Jones made a killing in Coke as an investor.

These deceptions have no human toll. Media relations, on the other hand, have become significantly less cordial since the early days. The cattle pen I'd barely survived on Friday was the least of my concerns, because the threat of banishment is very real, and very constant. In '66, they booted the announcer Jack Whitaker for calling a group of fans a "mob"—the club prefers the term "patrons." Gary McCord famously joked that the club used "bikini wax" on the greens, which led Tom Watson to rat him out. McCord hasn't been back since, which is so petty it makes my head spin. And there are smaller stories of journalists being kicked out for sending a text message steps outside the media center—a fate that befell Westwood One's Charlie Rymer was one—or players' wives being detained in special buildings for having the audacity to take photos at the par-3 contest. Alan Shipnuck was once banned for a year for following the champion into Butler Cabin for the final interview—which is to say, doing his job as a feature writer.

On *my* first day, I discovered that they didn't even trust us to walk to the media center on our own, opting to drive us by cart from the entrance instead. And when I walked on a patch of grass to reach the cart, an employee yelled at me to stay on the paved path. Big Brother is everywhere.

For the "patrons," the list of rules and regulations is so extensive as to be absurd, as Bill Pennington pointed out in *The New York Times* in 2013:

> "There is so much you cannot do at Augusta National, it is a wonder the place was not named the Country Club of No.
>
> No running anywhere on the grounds. No sitting on the grass near the greens. No bare feet (even when sitting down). No chairs with arms. No folding chairs. No flags. No signs. No banners. No coolers. No strollers. No radios. No standing in officially designated sitting areas. No sitting in the standing areas. No cameras. No rigid chairs. No hats worn backward. No metal golf spikes. No outsize hats. No carts. And absolutely no lying down anywhere."

Members aren't immune—their dues change year by year without warning, depending on what the club happens to need, and anybody can be evicted at any time without explanation. Stories like the following float round the ether at Augusta: A member brings a guest who doesn't behave with the proper reverence for the club, and at the end of the year, said member receives a letter in the mail. "Thank you for your membership at Augusta National," it says. "We wish you the best going forward." And that's that.

Even the players feel strange during Masters week, though it's rare for any of them to mention it. David Toms was one of the few to speak out, telling reporters in 2006 that players had to walk around "on eggshells."

"They're worried about their cell phone being on, having to stop by the hut on the way in to scan your ticket, making sure you only have one parking pass and somebody else doesn't get in there," he said. "It's like C.I.A. stuff, you know what I mean?"

In this kind of oppressive atmosphere, how could I be expected to appreciate the surroundings, stunning though they may be? For most of the week, I felt like a tourist in North Korea, watched with suspicion by armed soldiers. One false move, I thought, and I could be thrown in the underground bunker where they keep all the dead birds.

For some, all this rigorous pomposity is cause for praise. Augusta National is the last bastion of some sacred, vanishing way of life, the theory goes, although what that way of life might be is beyond me, since self-important old rich people who make life hell for everyone else are too common to be considered sacred, and too entrenched to be vanishing.

Nevertheless, it's a rule of life that all despots attract lackeys, and the Masters attracts more than most. The way the bootlickers carry on about the sacrosanct nature of the tournament, and seem to get such a perverse delight at the innocents who run afoul of the honor code, is enough to make you want to retch. I only mention them to point out that in this debate, unreasonable people can disagree.

Ask any American golfer to name his dream, and he'll say "winning the Masters." Maybe there's something to admire in how the prestige has built over the years to the point that it's now an inescapable spring television ritual, complete with tinkling piano music and the reassuringly dulcet tones of Jim Nantz. But when I hear the words "a tradition unlike any other," the only tradition that comes to mind is the exclusive, silent power of men who take themselves too seriously.

Needless to say, the words I've written in this chapter will have no tangible effect on Augusta. If it's true that they read everything written about them from here to the remotest regions of Indochina, my chances of ever going back as a working journalist will be quite, quite dim. On this point, I called up Curt Sampson after reading his book and asked if he'd ever been issued another media credential. I could hear a small laugh on the other end of the line. "Oh, *Shane,*" he said, as if I were a nineteen-year-old who still believed in Santa. "No."

But that's okay—the golf is terrific, and the course is stunning, but the sanctimony is a real downer. Some people worship the paranoia and pieties. Personally, I couldn't shake the feeling, as I walked among the rabid mobs and past the bikini-waxed greens, that the tyrant Cliff Roberts was sneering at me from beyond the grave . . . eagle-eyed and prissy as he probed for the slightest hint of impropriety; marshaling his living minions to show me exactly how I didn't belong; moving all the pieces like a conductor until the whole slick operation became a secret, choreographed homage to a shrewd old bigot with a toady's cunning instincts and a disturbing fetish for absolute power.

10

ONE LAST MOMENT AT AUGUSTA

Late in the front nine on Sunday, after failing to mount a charge from eight shots back, Rory McIlroy noticed that he was consistently putting the ball left of the target. He ultimately missed fifteen putts inside eight feet that week, and a 77 on Friday killed any chance he had of winning the tournament. By the sixth hole on Sunday, it finally got so bad that he decided to play detective. As an experiment, he drew a line on his ball and aimed it a few inches left of the hole.[10] When he stood up and addressed the ball, he was staggered by the results. It looked, and felt, like he was aiming at the *right* edge, even though he knew exactly where he had lined it up.

The difference wasn't huge—three inches or so—but it was plenty big enough to diagnose the problem. Every putt was doomed from the beginning. The idea that he'd been playing this way for who knows how long annoyed him to distraction. It had cost him a slew of bad misses on the mid-range putts, while anything longer was completely hopeless.

After the adjustment, he birdied his next three holes. By the end of the round, he had fought back to even par for the tournament and finished in a tie for eighth place.

---

[10] Some players use this technique on every putt—Rory does not.

What he found, when he analyzed things later, was that he had been standing so close at address that his eye-line fell on the far side of the ball. His body had understood the problem instinctively, even if the brain did not, and he'd unconsciously opened his stance slightly to allow his left hand to push at the ball in an attempt to compensate.

It boggled his mind that a mistake like this was possible for a professional golfer, much less one of his capacity, and he was unpleasantly surprised that nobody else in his camp had picked up on the problem.

After the Masters, he spent weeks using putting mirrors and chalk lines in an attempt to retrain himself to see a straight line from a proper stance. In those monotonous hours of adjustment and repetition, he hoped the work would pay dividends in the summer. He told us this story at the Wells Fargo a month later, and none of us knew at the time that his epiphany at Augusta would prove to be one of the most important moments of the entire season.

11

NEW ORLEANS, LOUISIANA

The Loneliness of Seung-Yul Noh; The Embattled Keegan Bradley;
A Showdown in Big Easy

ME: Do you like America?
NOH: Mmmmmmmm . . . no.
    —Exchange with SEUNG-YUL NOH

Tell me everything you know about twenty-two-year-old Seung-Yul Noh, who finished first on the Asian Tour money list in 2011 and, unlike Jordan Spieth or Rickie Fowler, won on the PGA Tour in 2014. Or what about Hideki Matsuyama, even younger than Noh, also a 2014 winner, and one of twenty-nine golfers who made it to the Tour Championship in Atlanta? Or what about K. J. Choi, or Ryo Ishikawa, or Sang-Moon Bae, all of them Tour fixtures? And since we're here, what do you *really* know about Y. E. Yang, the only golfer in history who has ever chased down Tiger Woods when he held a lead in the final round of a major championship?

You get the point—in terms of American and European media coverage, there's an Asian vacuum. Professional golfers from east and southeast Asia—mostly Japan, Korea, and Thailand—exist behind a veil, posting results that would attract far more attention had they been born in the western world. Whatever else factors into this phenomenon, the primary issue is language.

European golfers from outside Great Britain and Ireland have studied English for years, and most are fluent. For most Asian golfers this isn't the case, which makes it difficult for reporters to conduct snappy interviews, or to ask the type of personal questions that produce the best background details. Meaning is often lost in translation, leading to exchanges like the following, with Korean Sang-Moon Bae:

REPORTER: What's the key to your success this week?
SANG-MOON BAE: Uhh. . . . yes.

Later in that same interview, when asked about his patience, Bae responded by saying he wasn't angry, and then asked the speaker to slow down.

Consequently, interviews with Asian golfers tend to run about half as long as interviews with English speakers, and the questions remain more superficial. This creates a feedback loop—the public expects less information about these golfers, reporters put in less effort, and the veil thickens.

The same phenomenon that isolates Asian pros from the media also sets them apart from their fellow professionals.

When I spoke with Seung-Yul Noh at the Wells Fargo in Charlotte, he told me he wasn't very happy in America. "Is fun because my dream is playing PGA Tour when I start playing golf," he said, "but not many friends here."

"Is it lonely?"

"Very much, yes."

"Do you mostly hang out with the other Koreans?"

"Yeah, very good friendly all the Korean players, we probably ten guys playing in Tour, Koreans, so we eat dinner every night. Almost every dinner."

"Are you sick of being around the same people all the time?"

He laughed and nodded.

On the other hand, Asian golfers deal with an almost oppressive amount of attention from their home media. While American journalists might focus on any of a hundred golfers in a given week, Korean and Japanese media will always tailor their coverage to the native sons. The result is that players like Noh and Matsuyama often find themselves in the midst of huge circles of writers and photographers, where an American golfer would experience this only after winning a tournament—or if he happened to be Tiger Woods.

For Korean golfers, playing in America is a prerequisite for earning a high public profile back home, as Noh himself knew all the way back in 2010, when he earned his way into the PGA Championship and opened with a strong 68-71:

> Q. Dealing with both the Korean and American media, how different has it been and how are you gaining some celebrity status back at home?
> SEUNG-YUL NOH: I don't play much on the PGA Tour so that's why I'm not very famous back in Korea. But after this, maybe I'll be famous.

Noh grew up in the northernmost part of South Korea and began golfing at age seven. Noh's English is slightly better than most, in part because he began traveling to America every winter to train when he was eight. His parents both worked in banks, but his mother quit her job when he was twelve to drive him around the country to golf tournaments, and his father followed suit four years later to become his son's caddie. Noh turned professional at sixteen, qualified for the Asian Tour that same year, and won a tournament in China the next season. By 2010, he had topped the money list there and become the second-youngest winner ever in European Tour history when he beat K. J. Choi to take the Malaysian Open. After making the cut in three majors in 2011, he decided to come to America to try out Q-School.

He made it, and his life changed in a hurry. He settled in San Diego at his uncle's house, traveled with his sister while his parents stayed in Korea, and began working with swing coach Sean Foley—

who overcame the language barrier by showing Noh pictures of how he wanted him to swing. He felt lonely, but he liked the conveniences of America, with laundry services and courtesy cars and Korean restaurants in almost every town he visited.

On the course, fans mistook him for other Asian or Asian-American players—especially Kevin Na—but it was a headache he could bear. He ended his rookie season with a forty-ninth-place finish in the FedEx Cup standings. Though his mental game suffered in 2013 and his scores ballooned, he redeemed himself with a fourth-place finish at the Web.com Tour Finals to keep his Tour card. He bought a condo in Dallas and now spends his free time watching Korean movies, but he still doesn't know if his adventure in American golf is permanent.

"You know," he said with a deep sigh, when I asked if he'd eventually head home and play on the Asian Tour, "I'll make a lot of money for the U.S. and then maybe playing in Korea. Spend money in Korea."

Noh remembers watching Y. E. Yang beat Tiger Woods at the PGA Championship, which made Yang a hero in Korea and went down as one of the great major victories ever. Yang was the first golfer in fifteen tries to beat Tiger Woods at a major when he led on Sunday, and also became the first Asian-born player to win a major title. He's still the only one.

When Noh came to America, he became friends with Yang and ate dinner with him frequently. He had countless questions about that epic Sunday. Noh had watched the video over and over, knew every hole, and asked Yang about all of them—why had he hit that particular shot in that particular situation? What was he thinking about before the round, knowing he was playing against Tiger and facing a deficit? How did he feel as the round wore on, and he had a real chance to win?

Yang opened up to him, and Noh started to dream of winning on Tour himself. It wasn't far-fetched; Noh and Matsuyama represent a new breed of Asian golfer. As Rory McIlroy pointed out in Charlotte, the stereotype of Asian players is that they come to America and Europe with mechanically flawless swings, but generate little speed and hence have little power. The first time McIlroy saw Noh swing, he was blown away—he swung hard, and the ball jumped off his club. In

2014, Noh and Matsuyama each finished with a driving average of about 295 yards, good for fortieth and fifty-first place, respectively—well into the top half of Tour pros.

At the Zurich Classic, two weeks after the Masters, Noh opened with a 65-68-65 three-day stretch, free of bogeys. It gave him the first fifty-four-hole lead of his career, and a two-shot lead on his playing partner for the final day, Keegan Bradley.

"I'm amazed looking back at how many people were outright telling me how ridiculous it was to want to play on the Tour. But I remember those people. I remember who those guys are. I'll never forget."

—KEEGAN BRADLEY

Keegan Bradley taught me an important lesson in 2014, which is that if you have to ask a golfer for an interview more than three times, you're better off just forgetting the whole thing. By the time our endless miscommunications reached a climax at Bay Hill, we were both so annoyed at each other that a good outcome was basically impossible.

I approached him anyway, on the range, and with a sigh he agreed to make good on our plan to talk. I know now that I should have cut my losses and moved on; instead, we marched to an equipment trailer and I made small talk that he ignored while texting his girlfriend. When we sat down, I tried to salvage some goodwill by apologizing for using up his time—a move that he probably saw as insincere, and only made things worse.

On the other hand, the fact that our interview was conducted under duress allowed me to observe a trait of Bradley's that rarely sees the light of day—the chip on his shoulder. He is a connoisseur of old insults, and uses his resentment as fuel.

Those who watch Bradley on television miss this aspect, but they notice a few other traits: his distinctive blue eyes, his bounding energy, his tense posture—shoulders hunched up into the neck, torso ramrod straight—and, of course, the OCD-like behaviors. When Bradley faces an approach shot, he glares at the ball with an intensity that verges on fury. He places one foot ahead of the other, as though he's gathering his courage before taking a running start to leap over a creek. Then he hazards a step forward, decides it doesn't feel right, and steps back. When he repeats the motion, it becomes a strange, rocking dance of hesitation. Sometimes he'll hit immediately, and other times the routine will go on without end. On putts, Bradley twists his head to one side, contorting himself so that he stares at the ball with just his right eye, ogrelike. Other habits, like persistent spitting, have forced him to make a public apology; he didn't even realize he was doing it.

Later that year, at the U.S. Open, Martin Kaymer said what everyone was thinking: Bradley made things difficult for his playing partners. They never knew if he would play fast or slow, and it disturbed golfers who were accustomed to predictable rhythms.

On this topic, I thought Bradley and I might form a bond. As a child, I washed my hands repetitively until they became cracked and bloody, flipped light switches off and on for minutes at a time until it "felt" right, and obeyed odd counting rituals. These habits ebbed away in my teens, but the impulse remains, and my brain is conditioned to think and behave obsessively. Unlike most spectators, who are inclined to make a joke of Bradley, I at least had a sense of what he was going through. When I asked him, though, I might as well have been speaking Greek.

"I think it's more of a Northeastern, New England thing," he said. "I'm very stubborn."

I had no idea how geography applied at the time, and I still don't.

What really matters about Bradley is the way he views *himself* in the world. He grew up in Woodstock, Vermont, the son of Mark Bradley, a golf pro, and the nephew of Pat Bradley, who won three majors on the LPGA circuit in 1986, the year Keegan was born. Vermont isn't exactly a hotbed of professional golf, but Keegan began playing golf at age five, and could practice for free at the nearby Crown Point Country Club, where his father worked.

His competitive fire took flame at an early age, and at times he pushed it to absurd lengths. In a 2012 *Golf Digest* story, his high school coach remembered how Keegan would always make sure to walk ahead of his opponent during a match, on the advice of his aunt. But true to his obsessive nature, Bradley would make sure he was ahead even when he teed off *second,* which meant he had to stow his driver, grab his bag, and sprint off the tee box to race ahead of the other player—who must have been a bit puzzled, watching Bradley sprint by.

The only thing that limited him was the Vermont winter; in the junior golf world, that was enough to keep him a step behind the Southern prodigies.

"I went underlooked coming out of Vermont and New England," Bradley told me, "and I never really got that much credit."

Bradley's parents split up when he was seventeen, and while his mother and sister stayed in Vermont, he moved to Massachusetts with his father. Low on money, they lived together in a trailer park for seven months, which has become part of Bradley's lore. In a 2012 interview with *Golf.com*'s Alan Bastable, Bradley described the layout:

> "It was like something out of a movie. My dad is 6' 4", he's taller than me, and we were living in this trailer with bunk beds. He slept in the bottom bunk. I slept on the kitchen table—the table folded down and had cushions; that was my bed. We had communal showers and bathrooms; I wouldn't be able to do that now. [Laughs] I remember one night the A.C. wasn't working and it was so hot that I slept in my car. But I never remember it being terrible. I remember loving it."

In Massachusetts, Keegan's trajectory only increased the size of the chip on his shoulder. He wasn't even considered the best player on his high school team—or the second-best. Those honors went to Jon Curran and Kim Donovan, both of whom went on to play big-time college golf. Even when Bradley bested Curran—and everyone else in Massachusetts—to win the state title his senior season, he didn't attract much attention from the big golf schools.

But Frank Darby, the St. John's coach, got a call that autumn from a friend involved in New England junior golf who told him he needed to check out this kid from Vermont. Darby was an opportunistic recruiter, so he went up to Fairfield to meet Bradley the next day. The coach liked the kid's pedigree, and Keegan liked the fact that St. John's had developed Andrew Svoboda, a local legend who had nearly won the U.S. Amateur. He didn't even need to see the campus—he committed on the spot.

St. John's was an underdog school—they don't have a home course, and Darby has to maintain connections with many local courses in order to make sure his kids have a place to play. Every day, Keegan and his teammates piled into cars and headed to whichever club would have them. The schedule was unpredictable—sometimes they'd have to start on the third or fourth hole, with a plea from the club pro to behave themselves and avoid the members. On the other hand, some of the courses were excellent, and the players saw a wide variety of tracks— windy oceanside golf, tree-lined courses with narrow fairways, and everything in between.

The wiry Bradley, incredibly long off the tee—even longer than he is today, he claims—benefited from the play-not-practice mentality that Darby fostered. After struggling through his freshman season, his game improved drastically. He would win nine tournaments in total before he graduated in 2008, and the idea of the unheralded kid from Vermont making the Tour started to look realistic.

"He needed to be behind the pack and see what was out in front of him," said Darby, who began to see the career patterns emerging in Bradley even in those early days. "He needs a little adversity, and all the sudden you can see it kicking in, he starts charging. He's relentless. I wouldn't want him on my tail, I'll tell you that right now."

The same story repeats—even on the course, Bradley needs to feel slighted, beaten down, wronged in some way. Then he's like a cornered animal, dangerous and aggressive.

Socially, he had a one-track mind. No drinking, no partying, no nothing—just golf. "They used to call him 'grandpa' half the time because he'd be asleep by seven thirty," Darby remembered.

When I asked Bradley about his college career, it didn't surprise me to learn that his chief memory is a bitter one. "I won a bunch of times, I never finished out of the top ten my senior year, and had one of the lowest stroke averages in the country, but I didn't get an All-American," he said. "It was a shock. I thought I'd get second team or third team, but I didn't even get honorable mention. I was really upset about that. Little things like that have happened my whole career."

Bradley played the Hooters Tour out of college, and though he kept winning money, it wasn't enough to sustain him. With the second stage of Q-School looming in 2009, he was well short of the money needed to enter. He turned to a friend he had met during one of his college summers and explained the situation. The friend came through with six thousand dollars, and Bradley made it through second stage before earning his Nationwide Tour membership with a thirty-fourth place finish in La Quinta at the final stage.

At the start of his rookie season on Tour in 2011, he says, he read articles from writers who argued he wouldn't be any good, or that he'd lose his card, and he took those to heart. In May, already with two top tens in the bag, he forced a playoff with Ryan Palmer at the Byron Nelson and beat him on the first playoff hole. It meant all the usual perks—Masters, two-year exemption, a million dollars.

It would have been a career-defining moment for any PGA Tour rookie. For Bradley, though, who felt disrespected on Tour, the lack of change in player attitudes left him with a sour taste. "I was just kind of under the radar, same thing as my whole career," he said. "And when I won, I thought things would be different, but they were pretty much the same."

The turning point came at the PGA Championship later that season—the first major Bradley ever played.

At the Atlanta Athletic Club, a second-round 64 put him squarely in contention, and after a Saturday 68 and a solid start to Sunday's round, he stood on the 15th tee just two shots off the lead. He didn't realize it, but he was about to embark on one of the strangest finales in major golf history.

The day began poorly—Bradley chipped a ball into the water on 15 and ended up with triple-bogey. Suddenly, he was down five shots—

lights out, or so it seemed. His hard work with sports psychologist Bob Rotella paid off, though, and he grounded himself enough to birdie two of the last three holes. It shouldn't have been enough, but behind him, something remarkable happened—Jason Dufner, with the tournament in his back pocket, made three straight bogeys from 15 to 17, and finished in a tie with the man who would become his good friend.

They headed to a three-hole playoff, where Dufner stuck his approach on the 16th to six feet, then watched Bradley respond with an even better shot to four feet. Only Bradley made his birdie putt—Dufner's putter, bad in normal circumstances, can be hazardous under pressure—and a three-putt bogey for Dufner on 17 stretched the lead to two. The kid from Vermont was now just a hole away from becoming a major champion, and his hand shook violently with adrenaline as he tried to sip from his water bottle.

He composed himself well enough to make par, and somehow emerged victorious by a single stroke—a winner in the first major he'd ever played. At age twenty-five, he seemed to have it all—a major championship, lots of money, and, at last, the respect of his peers. He even got a congratulatory text message from Tom Brady, which made his year.

The good life continued in 2012, when Bradley won the WGC-Bridgestone by chasing down Jim Furyk and Steve Stricker with a Sunday 64, and formed a dynamic team with Phil Mickelson at the Medinah Ryder Cup, going 3-0 in pairs play. Even the sour ending on Sunday, when the Europeans stormed back for a dramatic win, couldn't dim Bradley's bright star.

Still, this is Keegan Bradley we're talking about. He wouldn't be himself if he couldn't fuel his own fire with slights both real and imagined. At the 2012 Northern Trust Open, which he lost in a playoff to Bill Haas, his compulsive spitting gained so much attention that Bradley was forced to quit cold turkey. He almost quit Twitter, too, in response to the number of insults that filled up his feed. In December of that year, after the USGA and the R&A proposed a rule that would ban anchored putters—Bradley's weapon of choice—he heard a spectator on the 18th hole of the World Challenge in California call him a cheater.

"That's unfortunate," he said in his post-round presser. "It's very disrespectful. But it's fine with me. I've got to try and look at it as motivation to help me try to win this tournament."

Heckling is common in golf. In 2013, in Philadelphia, I watched a lone idiot on the 16th hole scream at Justin Rose—"It's wet! Don't chunk it!"—as Rose tried to win a tense U.S. Open. When David Toms won the 2001 PGA Championship, playing with Phil Mickelson in the final round, a girl followed him around the entire day, screeching, "Phil will get you! Phil will get you!" between holes. It got so bad that he asked his caddie to take her out with an umbrella the next time she showed up—and he was barely joking. Jim Furyk's favorite heckle came at the 2010 Ryder in Wales, as he peered through a thick fog on the first tee. "Just follow your nose, Jim!" yelled one of the Brits, mocking Furyk's larger-than-average beak. The fans in the stadium seats erupted in laughter, and Furyk actually applauded the heckler.

It's a rite of passage everybody endures, but nobody catalogs insults quite like Bradley. After the anchored putter ban was announced, a fan on Twitter advised him to send in his application to Burger King for 2016. That was the tip of the iceberg, and the abuse became constant. It bothered Bradley, as it does many players, due to the anonymous nature—you can't fight a faceless bully, and even if you block one, seven more will pop up in its place, like a digital hydra.

He also felt as though the USGA had put an asterisk next to his name, tainting his accomplishments. The organization went so far as to issue a statement denouncing the hecklers, but the fact is that by the nature of their judgment, they had essentially ruled that an anchored stroke gives players an unfair advantage and is against the spirit of the sport. Even if it remained legal until 2016, and *had* been legal when Bradley became the first anchored putter to win a major, the implication was impossible to miss—if he'd had to putt like everyone else, who knows what might have happened?

The proposed rule was eventually passed after a feedback period, and the PGA Tour followed suit shortly after. The long sunset of the anchored-putting era had begun. Once more, Bradley could inflate with righteous resentment.

He was asked after the round if the debate could actually help him because he was running out of chips to put on his shoulder.

"Absolutely," he said. "You hear guys like Michael Jordan talk about how he liked to play on the road. The guy called me a cheater on the last hole—that gets me motivated. I'm never running out of stuff to motivate me because I always feel like I need to get better. I never go into a tournament thinking I'm playing so good that I'm going to win. Every single tournament I've won, I had a borderline meltdown on Wednesday. That's what keeps me going. It's just how I am."

—Doug Ferguson, AP, Dec. 11, 2012

It's no coincidence that Bradley befriended Michael Jordan at the 2012 Ryder Cup; Jordan is well known as someone who remembers every negative encounter he's endured since childhood. And when Bradley needs motivation, he can summon them all: the fans who called him a cheater, the USGA who tarnished his greatest accomplishment, the pros who didn't respect him, the NCAA who snubbed him on the All-American list, the other colleges who didn't recruit him, the rich kids who got to travel the country playing junior golf, the people at his dad's courses who thought he was a joke, and everyone in Vermont who told him he couldn't make it.

It's Keegan Bradley vs. The World, and even though he's smart enough to recognize the good luck he's had and the favors he's received, none of that matters when it's time to win. At that point, he fixates on the snubs. He's Captain Ahab, another famous New Englander, chasing the white whale of universal respect that he'll never catch.

"I still play with a lot of anger," he told me. "I still feel like I've got a lot to prove."

Seven top tens followed in 2013, though it was also the first year that Bradley failed to win a tournament. Now, in 2014, the pressure was on to close the gap in the Ryder Cup standings—he desperately wanted to play in the Gleneagles Cup in September, and though he stood a good chance to earn a captain's pick, he wanted to make the top nine on his own merit. He nearly won in Bay Hill, finishing second to Matt Every, and as April wound to a close he had a chance to take down a young and winless South Korean named Seung-Yul Noh in New Orleans. And he was right where he wanted to be—two strokes behind, ready to attack.

In New Orleans, it all went according to plan for the comeback kid—at least for two holes. Noh came out with a nervous bogey, and Bradley made birdie on the second. The two-shot deficit was erased before the untested Korean had time to get settled.

The wind blew hard on the TPC Louisiana course, gusting up to 30 mph and reminding Noh of the windy coastal conditions from his childhood in Gangwon province. Home was very much on his mind that day—he wore a ribbon on his hat in remembrance of the MV Sewol, a ferry that had capsized earlier that month off the south coast of Korea, killing more than three hundred passengers. He had received another reminder from Korea that morning in the form of a text from his pal Y. E. Yang: If you play your game and lose, it doesn't matter. The only way you can truly lose is if the situation takes you out of your game.

Noh took the advice to heart, and his past experience with close calls on the Tour had taught him well. He needed a quiet mind. On the days when he failed, he had caught himself walking faster, swinging faster, and feeling just plain *different* in all facets of his game. As the holes wore on, and he made par after par, he forced himself to walk at a slower than normal pace, and not worry about how Bradley or any of the other players were performing. The minute he began to take a reactionary approach—*Keegan made birdie, so now I have to make birdie and stay ahead*—he'd be in trouble. The more he could think like he had the first three days, when he played fifty-four bogey-free holes, the more he could play like those days.

The bogey on the first hole didn't rattle him. He limited himself to one swing thought, and let the action on the course play out. When Bradley bogeyed the fifth, he regained the lead, and then, on the long par-4 sixth, Bradley's triple bogey woes struck again—a wayward tee shot landed in the water left of the hole, and after laying up from the drop zone and hitting a poor approach, he three-putted for a disastrous seven. If anyone could recover from triple bogey, it was Bradley, but that kind of magic rarely strikes twice. This time, he managed just two birdies to go along with two more bogeys in the rest of the round. Frustration manifested itself all over his face, and he faded into a tie for eighth.

Noh's real challenge came from the other St. John's alum, Andrew Svoboda. Two birdies on the back nine brought him to -17 for the tournament, close enough to put a scare into the twenty-two-year-old South Korean. After an uneventful front nine, Noh began to liven things up on the way home with an alternating series of birdies and bogeys.

Heading into the 17th hole, Noh stood at -19, two shots clear of Svoboda and everyone else. On the tee at the 215-yard par 3, he knew he had to avoid the water stretching along the left side of the hole, and the result was a weak tee shot that landed far right and shy of the green. From eighty-nine feet away, he pitched to fourteen feet, and faced a par putt that meant the difference between a one- or two-shot lead heading into the final hole. It's the kind of margin that means everything; with a two-shot lead, he couldn't lose, but with just one shot to spare, the pressure could crush him.

The putt looked left all the way, like a simple misread. The ball went so straight for so long that it came as a surprise when it slid right at the very end and barely caught the left edge of the cup. After he watched the ball fall into the hole, Noh gave an uncharacteristic fist pump, knowing what he'd just accomplished. He played it very safe on 18 for par, and won his first PGA Tour event.

As he celebrated his win, Y. E. Yang and Charlie Wi came out of nowhere to spray him with bottled beer—Yang had a 6:30 flight, but he made sure he was on the scene to congratulate his young friend.

Bradley would go another full year without a win, but he'd never stop campaigning for that coveted Ryder Cup captain's pick, and the chance to reclaim his Medinah magic with Phil Mickelson. For all his talk of being the flinty outsider from New England in a world of child stars, he knew how to make the right friends and be in the right place. His Tuesday practice rounds with Mickelson and Fowler put him in high company, and whether he deserved it or not, he knew how to capture Tom Watson's eye.

Seung-Yul Noh could barely capture anyone's eye. The Korean winner fielded questions in the interview room, told the reporters he loved his new caddie, and said that no, he never felt nervous. It ended quickly—as it always does for the Asian players—and the champ left the stage alone.

MAY

The Southern Pass

12

CHARLOTTE, NORTH CAROLINA

Derek the Fluke

"In high school, the music teacher said I should join the march-
ing band because I was getting good at the drums. I said, 'OK,
but I have golf practice.' She said 'Really? How far do you think
you're going to get in golf?' I looked at her and said, 'How far do
you think I'm going to get in the marching band?'"

—DEREK ERNST,
in *Golf Digest*, March 2014

I n second grade, Derek Ernst loved building forts so much that his
mother bought him a child's tool set. It had everything, including a
miniature saw. On Valentine's Day, he decided to make his mother a
gift—a tiny fence, so she could put her stuffed bears inside. He set up
in the driveway on a sunny day and began by cutting through a length
of PVC pipe with the saw. He got halfway through before the implement got stuck, and so he tried to dislodge it by slamming it on the
ground.

The pipe snapped in half, and a rogue piece flew up at his face.
Before he could react, it had sliced his right eyeball down the center.
Ernst ran screaming into the house, and later that night, at one a.m., a

doctor put ten stitches in his eye. The pain lasted for days, and the stitches stayed for six months. They saved the eye, but when the scar healed, it thickened. Today, at twenty-four, Ernst still can't read anything with his right eye. He demonstrated for me when we spoke at the Colonial—"See that sign?" he asked. "I see white blobs. Over there, that's probably a flag, but they're just blobs to me." At dawn and dusk, when the sky darkens, his depth perception suffers—bad business for a professional golfer who plays by feel.

When that kind of bad luck hits you as a kid, maybe good karma starts stacking up, waiting for a day when it can tip the scales back in your favor.

In May 2013, just twenty-two years old and with a skinny frame and a baby face, Derek Ernst was in a car on the way to Athens, Georgia, to play in a Web.com Tour event. He'd earned his PGA Tour card at Q-School the previous December, but his priority number was too low to make it into the Wells Fargo Championship that weekend in Charlotte. So he rented a car in New Orleans on the Monday after the Zurich Classic and started driving north. On the way, he got a phone call from the Tour—enough players had withdrawn, and he was now in the field in Charlotte.

At Quail Hollow, where the Wells Fargo is played, the greens were in horrifying shape. Nobody knew who or what to blame—a new course superintendent, maybe, or bentgrass with low heat tolerance, or poor maintenance due to "top-dressing" the greens with sand. Two of the greens were so bad that they had to be resodded just before the tournament, an extraordinary measure for a Tour stop. The rest looked like they'd come down with some sort of splotchy rash, and the discoloration was not purely cosmetic—rolls were uneven, putts were affected, players complained.

The poor conditions resulted in nine withdrawals in the week leading up to the tournament. The golfers all had their own excuses, but the circumstances went beyond "suspicious." As CBS's Kyle Porter reported, Ian Poulter actually tweeted about the horrid state of the greens, *flew to Charlotte to check them out firsthand,* and then flew back home citing "personal reasons."

When Mark Wilson pulled out, Ernst got the phone call—he was in. It had been a rough rookie year to that point for Ernst. Since finishing in seventeenth place at Q-School, he had missed cuts in five of seven tournaments, and he came in to the Wells Fargo ranked 1,207th in the world.

He had begun working with a mental coach named Susie Meyers, who also worked with Michael Thompson, and many writers would later give her credit for Ernst's opening round 67 in Charlotte. He followed that up with 71 and 72, and heading into Sunday, he trailed Phil Mickelson and Nick Watney by two shots. What happened next, for a player of his stature and ranking, almost defies belief. In wet, rainy conditions, the self-admitted "fidgety player" slogged his way through the damp fairways and damaged greens, playing steady, unflappable golf. By the time he reached the 18th fairway, he stood at -7. In the group behind him, Mickelson still led by a shot, and Ernst figured he'd need at least a birdie to win the tournament.

From 183 yards away, he choked up on a six-iron and struck the shot of his life—a gorgeous approach that landed near the back left pin and stopped less than five feet from the hole. No sooner had he made the birdie putt to reach -8 than news reached him from the group behind—Mickelson had bogeyed 17. When the lefty couldn't sink his birdie putt from the fringe on the last hole, it left just Ernst and David Lynn in a two-man playoff for the championship.

It was the kind of moment that the average golf fan watching on TV would hate—why couldn't Phil have made the playoff? Who are these nobodies?—while for Ernst, there was a possibility that his life would change completely.

He and Lynn went back to 18, where Ernst hit another incredible approach, this time from thirty yards farther back, to set up a birdie putt. Lynn's drive ended up on the banks of a small creek, and he had to stand on a rock in the middle of the water as he took ambitious aim at the green. The ball landed in the bunker, where he blasted out over the green, and couldn't hole the chip coming back.

Ernst's birdie putt lipped out, but it didn't matter—one tap-in later, and the 1,207th-ranked player in the world had completed one of the greatest long-shot stories in PGA Tour history.

For most players, the maiden win launches a career. In Ernst's case, the trajectory was quite different. Almost from the very start, the larger golf world viewed his triumph as a bizarre fluke. At his very next tournament, the Players Championship, the first question he faced in the media room was about whether he felt bad that his win in Charlotte had knocked Scott Langley out of the Jacksonville field. An unfair question, at best, but it was an accurate forecast of what Ernst would face.

The pundits weren't wrong. He finished the 2013 season by missing nine of thirteen cuts, and never finished better than forty-fourth in a single event. The fluke narrative had legs to stand on, and Ernst did nothing to disprove the doubters. Maybe he wanted to be grouped with the emerging young stars of the sport, but he found himself in a race against time.

The PGA Tour gives tournament winners a very generous two-year exemption, and the two-year countdown doesn't actually start until the following season. For Ernst, it meant he could spend all of 2013 floundering, and still have the full 2014 and 2015 seasons to elevate his game and try to break into the top 125. In the aftermath of his victory, it began to look like he'd need every last minute.

He sunk below the radar, and anytime he lifted his head up with a good round, he found himself taking potshots from fans and media. They all believed the fluke of the century would be off the Tour in two years, and in the meantime, they intended to let him know exactly how lucky he'd been.

Meanwhile, his handlers cost him money that Ernst would have preferred not to spend—Ernst told me that the total had exceeded $100,000 in less than a year. Much of that went to Susie Meyers, the mental coach who Ernst mistakenly thought was a traditional swing coach when they first met. They'd worked together for about four hours total before the Wells Fargo, Ernst said, and it cost him $75,000—not to mention the fact that she took a huge share of the credit for his win in Charlotte. He switched agents, switched caddies, switched swing coaches.

All the instruction only made him worse, and by the start of 2014, at the Hyundai Tournament of Champions in Hawaii, he hit rock bottom. The Hyundai is an event exclusively for players who won on Tour the previous season—designed to kick off the year with a showcase of the best and the brightest. Of the thirty players in the 2014 field, twenty-nine of them finished the tournament at even par or better. Derek Ernst finished at +9.

There were extenuating circumstances—Ernst had gained twenty pounds of muscle in the off-season, attempting to bulk up his slender frame, and was still adjusting to his new body. He also had a new caddie he'd met just three days before the tournament began, so the timing wasn't perfect. Nevertheless, he knew the result was embarrassing, and if he didn't, the Internet was about to inform him.

In *Sports Illustrated,* he made the wrong half of Alan Shipnuck's "Heroes & Zeros" column. *Golf Digest*'s Alex Myers pointed out that Ernst's $61,000 payday for finishing dead last was by far the best he'd had since winning in Charlotte, and put his odds of winning a tournament in 2014 at 1,207-to-1—a reference to his world ranking when he won in Charlotte. In the *San Jose Examiner,* Gary McCormick chronicled these criticisms and more in a piece ostensibly supporting Ernst, but which mostly served to highlight his slow decline.

The commentary on Twitter, as usual, was far less polite. "I'm sure Phil doesn't dwell on such things," wrote the *Augusta Chronicle*'s Scott Michaux, "but every now and then he must wonder how Derek Ernst possibly beat him at Quail Hollow." Outside the media, as Ernst prepared to head to Charlotte for the one-year anniversary of his big win, the discourse devolved into scathing insults and cruel taunting.

For Ernst, this was nothing new—he'd been picked on his whole life. Growing up in Clovis, a city just outside Fresno in California's San Joaquin Valley, Ernst was tiny—he stood five foot two and was rail-thin for most of his childhood, only hitting a rapid growth spurt at age seventeen. He played baseball, but classified himself as "a short guy that was never tough enough," and some of his larger teammates would pick on him for his size.

Socially, Ernst was so shy that he wouldn't talk to anyone in high school.

"Literally," he told me, "I wouldn't say *anything*."

When I asked why, he attributed the shyness to a crushing fear of what other people might think of him. Golf was his escape. He mostly stayed local since his parents didn't have enough money to send him around the country or enter him in many AJGA tournaments. While the young jet-setters made their way around the country, Ernst played in thirty-dollar tournaments with players of all ages, most of whom shot in the 80s. And though he lacked the high-level national competition, he learned how to win.

At seventeen, he sent a minor shock through the golf world when he made the knockout rounds at the U.S. Amateur tournament and met Billy Horschel, already a college star at Florida and one of the best amateurs in the country.

"I had no idea who he was," said Ernst, "which was good, because I would've fallen over."

On the first hole, a par 5, Ernst hit a soft 3-iron into the fairway, and watched as Horschel bombed a driver almost one hundred yards past him. Unfazed, Ernst won the hole with a birdie, and went on to win the match 4&3.

His freshman year at UNLV began with great difficulty. Ernst had been a Christian since his early days, but when he arrived at college, still very much an introvert, another student in his freshman dorm began bullying him about his Christianity. They were nominally "friends," but the other student would bash him so regularly about his faith that it created intense feelings of stress. He spent all his free time at the golf course just to get away from the abuse, but the minute he returned to his dorm, it would start over again. It made an already difficult journey even harder, and he wanted to leave Las Vegas.

"I still know him today," Ernst said of his tormentor. "He does nothing but smoke weed and climb rocks."

"Sounds like a bad combination," I offered.

"Yeah, right?" he said. "That doesn't seem safe."

Ernst gradually came out of his shell, and his golf game blossomed—he made All-American four straight years, and finished as Mountain West Player of the Year twice. When he graduated, he turned pro and won four thousand dollars at a Pepsi Tour event, and then it was off to the last Q-School in PGA Tour history. Six days later, he had qualified for the PGA Tour.

"What do Craig Stadler and Derek Ernst have in common? Both playing in their last Masters."
                                    —Twitter volley, launched at Ernst in April 2014

When I told fellow journalists that I wanted to speak with Derek Ernst, the two most common reactions were laughter and confusion. Ernst, too, was wary of me. His new agent helped me arrange time to talk, but Ernst couldn't understand why anyone would want an interview unless they were writing a sad story about a kid who got too much, too soon.

I didn't see him that way. To me, he represented the underbelly of the Tour—a perfect example of golf's fickle nature, where you can be plucked from obscurity in a moment of glory, and then spend years fighting like hell not to lose your dream. I saw Ernst not as a subject of pity, but someone in the midst of a desperate war that would reach its conclusion in 2015, his last chance on Tour. Until then, the preparations for that moment fascinated me—a statistical outlier trying to capitalize on his good fortune.

When we finally met up, he was open about how the negativity had hurt his feelings. You can read the sensitivity on his face, and if you didn't know any better, you might guess he was too soft for the competitive life. When people are mean to him, as they have been his whole life, it hits him right in the gut because he actually *can't conceive* of why it's happening, and he reacts with childlike astonishment. While most of us grow tough hides when we encounter cruelty, and maybe even become a little mean ourselves, the whole process seems to take longer for Ernst.

"It's kind of like, wait, what did I do?" he told me. "It *hurts,* you know?"

His confidence had taken more than a few hits, and he didn't expect much in the way of credit or fan support. It had gotten to the point that when somebody was nice to him, it came as a shock. At the Byron Nelson a week before our chat, I watched his caddie walk up and tell him that a couple of girls standing nearby wanted his autograph. Ernst couldn't hide his surprise: "They *do?*"

As the defending champion in Charlotte, he had to face the media room on Wednesday, which was a hot seat he'd mostly been able to avoid during his rough stretch—perhaps the only silver lining of playing bad golf. He knew the hard questions were coming, but the rapid-fire process still came as a shock. They felt more like insults, flying in one after another, targeting his failure.

Q. Derek, if you could expand, how difficult has it been? The Cinderella story, you win the monster tournament, then struggles. How difficult was it for you in the last year?

Q. Do you still remain as confident now as you were a year ago?

Q. Derek, why the need to make a change? All the changes?

Q. Rocco Mediate once said when you win you shouldn't change anything except perhaps underwear. Do you regret any of the changes?

Q. Derek, with all the changes that you made, and not talking about regrets, but the results not coming as quickly, how have you fought off the frustrations of that?

Q. Had you decided to make these changes before you won? Is that something you knew you were going to do all along?

Q. Derek, what would you say to the people who say because of the greens the way they were last year that you were a fluky winner?

It wasn't much better with the fans. Around the course, they recognized his face from the year before, but kept calling him "David Ernst." He patiently reminded them that his name was Derek, and he tried to stay optimistic. This week, at least, it worked—he went out and shot a Friday 68 to make the cut and eventually finish in thirtieth place. It was his best result since the Cinderella weekend a year earlier.

But the feel-good ending, if it happens at all, was still months and perhaps years away. He followed up the strong showing in Charlotte with six more missed cuts, and stumbled into July still preparing for a battle that had begun to look hopeless.

13

PONTE VEDRA, FLORIDA

Fifth Major or First Minor?; Jordan, Martin, and the Third Wave

The Players Championship is the most prestigious tournament run by the PGA Tour, and is colloquially known as the "fifth major," though it enjoys no official status with the real majors. This fact has always struck me as cruelly ironic—the PGA Tour bears more responsibility for the health of professional golf in America than any other organization, and they run more than forty events each year with the kind of efficiency that every other organization aspires to. Yet due to the vagaries of history, the four most important tournaments each year are run by outside bodies— the USGA for the U.S. Open, the PGA of America for the PGA Championship, the R&A for the British Open, and Augusta National for the Masters. The PGA Tour deserves a major, but the Players Championship is as near as they come—close, but no cigar.

Held at TPC Sawgrass in Ponte Vedra, Florida, the Players also occupies a strange headspace for golfers. In the days leading up to the event, and during the event itself, there's absolutely no questioning the event's magnitude. Forget the official stance—to these guys, it's a major, and they're willing to say so. The tournament boasts one of the year's strongest fields—by the world rankings, even *stronger* than the other majors, since there are no amateurs here—and TPC Sawgrass is home to the most famous hole in American golf. The par-3 17th, with its iconic island green, has served as perhaps the most anxiety-provoking tee shot in the sport for forty years, leading to triumph and tragedy in equal measure.

The most famous success came in 2001, when Tiger Woods's tee shot on Saturday barely remained on the fringe, leaving him a treacherous sixty-foot downhill putt. As it began its journey to the hole, NBC's Johnny Miller asked Gary Koch how he'd done. "Better than most," Koch replied. The ball began breaking right, and when it dropped in the hole, Koch seemed to jump out of his shoes. "Better than most!" he cried again. Tiger went on to beat Vijay Singh by a single stroke, and Koch's call has become iconic.

On the flip side, it's hard to forget Sergio Garcia's 2013 meltdown. On Sunday, tied with Tiger Woods after a tense weekend, which saw Sergio accuse his rival of trying to distract him on Saturday by pulling a wood out of his bag when Sergio was about to hit his ball, Sergio needed a good tee shot on 17 to keep pace. Instead, he dumped two straight wedges into the water, made a quadruple bogey 7, and watched as the man he couldn't beat took home yet another title.

It's an interesting exercise to imagine the Players Championship as a major. How many careers would be changed? Sergio, for one, would have removed himself from the top of the "best to never win" list with his playoff victory over Paul Goydos in 2008. Greg Norman's '94 win, with a record score of -24, might mitigate his history of choking in critical moments. Henrik Stenson and Matt Kuchar would have the enormous major monkey off their backs, and we'd look at players like Tim Clark ('10), Stephen Ames ('06), and Fred Funk ('05) in a completely different light. Four golfers—Fred Couples, Steve Elkington, Davis Love III, and Hal Sutton—would increase their major totals from one to three, taking a significant step toward legendary status. Craig Perks ('02) would join the ranks of the flukiest major champions in golf history. And Tiger Woods himself would be two wins closer to Jack Nicklaus's career record, except for one problem—Nicklaus's total would grow to twenty-one majors after *his* three wins, including the first ever Players Championship in 1974.

But this is revisionist history—it may be the fifth major in the players' minds while they're *at* Sawgrass, and the tournament itself may be endowed with the same tension and meaning—but the minute it ends, so does the fantasy.

Looking backward, reality asserts itself. This is not a major. Regardless of what transpired on the course, among the best golfers in the world, nobody thinks of Henrik Stenson or Sergio Garcia as major champions. None of the Sawgrass winners receive the same accolades as the heroes who win the real ones. All they have in common—the lonely sliver of equality—is the goddamn suffering.

On Thursday, Russell Henley finished two shots off the lead after a near-flawless 65, and a stacked group that included Justin Rose, Jordan Spieth, Lee Westwood, and Sergio Garcia loomed at -5, four shots off the lead. On Friday, only Spieth kept pace, shooting a 66 to move to -11, just one shot behind the leader. It's foolish to call a tournament a two-horse race after 54 holes, much less 36, but that's how it felt on Friday night. Spieth would be the crowd favorite, and he'd be facing a man who had once been the best golfer in the world.

"You can play golf with a fade—you don't need to be able to hit the draw. You can win once in a while, of course you can. But standing here on the second tee and you can't draw the ball? Or on 16? You know, when you're that young, I was 25, 26 years old, how can you accept that you can't hit that shot?"

—KAYMER

Q. Back to the swing changes for a second.
MARTIN KAYMER: Please, no. I'm done. I'm done with it.

If there ever comes a point in your life when you have the urge and the opportunity to irritate Martin Kaymer, ask him this question: Why, after winning the 2010 PGA Championship and reaching number 1 in the world early the next year, did you decide to retool your entire swing? Why change, Martin, when you were the best golfer on the *entire planet*?

It's a question he's faced for three years, over which time he's come to hate it deeply, and the answer isn't always satisfying. On a practical level, he wanted to make a few subtle changes—a shallower backswing, for one—that would allow him a bit more length, and help him hit a right-to-left draw to go along with his natural fade. The draw is particularly helpful at Augusta, and it's no accident that Kaymer began to make serious changes after his fourth straight missed cut at the Masters in 2011. Still, the nagging fact remained—he was already the best player in the world.

The real answer gets to the heart of what makes Martin Kaymer one of the game's most fascinating golfers: When he stood on a tee and realized he couldn't hit a draw, it violated his sense of what a golfer should be. There is an ideal vision of a "complete player" in Kaymer's mind, and it goes beyond winning and losing. It delves into the heart of talent and self-belief. He craved the ability to hit any shot, in any situation; he needed the absolute confidence that he could execute. Without it? Yes, he could win tournaments. Yes, he could ascend to the peak of world golf. But the victories would be shallow.

"To be honest with you," he told the media at the PGA Championship in 2013, "when I became number one, it was a surprise. I was not playing like the best player on the planet. I didn't feel like the best player. And therefore, I needed to change things."

You could almost argue that he's an aesthete—he wants to play the beautiful game, results be damned.

Which is a surprise when you consider Kaymer as a physical specimen. He's a square-jawed German, and with his easy grin and athletic posture, he looks like the sort of man who breezes through his days and months and years on a cloud of self-assurance while the rest of us toil on earth. What you *don't* expect is an artist who behaves with the perfectionism of a half-mad painter who has worked on the same canvas for an entire lifetime.

In art, there is no objective way to measure superiority, but even so, we have an instinct about which artists are masters of their craft. Kaymer was like a young, creative wunderkind who received every possible award, but knew in his heart that none of it mattered—his art was asking more of him, and he had yet to achieve his potential. Fulfilling that idealistic vision meant everything, and the trappings of early success—world rankings, trophies, accolades—meant far less. If he had to give up these decorations, so be it. He would be true to himself.

"We are out here to have fun and play good golf and show the people that we do our job with passion and love," he said in early 2011, just days before he rose to number 1 in the world. "It's not about winning or losing."

There are not many golfers who would use the word "love" to describe the way they play, and I came to realize that the German is one of the few who truly believes he can transcend his results.

Kaymer struck me as intelligent from the beginning, but uniquely so for a professional athlete. His words demonstrate a deep understanding of human behavior, and a sharp insight into the subtle ways the mind works. He's the kind of person who simultaneously wishes his lifelong coach Günter Kessler got more attention, for instance, but loves him for the fact that he doesn't want it. You can always count on him for a terrific quote, and where others resort to clichés, Kaymer is expansive and creative. Even the simple questions generally yield thoughtful responses.

"I don't really believe in taking momentum into the next day," he said after his opening round 65 at the Players Championship, answering one of the most commonly asked questions on Tour. "Because you sleep, you wake up with a different body feel, everything is a little bit different. I think the most important thing is that you lower your expectations. Everybody else thinks you keep going like this, and subconsciously you think you *should*, but I, fortunately, I shot a few of those rounds in the past . . . I know that the next day is very difficult."

This is another Kaymer trademark—learning from every situation, whether it involves him or not. One of his favorite hobbies is watching professional sports, but even on this front, Kaymer takes a unique angle, monitoring the other players for "behavior, attitude, momentum swings" in order to find something he can use in his own competitive life.

The world interests him, and everything he encounters represents a learning opportunity, or at least psychological material for perfecting his game. In golf, he's as close as anybody comes to the Greek ideal of athlete-as-philosopher.

Kaymer was born in Düsseldorf, an international financial hub on the Rhine River near Germany's western border with the Netherlands. His father, Horst, was an accountant, and his mother, Rina, stayed at home to raise Martin and his older brother, Philip. Horst was a tough man; the kind of father who would force his sons to fight their way through difficulty rather than helping them out. The warmth at home came from Rina, who did her best to offset Horst's stern attitude.

"To simplify things and try to keep it a bit shorter," he wrote to me in an email, "I would say that our father was the tough one and our mother was the softer one. Perfect combination if you ask me."

Like many Germans, Martin grew up loving soccer. As a child, he and his friends spent most of their free time in the fields outside Düsseldorf, and Martin dreamed of playing professionally well into his mid-teens.

When his father brought him and Philip to the golf course, it was not love at first sight. He mostly played with Philip, and between the brothers, every round was competitive. The matches never devolved into fights or other ugliness, but they shared a fascination with winning, and found that they could make a competition out of anything.

He [Horst] and his wife, Rina, extracted a promise from the boys that they would not compete against each other in tournament play, but as teens Martin and Philip secretly entered a club championship on opposite sides of the match-play bracket. . . . The match was all square arriving on the 18th hole, a tough par-4. Martin reached the green in regulation, while Philip missed it and had to

chip up, giving his baby brother a putt for the victory. Martin pro-
ceeded to four-whack, handing the title to Philip. "It is a favorite
story in our family," says Philip. "It is useful when we are, as you
say in America, talking s——."

—ALAN SHIPNUCK, *Sports Illustrated*, 2010

When explaining his success today, Kaymer often cites the "German character," attributing his patience and perfectionism to a national
attitude. But as a child, he told me he could be "crazy and uncon-
trolled." That wildness faded as he grew up, and slowly he started believing he could play golf professionally. He won the Club Mettmann
Championship at age fourteen, and attended a sports academy for high
school. At fifteen, he hung up his soccer boots for good—training for
both sports was burning him out—and began to dominate the amateur golf scene. In 2003, his last year as an amateur, he won the German Masters double—the country's match play and stroke play
championships.

That year, at just twenty years old, he turned pro, and less than five
years later he had worked his way onto the European Tour and won his
first event at the Abu Dhabi Golf Championship. Four more wins in
the next two years set him up as one of Europe's brightest young stars,
but the most emotional win by far came in his home country.

His mother had been diagnosed with cancer in 2006, just before
Martin played his first Challenge Tour event at the Vodafone. Philip
had convinced him not to abandon the tournament, and took up the
bag for his younger brother as Martin won the event that launched his
career. Now, two years later, Rina was losing her fight. Playing at home
once again in the BMW International Open, Martin took a six-shot
lead into Sunday, but lost it all by the 11th hole and found himself
trailing by a shot. He fought back, and defeated Anders Hansen on the
first hole of a playoff with a seven-foot birdie putt.

He dedicated the bittersweet victory to Rina, and his family headed
home to Düsseldorf. Not long after, Kaymer lost his mom.

· · ·

In 2009, he bought a second home in Arizona, broke his foot in a go-karting accident, and came back in January 2010 to win his second Abu Dhabi Championship. That August, at Whistling Straits in Wisconsin, he entered the final round of the PGA Championship four shots behind Nick Watney at -9.

Watney faded badly, shooting 81, and he left the tournament wide open. Bubba Watson put together one of the day's best rounds, reaching -11 for the tournament, and Kaymer faced a fifteen-foot par putt on the 18th hole to finish with the same score. He holed it, and after Dustin Johnson's error on the 18th hole, Kaymer and Watson were the last men standing.

Bubba would have won in a traditional one-hole playoff after he bombed his drive just short of the green on the par-4 10th and made birdie, but the PGA Championship uses a three-hole playoff system. Kaymer struck back on 17, sinking another fifteen-footer to level the score.

On the third and final hole, the par-5 18th, Bubba went into full "Bubba Golf" mode and tried to hit his second shot 206 yards to the green from a bad lie in the right rough. He struck a nice pose after swinging his 6-iron, but the ball landed in a creek. The mistake allowed Kaymer to lay up from his own bad lie, after which he hit what he told me was "one of the purest strikes of his career" into the green. He two-putted from fifteen feet for bogey, and became only the second German after Bernhard Langer—one of his childhood heroes—to win a major championship.

Kaymer was fully in the zone, and the following February, the twenty-six-year-old became the number 1 golfer in the world.

His reign lasted eight weeks. Along with the swing changes he implemented after another missed cut at Augusta, Kaymer also struggled to cope with the fame and attention of becoming the public face of golf in Germany. He rarely opens up about the specific difficulties of this time, aside from the heightened fan and media scrutiny, but old interviews provide a few faint clues. After a two-day tournament in Germany, for instance, fans stalked him to his father's house and were still waiting there the next morning.

"I got more attention, became a little bit more popular," he told reporters that December. "No one from my, let's say, the people I work with, was used to [having] a player who is number one in the world. So it was a matter of getting used to a lot of things, and for me, only twenty-six years old, all of a sudden being in the spotlight wherever I go in America, in Germany, it takes some time to get used to the situation and that role that you have."

The pressure, the expectations from himself and others, and the startling lack of privacy knocked Kaymer back just as he recalibrated his swing. He did manage one big moment during this period; despite sitting out all but one pairs session at the 2012 Ryder Cup due to his struggles, he hit the putt to beat Steve Stricker on Sunday that capped off Europe's miracle comeback and allowed them to retain the Cup. Even as his game suffered, he understood the magnitude of that moment—any other result might have crushed him.

"I think a lot of people don't realize that it can change a career," he said. "You think about it in the negative way and think about if I would have missed the putt, it could break an athlete."

When he began to adjust his game after the 2011 Masters, he thought it would take six months before he won again. Three years later, he was still waiting, and had reached a low of number 63 in the world. He agonized over whether he'd made the right decisions, and whether the media were right when they called him a flash in the pan. The journey had soured.

Slowly, though, his long game began to take shape in 2014, and when it did, he devoted more energy to the short game that had abandoned him. Top-twenty-five finishes at Hilton Head and Wells Fargo were the first signs that something was changing. At some point after Augusta, Kaymer finally felt confident enough to stop leaning on his caddie like a crutch, and stop overthinking every shot. At last, he could trust his instinct and stop playing like a "weiches ei"—German for "soft egg," a wimp.

"I can say confidently that I can hit any shot," he said at the Players

Championship. "It's just a matter of if you can handle the pressure, if you can hit the right shot at the right time when you need to. That's the tough part . . . even if you screw up once in a while, that's okay, everybody does that once in a while. But at least you play brave."

In the first round at Sawgrass, he stood on the second tee needing to hit a draw with the wind off the left. Here was the complete artist, forced to work with his least favorite brush. He reminded himself of that idea. Be brave. Trust your ability to hit every shot in the arsenal. This is what three years of work had been building toward, and if he didn't attempt it, what was it all for?

He pulled off the draw, gave himself an eagle opportunity, and made birdie. He shot 29 on the front nine and finished with a 63, tying the course record. The German was back.

Kaymer and Spieth were paired on Saturday, and passed the front nine in style, consolidating their lead. Spieth had yet to make a bogey in forty-five holes, but when he missed a short birdie putt on 10, it didn't stop a fan from yelling "geez!" like his own son had just let him down. Such are the pressures of life as the great white hope.

As the two players walked down the 11th fairway, Kaymer put his arm around Spieth and advised him not to worry—this, he said, indicating the course, the lead, and everything else, is just where he wanted to be. Spieth appreciated the gesture, and marveled at how Kaymer never seemed to react to a bad break. When rotten luck hit, he just smiled and kept moving on. Spieth knew that was a weakness of his, but whether he could learn from the example was another matter.

They moved on, past the cabbage palmettos and the magnolias, the clumps of crown and cordgrass lining the fairways, the sandy mounds topped by pampas grass, and the ubiquitous pines and live oaks. I heard two fans coin a nickname for Spieth—"Heir Jordan"—even as he began to lose control of his driver. He flew it right on 14, but recovered with an incredible hybrid to the green. He managed to save par again on 15 after blasting his drive left.

I caught a glimpse of Spieth's grandfather following the group on a motorized wheelchair as the golfers survived the island green with two more pars. On 18, with Kaymer up a stroke, it looked like Spieth's bogey-free streak would end when he left himself a lengthy par putt from the fringe. Instead, he buried it, and it was Kaymer who blinked, missing his short par putt to sink to -12, in a dead heat with Spieth. A cheer rose up from the adamantly pro-Spieth gallery, but Kaymer wasn't offended. He just tapped in his bogey, smiled, and waved—and again, Spieth was amazed at his equanimity.

The situation after the round must have struck Kaymer as a bit odd. The man who had been overwhelmed by attention when he rose to number one now sat before a very small cluster of reporters in the interview room. Meanwhile, outside in the gathering dark, even Spieth's *caddie* commanded more attention. You could hear the girls behind the ropes scream Jordan's name—his youth, and his showing at the Masters, had elevated him close to the Beatles-esque status enjoyed by Rickie Fowler and Rory McIlroy.

Their cries, and the cheers for Kaymer's miss on 18, signaled to the German that he would face a Ryder Cup–type atmosphere on Sunday. The diverted attention came with a silver lining—he could go about his business while the crowds and journalists flocked to Spieth. He'd need to be brave and to trust his game; he also knew that a bit of luck wouldn't hurt. In order to close the book on three years of struggle, Kaymer would take every advantage he could get.

As for Spieth, Sunday presented a chance to redeem his final round at the Masters. A few very important questions loomed. What had he learned from Augusta? Could he control his drives under pressure? Was Jordan Spieth a legitimate winner, or was he just another talented young kid years away from rounding into form? Was he the next big thing, a Tiger in the making, or the living embodiment of a hopeful idea that couldn't stand up to the cold truths of competitive reality?

The next afternoon, both players would try to put a capstone on an era of their professional lives. One would succeed, and the other would continue to languish in uncertainty.

"Well, I think golf, you know, you should play for the right reason. You should not play golf to make dollars. And, for me, the nicest thing is just to get up in the morning—for example here, to get up in the morning 6:30, 7:00, get on the range and see the sunrise, that is the best moment. Those things, I think, that is life quality. And for me it doesn't really get better."

—KAYMER

Sunday was Mother's Day, but Kaymer didn't need the holiday to remember Rina. He thinks of her each time he sees the sunflower on his golf bag. It was her favorite flower, and it opens to the sky in her memory.

Spieth came out at 12:20, giving himself an hour longer to warm up than he'd allotted at the Masters. He wore a salmon pink shirt and gray pants, and started out on the putting green, using three balls.

"He's incredible," a woman watching remarked to her friend. "So many *adults* I know don't have that composure."

In other words: Here we go again.

An overcast sky brought a faint humidity that thickened as the day went along, choking the air as the Spanish moss choked the branches of the oaks. Martin Kaymer and Sergio Garcia emerged from the clubhouse together, with the German dressed in pink and blue. He set up behind Spieth on the range—he could see the young American, but all Spieth could feel were the eyes on his back.

Kaymer wore a tennis ball on a lanyard around his neck to help him keep his forearms together—"a smart way of being lazy," he called it, since the lanyard kept him from having to chase the ball if it came loose. Sergio hit the range picker by accident, delighting the fans.

As the players approached the first tee, Spieth pounded fists with the fans along the ropes. Kaymer looked bigger and more athletic, with his usual sheen of sweat or sunblock covering his face and forearms. The two shook hands and had a very short talk—Kaymer was no Bubba Watson, and he wouldn't be keeping up a stream of nervous chatter throughout the day. From the stadium seats at the first tee, the fans roared for Spieth, and clapped politely for Kaymer.

Spieth lost his drive to the right off the first tee, but had a clear shot to the green on his approach, and saved par. Kaymer gave himself a good early birdie look, and took par after missing the nine-footer. On two, the long par-5, Kaymer couldn't pull off the draw and left his drive right. He dried his palms on Craig Connelly's towel, and Spieth dipped his head into his shoulders, first one side and then the other, wiping off his own sweat.

Both made birdies on two, and followed with pars on the par-3 third. The fourth hole saw the day's first separation, when Spieth hit an approach to seven feet on the short par 4, and knocked in the birdie for a one-shot lead. On the next hole, his drive found the left rough, and he decided after much discussion that the lie was too thick to go for the hole, which was guarded in front by a series of difficult bunkers. He laid up, but his approach from 108 yards was mediocre, leaving him twenty-seven feet for par. The putt came up a foot short, and Spieth gave a dirty look at a fan who yelled, "Pick it up!" He fell back into a tie, and snapped his bogey-free streak at fifty-eight holes for the tournament.

On the sixth, Kaymer made his first real error of the day, hitting a weak uphill putt from thirty-eight feet that stopped ten feet shy of the hole. Spieth had just a foot longer for birdie, and it looked like a two-shot swing could be in the offing. Instead, Spieth missed, Kaymer holed a huge par putt, and the two remained deadlocked at -13.

Elsewhere on the course, Jim Furyk was making some final round noise with four birdies on the front nine, but at -10, he was still three shots off the lead. Sergio was one closer as he neared the turn, and Rory McIlroy and Jimmy Walker were unleashing back nine runs that would prove to be spectacular, but not quite good enough to erase the gap. For the moment, Spieth and Kaymer were the only show in town.

On the 8th, a tough 237-yard par 3, Kaymer looked almost anguished as he watched his ball land, but it fell safely on the green, twenty-seven feet away. Spieth wasn't so lucky. His tee shot came up well short, landing in the left rough thirty yards in front of the hole.

"I can't get up and down from there!" he moaned. "It's the worst place to be." As he stowed his club, he continued to complain about his shot. "Anywhere right is fine . . . not *there!*"

He managed a good flop shot that got him within eleven feet, but he couldn't hole the putt. When Kaymer two-putted, the German held his first lead of the day. The lost stroke wasn't a killer for Spieth, but for those who knew his on-course style, the sudden attitude change was an urgent cause for concern. Just like at the Masters, he gave in to the woe-is-me lamentations that rocked his focus—as if fate was against him, and all he could do was curse the cruel universe.

The last hole on the front nine is a 583-yard par 5, and Kaymer led off by bombing a 322-yard drive that stopped just shy of the creek bisecting the hole. Spieth hit a nice drive of his own, and since the wind was helping, he took out a hybrid and went for the front of the green 260 yards away. He hit the ball slightly on the heel, and just missed his landing spot. He wound up in the right rough, while Kaymer put his second shot into the greenside bunker. The German's shot from the sand was perfect, stopping seventeen inches from the hole for an easy tap-in birdie. Spieth pitched out to the front of the green and took a decent line, but the ball tumbled off at the last moment. He wrenched his club angrily, and had to settle for par and a two-shot deficit.

The Augusta parallels continued—Spieth's hot start had carried him to an early lead, and he lost it before he had even made the turn. Now he had a chance to show courage and resilience, and to respond to his bad luck with a bit of Kaymer's combination of stoic resolve and aggression.

The rain began to threaten on the tenth, and when Kaymer hit his tee shot right, a few fans began to heckle, albeit lightly. His muscular forearms glowed with perspiration as he hacked out of the rough and onto the green. Any chance for a reversal was lost when Spieth's approach sailed left of the hole. The young Texan sent the ball across the green on the way back, and took yet another bogey. Thunder sounded in the distance as Kaymer grabbed a three-shot lead, and Spieth's hopes began to fade. On number 11, he looked about as overcast as the sky, and I thought for a second that he might throw a club.

At that moment, it was clear that the tournament was over—at least for him. In less than two hours, he had shown yet again that he wasn't ready for the big moment. I wondered whether it might be good for him to go ahead and hurl that club. He tried so mightily to curb his anger—to act like the upright savior golf so badly wanted—but was it natural? Did it make sense, to curb those youthful impulses? Was it healthy, or even instructive? Instead of the tepid whining that led him to slow, agonizing defeat, maybe he should break a club over his leg and come back angry, ready to tear down the course or die trying. Instead, he let himself fade, moment by moment, watching the victory dissolve.

Kaymer birdied 11 to take a four-shot lead, and though Spieth held on by his fingertips to make par on 11, 12, and 13, the story had already been written—the rest of the round would be an act of suffering. Sensing his resignation, one fan began chanting "Europe!" at Kaymer—a noise Spieth would hear again that year. The German marched off instantly after each shot Spieth made, keeping him behind all the away, maintaining honors on every tee. The crickets started to chirp, the thunder grew louder, and Spieth grew darker.

"You gotta give me a bounce! One bounce!" he cried on 14, after hitting his drive into the right rough. He turned his head to the woods, away from the gallery, and screamed silently at the trees. On the green, he read the birdie putt obsessively, lined it up, and prepared to strike. At the last moment, the weather horn went off. Spieth's whole body sagged, and he fell to his knees in frustration. When he came back to the putt later, he three-putted, and another bogey on 15 buried him for good.

When the weather horn sounded, Kaymer had the tournament wrapped up and ready to carry home. At -15, he had left the field in his dust, and when he returned to the course, he was playing not against Spieth, but against the ghost of Jim Furyk, who had finished with a blazing 66 to steam ahead into second place at -12.

Kaymer made his par on 14, and simply needed to play par golf the rest of the way to win comfortably. His form had been brilliant up until the weather struck, but as the downpour began, complete with thunder and lightning, it not only interrupted his flow, but threatened to delay the finish until Monday. After ninety minutes, the Tour sent him back out in a race against darkness, and on the 15th hole, after hitting his approach to the left rough just twenty-five yards from the hole, Kaymer made what could have been the mistake of his life.

Instead of playing it safe and making sure the shot landed on the green, he attempted to hit a perfect flop over a bunker and at the pin. It came up short, landing with a soft splash in the sand. It was the worst place to be, and when he failed to get up and down, he'd taken a double bogey, and suddenly his three-shot cushion had been reduced to one. The phantom figure of Furyk loomed closer.

The gulls circled on the 16th green near the water, and Kaymer hit his second shot on the par 5 to the left side of the hole. An up-and-down would mean birdie and a crucial two-shot cushion, but facing a downhill chip—not his favorite shot—he decided to putt from off the green. He later called this a "soft egg" moment. He lost his bravery, and paid for it with a putt that came nowhere near the hole. He left himself thirty-seven feet, and could only two-putt for par.

On the tee at 17, retaining his one-shot lead, he stared out at the island green. So many tournaments had been made and ruined here, and now he'd have to survive the same test. It was, without a doubt, the most important shot he'd faced in three years, and he was between clubs. He couldn't decide between pitching wedge and gap wedge, but he knew how his adrenaline would be flowing, and he figured it was smart to take the shorter of the two. He grabbed the gap wedge. The pin was in its traditional Sunday location, to the front right, and Kaymer aimed his shot safely at the center, over the small front bunker. Par would be plenty.

The shot rose up into the gray sky and came down dangerously short. Kaymer watched in something like shock as the ball hit the left side of the green and began rolling down the ridge. The noise of the crowd grew—some were begging for it to stay, but many more watched with the kind of fascination that precedes a car crash. They would have loved to see it roll forever, all the way into the water, and Furyk wouldn't have minded either. The ball gathered momentum, trickled on, and then began slowing as it got closer to the ledge.

At the last possible moment, it stopped, held up by the fringe. A combination of gasp and groan rose up from the crowd that remained.

But Kaymer's adventure was far from over. He had to stand in the Bermuda grass close to the water, giving himself an awkward chip shot—there was no avoiding it now. He aimed for the top of the ridge, hoping to let it run down to the right and close to the hole, but to his frustration, the ball stopped at the very top. Now, just one shot clear of Furyk, he had left himself twenty-nine feet for par. The daylight was holding on by a thread, and this made it harder for Kaymer to read the putt. He told himself that even if he missed, it would be okay. He could go to 18, hope for a birdie, and at the very least make par and get into a playoff. "Obviously," he said after, "you cannot expect yourself to make that putt."

He analyzed it as best he could—downgrain, downhill, maybe three feet of break. Three and a half, at a stretch. He picked his line, hoped for a bit of luck, and brought the club back. A light rain fell, making soft splashes in the water behind him as the ball rolled to the hole. The speed was perfect, and the closer it got, you could see that the line was, too. Across the lake, the hum grew—was the man who had holed the fifteen-footers at Whistling Straits, and the Ryder Cup clincher, about to do it again?

He was. The gallery exploded when the ball tumbled into the cup. Kaymer pumped his fist twice—his face flushed and his eyes shone. The German had another iconic putt for his résumé.

On 18, the last slanting rays of sun peeked through the clouds above the clubhouse, and even those had vanished by the time Kaymer reached the green. The only real light came from the giant score-board. Even in the near-dark, the hole was a formality—fairway off the tee, hybrid approach coming to rest just shy of the green, a two-putt from forty-two feet—and Kaymer's long journey had entered a new phase.

·   ·   ·

After his 74, Spieth played the mature young man for the media yet again. "It's just tough right now," he said, in the darkness by the clubhouse. "You guys catch me five minutes after the round, and it just really stings. . . . I hope I look back at today and laugh at these moments."

When I spoke to him at Congressional, though, he called that Sunday the hardest moment of his career. "I felt like I learned from Augusta, and I hit the right shots," he said, "and I just got really, really, really bad bounces. I mean, I landed a couple balls right next to the hole, and they were supposed to stop there, and they found their way into spots where I couldn't even make par."

Those words came a month later—a month after he had admired how Kaymer adapted to his own bad luck—and it was hard not to notice his lack of self-awareness. The smart golfers know that if you believe the world is against you, it will be, but the lesson hadn't sunk in for Spieth.

A harder one was still to come—in the rest of 2014, he'd muster just two more top tens. Opportunities can dry up in a heartbeat, and Spieth would have to wait until September, at the Ryder Cup, for his third and final moment on the biggest stage.

The Bubba Wave had hit its apex in Augusta, and washed up in the month that followed. Golf was looking for someone to fill the void, and it happened at Sawgrass. The lost years had passed, and the Kaymer Wave of 2014 had begun.

After the trophy ceremony, and the media gauntlet, and the autograph hounds, Kaymer got a text from Paul McGinley. Would Martin care for a drink? the Ryder Cup captain wondered.

He would. They met at a nearby bar and settled in, letting the conversation wander where it wanted. McGinley knew how lonely it could be to win a golf tournament—how empty it feels when you return to your room and there's nobody there. His company was just what the German needed to wind down.

14

FORT WORTH, TEXAS

Tiger Relinquishes Number 1; Adam Scott, the Aussie King of Texas

"When people think you've got potential, they can be fairly harsh. When you're busting your ass and not getting anything out of it, you do get tired of hearing it."
                                   —ADAM SCOTT, in *Golf Digest,* 2011

On we marched, westward to Dallas, Texas, where Brendon Todd won the Byron Nelson, and then to the other side of the great urban sprawl, to Fort Worth. A simple trip, except for the fact that Dallas rivals Boston for sheer difficulty of driving. For anyone stupid enough to brave the highways, like me, there's peril and death in every direction. Roads merge without warning, lanes disappear, and the minute you start to sense order amidst the chaos, the city drops a random cloverleaf or sudden exit in an apparent attempt to divert all newcomers to Oklahoma or Mexico or back into the Louisiana swamps.

Colonial Country Club, though, is a sanctuary. It's the home of Ben Hogan—a sort of Lone Star spiritual oasis for the sport, sheltered from the madness of the home city in a way that reminded me of Augusta, minus the sinister history and the weird lingering paranoia.

To survive this course, you have to survive the trees. And the trees are everywhere, lining the narrow fairways, their drooping branches obstructing the approach to greens that are practically surrounded by moats of white sand. Burr oaks and red river oaks and cedar elms and cottonwoods and warty hackberries are the culprits, but no tree is as ubiquitous as the pecan, which doubles as the Texas state tree. These beasts are old—so old that Dan Jenkins called them old forty-nine years ago, and today they're even older, and even bigger.

Along with Pebble Beach, Riviera, Innisbrook, Pinehurst, and Valhalla, it was one of the most beautiful tracks I saw all year, and it made sense that it played host to the longest-running PGA Tour event held at the same course, dating back to Hogan's first of five wins in 1946. Since that inaugural year, the tournament's champions have included Sneak, Nicklaus, Palmer, Trevino, Crenshaw, Casper, Weiskopf, Baker-Finch, Watson, Price, Mickelson—legends galore, with the notable exception of Tiger Woods.

In 2014, Colonial would welcome the best golfer on earth in his first week holding the title. All through the spring, with Tiger sidelined, the honor of the world's number 1 golfer had been up for grabs. The rankings take each player's results from the last two years into account, and Tiger's eventual fall was inevitable. Adam Scott had been chasing it for weeks, and the irony was that his ascension came, at last, on an off week—he didn't play the Byron Nelson, but that's when his point total finally eclipsed Tiger's. How that happened may seem confusing, which is why I quickly arrived at a good rule of thumb for the world rankings: They make total sense, as long as you never try to understand them.

The rise to number 1 had been a career-long dream for the thirty-three-year-old Aussie, just as winning the Masters had been before he defeated Angel Cabrera in a playoff at Augusta the year before. Now Fort Worth awaited, where he had the chance to become the first golfer in history to win the "Texas Slam"—he had already won the Houston Open, the Texas Open, and the Byron Nelson, and only Colonial remained. With number 1 secured, he arrived like a king.

On Sunday, I followed Brian Harman until the 11th fairway, where I heard a roar over my left shoulder and hurried up a small

knoll overlooking the 12th green. The noise had been for John Senden, who had just sunk a thirty-seven-foot birdie putt. By the time I
reached the crest, Scott was standing over a birdie putt of his own,
this one considerably shorter at four feet. It fell, and the standard
bearer confirmed that Scott stood at -8, just a shot behind the leader,
David Toms.

He took dead aim on the par-3 13th, hitting his iron over the Trin-
ity River. The twirl of his club meant he liked it, and with good reason—it stopped on a small shelf of green eleven feet from the pin.
Framed by the trees growing from the far riverbanks, he placed the end
of the long putter in his sternum, gripped it with his left hand, and held
the middle of the shaft lightly between thumb and forefinger as he
drew back and struck. He missed—barely—but walking to the 14th
green, he was one of the few players on the course moving with any
swagger.

"Adam, my wife loves you!" a man shouted as he moved past. He
could have been speaking for a whole country of golf fans.

After a solid drive on 14, he chewed on a bit of food and ignored
the cries of "Aussie!" and "G'day, mate!" from the gallery. Wearing his
Titleist hat, white shirt with Uniqlo and Mercedes logos, and gray
pants, Scott walked with the erect posture mothers dream of when
they harass their children. If anything, his torso shifts slightly forward,
and his legs do all the work—his still upper body is a living experiment
in motion efficiency.

He didn't realize Toms had dropped to -8, and he was tied for the
lead. Nor did he realize, as his thirty-nine-foot putt tracked toward the
hole a moment later and fell, that he now had sole command of the lead.
As the air thickened on what was already a humid day, and the dark
clouds sent a few speculative raindrops to earth, he protected the lead
with par on the 15th and 16th. Dufner, at -8, had just one hole left,
while Toms held the same score several holes behind.

As Scott approached the 17th tee, a loud roar echoed from the 18th,
just one hundred yards away. Bleachers impeded the view, but when he
reached the green, a digital scoreboard broke the news—the roar was for

Dufner, who birdied the last hole to reach -9 for the second time. "That would be a fucking awesome playoff," a volunteer murmured.

Why do all the modern Aussie golfers underachieve? Why do they waste their talents, and stumble under pressure, and let brilliant careers pass without resplendent moments?

It's not exactly a fair question—and it's also not 100 percent true—but we're dealing with perceptions here. For the Aussies, that perception begins with Greg Norman, who is universally acknowledged as one of the most talented golfers ever to live, a two-time British Open winner, and one of the greatest repeat choke artists in the history of modern sports.

A cruel analysis, maybe, but his collapses at Augusta are the stuff of legend. Adam Scott grew up idolizing "The Shark," and it's easy to imagine that the reason he values Augusta above all other majors—and why he would pretend, as a kid, that each putt was for the green jacket—stems from the times he watched the tournament elude Norman. The Masters remained tantalizingly out of reach for his hero, and the sheer brutality of those losses must have looked like a judgment on an entire nation.

Of course, this "Australian pattern" doesn't always hold. Steve Elkington took the '95 PGA Championship with a final round 64, and Geoff Ogilvy won the '06 U.S. Open with three clutch pars on the final holes. Golfers like these may only get one or two opportunities at a major in their careers, and they went against type by seizing the chance.

Those examples aside, the Aussie failure narrative mostly stands the test. Stuart Appleby rarely played well in majors, and never won, and the country's two young stars—Scott and Jason Day—have had wavering careers, with disappointment at the majors undermining their usual brilliance.

On one hand, it's tempting to laugh at the whole notion. Winning a normal tournament, much less a major, is absurdly difficult even for the best players, and that's especially true when you consider how golf differs from other sports. In America, almost all of our professional leagues culminate in a playoff, where players or teams compete against each other in a one-on-one setting, allowing for clear results and a well-defined historical legacy.

Golf, on the other hand, can seem arbitrary—the "important" tournaments are held throughout the year, during weeks that are otherwise insignificant, and the courses are so different that the advantages to any given player are random at best. Only one of the tournaments, the Masters, is held at the same venue, and the layout there benefits long hitters who can play their ball from right to left, which arguably makes it even *less* fair at determining career greatness.

That's the paradigm of golf, and what's most surprising is that the players all seem to accept it, including Scott.

"No, I like majors," he told me, in Akron. "That's just the way the game's evolved from whenever they were labeled majors in the forties or fifties. You know, history has shown that the greatest players have ended up accumulating the most of these tournaments, and I think it's probably a fair assessment of who the greatest players over time have been in each decade and each era. So I'm happy with the way everyone sees that."

And he's right. Arbitrary as the system may be, the accidents of history that produced four majors have indeed painted an accurate picture of the game's legends. Most critically, the pressure associated with these events has *made* them important in players' minds, so that each one becomes a sort of crucible that can only be survived by the best. It matters less how the majors came into existence—the fact that the players accept them as the premiere events of the season is enough.

That's why Scott's win at Augusta was so big. The Aussie Masters curse was over, and Scott finally shrugged the monkey off his back. But for many, it didn't quite cut the mustard—they wanted more.

Here again, Scott sided with his critics, saying that if he ended with twenty fifth-place finishes and just one career major win, he'd be disappointed. For players like Ogilvy and Elkington, one major win seems appropriate, even lucky, but Scott had always flown a bit higher. He won his first tournament on the European Tour at age twenty, and as far back as 2008, articles were being written with headlines implying his ascent to greatness, like *Sports Illustrated*'s "Adam Scott Is Ready to Win a Major Championship."

He'd been tabbed as the next great thing from the start, and to cement his status as an all-time great, he'd need to fit a lot more wins into his prime.

In this game, unfair expectations abound. But then again . . . not really.

"I have three daughters that are now 25, 23, and 21, they never showed any interest in the game at all, until one day Adam Scott won the Players Championship. Then all of a sudden, they said, 'Dad, can we meet Adam?'"

— Commissioner Tim Finchem

Whenever I see Scott in the flesh, I think of a Beatles lyric:

"Got to be good looking 'cause he's so hard to see."

Scott is a kind person (and a smart one), but he speaks so quietly, and with such a measured cadence, that it's easy to come away without a solid impression. A fellow journalist captured the feeling best when he told me that after he'd conducted a solo interview with Scott, he left discouraged, certain it had been a dud. It was only later, when he transcribed the talk, that he realized Scott had given him pure gold.

It was a feeling I could relate to, at least from press conferences. It's hard to appreciate the intelligence and insight of what he's saying in the moment, because it feels so reserved. From his body language, you get the sense that he's withholding something, and that the *real* Adam Scott is hidden somewhere behind the words. It takes a bit of time and distance to see that you were wrong, at least about the content. As far as his demeanor, the impression remains—he is guarding his privacy, you think, fighting a cold war against anyone who wants to break down the walls.

So what is he *really* like? That's a question I tried to answer all year, but his agents wouldn't let me anywhere near him in a one-on-one setting. Even if they had, I can't imagine what deeper truths I could have unearthed that others hadn't already tried and failed to find. Adam Scott simply doesn't slip.

I know that he has a beautiful swing that often drew comparisons to Tiger Woods in his early days. I know that women love him—you read anecdotes everywhere from *SI* to *Esquire* about the lengths women go to for his attention—sending panties to be autographed, fighting over his discarded banana peels, and God knows what else. Even Tim Finchem's daughters are in on the act.

I know he makes around eight million dollars annually—off the course—which in 2013 made him the fifth-highest earner among active players behind Rory McIlroy, Henrik Stenson, Phil, and Tiger. I know he has a philosophical side—when asked about the Eisenhower Tree's demise, he said, "Anything that lives will eventually die, I guess, and this one maybe early." I know he likes wine—he was excited for his fellow golfers to try his selection at the champions' dinner at Augusta— and I know he carries himself with a dignified reserve, but that he's generous and empathetic in his rare public moments.

Beyond these impressions, I never learned very much, and I get the sense that although many like and respect Scott, the list of people who really *know* him is quite small. Even the man's marriage was conducted with extreme privacy; nobody in the public eye even realized he had wed his longtime girlfriend, Swedish architect Marie Kojzar, until weeks later, when he mentioned a secret ceremony in the Bahamas to an Aussie reporter. He invited some friends, but he didn't even tell them what sort of event they'd be attending—they only learned it was a wedding when, and *if,* they arrived. Justin Rose, probably Scott's best friend on Tour, declined the party invitation, having no idea what he was about to miss.

His reserved nature extends to all walks of life. It's very difficult, for example, to get much sense of his childhood. He was born in Adelaide, on the south side of Australia off the Gulf St. Vincent inlet, and played his first round there at age four. The family moved to Queensland's Sunshine Coast when Adam was seven, when his father, Phil, landed a job as the golf pro at a resort called Twin Waters. He worked in the town of Maroochyadore manufacturing clubs—he had considered a playing career himself, but a motorcycle accident at age nineteen finished that dream—and his wife, Pam, worked in a "uniform shop" at a school.

Pam's mother came from Wales, and Phil had roots in England, but their son was 100 percent Aussie. In Queensland, he went to school at the Matthew Flinders Anglican College in Buderim, and later the famous Kooralbyn International School.

Scott modeled his game after Greg Norman's from the time he was seven years old, and first broke 70 and beat his dad at age thirteen. He went on to play junior golf in and around the Gold Coast in Queensland, and came to represent both his state and country in international competitions. All the while, he idolized the Shark, and was glued to the television whenever Norman contended at a major, even if that meant rising in the predawn on a Monday morning to watch the final round at Augusta.

After a stellar junior career, he decided to head for the States, where he attended UNLV for roughly eighteen months starting in 1998, the year after the Rebels won the national championship. This is a part of the Adam Scott story that many people don't know, and that obfuscation seems purposeful. Details are murky, but there was some sort of disagreement between him and coach Dwaine Knight when Scott decided to turn pro. Since then, he's resisted any overt ties to the school. He did, however, join a fraternity, and in November 1999 he golfed with Bill Clinton. He also met Butch Harmon, the man who would coach him for the next decade.

A couple of top tens as an amateur on the European Tour in early 2000 convinced him to make the leap to the professional ranks, and after a rough year spent between the PGA and European Tours, he came out the next season, at age twenty, and won the Alfred Dunhill Links Championship in January. He won twice more in Europe in

2002, won the Deutsche Bank Championship for his first PGA Tour win the next year, and made a splash in his first full season on the PGA Tour by winning the Players Championship in '04.

That was his biggest title yet, but he nearly blew it—with a two-shot lead on the 18th, he found the water on his second shot, and had to go up-and-down from forty yards to save bogey and win by a stroke. Even with the sloppy finish, the win turned him into a golf celebrity, and vaulted him into the top fifteen of the world rankings, where he'd remain through the end of 2008.

By this time, he was dating Marie Kojzar, whom he first met when she served as nanny for Thomas Bjorn's children, and living with her between Australia and London. He'd built his dream home on the gold coast in Queensland, and he also owned a place in Switzerland—in the same town as Sergio Garcia—that enabled him to escape Australian taxes.

The only things missing were those pesky majors. Aside from a T-3 at the PGA Championship in 2006, he never really came close to winning, and he missed a surprising number of cuts for one of the world's elite golfers.

On his first trip to Augusta, he played a practice round with Norman. When the older Aussie poured out a stream of water on the 16th green, Scott was amazed to watch it trickle all the way off the green, never sinking into the grass. The atmosphere felt charged and tense that day, and perhaps the feeling persisted to the other majors. Whether it was intimidation, nerves, or just bad luck, he couldn't seem to muster his usual talent at the year's biggest events.

By 2008, the whispers had reached full volume—was he tough enough to win the big tournaments? As far back as 2003, he'd faced questions about his so-called "killer instinct," which even his coach, Harmon, had called into question. The comparison to Tiger went through its own evolution—in the early 2000s, the media had focused on whether he would challenge Tiger for world dominance. By the middle of the decade, he was being asked whether the pressure of trying to fill Tiger's shoes kept him from achieving his best results. And by the end of the decade, the questions disappeared entirely. He might challenge Woods for number 1 someday, but his window to reach the American's extreme level of greatness had already passed—he would never win majors at anywhere near the same rate.

———————

Q. I think it was here last year somebody was asking you about whether or not you were too nice out there. Have you gotten any meaner in the ensuing year?

ADAM SCOTT: I don't know, you tell me. I mean, yeah, I think it's an inner thing. You've got to be mean inside. Some of my experiences over the last year have showed me how these big guys really have to have burning fire inside of them just to squash everybody else out there, and I think you have to have that or they'll do it to you. I'll be ready to go tomorrow. I'll be Mr. Tough Guy tomorrow (laughter).

—Players Championship, 2004

In some ways, you could look at Scott as part of a lost generation. There's an old quote from him at the '04 Booz Allen Classic—where he beat Charles Howell III—identifying himself, Howell, and Sergio Garcia as the best players under twenty-five. A decade later, only Scott would hold a major championship, while Howell had essentially dropped off the map and Garcia bounced from crisis to crisis.

Most players in their mid-thirties today who have excelled in major championships are not the ones anybody expected—Bubba Watson and Jason Dufner came from nowhere—while the child stars either flamed out, spent a career floundering under pressure, or bloomed far later than expectations, like Scott and Justin Rose. It's almost as if Tiger Woods's star was so bright that anybody within five years had no chance to shine—greatness skipped a generation, falling instead on the likes of Martin Kaymer and Rory McIlroy, while old-timers like Ernie Els and Mickelson scooped up any stray majors left hanging around.

Still, by any normal standard, Scott found great early success, and his first real stumble didn't come until 2008. After winning the Byron Nelson, a series of events shattered his focus, beginning with the end of his seven-year relationship with Kojzar. Unlike many Tour wives, who build their lives around their husbands and serve a sort of auxiliary role, Kojzar had ambitions of her own—she studied architecture—and the constant travel put a strain on the couple that eventually drove them apart.

Shortly after the breakup, Scott broke his hand in a freak accident when a friend slammed it in a car door, and became so sick with a recurring fever and throat troubles that he had to take antibiotics and steroids just to be able to play—and sometimes, to breathe.

His results suffered for a year, as Scott split from Butch Harmon and only returned to the winner's circle at the 2010 Valero Texas Open. In 2011, he nabbed Steve Williams, Tiger's old caddie, and together they won the WGC-Bridgestone Invitational that August. That elevated Scott back into the world top ten, and with his career rebound complete, he turned his eye to the majors. Slowly but surely, his play improved.

Finally, at the 2012 British Open at Royal Lytham & St. Anne's, he took a four-shot lead into the final round. This, it seemed, would be his big breakthrough.

He was shaky on Sunday's front nine, finishing with a two-over-par 36 on a difficult day, but his nearest competitors faltered as well. With a birdie on 14, he got back to -10, and held a four-shot lead over Ernie Els. The tournament looked all but over with four holes to play, but then Scott suffered through the same kind of nightmarish collapse he had watched his hero endure as a child. With three straight bogeys, he sank to -7. Els birdied the last hole to tie him at that number, and the sure victory had dissolved into thin air.

With just the final hole to play, Scott put his tee shot into the bunker, laid up into the fairway, and hit his approach to eight feet. The mistake put him in a horrifying position—now he needed to sink a tough par putt just to force a playoff. He tried to gather himself, but this meltdown wasn't meant to have a happy ending. He missed, and Els took home an unlikely Claret Jug.

It was the sad Australian narrative playing out all over again, and after answering the same old questions for years, Scott was devastated at missing his chance to finally win the big one. He responded to the situation with grace—he had learned from Norman's example all those years ago—but he knew that everyone who had called him a choker before had more ammunition, and the pressure would only mount.

By April 2013, he was back with Kojzar—now a full-fledged architect. On the course, he did his best to maintain his focus, and was lucky enough to get his next shot at major glory at the 2013 Masters, less than a year after his British collapse.

Trailing by a shot heading into Sunday, he turned on the burners, and finished an excellent day by sinking a twenty-five-foot birdie putt on 18. In the background, showing how much the tournament meant to Australia, his playing partner and fellow Aussie Marc Leishman pumped his fist as Scott roared in celebration. They both thought it was a winner, too—right up until the moment when Angel Cabrera came up in the final group and stuck his approach to three feet. He made his birdie, and Scott's work continued.

Rain fell on the second playoff hole, no. 10. Scott bombed another tee shot, getting a great downhill bounce, and Cabrera matched him again. In the valley, with the sky darkening, Cabrera hit a 6-iron that stopped just below the hole. From 196 yards, Scott did him one better, finishing hole high and fifteen feet away. Cabrera's birdie putt missed by inches, and the Argentine flipped his club in the air in frustration. It left Scott with a putt to win the green jacket, and bury a national curse, along with his own demons, for good. Behind him, the rain poured down, and Williams stood next to Cabrera, both men with their hands on their hips. Scott anchored the putter in his chest, breathed deeply, and swung.

The ball seemed to linger forever on the green, but finally it dropped. The roar from the greenside mob eclipsed his own as he leaned back and screamed to the sky.

. . .

The only hiccup through the rest of that season came at the Australian Open in November, when Scott entered the 18th hole a stroke up on Rory McIlroy. The Northern Irishman had fought back from four strokes behind on the day, and on the 18th hole, Scott bogeyed while McIlroy holed a ten-foot birdie putt to steal a dramatic victory.

The result stunned the fans in Sydney, and it ate at Scott—he badly wanted to complete his season with a win at home, and finish off the triple crown he had started by winning the Australian Masters and PGA.

At the time, there was no way to know that we were watching a blueprint for what would happen in 2014—all anyone knew was that Rory had just won his only tournament of the year, and maybe it meant he could rediscover his old form. Maybe.

In the meantime, Scott ascended to number 1, and set his eyes on Colonial and the Texas slam.

Scott had his chances to reach -10 and win the tournament outright—twenty feet on the 15th, thirty-two feet on the 16th, thirty-six feet on the 17th, thirty feet on the 18th—but none of the attempts were great, and he took his pars and moved on. As he made his way to the final green, a clanking sound came from the manual scoreboard by the water, where a metal tile was replaced with another—it was down to Dufner and Scott.

After making his par, with the skies darkening, Scott gave his tired standard bearer an autographed ball. He walked past the statue of Ben Hogan, told CBS's Peter Kostis that he could use "a couple of bottles of wine to go," and drove with Steve Williams to a low brick building with a sign on the front that read "caddie registration." They sat for a bit on a couch, feet on the green felt carpet, watching a television feed of the tournament. A television crew lurked in the doorway. He and Williams soon appeared on the screen, which created an odd tableau—there they sat, watching themselves on a seven-second delay. That spurred Scott to action, and he and Williams fled.

Dufner was already on the range, and the two didn't exchange so much as a nod while they hit on opposite sides, moving from short irons to long irons to driver. Back on 18, Dufner—looking miserable as always—reached into a hat and drew out the number one. The two major winners shook hands, and both ripped their drives into the center of the fairway.

Dufner's eyes drifted to the clouds, more menacing by the second, and both players hit wedges to safe spots on the green. When they moved down the fairway, the first chants of "U-S-A" descended from the galleries, now well-oiled from a day of drinking in the sun.

It was pars all around, and then on to 17, where the impending afternoon storm brought an early darkness. After a safe shot into the fairway, Scott's approach flew straight at the flag, stopping in the fringe fourteen feet past the hole. As Dufner stood over his ball, his caddie threw four fingers down into the ground at a CBS spotter, who made the same gesture to David Feherty across the fairway: 9-iron. He made his best shot of the day—the ball sailed over a greenside bunker and stopped four feet from the hole. In the stands behind the green, the gallery shouted chaotically before organizing themselves into another U-S-A chant.

With a short, uphill putt awaiting Dufner, Scott knew his putt had to go down. As he stood over the ball, a train whistle blew in the distance, so he backed off and began the routine anew. He straddled his ball, legs wide like a colossus, and held his fingers in a V. When he was ready, he struck his putt and watched it move down the hill.

It curled left as it neared the hole, caught the right edge, and dropped. There was defiance in Scott's fist pump, and in the clenched muscles of his face. Dufner tapped in his own birdie and exhaled with relief as it fell—with him, there's no such thing as a gimme—they were off to 18 again.

Scott's 3-wood was identical to the one he'd struck moments earlier; the ball came to rest two feet from his previous divot. Dufner's drive stopped short of Scott's, and the reigning PGA Champion had his first hiccup of the playoffs as he flirted with the bunkers on his approach and left the ball almost forty feet from the hole.

Scott did better—his previous pitching wedge had been cautious, and tight. He said later that even after coming through in a Masters playoff, there's still something to learn from each new pressure situation. His normal instinct would be to hit a full, hard shot, but now he could suppress the tension, soften his hands, and let his natural feel take over.

His previous wedge had settled twenty-one feet from the hole. This one left him with just seven. When Dufner missed his birdie putt from a distance, Scott focused through the hushed conversation and the unfriendly skies. Something about the place reminded him of Australia, right down to the dirt. It's why he'd won the three other Texas events, and why the so-called Texas Slam was within his reach. So why not hold the massive trophy amid the club members in their red tartan jackets? Why not see your name in calligraphy on a giant check? Why not make the putt, and why not win?

When the ball rolled in the hole, he had it all—at least for the moment. But there's always someone coming to take it away.

JUNE

America's Major

15

BEYOND THE BRAND

Rickie Fowler

"My parents never drank, so I wasn't really around it. I just never really felt like it was something that needed to be done, and I was focused on what I wanted to do. There might have been three nights in the two years I was in college when I drank, and even then, nothing crazy. I was designated driver pretty much every weekend, Friday, Saturday, Sunday. I was around having a good time, and able to make sure my teammates got home and they were all good, so that was fun for me."
—RICKIE FOWLER

Rickie Fowler's childhood home stood on the Santa Rosa plateau in Temecula, California, twenty miles inland from the Pacific Ocean. His family moved from the lowlands when Rickie was eight, and there, in the shadow of the Santa Ana Mountains, he could lie in bed, stare at the poster of Motocross champion Jeremy McGrath on his bedroom wall, and listen to the coyotes howling in the hills and ravines.

Rod Fowler, the boy's father, had been a talented rider himself, and the Murrieta-Temecula area is considered the Motocross capital of America. At the time, it was also small; in 1988, when Fowler was born, Murrieta had fewer than 20,000 residents. The population explosion that would see the town quintuple in size and grow to over 100,000 people—spurred on by coastal congestion, rising real estate prices, and a surge of immigration—was still a few years away.

For work, Rod ran a trucking business that he started after high school, hauling sand and gravel across Southern California. He introduced Rickie to dirt bikes at an early age, and was thrilled to have a partner in crime—together, they'd go to the local track on Wednesday nights and ride for hours. Rickie showed a capacity for skilled, fearless riding, even after he broke his leg at age three. He'd be the first to hit every jump with speed, navigate risky terrain, and launch off the steep dirt hills with the confidence of a much older rider.

Rickie loved the colors on the racers' uniforms, too. He painted his room blue, and he gravitated toward flashy designs. Fowler was a quiet kid, and the colors gave him a way to express himself. He later brought that aesthetic to the golf course, where he'd enter junior tournaments clad in white pants and a white belt with a bright shirt.

Rod was the easygoing parent, the kind of guy who could talk to a stranger for hours. His wife, Lynn, another dirt bike racer, brought order to the family. They complemented each other, with Rod earning the money to give his children opportunities outside Temecula, and Lynn making sure everything ran on time. They weren't rich, but they were supremely disciplined—not the kind of people who left much to chance.

Rickie is the product of a unique blend of West Coast cultures, mostly due to Lynn's heritage. Her mother was born to the Sage Brush Hill clan of the Navajo nation, and her father, Yutaka Tanaka, was a Japanese-American who was sent to a World War II internment camp as a child. When I asked Fowler about this lineage—his middle name is Yutaka, in homage to his grandfather—he pointed out that while his grandfather was being imprisoned, the Marines employed Navajo "code talkers," who transmitted secret messages based on their native tongue. When Jeanie and Yutaka married, it was also a union of two cultures with complex places in the American narrative—particularly during the defining war of the twentieth century.

The Fowlers didn't have much money, and they didn't belong to a country club, but they would take family vacations in winter to Ocotillo Wells, a town in the Colorado Desert outside San Diego. They'd all ride their bikes on the open terrain, including Rickie's younger sister, Taylor. Like both of his parents, Rickie became an adrenaline junkie—a craving that would stay with him the rest of his life.

Against this backdrop, it's hard to imagine golf entering Fowler's world. The unlikely addition came from Yutaka, who began to play when Rickie was three years old. He practiced at the Murrieta Valley Golf Range, and one day he brought his grandson along. Rickie loved everything about the sport, though it was miles away from the speed and thrills of Motocross. Lynn even told *USA Today* that he got a kick out of the etiquette and rules, which is precisely the element that turns some kids away.

When Rickie was seven, he met a man who would become incredibly important to his development—Barry McDonnell, a PGA pro at Murrieta Valley. They began working together, and the partnership lasted for the rest of McDonnell's life. They kept their sessions simple, making sure Rickie was armed for any situation he'd encounter on the course. He learned to hit it low, and high, with a fade and draw, and to execute each shot by feel. When he turned pro, Fowler would credit McDonnell for his intimate knowledge of his own swing, a quality he felt was missing among players who became too reliant on rigid technique and video-oriented training.

"He was a man of very few words," Fowler said of McDonnell. "Even with me, where he was open and we'd talk about things, he'd get his point across with as few words as possible."

Taka and Lynn, meanwhile, had the most influence on how he behaved on the course. Fowler told me that sulking or throwing a tantrum would have been totally unacceptable. His mother even set a rule: If he broke a club, that club would not be replaced.

But the truth is that Fowler wasn't like most kids. He rarely had to be told to keep his cool, and even though he had a strong competitive instinct from his earliest days, it never manifested in anger or self-pity.

He even admitted to reporters that he went through his whole life without ever throwing a club—at least until he hurled one at a palmetto tree during a friendly round in Florida as an adult, just to see what it felt like.

Rickie played out of state for the first time when he was twelve years old, and from then on, his mother became his travel agent. Lynn still works with her son full-time, along with Rickie's sister Taylor, and they approached his junior days with the same sense of professional dedication they maintain today. If golf was Rickie's dream, and he had the talent and passion, then why not?

He quit bike racing for good after he hurt his knee during a wreck in high school, and from then on, golf was his full priority. "I was bummed out," Rod admitted to *Yahoo Sports* in 2012. A few years earlier, Rod had met Rickie's hero, Jeremy McGrath, and the two became friends. McGrath spent time with Rickie, and thought Rickie had a bright future in racing. Rickie's choice may seem obvious now, but putting his bike to the side was a drastic move, and the end of a lifelong passion.

When Kevin Tway went to Oklahoma State last fall, his father, Bob, had some advice for him.

"I told Kevin to play golf with Rickie Fowler every day," Bob said. "Play for dinner or for $5 because when you get tired of getting beat by him you'll get better."

—USA Today, June 12, 2008

Mike McGraw was coaching the women's team at Oklahoma State when he first heard about Fowler from his assistant, Alan Bratton. He saw a picture—the long hair, the white belt—and took note. When he was named the head men's coach the next summer, he made the California kid a high priority.

Rickie visited that January, and McGraw didn't know what to expect. McGraw coaches at Baylor now, and had no problem telling me that Stillwater, Oklahoma, is a dull town. It can be a sticking point with recruits, but to his surprise, Fowler saw the place as an asset—nothing would get in the way of his development as a golfer. The kid didn't even drink, McGraw learned. He paid a visit to the Fowler home that summer, up in the Santa Ana foothills—he still remembers the sound of the coyotes at night—and the more he learned about Rickie, the more he wanted him in Stillwater.

Fowler committed, and put together a spectacular freshman season that culminated in a Big 12 individual championship at Whispering Pines—"He was playing a different course," McGraw remembered—and fourth place in nationals. At season's end, he became the first freshman to ever win the Ben Hogan Award as the country's best golfer.

"He's probably got one of the best attitudes of anybody I've ever seen," said McGraw, "and that's why he's so much fun to watch."

That summer, Fowler made the cut at the U.S. Open. A few months later, he teamed with Peter Uihlein, Kevin Tway, and Morgan Hoffmann in his sophomore season, leading an Oklahoma State team that was considered the best in the country. They lived up to their billing all season, and by the time spring rolled around, they had the look of a juggernaut. At the national championships at the Inverness Club in Toledo, they crushed the nearest competition in stroke play, with Fowler finishing third individually.

A year earlier, those three brilliant days would've put them one round away from a national championship. But the format changed that year, and 2009 marked the start of the new match play era in college golf.

By his own high standards, Georgia's Brian Harman—a diminutive firebrand who would "rather chew a nail than lose," per his coach Chris Haack—hadn't had a very good senior season. He'd grown sick of college, and was ready to move on. Harman needed the competitive fire in his life—it had always been his fuel, sometimes to his detriment—and the well of inspiration at Georgia had run dry.

When his Bulldog team faded to an 8-seed in Toledo, though, it meant that the dream match-up—Georgia vs. Oklahoma State—would be pushed ahead to the quarterfinals. Worse, Georgia would face a team that had routed them by twenty strokes over the three previous days.

When the morning came, Harris English and Hudson Swafford continued to struggle, and both lost their matches 4&3. Three losses meant elimination, and when Georgia's Adam Mitchell was penalized two holes during his match against Kevin Tway for keeping too many clubs in his bag, it looked like the fatal blow—an embarrassing 3-0 drubbing for the number 2 team in the nation. But Mitchell played scorching golf all day, beating Tway 5&3 despite the penalty, and Russell Henley came through—as he always did—with a 2-up victory, knotting the match at two wins apiece.

That left just one match on the course—Brian Harman vs. Rickie Fowler.

A huge contingent of fans, larger than anyone had seen to that point in college golf, converged on the final pair. By the 15th, trailing by a hole, Harman's competitive juices were flowing again. On the green, Fowler two-putted for his par, and Harman had to make an eight-footer to avoid going 2-down with just three holes to play. He tuned everything out, and knocked it in.

When he looked up, he saw that Fowler and McGraw had already left the green, and were standing on the 16th tee. They hadn't even stayed to retrieve the flag—a standard bit of etiquette in college matches. Harman, already keyed up in the high-pressure atmosphere, saw red. The anger overcame him.

"You mother*fucker*," he thought to himself, staring at Fowler.

He paced across the green, picked up the flag, and slammed it in the hole. He walked up to Chris Haack, barely containing his rage.

"I'm about to kick this guy in the teeth," he said.

Haack liked what he saw—he knew that unlike some players, Harman got better when he played with rage. With the match on the line and trailing by a hole, Haack knew they needed a spark.

Harman had blood in his eyes for Fowler. He struck immediately with an eight-foot birdie on the 16th, and though Fowler matched him there, he couldn't keep pace when Harman made another birdie on 17—a twelve-footer, this time—to square the match. On the 18th, Harman's drive flew into the left rough, but he struck a beautiful approach to eight feet. Fowler nearly matched him, setting up a twelve-foot birdie chance of his own.

Fowler went first, but left his putt short. The stage was set for Harman. He had enough residual anger for one last shot, and enough to carry his team to a win. His putt tracked toward the hole, caught the right lip, and dropped.

The incredible flourish capped Georgia's comeback, and Harman leaped into his teammate's arms. Fowler never understood what happened, or why Harman seemed so upset toward the end of the match. It's unlikely that he left the 15th green for malicious reasons, but it didn't matter—Harman had found the motivation he needed. McGraw, the Cowboys coach, would only learn about their faux pas five years later in a conversation with Haack. All he knew, at the time, was that Fowler had never been more devastated in his life.

Later, Harman and Haack would laugh about the final match.

"That sucker should've gotten that flag stick, shouldn't he?" Haack asked. Harman just smiled.

"It's true," he told me. "He should have. He might've beat me if he had just gotten that flag stick."

Fowler broke down in tears as Georgia celebrated in front of a large gallery—it was his last round of golf for Oklahoma State. That fall, he turned pro.

"I love the position I'm in, and I definitely wouldn't change it. But yeah, there's times where it would be cool just to be out and blend in. But uh . . . I guess that's not going to happen."

—Fowler

Titleist had been Fowler's club of choice for most of his career, and he was friends with the Uihlein family, so a sponsorship deal was a no-brainer. But it was his contract with Puma that would come to define him as a golfer. Fowler had chased the apparel company as much as they chased him, and the partnership was one of those rare moments of corporate synergy that sends marketing departments into euphoric spasms.

Puma's edgy style and Fowler's Motocross background made a perfect match. What many don't realize is that Fowler actually requested the orange outfit with the white belt—a nod to Oklahoma State—which, along with a flat-brimmed cap and a puma bounding across the front, would quickly become his signature look.

"They didn't really have any orange in the line," Fowler told me. "So I've had to make it all."

In the flashy new duds, Fowler became a hot commodity for the PGA Tour, who desperately needed young stars as they prepared for a future without Tiger Woods. Fashion-wise, Fowler was an immediate success, and it wasn't long before kids at every PGA Tour stop came decked out in orange Puma gear from head-to-toe—not to mention a few adults. The company was thrilled, and Fowler quickly gained a reputation as a player in Phil Mickelson's mold, who went the extra mile with his sponsors and didn't mind turning himself into a walking advertisement.

The clothes came with a few side effects. He gained legions of detractors, and the image he conveyed bore no resemblance to the humble, easygoing kid from Murrieta with a strong family foundation. Based on your perspective, he either looked like a hip young emblem of the counterculture, a sneering punk who thumbed his nose at the golf establishment every time he donned his garish orange duds, or a cynical clothes horse cashing in on his looks. Neither one came close to the truth, and almost everyone who came to know Fowler personally understood that the dichotomy was false. But even among some of his fellow pros, annoyance brewed—especially when the fashion campaign proved incredibly successful.

By 2013, Fowler was making an estimated $4.5 million off the course annually—he's had sponsorships with everyone from Cobra to Red Bull to Farmers Insurance—which eclipsed almost everyone in his age bracket, and put him in a class with major winners and national icons. It was a gaudy sum for a kid who had won just a single PGA Tour event and managed only one top five in the majors, and it's easy to see why it bred resentment.

Not that his golf game didn't merit praise—in 2010, Fowler won the PGA Rookie of the Year award, and earned a captain's pick for the Ryder Cup. In 2012, he earned his first PGA Tour win at the Wells Fargo Championship, hitting a risky fifty-one-degree wedge over the water and into the green on the 18th hole. It stopped four feet from the pin, and he made birdie to top McIlroy and D. A. Points in a playoff. In the budding Rickie-Rory rivalry, the early rounds had gone to the American.

The win carried emotional value, too—a year earlier, he'd suffered a heartbreaking loss. In the early days of his professional career, he would return to Murrieta a couple of times each year and visit Barry McDonnell, the only coach he'd ever had. He'd hit balls while McDonnell smoked a cigar or sipped a beer, and they'd chat about his game. Being home was like therapy for Fowler, and he enjoyed those moments with the quiet instructor who had helped define his playing style.

In May 2011, McDonnell passed away at age seventy-five after a heart attack. McGraw was with Fowler a week later, and the pain he witnessed was intense. That feeling stayed with him through the next year, and through his first PGA Tour win. The closest he came to crying in Charlotte was when a reporter mentioned his old mentor.

"I tried not to mention my swing coach Barry a whole lot," he said, "because that definitely pulls a whole lot out of me."

After struggling in 2013, he began to think about working with Butch Harmon. His only hesitation came when he thought about McDonnell. Would it be the right career move to use another coach? Would it be disloyal in some way to the man that had guided him since he was seven?

In the end, he decided to approach Harmon, and his pitch to the legendary coach became the centerpiece of countless stories in 2014: "I want to be known more for my golf than my clothes and my hat." Despite Fowler's insistence that his well-cultivated image is only positive, that desire tells you all you need to know about the effect the criticism had on his psyche.

Harmon sought the permission of his other students, and the two began working together after Fowler's dismal 78-76 missed cut at the British Open. *PGATour.com*'s D. J. Piehowski reported that shortly after the relationship started, Fowler got a message from Bill Teasdale, the owner of the range where McDonnell had worked. Just before his death, the old instructor had sent a text to Teasdale with an eerily prescient message: "When the time is right, Rickie should go work with Butch Harmon."

The text gave Fowler confirmation and closure—he knew he was doing the right thing, and it was a load off his mind. He gave Harmon his full commitment, and together they made his swing more efficient and gave him room to generate speed and distance. He cut his hair short in February, made the Match Play semifinals before falling to Jason Day, and earned his second top-five major finish at Augusta in April. But he also suffered seven cuts before June, and to the doubters, Fowler still had a lot to prove.

Bubba Watson, whose tightly wound personality keeps him distant from most players, feels so close to Fowler he calls Rickie his "little brother.". . . According to longtime Mickelson caddie Jim Mackay, "Rickie is like Steve Stricker: There is literally not one person on tour who has a bad thing to say about him." Adds PGA Tour commissioner Tim Finchem: "You look at Rickie, and if he were self-centered or whatever, you'd say, well, anyone at his age and ability level would go through that phase. But he's got none of that, and it's why his connection to people is automatic."

—Jaime Diaz, *Golf Digest*

I didn't know quite what to think of Fowler at first. If you buy what you see on television, he's the amiable, loose character who makes fun of himself in SportsCenter commercials and plays a mustachioed PI for State Farm ads. Even before I knew his story or had ever interacted with him, though, I got the sense that this image couldn't be very accurate.

As much as Puma and the PGA Tour might want to present him as the young, carefree face of golf, the fact is that nobody makes it very far without intense levels of obsession and focus. The simple fact that Rickie had made the big time meant he couldn't *really* be the free-spirited rebel they were trying to sell, and though his people like to use the word "edgy" whenever possible, the only thing edgy about him is his love for speed.

The truth, I found, is that he only really stands out in certain controlled contexts. Bright clothes, funny videos, and great golf? Sure. But that's it. He made the usual sacrifices along the way, eschewing a social life in service of a larger goal. He doesn't flaunt his money. He's not much of a joker, and though he may have played a prank or two in college, there's nothing cruel or confrontational about him. In a sport dominated by anger, he's remarkable for the fact that you barely ever see a hint of rage in his face. His unusual comfort with himself also explains why he avoided some of the standard growing pains—unlike an average pro, he never spent endless wasted hours on the range, or felt a compulsion to change his swing.

The best word I can come up with for Fowler, to describe his style and nature, is "gentle." Beneath everything else, there's an undercurrent of empathy. That's why kids love him, too—they follow Fowler like the pied piper, and while women of all ages are drawn to Rory McIlroy, with his intense energy smoldering beneath the face of a teen idol, Fowler is the mellow soul that captures young imaginations.

Early on in the year, I was dying to ask him a question that I thought would be very profound: Does he ever feel imprisoned inside his image? Did the glaring nature of the Puma brand overshadow his true personality? It turns out, though, that he'd heard this question a million times, in a million different ways. And each time, Rickie refused to blink. He knows who writes his checks and, money aside, he truly seems to believe that Puma gives him the best chance to represent himself to the wider world.

When he turned pro, Fowler signed with the Wasserman Media Group, and is managed today by a man named Sam MacNaughton, a former Oklahoma State golfer who enjoys a high status in the world of agents. If you want to talk to Rickie, you go through Sam—even Mike McGraw, Rickie's college coach, has to take his requests through MacNaughton—and there are so many requests for Fowler's time that no sane journalist expects very much.

There are a few agents who are so stingy with a player's time that they earn the nickname "Dr. No," and MacNaughton is one. The tight circle Wasserman forms around Fowler also serves to keep the details of certain stories quiet—like his car crash on July 1 in Palm Beach Gardens, which left him with cuts near his head.[11]

Time with Rickie isn't just a hard sell for small-timers like me, either; in mid-October, as the 2014 season wound to a close, Karen Crouse of *The New York Times* got so fed up that she took the unusual step of tweeting at Fowler to draw public attention to the stonewalling:

> "Hey @RickieFowlerPGA, I proposed in-depth profile on you 4 NYT, your agent told me 'don't get your hopes up.' What gives? Won't u sit w/me?"

Crouse is one of the few journalists to get the in-depth goods on Bubba Watson, and the fact that a strong writer working for the world's

---

[11] The severity of his injuries, which may have required stitches or staples, never came out, though the police report from the incident outlines the sequence of events. Fowler, driving a gray 2011 Porsche 911 with an eighteen-year-old junior golfer named Morgan Hobbs in the passenger seat, took a turn too fast off an I-95 exit ramp on a rainy night, jumped the curb, crashed through a chain-link fence and into a housing development, and hit a tree. Nobody was hurt, and Rickie couldn't have blinked at the four thousand dollars in property damage . But he proved that his need for speed is alive and well when he admitted to the cop that he had been driving "a little too fast."

most respected newspaper couldn't get any time with Fowler is a clear indication that he's essentially off-limits to anyone without a video camera.

I had been through the same process with MacNaughton, and we had developed what I thought was a fairly comical relationship. I'd approach him on the range, endure his gruff but subtly humorous glare—he has the uncanny ability to intimidate while still giving the impression that, deep down, he *might* like you—exchange a couple of awkward pleasantries, and then make my latest pitch. He'd balk, ask for something clearer, watch me stutter, and then give an answer that wasn't quite "no," but was very far from "yes." My favorite response came at the PGA Championship, when he looked up from his phone and said, "To be honest, I'm not engaged in your story." I didn't know how to respond, but I knew what it meant—yet again, I'd be forced to approach him a week or two down the line, and repeat the process.

This went on all year, and by July I had resigned myself to the usual Plan B—asking Rickie my questions in press conferences, and hanging out by the flash area after his rounds in an attempt to salvage a spare minute or two. I held out a faint hope of something longer down the line, but when he declined *The New York Times,* I realized my own chances were laughable.

Which is why it shocked me, in early November, about a month after I had last emailed MacNaughton—and nearly eighteen months since our first exchange—when I got the okay to do a twenty-minute phone interview with Fowler.

This kind of access is worth its weight in gold, at least in theory, but in practice it's only as valuable as the player. I knew Rickie well enough to hope for the best, and when we finally spoke, I wasn't disappointed. What stood out to me, over the course of that call, was his unpretentious sense of himself and his past. We spent a few minutes talking about Rod and Taka's businesses, and it became clear that he could go into as much detail as I wanted—a stark contrast to the many golfers I spoke with who were only dimly aware of what their parents did for a living—"something in finance, I think"—and couldn't care less. For

Fowler, there was never a point when his own rising star cut him off from the world he knew.

He also cares about his lineage, and not just as an interesting auto-biographical detail to throw at reporters. When he learned that his grandfather had been in an internment camp as a child—it wasn't a topic the old man brought up or talked about very often—it interested him enough that he wrote a book report on the topic at school. On his grandmother's side, he was able to tell the *Navajo Times* exactly which clan she came from, and to relate memories of visiting Tuba City, Arizona, the largest community in the Navajo Nation. There's also a spiritual side to him—he was raised Catholic—but it's a silent part of his life.

I knew, by the time we spoke, that my question about losing himself behind a brand was neither original nor interesting. When I asked a modified version—is there any consequence to being so closely identified with such a specific style?—the most I could get was that he didn't always like the fact that he has to watch his step in public.

"I don't want a publicity disaster," he told me. "I want to make news on the course, not off."

But that's not particular to his life, or to the Puma brand, and he said it without much regret—he knows it comes with the territory, and it's not like he'd change his situation if he had the chance. The clothes even come in handy at times, creating a sort of separation between Fowler the public figure and Fowler the private individual.

"There's definitely a lot of people that don't know me," he said, "but it's not that I'm hiding. It's not that I don't want people to know me. But I've enjoyed keeping my personal life and family life away from the course. I don't want it to blend together."

That's true of his friendships and love life, too—he dated Alexandra Browne, a singer and the daughter of former pro golfer Olin Browne, for years, but that relationship ended. He now lives in Jupiter, Florida, with fellow pro Cameron Tringale now, and hangs out among the robust golfing community in Jupiter, including Rory McIlroy. The two rivals golf on occasion, but only among larger groups. He's also good friends with Bubba Watson, which is as puzzling a duo as you'll find anywhere, but which speaks to Rickie's ability to relate to almost anyone.

Like everything else in Fowler's life, there's no dramatic answer to the brand problem. It may rub you or me the wrong way—or feel like an insidious corruption of a grounded golfer with a unique past—but he approaches it earnestly, without much calculation. The fact that it masks him, and affects the way America views his personality, is more of a fault with our culture, and the way television tends to reduce everything to a simple formula.

There is nothing sinister to Fowler himself—he's the same as he's always been. He's the quiet Murrieta boy who likes bright colors, who works like hell, and who hasn't changed his essential nature despite a life that couldn't be more different from his childhood on the Santa Rosa plateau, with the coyotes howling off in the dark hills.

16

PINEHURST, NORTH CAROLINA

The U.S. Open; Cruel & Unusual Punishment at the USGA;
Martin's Run; Restorations

"Charlie Price, the great writer, he'd say Pinehurst in his day was fairways, and the fairways were oases within sandy country. The wispy rye grass, pine needles and sand, the little tufts of ground, that's what Pinehurst was."

—BEN CRENSHAW, to PGATour.com,
on the restoration of Pinehurst no. 2

The United States Golf Association might be the cruelest organizing body in the entire sport, and when they take center stage each June at the U.S. Open, they set out to punish and humiliate any golfer with dreams of winning America's oldest major championship.

The USGA's unofficial goal at each U.S. Open, at least in the past decade, is to stage an event so challenging that the winning score is close to even par—ideally on the high side. Sometimes the courses they choose aren't quite difficult enough on their own, but that doesn't faze the USGA. They simply doctor the course in the weeks leading up to the event, using some tried-and-true methods to rig the whole event. For starters, they grow out the rough, creating gnarly patches of grass that you'd need a machete to hack through. Then they deprive the fairways of water, speeding them up so that even decent tee shots run forever and eventually find their way into the dense thickets along the side. They do the same to the greens, making it impossible to stick an approach, or to putt on them even if you do. They'll even use artificial methods, like turning a normal par 5 into a laughably long par 4, so that a birdie becomes a par, and par becomes bogey. And if all else fails, they can simply push tees back to lengthen their holes, or set the pins in diabolical locations, near the highest point of the humped, turtle-back greens they love so much.

There are players, believe it or not, who appreciate this type of setup. The one thing you can always say about a U.S. Open is that it will be a true test of golf, and it will never devolve into a putting contest of the kind you sometimes see on the PGA Tour. Players like Adam Scott, Martin Kaymer, Justin Rose, and Tiger Woods would take this setup every week, because they're among the most complete golfers in the world, and any course that demands every single shot from your arsenal will benefit the player with no weaknesses. And the U.S. Open comes with one absolute guarantee—if you have a weakness, it will be exposed.

In the nine years preceding the 2014 U.S. Open at Pinehurst, the winning score was even par or worse six times. Two of the three winners who actually went *under* par—Tiger Woods in 2008 and Lucas Glover the next year—stayed nice and close, at -1 and -4, respectively. The only exception came in 2011, when Rory McIlroy put on a historic show at Congressional Country Club, decimating a difficult track to the tune of -16 and asserting himself as one of the world's best players.

The first winner in that difficult stretch was Michael Campbell, who won at the Pinehurst Resort in the Sandhills of North Carolina with even par in 2005. Campbell has largely been forgotten—he's a member of golf's one-hit wonder club, and you can barely find a mention of him at the club—but the previous Pinehurst champion in 1999, Payne Stewart, has become an important part of the resort's identity. Less than six months after he won the event, he died in a plane crash, and he's honored today with a large statue outside the clubhouse that captures the moment when he sunk the winning putt on 18 to beat Phil Mickelson—clad in his famous knickers and tam-o'-shanter cap, right foot off the ground, fist extended in triumph.

The U.S. Open returned to Pinehurst in 2014, and the three biggest stories going were Stewart, Mickelson, and the course itself.

Payne was the legend who had won the first U.S. Open ever played at the course, and his name was already on everyone's lips in the week leading up to the event. On Thursday, Rickie Fowler upped the ante with his own moving tribute. Stewart had been one of his heroes growing up, and Fowler still remembered the moment when he heard about the plane crash in October of 1999. He was in the car with his mother, and news of the tragedy was broadcast over the radio. He broke down crying, and fifteen years later, in his first round at Pinehurst, he wore white knickers and a pair of teal argyle socks, Stewart's signature outfit.

Phil Mickelson, runner-up to Payne, had gone on to five more second-place finishes at the U.S. Open—the kind of success that you can only call brutal. It's the one tournament that eluded him, over and over, all the way up to 2013, when he had started the final round in the lead, only to shoot 74 and lose to England's Justin Rose. He was viewed as something of a tragic figure after that event—someone destined never to fulfill his dream at his country's national tournament. He spit the pity right back in everyone's face later that summer, though, winning his first ever British Open. Now the U.S. Open was the only tournament standing between Mickelson and a career grand slam, and he arrived at Pinehurst as the overwhelming crowd favorite.

Unfortunately for him, his past success at the course meant very little. The Pinehurst no. 2 that greeted players this time was miles different from the track they'd played in 1999 and 2005. Back then, it looked like a typical U.S. Open course—very green, with thick rough and the usual USGA trapdoors. Some of that remained the same—the "par-4" fourth hole, at 529 yards, was the longest par 4 in U.S. Open history, just edging out the "par-4" 16th, a 528-yard beast. Both play as a par 5 at every other time of year, and are changed only to make everyone's score eight shots worse by the end of the week. The par-3s, too, were punishingly long, with the shortest clocking in with a standard length of 191.

Beyond those USGA special effects, though, the course looked nothing like its previous iterations.

In 2010, the resort took the bold step of commissioning a total restoration to Pinehurst no. 2—a return to the course as it looked before the U.S. Opens, and to the 1935 design undertaken by legendary designer Donald Ross. The team of Ben Crenshaw and Bill Coore were hired to handle the job, and in the broadest sense, the aim of their project was to make Pinehurst no. 2 reflect the natural terrain of North Carolina's Sandhills, as it had all those years ago.

The Sandhills represent an interesting geographical phenomenon—a holdout from a time, twenty million years ago, when the ocean encroached farther inland, and places like Pinehurst were still a beach. Sandy dunes built up on the shores, and they remain as remnants of an ancient era. Today, they fight for turf with towering pine trees, and form a boundary between the plateau region called the Piedmont and the coastal plain that extends to the ocean. The land is dry and hard-baked, covered with pine needles and sand, and it doesn't have the kind of soil that can produce acres and acres of green rough without enormous amounts of water.

The restoration came at the head of a broader water conservation movement in golf, and the first big move that Crenshaw and Coore made was to get rid of the Bermuda rough altogether—forty acres of it, in total, along with hundreds of sprinkler heads. They let the "native area" take over where thick grass once soaked up endless gallons of water, and to make the course more difficult, they imported more than eighty thousand clumps of *aristida stricta*—the wire grass that was used to fill the areas outside the fairway. This move introduced an element of chance to a player's round. Full recovery was now possible from the new native areas, far more so than it had ever been in the dense rough, but a ball could also land beneath one of the many clumps, and force a player to chip out sideways.

Crenshaw and Coore used old archived aerial photographs, as well as an old mainline irrigation system, to restore some of the curves of the old course that had been straightened in the modern era. They widened fairways to reward players who drive down the proper side. They kept the greens' domed shape that had developed over the years, choosing not to flatten them to '36 standards and thus lower the difficulty, and they accentuated old bunkers, humps, and swales that had been forgotten with the narrowed fairways.

Pinehurst no. 2 was never meant to be a so-called parkland course, with verdant expanses of greens. As Coore said, the course had its origins in the rough-and-tumble style native to the Sandhills, and if it didn't represent that visual style today, right down to the plants lining the fairway, it would be a geographical impostor.

The final product looked a little like a links course, but a lot more like something you'd see in the hot, desertlike climates of Australia. In what became their most controversial choice of all, Coore and Crenshaw allowed the climate to determine the color of the Bermuda grass. The dry, midsummer heat produced more than a few patches of brown and yellow—especially at the fairway edges, where the center row irrigation system distributed water unevenly. They liked the way the grass faded by the native areas, but they also knew how it would look on television, and they knew that the beauty of their restoration might be compromised with the flattening perspective of cameras. The owners and executives of the course knew it, too, and they took a big risk in order to produce one of the country's most unique courses.

To those who understood and appreciated golf, the restoration of Pinehurst no. 2 was recognized as a progressive, sepia-toned masterpiece, and one that succeeded brilliantly in balancing the sport's future with its historical roots. In December, the course won *Golf Digest*'s Green Star Award for Outstanding Environmental Practices, and in 2015, the resort estimated they would use fifteen million gallons of water on the course, compared to fifty-five million in 2009.

Nevertheless, no good deed goes unpunished. For the legions of simpletons who were conditioned to expect nothing but miles and miles of generic parkland green, the course became a target for uninformed vitriol. It should come as little surprise that Donald Trump emerged as the ringleader of the buffoons and blowhards.

"I'd bet the horrible look of Pinehurst translates in poor television ratings," he tweeted. "That is not what golf is about!"

Bubba Watson was the most critical of the players, calling the natural areas "weeds," and expressing his disappointment with the difficulty of landing an approach on the greens. But even he admitted that the blind tee shots simply didn't fit his style—Watson is a player who wins tournaments by bludgeoning long courses to death, and the events that require a great amount of finesse around the greens will always be difficult.

Naysayers aside, Coore and Crenshaw earned heaps of praise for the job they'd done. Pinehurst had its character back, and though it didn't look the same as most American courses, it only took a second glance to recognize the beauty in the difference.

A few interesting stories cropped up before Thursday's opening round. For one thing, the USGA decided to get a bit cheeky with its pairings. They've been known to group golfers "thematically" over the first two days of U.S. Open competition, but this time they decided to really flex their creative muscles with one threesome.

When Kevin Stadler, Brandon de Jonge, and Shane Lowry saw themselves in the same group, there was no mistaking the intent of those rapscallions behind the USGA curtains: They had created a fat group.

The Golf Channel's Jason Sobel got on the story first, and all three players had different reactions. Stadler didn't appreciate the "five-year-old sense of humor," but it wasn't the first time it had happened to him, and he accepted the situation with as much good humor as he could muster. "It's not like I don't pretend that I'm not a fat-ass," he told Sobel. Lowry, on the other hand, had been trying to get in shape for most of the year, and was seriously frustrated with the USGA, calling the move "a mockery" in a weekly column for the *Irish Times*. Brandon

De Jonge completed the emotional triangle—he thought the whole thing was funny.

Of course, the USGA didn't cop to anything, but this was old hat for them. As Chris Chase pointed out in *USA Today*, they once put three women together at the women's U.S. Open based on the fact that all three were in therapy. In a way, you had to admire them for staying true to character—if they were abundantly cruel in their course setup, why should the pairings be any different?

That drama aside, some things stayed the same. Patrick Reed and Victor Dubuisson played practice rounds by themselves, questions were asked about Tiger's absence, and the players predicted a collective catastrophe as the brutal North Carolina heat baked the course and hardened the greens. Martin Kaymer told reporters that he'd be happy with +8 for the week.

The forecast called for rain on Wednesday night, but though storms raged across North Carolina, very little fell on Pinehurst. This had a paradoxical effect—in a rare act of mercy, the USGA took the unprecedented measure of actually making the course *easier*. The complaints had reached them—they watered the greens that night, and again before the first tee times on Thursday, and suddenly, Pinehurst no. 2 could be had.

The whole organization must have looked on in abject horror as players actually *scored* on Thursday, and they were probably near suicidal that night, when the rain came and softened the course yet again for the second round on Friday. When the dust settled at day's end, an ungodly thirteen players had finished under par, including McIlroy, Spieth, Dustin Johnson, Keegan Bradley, and Brendon Todd.

Towering above them all, Martin Kaymer had ravaged the course in an unrepentant, one-man blitzkrieg. In two previous U.S. Opens at Pinehurst, no golfer had ever shot a 65. On Thursday and Friday, Martin Kaymer did it twice. He finished the second round at 10-under.

That put him six shots ahead of Brendon Todd, his nearest competition, who *thought* he had played terrific golf. When he watched coverage Friday morning, though, he saw Martin Kaymer hit a shot that landed ten feet left of the pin on the par-3 17th, and was shocked to see

The resilient, star-crossed Jason Day walks ahead of Tiger.
Scott Halleran/Getty Images Sport/Getty Images

Victor Dubuisson, the man of mystery, escapes from the desert at the WGC Accenture Match Play Championship.   Kohjiro Kinno/*Sports Illustrated*/Getty Images

Tiger tries to fight off Father Time in what will be his last tournament for three months.
Fred Vuich/*Sports Illustrated*/Getty Images

Patrick Reed, the sport's rising villain, shares the WGC trophy with Donald Trump.
Fred Vuich/*Sports Illustrated*/Getty Images

The irrepressible Matt Every from behind a tree at Bay Hill.
Sam Greenwood/Getty Images Sport/Getty Images

Bubba Watson at Augusta hours before his big win.
Robert Beck/*Sports Illustrated*/Getty Images

Seung-Yul Noh and Keegan Bradley with a soul shake in New Orleans.
Marianna Massey/Getty Images Sport/Getty Images

Martin Kaymer and Jordan Spieth on Sunday at the Players Championship.
Chris Condon/US PGA TOUR/Getty Images

The fluke, Derek Ernst, hard at work.   Maddie Meyer/Getty Images Sport/Getty Images

Sunday at Pinehurst with Rickie Fowler and Kaymer.
Ross Kinnaird/Getty Images Sport/Getty Images

Rory McIlroy at Hoylake, with a sneer for the competition.
Angus Murray/*Sports Illustrated*/Getty Images

Dustin Johnson at Hoylake, trying to chase down McIlroy.
Ian Walton/R & A/Getty Images

The wolf and the lamb.   Sam Greenwood/Getty Images Sport/Getty Images

McIlroy basks in the camera glow as night falls on Valhalla.
Fred Vuich/*Sports Illustrated* Classic/Getty Images

Billy Horschel celebrates after a clutch putt brings him closer to $10 million.
Sam Greenwood/Getty Images Sport/Getty Images

that the German looked upset. "Those were my *good* shots this week," he marveled later.

On Saturday, the crushing heat had returned just in time to coincide with the USGA's remorseless campaign to avenge the results of the first two days. The course was naturally faster, and they augmented the challenge by pulling out their toughest pin locations yet. Nobody was sure how this would affect the huge gap at the top of the leaderboard. Did it make it harder for Kaymer, since he was more likely to shoot a huge number and come back to the field? Or did it essentially close the barn door after the thoroughbred horse had sprinted away, making it impossible for anyone to catch him?

Of the sixty-seven golfers who made the cut, only two shot an under-par round on Saturday—Rickie Fowler and Erik Compton. Both posted 67s, which amounted to a heroic effort under the circumstances. It vaulted both men into a tie for second, but the bad news was that Kaymer, who wore the same pink shirt with blue trimming that had seen him through the final round at Sawgrass a month earlier, survived some early trouble and posted a 72. He had lost just two strokes, and maintained a five-shot lead with only Sunday's round remaining. It never looked quite as easy as the first two days—on the fourth hole, he pulled his tee shot into the pine straw on the left, where it rested in a "wash out" area, which left his ball obstructed by a ridge of needles. When a rules official told him he was allowed to move "loose impediments" as long as his ball didn't move, Kaymer stared at the man in disbelief.

"It's *all* loose," he said. "How should I know?"

"Be careful," the man advised.

Kaymer shook his head and turned to his caddie, Craig "Wee Man" Connelly. "If you have any idea how to play it, I'll follow you."

Wisely, they took a drop. The ensuing bogey dropped him to -8, but a spectacular approach out of the waste area on the par-5 fifth gave him a five-foot eagle putt, which he canned to return to even on the day. On the sixth, Pinehurst struck again when he sent a birdie putt past the hole. It rolled and rolled, all the way down a slope and off the green. Kaymer just laughed, rolled his par putt up to the hole, and took a happy bogey. He dropped two more shots on 13 and 15—a drunkard screamed his name as he stood over his putt on 15, forcing him to retreat—but on 18, he scrounged a final shot back with a birdie.

Kaymer had watched *Bagger Vance* the day before, and maybe that's why he managed to keep his perspective even as the course threw its first curveballs of the week. For Brendon Todd, playing in the last group of a major for the first time, the pressure and the course proved to be a deadly combination—he spiraled down the leaderboard with a 79. Even his trusty putter abandoned him, and by day's end, he had played his way out of contention. He chalked up the 2014 U.S. Open to a lesson learned.

"I like to be in control of things. It's the way I think a lot of Germans are. But at the end of the day, you have to feel on the golf course. You have to create that feel and trust your skill and all the work. And today when I was standing on 18, that's a tough tee shot. There's pretty much no fairway. It's very difficult to see any fairway from the back tee. So you stand there, and for me it was such an enjoyable shot, because I knew exactly where I wanted to aim and I thought, what a great position this is now. You are 7-under par at the U.S. Open, playing your third round . . . and it's about that feel, that touch, that you play with your heart, that you can't control too many things. That's what I was trying to do the last three years. Now I just play."

—Martin Kaymer

"He kind of killed the event in the first two days."

—Henrik Stenson

Kaymer told reporters on Saturday night that he wanted another tough track for Sunday's round, thus resolving a media room debate. The bigwigs at NBC likely disagreed, as it was the network's last year broadcasting the event after losing a bidding war the previous summer to FOX, who earned the rights in a twelve-year, billion-dollar deal. They wanted drama, and Kaymer was depriving them. The best thing that could happen would be for the German to falter early, while Fowler or Compton made a run to close the gap.

Their margin for error was incredibly slim, and there was a definite feeling on Sunday morning that the only real battle would be for second place. Kaymer had already played his bad round, and *that* turned out not to be very bad at all—just two shots over par, and barely a dent in his nice lead.

For Erik Compton, even second place would be quite the coup. His story, which spread like wildfire that week, was enough to make you cry. Not that he'd want the pity. Compton is perhaps the most resilient golfer in the world, judging by the fact that he's still competing at the highest levels despite undergoing two transplants of the most vital organ of all. All other hardships pale—the man is on his third heart.

Ian O'Connor, among others, chronicled the story on *ESPN.com,* and NBC ran a tearjerker of a feature during Sunday's round. When he was only nine, Compton found out he had come down with viral cardiomyopathy. Doctors tried to pump him with steroids to keep him alive, and as a result, his face swelled up to twice its normal size, hair grew everywhere, and he became a social pariah. Deep inside, he knew he still had the body of an athlete, but he didn't fit in with the other kids, couldn't go back to school, and felt like a grotesque freak—a self-image that was confirmed when other kids mocked him relentlessly whenever he went out in public. It became clear that the steroids wouldn't work, so at age twelve, he received a heart transplant from a girl who had been killed by a drunk driver.

He became a great golfer, and as he made his way through Georgia and into the pros, he thought he would live forever on the new heart. It lasted just sixteen years. In 2007, he felt intense pain in his chest as

he was driving home from his home course, and he knew exactly what
it meant. He made a dash for the hospital, but deep down, he didn't
think he could make it. He phoned his mother on the way to say goodbye—a last goodbye—and continued to speed to the ER. He made it
just in time, staggering in as he coughed up blood, and they saved him
again. Seven months later, a twenty-six-year-old motorcyclist named
Isaac Klosterman was hit by a Dodge truck on a Florida highway, and
the crash killed him. His heart was transplanted into Compton's body,
and it was this heart that he carried to Pinehurst.

Rickie Fowler came out to the range at two thirty, dressed in orange and
white, with a bright white hat, and Kaymer followed ten minutes later.
The temperature was threatening ninety degrees, and the humidity
struck just as hard. The German, despite the slick sheen of sweat on the
back of his neck and arms, looked cool as can be. He told a TV crew that
Sunday would be the "toughest day in my career," and a comedian in the
gallery shouted out, "World War Two!" Kaymer wore a white shirt with
the usual logos—Mercedes, Hugo Boss, and SAP, a German software
company, emblazoned on his hat. German legend Bernhard Langer had
been texting him throughout the week, and though he knew the American fans might be slightly hostile on this final day, he seemed comfortable in his own skin.

He made his way to the putting green, where an LPGA golfer
named Jenny Shin, preparing for next week's women's Open, was using
a putting device. Kaymer eyed it with interest, and Shin offered to sell
it to him for a million dollars. With just the hint of a smile, Kaymer
declined.

The red rail cars of an Aberdeen Carolina & Western train slum-
bered in the background, and Butch Harmon stood watching Fowler
hit shots on the range. Kaymer settled two spots down, with his dingy
old club covers—a lion, and one that may have been an otter, or beaver,
or gopher. He and Fowler never exchanged a word. Erik Compton
came out wearing Georgia red, and gave Fowler a fist bump on his way.

Kaymer left soon after, worked his way back to the giant scoreboard, and chipped up to the practice green.

After an hour, Fowler left the range first—Kaymer always makes them wait. When they finally shook hands at the first tee, it was quick and formal. The air was already thick with dust from and pollen from the massive pines, and at 3:35, they stared down the first fairway, ready to battle each other and the elements.

Church bells rang as Kaymer struck his opening drive a day earlier, but all you could hear Sunday were dragonflies coasting lazily in the heat and the distant drone of NBC's blimp as the German put his first shot on the fairway. As was to be expected, nobody in the early groups had made any kind of run at his lead. The course would play easier, but not much easier—there were certainly no 63s to be had. The field might have entertained delusions of catching him on Saturday, but now it was clear that Kaymer could only beat himself. The course could help in that regard, and so could the fact that he would be facing another Ryder Cup atmosphere; he had taken down one of America's young darlings in Jordan Spieth at the Players Championship, and now he was drawn head-to-head with the other.

The day would be defined by mistakes, as with most U.S. Opens, and Fowler made the first on his approach to the opening green, which came up well short and fell off the front slope. His chip was mediocre, but he holed the eight-footer for par to match Kaymer's easy two-putt. A reprieve, for now, and up ahead, news came slowly—Brandt Snedeker had bogeyed, Compton was still at -3, and neither Dustin Johnson nor Henrik Stenson were making any waves.

On the long par-4 second, with its impossible angled green that only 30 percent of players were hitting in regulation, Kaymer found the waste area with his drive, then hit his approach over the green. Intimidated by the speed of Pinehurst's greens, he grabbed the putter to avoid a hazardous chip, his least favorite shot. Soft egg or not, the shot set a pattern for the day—when in doubt, facing a hard green, Kaymer chose to putt. He executed the up-and-down, sinking a brutal twister for par, and Fowler missed his birdie attempt after an excellent approach and had to settle for his own par.

The third hole, a drivable par 4 at 308 yards, demonstrated yet again that fate was smiling on Kaymer. A player aiming for the right side of the green would have to clear the bunker by a foot or less, and hope that it wouldn't roll off the back of the slick green. The landing space was probably a yard or two wide at best, but from 290 yards away, Kaymer's tee shot touched down right in its heart. That gave him two putts for birdie, and he gained a stroke as Fowler settled for par. Now, at -9, leading by six shots, Kaymer was in his strongest position yet.

Fowler couldn't afford to make even the slightest mistake, but he made a big one on the fourth. With his approach 227 yards away on Pinehurst's toughest hole—and the longest par 4 in U.S. Open history—he pushed his shot toward a scoreboard, among a deep bed of pine needles. Fans had cheered when Kaymer's drive went left, hoping for a Fowler surge, but now they grew silent. Kaymer's approach, a lovely draw, hit the green and rolled off, but set up another long lag putt for par.

For Rickie, the hole was just beginning—his pitch from the pine straw was disastrous, flying over the green and coming to rest behind a tree that blocked him from the green. He had to chip out sideways, and only then could he pitch up the slope and onto the green. By the time he finally reached the putting surface, he was staring down twenty feet for a double bogey.

He made the putt, and the fans tried to rally him, but he had dropped to -1 for the tournament, eight shots off the lead. His chances, slim as they were, had come to an end, and everybody knew it. He looked a little crestfallen, and Kaymer patted him on the chest with the same sympathy he'd shown Spieth at the Players Championship.

Fowler picked himself up quickly, though, and here you could see the difference between him and Spieth—it's not in Fowler's nature to sulk or complain. The tournament was lost, but Fowler bore that reality with stoicism and grace as he fought on through the back nine.

As the leaders walked to the fifth hole, Phil Mickelson finished his day with a bogey to sink to +7—another U.S. Open dream deferred for the six-time runner-up.

I walked with Philip Kaymer, Martin's brother, for a while, and he told me that no, he wasn't nervous, and that the unidentified animal among Martin's club covers was a beaver that had lost its teeth. Mystery solved.

Erik Compton made birdie on the fifth hole, and when Kaymer missed his own birdie chance, he had just one challenger left to vanquish before he could bag his second major title. On the seventh, faced with a dicey pitch over a bunker after pulling his approach left, Kaymer again let caution be his guide, putting to the right of the bunker and essentially accepting bogey rather than flirting with disaster and the sand. His mind must have been back at the Players, and the 15th hole, when he turned an easy win into a nervous finish when he tried to play too perfectly into the green. Compton fought back to -4 with a birdie on the ninth, and for the first time all day, the deficit had hit four shots.

The margin waffled back and forth between four and six over the next four holes. Compton needed something special, but when he bogeyed the 11th and 12th holes, it gave Kaymer, now at -8, the chance to close the door for good. On the 13th, with the tees moved up to make the par 4 almost reachable off the tee, Kaymer drove into the right bunkers, played up softly from the sand to leave himself a birdie putt of about twenty feet underneath the hole, and sunk it. One hole later, on the long par-4 14th, he hit a metal wood off the tee, barely reached the green on his approach, and poured in a twenty-eight-footer for birdie to reach -10.

He pumped his fist, and allowed himself a small smile. With his nearest competition eight shots behind with four holes to play, it was finally over.

Compton and Fowler finished tied at -1, the only two players other than Kaymer to beat par. It was Fowler's second straight top-five major finish, and the latest demonstration of how his game had rounded into complete form under Butch Harmon. The finish was a triumph for Compton, too, who had prevailed under the toughest possible conditions to show that he belonged with the best players in the world, third heart and all. "It felt like a sacred place," he told NBC, taking one last glance at Pinehurst.

But the championship belonged to the German. He holed a fifteen-foot par putt on 18, leaned back in an expression of relief, and hugged his caddie. The fans roared. He had whipped their young American, but it's hard not to appreciate greatness of that magnitude. And of course, he was the toast of his own country—at least until noon the next day, when *Die Mannschaft* kicked off their World Cup campaign against Portugal, and Germany entered a monthlong soccer fever that culminated in the biggest championship of all.

For now, though, it was all Kaymer. His face went up on all the German websites, and he had struck another blow for German golf. In America, they cheered in the stands, along the ropes, and beneath the white arches of the clubhouse veranda. The day had been more stressful than Kaymer let on, but now he could wave at them, and laugh, and disappear down the stairs to sign the winning scorecard.

Kaymer was restored to his former glory, just like Pinehurst, but the stress and the heat had taken their toll. The time for enjoying the victory would come later—at the moment, exhaustion set in, and his work wasn't finished. The ceremonies and the interviews dragged on, and at the very end of his final press conference, someone asked the question he hated more than any other: What about those swing changes?

He answered calmly enough, at first, but he had reached his breaking point. What happened next was the closest I've ever seen Kaymer come to losing his temper.

"So why is that? So why do you change?" he asked the room, a hard edge creeping into his words. "So you have to answer all of those questions, and you don't want to answer those questions all the time. You answer them once or twice and then that should be enough. But people keep going and I keep answering and answering. *'Why do you change if you win a Major, you become number one in the world?'* And it's annoying. You don't want to talk about that all the time. . . . And, you know, I don't want to be rude to people, so that's why I kept answering. But I want to say that's enough. I think we talked about it many times before and now I'm sitting here with the U.S. Open, so there's no change."

Mercifully, then, they let him go—off through the glass doors, into the Carolina night. And somewhere in that darkness, the Kaymer Wave of 2014 crested and broke.

17

BETHESDA, MARYLAND

Congressional; Tiger's Return, Jason Day's Dystopia;
Reed and Rose

"I feel old."
—TIGER WOODS

The greatest golfer since Jack Nicklaus sighed as he sat behind the microphone in a jam-packed media room in Bethesda, Maryland, on the grounds of Congressional Country Club. He fielded questions with a forced smile. Did he believe he could win, in his first tournament back from serious surgery? Well, yes, but it would be hard. Had he changed his swing to protect himself from further injury? A bit, here and there. Was he truly pain free?

"Other than the headache of coming in here?"

We laughed at the tepid joke, bound by duty, but our hearts weren't in it, and his wasn't either. After boasting about how fast he had healed, thanks to an army of physios and nutritionists and surgeons and shamans and God knows what else, Tiger admitted that he wouldn't even be *playing* at Congressional—now with a brand-new sponsor in Quicken Loans—if it wasn't *his* tournament, benefiting *his* foundation. Business aside, he would have targeted the British Open for his return.

That Tuesday, the truth became clear long before he stepped on the course: This would not be a triumphant return. He had barely even begun to take full swings, he lacked his former explosiveness, and until recently he'd been forced to stand on the back of moving golf carts during rounds, because it was too painful to endure the bumps when he sat down.

Watching Tiger was to see a living, breathing paradox. As he compared himself to an aging Michael Jordan—"I've got a fadeaway now," he said, with a halfhearted grin—his shoulders seemed to slump with fatigue. While he bragged about his healing powers, his body language told the real story—Tiger wasn't ready, and shouldn't have been playing. Around the media room, two schools of thought emerged. The first gave Tiger the benefit of the doubt, and assumed, on the basis of his greatness, that he'd find a way to rise to the occasion. The rest of us, looking at the situation dispassionately, saw the facts: There was no way in hell he was making the cut, and he'd be lucky not to aggravate his damaged back.

Tiger shot 74-75 and missed the cut, but he managed not to hurt himself. That would come later.

———————

"There's an old joke—um . . . two elderly women are at a Catskill mountain resort, and one of 'em says, 'Boy, the food at this place is really terrible.' The other one says, 'Yeah, I know; and such small portions.' Well, that's essentially how I feel about life—full of loneliness, and misery, and suffering, and unhappiness, and it's all over much too quickly."

—Woody Allen

In stark contrast to Tiger's performance, in a sparsely attended presser later that day, Jason Day looked back on a difficult year with his usual honesty. After the win at the Match Play Championship over Dubuisson, he thought he had a real chance to rise to the world number 1 ranking and contend at majors. If you watched the patterns of Day's life, though, you might have predicted what was coming around the bend. A fluke ligament injury in his left thumb—painful enough to make him flinch at impact, which is death to a golf swing—led to a withdrawal at Bay Hill, a cortisone shot in Columbus, a reaggravation at the Masters, and subsequent rehab that kept him out until late May. He managed a backdoor fourth at the U.S. Open, well behind Kaymer, but even with that top-five finish, his year felt like a letdown.

In his time off, Day would watch golf at home, and each new Sunday delivered a hard reminder that he was far from the course. He became moody on those days, as his fellow pros fought for a win. I asked him about the contrast—life on Tour can be a circus, with never-ending obligations and very little downtime, but I suspected it didn't seem quite so bad from the other side of things.

"It's just funny," he said. "Sometimes when you're out here, you're like, 'Just leave me alone.' But then you're by yourself on the couch alone, you're like, 'I want to get back out there.' It's kind of like a double-edged sword. . . . I was playing a lot of things over in my head, a lot of negative things."

It's the kind of vulnerable sentiment Tiger would never share—the million little headaches that dog them from week to week pale in comparison to the big depression of missing out entirely.

Professional golfers can sometimes embody the old ladies in the Catskills from Woody Allen's bit—kvetching about the day-to-day problems, getting tied up in petty angers and complaints, and rapidly losing sight of the fact that they play a game for a living. But the minute it's gone, they come face-to-face with the horror of the abyss. Life without golf, away from the rush of competition, can hit a player hard, and that's the dystopian future Day and Woods had to contemplate in their time off.

In contrast to Day's honesty, it's hard to know how Tiger tangled with those moments. Ever since Charlie Pierce wrote a story in *GQ* about Tiger making a racial joke, way back in 1997, he's been a closed book to the media. All we get is accidental glimpses—his fierce anger, or the slew of dirty text messages he sent to his mistresses. Most revealing of all was a text he sent to porn star Joslyn James, which showed his deep fear of being exposed and gave us a hint of how he must have felt less than a month later, on Thanksgiving:

"Don't Fucking talk to me. You almost just ruined my whole life. If my agent and these guys would have seen you there, Fuck."

Then there are the times when he tries to get media figures fired for criticizing him, as he did with Brandel Chamblee, who essentially called him a cheater, or Dan Jenkins, who wrote a satirical conversation with Woods that Tiger thought would be misinterpreted.

Aside from these dramatic exceptions, we get very little emotional honesty from Tiger. Maybe humility and perspective just isn't possible for him—after all, he grew up with a father who repeatedly told people that his son would be the next Gandhi. And maybe his tremendous ego, bolstered by years of unbelievable results, makes him somewhat delusional in the twilight of his career. Maybe he really *did* believe he could win at Congressional, or that he could catch Nicklaus with eighteen majors.

But watching him on the stage that Tuesday, he looked like someone who had been worn down by the sheer magnitude of his own life. I think he knew, at least intuitively, that the ride was coming to an end. He'll never be capable of assessing himself honestly and taking a broader view of life—he's too wrapped up in his own mythos, even after the crash—you get the sense that it will be difficult for Tiger to handle his descent into mediocrity.

More than anything else that day, I wondered about his happiness—is he capable of stepping outside himself, and the larger-than-life realities that being Tiger Woods entails, and experiencing joy? Or does he just waver between grim satisfaction and anger, depending on his results?

Tiger would never be Day—by this point, his life has become too constricted. By the same token, Day could never be Tiger, because how many human beings can exist at that exhausting level, even for a year? The hyperbolic greatness that Tiger has achieved requires unflinching self-belief and a sacrifice of some basic humanity—especially in the modern technological bubble—while Day's ability to retain a more nuanced, healthy mind-set may limit what he can achieve on the course.

And the real puzzle is this: Would either of them change places, if they could?

Congressional Country Club, a few miles northwest of the nation's capital, has been home to presidents, captains of industry, and four major championships. Rory decimated the Blue Course to the tune of -16 at the 2011 U.S. Open, but it generally plays difficult, and players in 2014 met the most challenging version of the track since the Quicken Loans National—formerly the AT&T National—began in 2007.

It didn't show its teeth right away. Patrick Reed, finally rounding back into form after a midseason slump that coincided with the birth of his daughter Windsor-Wells, posted two straight 68s to grab a tie for the thirty-six-hole lead. Others lingered close behind, with a 65 from Justin Rose setting the low mark on Friday.

The rough grew thicker over the weekend, and the bentgrass greens sped up in the heat. For the first time, it began to look like a U.S. Open course, and the scores followed suit. Reed made two straight bogeys to end the front nine on Saturday—and missed a slew of makeable birdie putts on the back nine—but the fact that he even had a chance at birdie put him above the competition. He fought back to -6 with a birdie at 16, and made an excellent sand save on 17 to preserve his lead. The one great round of the day belonged to Seung-Yul Noh, whose 66 vaulted him to -4, and a spot in the final group with Reed, two shots ahead.

After the round, I asked Marc Leishman, also at -4, whether he'd prefer to be in the final group or the second-to-last group in his situation, when his score would be the same either way. Was it better to have the leader in your sights all day, or to avoid the spotlight and sneak up from outside of the final pairing? His answer was the equivalent of a shrug—"I'm pretty happy with the position I'm in, to be honest, second last. Not a whole lot of attention . . . it doesn't worry me either way."

When I asked Reed to put himself in Leishman's shoes and ponder the same question, he didn't hesitate: "I'd definitely be in the last group."

Another bit of evidence, maybe, in the endless mystery of what separates the very good from the great.

The Congressional clubhouse is a stately, arresting Spanish Revival mansion with red-tile roofs and umbrella-dotted balconies that overlook the 18th green and its small lake—a body of water fed by Cabin John Creek, a tributary branch of the Potomac. The hole makes for such a dramatic venue that it was changed from the 17th to the 18th before the 2011 U.S. Open. Eastern red cedars with their pale blue berries spring up around the clubhouse, and give way to sycamores, dogwoods, and crimson king maples, along with a spectacular Norway spruce behind the 16th green.

Outside that clubhouse on Sunday, in the minutes before the day's final tee time, Seung-Yul Noh chipped and putted by himself. No caddie, no media, no fans—just a lone golfer, and his unreadable thoughts.

Reed emerged moments later in his Sunday best—black pants and Tiger-red shirt, complete with Tax Slayer and Callaway logos. In his presence, Noh almost seemed to shrink. Reed had held a fifty-four-hole lead three times in his career, and all three times, he'd gone on to win the tournament. He valued his reputation as a closer, and at this early stage of his career, it formed the basis of his identity.

Reed's meltdown began on the 10th, a downhill par 3 over the lake, when his tee-shot splashed lightly in the water. The fans standing on the stone wall above him groaned, and Reed smashed a tee box with his club—an unpatriotic move, considering there was a picture of the Capital rotunda engraved on each marker.

"Not a top-five shot!" yelled a loud voice from the gallery, and Reed's face flushed red.

From the drop zone, Reed hit into the right rough, dropped an emphatic "fuck!", and made double bogey. On the 11th, he pushed his drive hard right—there was now a definite trend of him missing in that direction—and proceeded to hit a fairway metal over a small arched footbridge and into the creek. By the time it was over, he had another double bogey, and dropped all the way to -2. Meanwhile, Noh failed to get out of a bunker, and made double bogey of his own. That was just the start of the carnage. The two players seemed to be following a mutual collapse accord, and they weren't alone—eyeballing the leaderboard, you only had to think someone's name, and *voilà,* they dropped. Reed and Noh had it the worst, though; by day's end, the man in red had shot 77, and Noh came in at 8-over on the back nine alone.

I followed Reed until the 13th, and made sure I was in the media flash area when he left the course. Noh came ahead of him, nodding politely to the media. As expected, Reed followed under a black cloud, seething with barely contained fury. As he signed his card, a Tour official asked if he could step out and talk to the media. He grunted an unfriendly no. "But they're all assembled right here, Patrick." Same grunt—no way.

Justin Rose—a kind of cipher, but one who carries himself with inscrutable politeness—would go on to win the tournament in a playoff. What I'd remember most about Congressional, though, was Reed, and our first indication that he may not be the second coming of Tiger. He answered two questions for TV, signed a couple of photographs, and then disappeared with Kessler and Justine. He cuts an intimidating shape when he wins, but that day, stomping off into the distance, he gave off a very different impression. He looked like a spoiled, churlish boy playing dress-up—the kind of kid who throws a fit when he doesn't get his way.

JULY

A British Midsummer

18

HOYLAKE, MERSEYSIDE COUNTY, ENGLAND

Royal Liverpool and the British Open; Biased Wind, Slanted Rain; The Rory Wave

Q. You said in April that the game was just waiting for somebody, for one of the best players to stand up and take it by the scruff of the next. Do you feel this is a platform to do that sort of thing?
RORY MCILROY: I hope so. I definitely hope so.
—BMW PGA Championship, May 25, 2014

"All the stories have been told
Of Kings and days of old
But there's no England now."
—The Kinks

On to England—England after the age of empire, with its profound identity crisis and lingering gentility. The Open Championship— call it the "British Open" at your own peril—is the oldest major in the world, and, to European golfers, the most prestigious. It's almost always played on links courses—"linksland" being the rolling, sandy stretches between the beach and the arable mainland. As David Owen wrote in *The New Yorker,* this is where, sometime around the start of the fifteenth century, Scottish shepherds invented golf on the terrain that would come to define the look of modern courses. Sheep and cattle grazed the fairways, coarse grasses grew wild in the rough, livestock huddled together in the bitter winds to form the sandy depressions that became bunkers, and hungry rabbits with low jawbones chewed the grass to the quick on the tees and greens.

Aside from that common history, there's not much thematic consistency to the Open from year to year, especially when compared to the U.S. Open. The courses can be relatively easy like St. Andrew's— where the last three winning scores have been -16, -14, and Tiger Woods's record-setting -19 in 2000—or they can be brutally difficult, in the Royal Birkdale mode, where Padraig Harrington's +3 carried the day in 2008. Even on the same course, conditions can vary wildly with the weather. When the driving wind and rain are working in concert, there is no such thing as an easy links course.

The 2014 Open landed at Royal Liverpool Golf Club. To reach the grounds, you have to leave the port city from which it takes its name, cross the River Mersey, and make your way to the west coast of the Wirral Peninsula and into the coastal village of Hoylake. It's a quaint little hamlet, and wealthy, but compared to the gaudy mansion communities lining the PGA Tour's American courses, you have to look close to notice. Next, take a walk down Meols Drive, beneath the privet hedges with their sweet, cloying odor, and past the brick-and-stone cottages with flower gardens and crawling vines. Here, the houses have names, and you can read them on the stone pillars marking each entrance, English to the core—Hatherleigh, Shearwater, the Coppice, Denewood, Chalgrove, Wentworth, Innesholme, Rothley, and my personal favorite, Nan's Nook.

Then it's on to the course itself, set alongside the River Dee— undulating, wind-beaten, and hard. The wild rough grows thick with tall grass, pinkish blooms of Yorkshire fog, dandelions, purple harebells, and the rough sorrel, which lends a reddish hue to the golden fescue. The wind mostly aids the golfers on the front nine, but there's an about-face starting on no. 11, when the course heads straight into the gales along the River Dee—a body of water that's more of an estuary, melding with the Irish Sea.

Look southwest, and you'll see the rocky hills of Wales less than five miles away. Look due west, squint your eyes, and use your imagination, and you may convince yourself that far out across the sea, you've caught just the faintest glimpse of Dublin—just two and a half hours away by catamaran, according to a friendly marshal.

Much was made of potential windy conditions in the week leading up to the Open, and for a good reason—Royal Liverpool needed it. Despite the rough, and the swales, this is one of the easier stops on the British Open circuit. Management tried to toughen it up a bit in 2014, still harboring a memory of 2006, when Tiger nearly equaled his own record with a score of -18. They built an extra hillock or two, but it was purely cosmetic—the greens stayed huge, and they stayed flat. As long as players managed to avoid the pot bunkers with their steep walls of sod, it was no difficult task to hit green after green in regulation, even from the rough.

All it would take from there was a few hot putters, and scores would soar. Against this fate, Mother Nature was Royal Liverpool's only protection.

Following his win at the Congressional, Justin Rose took the Scottish Open at Royal Aberdeen, and came in to Hoylake as the favorite. Adam Scott, too, had long targeted this British Open as the venue for his second major title.

Unfortunately for both of them, the bad weather did indeed hit Hoylake, and it did indeed protect the course from low scores—but only for half the field. The players who went off in the morning on Thursday had clear skies and minimal wind, and they tore up Royal Liverpool exactly as everyone expected they would. In the afternoon, though, the conditions got very ugly. The leaderboard after the first round paints the picture—of the top eighteen players, sixteen of them had teed off before noon. The only two exceptions were Shane Lowry and Adam Scott, who manfully fought their way to four-under on the day. Everyone else in the afternoon wave—all sixty-six who started their rounds after noon—failed to make an impact.

One of golf's best and truest proverbs is that you need to get lucky to win a major, but rarely do you see fate intrude this emphatically. Nevertheless, the system is designed to regulate these discrepancies, and the Open is no exception. The players who teed off in the morning on Thursday would go in the afternoon on Friday, and vice versa.

This particular safeguard, for all its good intentions, can't do anything about the vagaries of the weather. The unlucky golfers from Thursday afternoon looked on with dismay when they discovered the same conditions on Friday morning. Again, they fought wind and bouts of rain, and again, like a nightmare, the conditions became serene the minute they had finished, just in time for the afternoon wave.

By the end of play on Friday, the situation was even more exaggerated—seventeen of the top-twenty golfers had played Thursday morning and Friday afternoon, including ten of the top eleven. Adam Scott (-3) and Justin Rose (-2) were two of the three exceptions, and had arguably played some of the best golf in the field just to stay under par.

Their heroic efforts weren't good enough—nine shots ahead of Scott, and ten ahead of Rose, Rory McIlroy had taken advantage of his lucky draw. His success came with a bit of irony, since he had complained about the British Open in 2011, annoyed by how "the outcome is predicted so much by the weather." What goes around comes around, and he ripped Royal Liverpool to shreds, posting 66 on back-to-back days. He towered over the leaderboard at -12, and he had done it by burying the so-called "Friday curse." There was a feeling after Thursday's round that he might stumble the next day, as he'd done for most of the spring and summer. When he went low instead, it was like watching a wild animal break down the walls of his cage—the last barrier between the killer and his prey had collapsed, and now there would be carnage.

And the golf was exquisite. For those days in Hoylake, Rory represented the perfect confluence of finesse and power. Every swing had the imprint of genius, and the imperfections only made the entire performance more stunning. There were errant shots. There were drives that vanished into the fescue, with Rory vanishing right behind them, only to emerge moments later on the heels of a gorgeous recovery, marching up the fairway to the expansive green—an expanse he didn't need, incidentally, because his homesick ball, buried in coarse grass or resting on baked earth, would make a beeline for the pin, obstacles or bad lies or physics be damned.

Bit by bit, birdie by birdie, his score fell, and he seemed to move in his own sovereign, electric field. He glided along the fairways, up and down the laborious swales, while everyone else plodded step by heavy step. The old sensations coursed through the air, sharp currents that grew more acute with each brilliant par save, each mad scramble. The glory days of Congressional, and Kiawah Island, had come rushing back in our memories, and we knew the truth again—this virtuosity comes once in a generation, at best, and though we force the empty comparison on each new prodigy, you cannot fake the flush of recognition—the heightened awareness; the rush of greatness; the unmistakable impression that brings the name "Tiger" to the tip of every tongue.

"Ireland is the old sow that eats her farrow."
—JAMES JOYCE, in *Portrait of the Artist as a Young Man*

The life of Rory begins in Holywood, County Down, Northern Ireland, a small coastal town on the Belfast Lough, just a five-mile drive from the capital city itself. Gerry McIlroy, a onetime scratch golfer, married Rosaleen McDonald in 1998. Their only child, Rory, came along a year later, and was swinging plastic clubs before his third birthday. They weren't rich—Gerry was a bartender at the Holywood Golf Club—and they had to take on extra jobs to pay for their Rory's travels on the junior golf circuit. Gerry became a cleaner, and Rosaleen worked nights in a 3M factory, all to support their son's dream.

There is nobody born in that complicated nation who escapes the stain of sectarian violence that has battered the six counties since the partition of Ireland in 1920. While the rest of the island became the Irish Free State, and an autonomous republic in 1949, Northern Ireland remained under British control. Before long, it was a battleground in the fight between the Catholics who wanted to join the rest of Ireland and the Protestants who remained loyal to the crown. The history of the young country is one of murder and terror, of hunger strikes and bombs and broken truces. Even a young man like McIlroy, born just nine years before the Good Friday Agreement that brought a measure of peace to the nation, can't escape the ugly history.

Like many of his countrymen, Rory doesn't have to travel far back in time to find tragedy. Joe McIlroy, the brother of Rory's grandfather Jimmy, made the mistake of moving his family to a Protestant neighborhood of east Belfast in the late sixties, at the height of "The Troubles." The McIlroys are Catholic, and Joe was a computer technician who thought he and his wife and four daughters could live peacefully in the middle-class community. He was proven wrong almost immediately, enduring constant abuse as he stubbornly tried to forge an ordinary life.

In 1972, with his daughters sleeping upstairs, Joe came down to fix a washing machine in his kitchen. He didn't know that a group of gunmen from the Ulster Volunteer Force—Protestant paramilitaries—had camped out in his garden, and were waiting for him. They opened fire through the back door, and hit their target seven times. Wounded, Joe managed to fight his way into the living room, where he collapsed in the arms of his wife, Mary. She ran screaming into the street, his daughters rushed downstairs, and Joe McIlroy, thirty-two, died in his home—an example for any other Catholic who thought he could move into a Protestant neighborhood.

This was the most dramatic instance of sectarian violence affecting the McIlroys, but they were never far from the religious crucible that defined life in Northern Ireland. Rory's grandfather Jimmy repaired cranes on the Belfast docks, but was banned from the shipyards themselves, which were reserved exclusively for Protestants. He took up golf, playing at the Holywood Golf Club, where he and his sons were in the club's minority Catholic population. Even in Holywood, where the family settled, they were outnumbered by more than two-to-one.

Despite the specter of Joe's death as a haunting backdrop, the McIlroys never became extremists. Today, Rory maintains an iron silence on the political situation in Northern Ireland, and that mind-set seems to have begun with his father and grandfather, who strived to coexist in a fraught environment. Writing for *The New York Times,* Niall Stanage posited that this nonviolent approach is particularly prevalent in McIlroy's generation. You can see Rory as the most visible figure in a broad movement among young Northern Irish to let their religious affiliations fade into the background, so that they can be defined by something—*anything*—else.

At the Sullivan Upper School, Rory wore a blazer with the Gaelic motto "Lamh Foisdineach An Uachtar"—*With the gentle hand foremost*—an aspirational philosophy for a generation who were raised in the shadow of violence. This was no small gesture in Northern Ireland; personal identity has been a function of religion and politics for so long that divorcing from it seems almost revolutionary.

Then, too, Joe McIlroy's death might have played an instructive role for the family, one whose lesson resounded with greater clarity when Rory became a superstar: Maybe it wasn't the safest idea for a Catholic with a sizable platform to espouse controversial views—at least not as long as he wanted to live safely in Northern Ireland.

Rory takes this neutrality to an extreme. Before he won his first majors, it was difficult to discern whether he was Catholic or Protestant. The same could be said for Graeme McDowell, who was raised in a Protestant family—neither spoke about their backgrounds unless they were forced, and even then they used broad language, careful never to be pinned down to a single controversial view.

You can count on two hands the number of times Rory's religious background has infringed on his public life—a remarkable feat of discretion for one of the world's greatest golfers, especially considering his outgoing nature. The first big intrusion came after his triumph at Congressional Country Club, when the twenty-two-year-old won the 2011

U.S. Open by eight strokes for his first major title. What happened in the immediate aftermath—a brief, unremarkable moment for anyone who didn't understand the tensions of his home nation—reverberated back home.

As the *Daily Mail* described it, a fan threw an Irish flag at Rory as he walked away from the 18th hole. He caught it instinctually, the feed cut away, and when it returned a moment later, the flag was gone.

The mystery of the vanishing tricolor sparked an online furor, with loyalist Protestant populations praising McIlroy and nationalist Catholics accusing him of everything up to and including treason. Internet message boards burned with rhetoric and armchair analysis, Facebook pages sprouted up, and in some quarters, the whole episode overshadowed the stellar week of golf that had earned him his first major championship. Nobody actually knew what happened to the flag, but what became exceedingly clear in the aftermath was that Rory had been right to stay quiet—it proved, beyond a shadow of a doubt, that when it came to Northern Irish politics, he was damned both ways.

The two times McIlroy was asked whether he felt more Irish or British—first by the PGA Tour, second by Fox Sports—he answered with the same word: "Pass." Later, he gave insight into the thought process that had governed much of his career, saying, "I have to be very careful in what I say and do."

He would have liked nothing better than to avoid the topic entirely, but as it happened, the International Golf Federation successfully lobbied the IOC to have golf included in the 2016 and 2020 Olympics. For McIlroy, who had played for Ireland in World Cups, it brought up a dicey question: Who would he represent if he played in the 2016 Games?

"I'd probably play for Great Britain," he told *The Telegraph* in 2009. "I have a British passport. It's a bit of an awkward question still."

A rash comment by his standards, and it provoked the expected reaction. Ireland is known for turning against its brightest and best, and if they needed an excuse to vilify Rory, they had it. Stanage, in *The New York Times,* quoted another famous line from Joyce—"When the soul of a man is born in this country, there are nets flung at it to hold it back." As if to prove her point, rumors about Rory's Olympic decision, and all the reactionary condemnations that came along with it, forced him to write an open letter on his Twitter account in 2012.

"Having just won three out of my last four tournaments," he began, "including a second Major Championship, I was hoping that my success on the golf course would be the more popular golfing conversation today!"

By early 2013, he was considering not playing at all in order to avoid the controversy. That summer, Karen Crouse wrote a feature in *The New York Times* that seemed to encapsulate how Ireland took out its self-loathing on anyone with the audacity to strive for greatness. Like so many famous Irish artists of the past, McIlroy had by then left the country, settling in Florida. He had also left his Irish management company, Horizon Sports Management, to start one of his own, which sparked a feud with Graeme McDowell, a Horizon shareholder. His game was suffering, too, and had been since he switched from Titleist to Nike the previous November.

In Crouse's piece, a customs official called McIlroy a "snob," another deemed him a "spoiled brat," and fans at the Irish Open disapproved of his private parking space with—God forbid!—a special placard. To top it off, the general secretary of Ireland's Golfing Union was quoted saying that the public didn't support Rory like they once had because of the Olympics situation.[12]

For years, McIlroy tried to keep his cultural identity separate from his public image. That would be a very simple thing for most golfers, but for a kid from Northern Ireland, the effort alone was remarkable. And, of course, it couldn't last. It wasn't long before he was entangled in the same struggle that had defined his country for decades. He's handled it with as much grace and reserve as possible, but understanding this aspect of his background is key to understanding Rory as a

---

[12] The general ill will died down slightly in 2014, when Rory announced that he would be playing for Ireland after all.

person. Outside of his golf, there is always this lingering shadow—the one that he's spent a lifetime trying to escape, and the one he never will.

Rory learned golf from his father as a toddler, and loved it so much that he began watching instructional videos on his own. His talent was obvious, and the Holywood Club—a no-frills affair that stood in contrast to the haughty Royal Belfast Club nearby—changed its membership rules to allow Rory to join at age seven.

He began working with Michael Bannon, and the two have stayed together ever since—today, Bannon travels with McIlroy full-time. As *Golf Digest* reported in August, Rory stands out for the fact that his swing has remained more or less the same since his early childhood days. Unlike Tiger, who has undergone significant transformations at various stages of his career, Rory doesn't foresee the essential components ever changing.

YouTube offers a small archive of Rory's childhood, starting with a home movie shot in a dark living room, where the three-year-old takes full swings with a wedge, hitting a ball off the carpet and onto the couch while soccer highlights play on the small television in the background. There's also an interview from BBC Northern Ireland after the nine-year-old Rory won the World Junior Tournament at Doral, in what the anchor called "the searing Miami heat." Rory, all freckles and grins, has the same soft, lilting accent that's become familiar today—a contrast to the flat Northern Irish timbre you hear from the likes of McDowell and David Feherty. In another clip from that year, on Ulster Television's the "Kelly" show, he juggles a ball on his wedge, and then shifts the club between his legs without missing a beat. He chips a golf ball into a washing machine, and tells the host that Darren Clarke is his favorite Irish golfer.

"If the Americans have Tiger Woods," the host says in closing, "we have young Rory."

From Doral, he put together a sparkling junior career that included a wide array of tournament wins and honors, including a victory in the

2004 Junior Ryder Cup. He set a course record at age sixteen with a 61 at Royal Portrush, the Northern Irish course that hosted the 1951 British Open. That same year, he dealt with his only real crisis of faith in golf.

"I was ready to give it up," he told me in Akron, at the WGC-Bridgestone Championship. "I just won the Mullingar Scratch Cup, and I remember the drive home with my dad. It was like a three-hour drive. And I said to him, 'I don't like this anymore. I don't enjoy it. I just won, and I don't know, I'm not happy, I'm not excited.'"

His parents told him they just wanted him to be happy, and while they may have been experiencing a bit of panic inside, they advised him to do whatever he wanted. He went home, and didn't golf for three days. When those three days had ended, he decided that he loved golf again, and today he chalks it up to the hormonal issues of a "grumpy teenager."

"There was a teenage rebellion, yes," he said. "For three days."

The angst never returned, and his career took off with startling speed. In 2007, still just eighteen, he was the low amateur at the British Open in Carnoustie. After turning professional, he won his first European Tour in Dubai before his twentieth birthday. In 2010 he joined the PGA Tour as one of the world's top-ten golfers, and he wasted no time making an impact. He won his first event at Quail Hollow with a course record 62 in the final round, set another course record on Thursday at the British Open in St. Andrew's, and nearly joined Martin Kaymer and Bubba Watson in their playoff at the PGA Championship.

He made the strange decision in 2011 to return to the European Tour and to skip the Players Championship—choices he regretted almost immediately, and which led to him firing his agent Chubby Chandler that November and joining Horizon. Before he left, he nearly won the Masters, racing out to a four-stroke lead on Sunday before posting a disastrous 80 to drop out of the top ten. It was his hardest moment as a professional—he had lost his confidence on the back nine, and stopped trusting his putter. He faced the media, and all he could hope was that the next time he had a chance at a major, he'd handle the pressure with more aplomb.

He didn't have to wait long. At the very next major stop, he tore apart Congressional Country Club and won the U.S. Open running away. The next March, after a win at the Honda Classic, he ascended to the world number 1 for the first time. He held the top spot through a spectacular season that included wins in Dubai, two FedEx Cup events, and a record-setting eight-stroke win at the PGA Championship, his second major.

At twenty-three, he was the Player of the Year on both the PGA and European Tours, and unlike other child stars—Scott, Rose, Day—he was naturally aggressive, and had the transcendent game to put himself in the hot seat again and again until he could occupy it comfortably. Now, two years before his twenty-fifth birthday, he had become more than just a young superstar—he was the heir apparent to Tiger Woods.

There's a fearlessness and intelligence to McIlroy that transcends the course, and these are the qualities that place him above golfers of equal—or at least near-equal—talent. They also get him in occasional trouble. Northern Irish politics aside, Rory won't hesitate to speak his mind, especially when he feels threatened. It's almost as though he makes up for the gag order on politics and religion by letting loose with an added bit of volume on everything else.

Some of the controversies he's encountered are nonstories whipped into a froth by the media. When he called the Ryder Cup an "exhibition" in 2009, and admitted that he'd rather win individual tournaments, he was only saying what every golfer felt to be true. Many of them loved the Ryder Cup, and the atmosphere was unlike any other, but there's not one player who would trade a victory there for an individual major. In fact, you get the sense that some of the most passionate Ryder Cuppers, like Ian Poulter and Sergio Garcia, love it that extra bit *because* they've never won a major—it's a substitute high, in a way.

Other moments, though, have been truly tense. When a TV reporter and former golfer named Jay Townsend said on air that Rory should fire his longtime caddie, J. P. Fitzgerald, McIlroy took to Twit-

ter, firing off a harsh salvo at Townsend: "Shut up . . . you're a commentator and a failed golfer, your opinion means nothing!"

"I don't know if he's got something in for my caddie, J.P.," McIlroy
said in a presser later that week. "He's been going at him for the last
three years. And it was just one comment too far. I've got to stand up
for my caddie. J.P. is one of my closest friends . . . and I just had to say
something."

He was called immature in some corners for the reaction, but the
more you learn about Rory, the more you realize it wasn't youth or im-
maturity at all, but the cunning instinct of someone who realizes that
if you let someone push you once, they might keep pushing forever.

And Rory, despite the soft voice, freckles, curly hair, and the last
days of his puppy-dog looks—"I want to pinch his *cheeks,* he's so cute!"
I heard a young girl squeal at the Deutsche Bank Championship—is no
pushover. His fire is reminiscent of the man he's chasing, though Rory
on the whole seems more stable and less self-destructive than Tiger.

The two spent some time together late in the 2014 season in New
York, appearing together on the *Tonight Show* with Jimmy Fallon. The
next week, I asked if he could recognize a kindred spirit when they had
a private moment together—something they could see only in each
other, and that set them apart as psychological competitors.

"In some ways, yes," he said. "We talked about a few things, and
he's telling me like, I'm not going to let you win a green jacket next
year . . . and I might not look it, but I'm the exact same way. I've got a
very competitive spirit, but it would only be on a golf course. Like, I'll
let you win in a game of pool. I don't care about that. But golf, it's my
thing to be competitive at and it's my thing to succeed in, so of course
I'm really competitive. And even if it doesn't look it, on the inside I'm
trying to beat those guys to death."

But *trying* and *doing* are two different things, and it's the rare golfer
who masters both in his early twenties. There's a ruthlessness to Rory,
and watching him over the course of a year, I came to believe that his
ability to put others away with such cold efficiency boiled down to the
simple fact that he's *smarter.* He rarely makes the mistake of playing
recklessly, the way Mickelson can. He knows when to turn his analyti-

cal mind off and play with pure instinct, rather than linger in an intellectual funk or give in to anger. If Rickie Fowler takes a Zen approach to the game, McIlroy understands the art of war. He's equipped with the golfer's equivalent of street smarts, and at every moment, he's the biggest threat on the course.

That's why he defended his caddie. By firing back at Townsend, he didn't just shut up a lone commentator. He showed loyalty, and broadcast a clear signal to anyone who might be thinking of taking their own potshots. Speak carefully, he seemed to say, or you're in for a fight, and I'm not the kind to pull punches.

Rory has an intuitive understanding of power. How to earn it, how to wield it, and how to keep others from taking it away. Like Tiger, he'd also learned to sniff out weakness at a young age, and to conceal his own. It's too bad that the "Shark" nickname was wasted on Greg Norman, because Tiger and Rory are the ones who can truly smell blood.

By 2013, the war with Horizon Sports Management was in full swing, and the equipment change was sabotaging his game.[13] McIlroy contended that Horizon coerced him into signing an unfair "limiting contract" that cost him almost seven million dollars in related fees, which apparently occurred at a Christmas party in 2011. Forbes reported that Horizon's deal gave them 20 percent of "off-the-course income"—including the enormous contract with Nike, which was less than the ten years and $250 million originally reported, per *SI*'s Alan Shipnuck, but not significantly less. It's an incredibly high commission rate—significantly higher than the terms given to Graeme McDowell by the same company. But McIlroy's argument—that he was young, naive, and lacked legal counsel—sounded a bit thin, and Horizon decided to take the fight to him by countersuing for around $3 million in unpaid commissions.

The lawsuit was settled out of court in early 2015, but in 2013, the

[13] In a wonderful piece of irony, the *New York Times* ran a feature on how well Rory and Horizon worked together just two weeks before their acrimonious split.

confluence of stressors contributed to a decline in his game. It also hurt his friendship with Graeme McDowell, particularly when he announced in May that he'd be leaving to form his own company, Rory McIlroy Inc.

In details that emerged over the next year, Horizon accused Rory of timing his lawsuit to hit a day before McDowell's wedding in September 2013, which would be attended by Horizon agents—a wedding Rory skipped in favor of a Nike photo shoot. It later came to light that McDowell was a Horizon shareholder, which raised questions about his harsh comments toward McIlroy, as well as his initial recruitment.

Rory McIlroy Inc. took full effect late in the year, with Gerry McIlroy assuming a leadership role, but Rory's 2013 season dragged on with one mediocre result after another. At the Honda Classic, he withdrew in the second round after a 7-over start, and cited pain in his wisdom tooth—a dubious explanation at best, considering how frustrated he appeared with his game, though he did send a doctor's note from Belfast to the PGA Tour the next Monday.

He relinquished his number 1 ranking after holding it a year, and his low point came at the British Open in Muirfield, when Nick Faldo publicly lectured him about focusing on golf. McIlroy, looking irritated and a bit sullen, defended his work ethic and said, "Nick should know how hard this game is at times. He's been in our position before, and he should know how much work we all do put into it." Three days later, he finished up an ugly 79-75, failing to make the cut in a British Open for the first time in his professional career.

By late 2013, though, his game had started to round into something resembling its old form, and a one-shot win over Adam Scott at the Australian Open in December hinted at an imminent return to greatness.

In Sydney on New Year's Eve, he sat in a boat with his longtime girlfriend Caroline Wozniacki, the tennis star, in the harbor. Fireworks went off, and he was prepared to propose when a fellow passenger, quite drunk, jumped in the water and spoiled the moment. He saved the proposal for his hotel room, she said yes, and finally, it seemed as though his life had settled into a calm spell.

"I feel I have stability in my life now," he told *The Telegraph,* "and the engagement will only help with regards to knowing everything in my life is set. I mean, if you get engaged, you plan to spend the rest of your life with that person, so it is a big decision. But she's definitely the right girl for me."

Or, maybe not.

In May, a few days after they sent out wedding invitations, Rory called off the wedding. Worse, he broke the news to Wozniacki with nothing more than a brief phone call.

"The problem is mine," read a statement issued by Rory McIlroy Inc. "The wedding invitations issued at the weekend made me realize that I wasn't ready for all that marriage entails. I wish Caroline all the happiness she deserves and thank her for the great times we've had."

Rory's ice-cold method of deep-sixing his fiancée was particularly eyebrow-raising when you consider an excerpt from a *New York Times* article in May 2013:

> "At the end of last year, McIlroy sat down with his strength coach, Steve McGregor, who also works with the golfer Lee Westwood and has consulted with the Knicks and Manchester United.
>
> Citing scheduling difficulties, McIlroy ended their professional relationship. But to ensure that they would remain friendly, he chose to tell McGregor about his decision face-to-face instead of in a text message or an e-mail."

In other words, a trainer merits a sit-down dismissal, but a fiancée gets the kiss-off by phone.

McIlroy is a conscientious person, or he at least fakes it well. If a reporter asks him a question with a flawed premise, for instance, he'll correct the man obliquely in response, rather than pointing out the error in public as many golfers love to do. The courtesy he extended to McGregor in 2012 wasn't out of the ordinary.

Considering all that, the Wozniacki phone-dumping was a bizarre move, and inexplicable on its face.

Those who hoped that karma would punish McIlroy for the cruel breakup were disappointed. He made his key putting alignment fix at Augusta, and already his game was looking nearly as strong as it had in 2012. In his very first tournament after the breakup in 2014, he won the European Tour's BMW PGA Championship with a final round 66, chasing down Thomas Bjorn from seven strokes behind. The message had been received around the golf world—Rory was back, and he was shooting some very low scores.

What we knew, in the days leading up to the British Open, was that if he could beat his so-called "Friday curse," everyone else would be in serious trouble.

And Rory—shark that he was—knew it, too.

With three holes remaining in his third round Hoylake, the field had crept up behind Rory, like cagey assassins who move only when their target is facing away. A new feeling arrived, just briefly—something like vulnerability, but less pronounced. Rory had spent most of the day at even par or +1, not quite as transcendent under the gray British skies, with gulls circling the beach on the River Dee, and seals basking on the banks. The wind had kindly stayed away, and though Rory showed signs of fading, a few long par saves, and a few great approaches, kept the competition at bay.

At the end of the opening nine, Sergio Garcia caught fire with two straight birdies. On the 11th hole, Rickie Fowler—his facial hair cut into something approximating a Fu Manchu—sank a long birdie to pull within one. This broke the two-shot cushion, that mythical blockade that nobody had breached against Martin Kaymer at Pinehurst. Another birdie at 12 for Fowler, along with a bogey for Rory, and they were tied at -12.

It looked like the front-runner had faded, and would have to scrap and fight just to stay in Sunday's final group. Instead, Rory reacted like a sprinter who had turned off the jets and started to coast, only to see another runner catch up. It served as a reminder—*yes, that's right, I need to go!*

And go he did. A birdie on 14 propelled him back into the lead, and on 16, a par 5, he showcased the most devastating element of his game. Rory had packed on lots of muscle since 2012, and while he had always been incredibly long off the tee, now he had the core strength and the general mass to stabilize his entire swing—which gave him even more distance, and better accuracy. At the end of 2014, only Bubba Watson and Dustin Johnson had a higher average driving distance—remarkable, considering Rory's size—and even compared to those two, the margin was razor-thin. Considering the strength of the rest of his game, Rory became almost unbeatable when he could drive the ball straight; he was like an amalgam of Bubba Watson and Zach Johnson, strength and precision contained in a single golfer.

On the par-5 16th, he smashed one of his trademark drives, leaving himself 252 yards to the green. His 4-iron reached with ease, and he poured in the first eagle of the day on the hole. On 18, another par 5, a massive drive left him a simple 5-iron from 239. Again, he stuck it, and drained the first eagle of the day on *that* hole. The devestating closing kick redeemed what had been, for sixteen holes, a very mediocre round.

The contrast of how he finished, compared to Garcia and Fowler, brought to mind what Jason Day had said about the perils of being in contention. In that fight-or-flight moment, will a golfer retreat from the distress, sacrificing a few strokes to ease the tension, or will he surge forward, resolved to living comfortably in the flames? While Rory had set his jaw and thrived, Sergio had played even-par golf on the back nine, and Fowler made three bogeys as he stumbled to the finish. In the span of five holes, the tie at -12 had become a rout—Rory led Fowler by six shots, and Sergio by seven.

That stretch was just the latest example of the qualities that separate a "gamer"—someone who handles the pressure and excels—from everyone else. It comes down to a simple question of comfort: Do you believe this is where you're supposed to be? Each time a player like Rory beats an opponent in that circumstance, it creates psychological ammunition for the next battle—success builds on success, and failure on failure.

Rickie looked despondent in his post-match interview, while Sergio had adopted his usual "everything's fine!" demeanor, smiling and shrugging and even hugging Rory during a television interview.

By the time McIlroy came to the press tent, the rain was beating loudly on the roof, validating the R&A's choice to send the players off early that morning. The forecast on Sunday called for clear skies, but when Rory burst through the door, he was soaked from the walk. It didn't matter—he came in laughing, and he left with a smile. He had put his two closest competitors under his boot heel with the spectacular eagles, and he knew it. Now, he just had to grind them to dust.

"A decade ago, Rory McIlroy was a 15-year-old kid with some skill at golf and a dad who believed in him wholeheartedly. So much so, in fact, that Gerry McIlroy and three friends put together £400, just less than $700 in today's dollars, on an audacious bet: young Rory would win the Open Championship before he turned 26. The odds? 500-1. McIlroy is now 25. . . . The bet would pay £200,000, or more than $340,000, if McIlroy is able to win."

—Yahoo Sports

Rory had experience with big leads. The Masters he lost in 2012 had taught him the unease that came with holding a Sunday edge, and his comeback from seven shots down in May's BMW PGA Championship clued him in to the mentality of the chase pack. He had watched the scoreboard that day, and he remembered the precise moment, as he waited on the 11th tee, when Thomas Bjorn had come careening back to earth with a triple bogey on the sixth. He saw his opportunity—a few birdies would increase the pressure Bjorn was undoubtedly feeling, but they had to come now. Collapses of that magnitude happen because of negative momentum, and anything the trailing golfer can do to heighten the sense of impending doom will hasten the meltdown. Bjorn heard the cheers coming from ahead, and he saw Rory's name gaining ground on the scoreboards. Finally, stress and bad play got the better of him, and the impossible outcome materialized.

Except it *wasn't* impossible—it never was, and Rory knew it. Just two years earlier, Adam Scott had come into the final day at the Open with the same exact six-shot lead over Ernie Els that Rory would take into Sunday. Scott had blown it at the end, and Rory could, too. That knowledge, paradoxically, gave him power. He wouldn't coast, and as long as he didn't give too much ground, or panic when somebody below him made his inevitable run, he'd be leaving Hoylake with the Claret Jug.

He hit the driving range just after one p.m. after spending Saturday night relaxing and watching *Jackass Number Two*—the latest in a series of nightly films that had included *Django Unchained* and *The Internship*. He wore a pink-and-gray Nike top, and gray Nike pants. The English sky, too, was a palette of grays—a heavy gunmetal slate where the dense clouds massed, lighter shades of ash and silver where the faint light hinted at the presence of a sun somewhere behind the gloom. No surprises here—as Alistair Beggs, the captain of Royal Liverpool, told me, Hoylake actually gets less rain than almost everywhere on the east coast of the United States, but far less sunshine, too. It just mists with a depressing constancy, rarely yielding to clear skies or vigorous downpours.

Like Kaymer at Sawgrass and Pinehurst, Rory situated himself on the far left of the range—the high ground, so to speak, where he could see everybody, but they couldn't see him. In front of him, Rickie Fowler wore his Sunday orange and hit looping irons. His agent, Sam MacNaughton, stood beside him, eyes glued to his phone, mouth twisted in a half smirk. On the far right, Dustin Johnson, starting the day tied with Sergio in third place, stared blankly at the yardage markers while he hit.

Aside from the bleachers that rose behind the players, the range could have belonged to any municipal course in America, with its plain yardage placards placed at fifty-meter intervals. It was a far cry from the elaborate PGA ranges, with greens and bunkers and hills offering a simulation of shots the players might face on the course.

Sergio made the scene next, joining Rickie near the middle of the range. They gazed at the clouds and talked about the possibility of rain, while Rory, with his massive forearms and a swing like a liquid whip, bashed ball after ball with his driver. As the tee times approached, they left the range and made their way to the chipping green. Rory earned the loudest roar on his departure, offering a hint at the partisan atmosphere he'd enjoy all day. He muttered a few words as he passed Sergio, who issued a terse "yeah" in response—none of yesterday's post-round bonhomie.

They hit sand shots and short pitches next, ringed by black Mercedes cars and every equipment truck in the business—TaylorMade, Ping, Callaway, Cleveland, Mizuno, Nike, Wilson, Fleetwood, Titleist. Then it was off to the first tee, where Fowler, back in the final group on a major Sunday, gave Rory a quick soul shake as he prepared to stagger up his latest mountain.

Sergio came out hot. With three birdies in his first five holes, he served quick notice to Rory that the day would not be an easy coronation. The fist pumps and the cries of *"vamos!"* came in exhilarated bursts, and if you didn't know Sergio's past, you might think it was the start of a sustained charge.

Rory birdied the first to assert his control, but on the fifth, after an awful approach and a weak chip, he missed his par putt. The par-3 sixth brought more trouble when his tee shot rolled down into a hollow on the left side of the green. He stared at the leaderboard before he took his chip, and saw that he led Sergio by just five shots. The chip was adequate, but the par putt was not, and when the five-footer missed, his margin shrunk to four.

He nearly gave another shot away on the seventh hole after a wayward drive, but he recovered with a good sand save from the pot bunker. He walked on to the eighth tee, head bobbing, eyes staring at nothing and everything. On the par 4, a dogleg left, he made a standard par, and seemed to recover some stability. Fowler, meanwhile, was having a quiet front nine. Aside from a birdie on the second hole, he made all pars through the turn. He was playing solid at a time when solid wasn't quite good enough, and each missed birdie putt tightened the noose.

With the fans hugging the hillsides, Rory hit his tee shot on the par-3 ninth so close that it nearly hit the hole, and came to rest fifteen feet past. His birdie putt broke hard to left in the last three feet, but he hit it on the perfect line and moved back to even par for the round.

That's when Sergio struck the biggest blow of the day—on the par-5 10th, he hit a 6-iron from 228 yards to twelve feet. With Rory peering on from the fairway, and sailboats moving slowly past on the river, he buried the eagle putt. He trailed by just two strokes now, and had emphatically passed the first part of his difficult test—stage a furious charge over the first two hours and pressure the leader. With his first major victory looking more and more realistic, Sergio now had to accomplish the second, more difficult part of the task—maintain his fearless play, keep charging, and put up a score that could win the event *even if Rory didn't falter.*

And it didn't look like Rory would falter. After Sergio's eagle, his own approach cleared the front bunker on no. 10, leaving him a simple two-putt for birdie to extend the lead back to three. Fowler followed with a birdie of his own to stay five shots behind, still within shouting distance, but the fight for the Claret Jug looked increasingly like a two-horse race.

Starting on no. 11, the leaders turned back into the wind, marching along the river for four holes. Sergio hit a short approach into the green on 11, and began begging as he watched it fly to the hole. His voice reached the desperate upper registers—"Oh, be good, please, be good, please, *please, please!*"—but the wind prevailed, and he came up just short, leaving a long birdie putt that he narrowly missed. Rory followed by making par with a short but tricky left-to-right putt, securing another precious draw.

From the 12th tee, you could see the church spires and dark roofs of Hoylake reflecting in the afternoon sun. In the fairway off the tee on the par-4, Sergio found his ball behind a swale that made his approach shot practically blind. He had lost some of his spontaneity now that things were tight, and stood over each shot, analyzing obsessively. He backed off again when a cell phone rang out along the ropes. When he finally hit, the ball took off to the right, fading into the gallery. Sergio shouted a warning, and with a clang, the ball hit near the top of the metal bleachers.

British television feeds are notoriously poor at tracking balls in their gray native skies—especially when compared to the efficiency of American crews—so it took a moment for viewers to understand what had happened. In an incredible break, the ball had caromed back toward the green, running almost all the way to the putting surface. From there, Sergio went up and down, blew a kiss toward the gallery, and threw the ball back to them.

A hole later, on the 194-yard 13th, with the gulls swarming on the beach behind him, Rory hit one of his worst shots of the day. Sergio had barely avoided a nasty pot bunker to the front right of the green, and chipped up close to save par. Rory came up well short, landing his tee shot somewhere in the thick fescue to the left of the fairway. He did his best with his recovery shot, but the ball skipped on the green and nearly ran all the way to the same bunker Sergio had avoided. Rickie had come up short off the tee as well—the wind was knocking everything down—but he went up-and-down for par. No such luck for Rory, who two-putted for bogey to fall to -16. The lead was back to two.

The fans shouted vaguely Spanish words at Sergio—*"Ole!"* and *"Aye-aye-aye!"*—and gave him an enormous, sarcastic cheer when he emerged from a Porta-Potty between the 12th green and 13th hole. There was something familiar and almost friendly about these instances of near-mockery, but for the majority of the English, Rory was the chosen one. It reminded me of Andy Murray, a Scot, trying to win Wimbledon—he wasn't quite their own, but it was close enough for jazz.

Still, they stuck by the Spaniard as he climbed the hill to the 14th

tee, with a very English style of support that existed somewhere between sincere and derisive. He was moving now at a pensive pace,
brooding over each shot, and on his approach shot from 172 yards
away, he came just inches shy of carrying a ridge in front of the flag. He
gave his birdie putt a good run, but it missed, again by inches. Rory
played very safe, took his par, and Rickie got in trouble off the tee, laid
up in the fairway, and made an excellent up-and-down from eighty-
three yards away.

By now, all three players were showing the different sides of their
nervous personalities. Rickie was silent and stoic, resolutely focused
over each shot, playing the game with the utmost sincerity as he tried
to ignore the stakes. Sergio had gone antsy, yelling at every ball, hopping up and down nervously, and talking to anyone who would listen—
his caddie before shots, reporters between holes, and even his playing
partner, Dustin Johnson, who made a poor audience. Rory was pure
aggression, even when he chose to play cautious—eyes burning, stride
forceful, resolute with a dash of fury.

All three made pars on 14, and moved on to the par-3, 163-yard
15th, downhill and finally out of the wind. When Sergio is in contention at a major, and he begins to vibrate with that unstable, manic energy, we've been conditioned to wait for the other shoe to drop—for
disaster to strike. Even before it happened at Hoylake, you sensed that
the moment was imminent. On the tee, he took out his pitching wedge,
backed off once, and sent his ball high into the wind.

"Ohhhh," he screamed, "no!"

It came up short, hit hard, and rolled sideways into the bunker.
This wasn't the worst place in the world to be, but the catastrophe we'd
been expecting came next. As he began his downswing in the bunker,
with Rory looking on from the tee, Sergio dipped his shoulder in an
attempt to elevate the ball and lift it safely over the steep face of the
bunker. He made impact far too early, and got a load of sand for his
troubles. The ball popped up, peeked over the sod wall for just a moment, and came right back down in the hazard.

This was the shot he couldn't afford. He saved bogey, but it meant
that he'd need miracles on the finishing stretch—two eagles, proba-

bly—to have a chance. On the tee as Sergio holed out, Rory could be seen laughing with Fowler. He knew the heat was off, at least a little, and he hit a flat 9-iron into the wind that landed safely on the green. He made par from there when birdie would have secured the championship.

Sergio reached the 16th green, the par-5, in two, but somehow left his eagle putt short. Rory followed with a mammoth 360-yard drive, after which he spun on his heels to point out a heckler who had been dogging him all day, and who purposefully coughed on his downswing. Security dragged the culprit off the course, and McIlroy hit an easy approach to the green and two-putted for birdie. His three-shot lead was intact, and when Sergio missed his birdie putt on 17 after a low, line-drive approach into the wind, he knew that one more par would secure the win. It would require a tremendous pitch—his second shot on the par-4 17th ended up in the rough, on the wrong side of a pot bunker that guarded the hole. Rory struck it beautifully, high over the bunker, and an easy par putt sent him to 18 with the same comfortable cushion.

A birdie there would have tied Tiger's British Open record score of -18, but Rory chose to hit iron off the tee, nice and safe, to avoid the out-of-bounds area on the right. As he moved down the fairway, a few hopeful rays of sunshine shone down from above, fighting their losing battle against the dusk. With 257 yards remaining, he took aim at the hole and wound up in a bunker just shy of the green. Sergio failed to make eagle, and though Rickie hit a solid approach to reach the green in two, he was still far from the hole. One critical shot remained for Rory—all that could stop him now was a Sergio-esque error from the bunker.

He knew better. The shot rose from the sand with ease, landing on the green, and you could actually see the tension leave his body. When Fowler missed his eagle putt, the last bit of doubt drained away.

Flags from every player's home nation whipped in the wind above the grandstands as Rory tapped in for par and basked in the thunderous applause that rang from the stadium. The look of confidence on his face was almost brash as he pumped his fist twice, with emphasis. He had gone wire-to-wire, and become the first European in golf history to win three different majors. He was also just the third player ever, after Jack and Tiger, to own three major titles before his 26th birthday. He tossed the ball into the gallery, hugged his mother, and applauded the fans. Later, at the awards ceremony, holding the Claret Jug, a sly grin crossed his face as he addressed them.

"And to the fans, you've turned out in thousands and thousands this week and on behalf of all the players, I'd like to say thank you very much. The support has been absolutely fantastic all week, you've been a pleasure to play in front of, and even though I'm a Man United fan sitting here—"

They didn't let him finish the sentence. The boos rang down from the masses of Liverpool and Everton supporters, and Rory's grin only grew wider. After his speech, he sat on the lip of a pot bunker and posed for photos with the Claret Jug.

Under the gray sky, the last rebellious shafts of sunlight now quelled, he looked older. Time, and the storm and stress of the year gone by, had left its mark. The weary, battle-scarred face we saw illuminated by the stroboscopic flashes of a hundred cameras could no longer be mistaken for the naive, innocent prodigy that had once walked these fairways lightly, untouched by pain or adversity. This was the man who had emerged from the fire, battered but unbowed. With his legs pressed to the sod, he held the trophy like it could only ever belong to him. It was possible, at that precise moment, to see Rory unvarnished—flawed, brilliant, and deadly.

AUGUST

Last Chances

19

AKRON, OHIO

Dustin Johnson's Black Friday

"I am taking a leave of absence from professional golf, effective immediately. I will use this time to seek professional help for personal challenges I have faced. By committing the time and resources necessary to improve my mental health, physical well-being and emotional foundation, I am confident that I will be better equipped to fulfill my potential and become a consistent champion. I respectfully ask my fans, well-wishers and the media for privacy as I embark upon this mission of self-improvement."
—Statement from DUSTIN JOHNSON,
Thursday, July 31, 2014

On Monday, July 28, 2014, Dustin Johnson announced he would be withdrawing from the WGC-Bridgestone event in Akron due to "personal challenges." The formal tone of the statement, and all its attempts at self-reckoning and gravity, probably didn't benefit from a recent picture posted by his fiancée Paulina Gretzky on Instagram that showed a barefoot Johnson wearing a blue caddie's bib and reading her putt—but then, everybody figured the words had been crafted by his agency, and not Johnson himself.

By Thursday, the withdrawal became an extended leave of absence, and his agent David Winkle confirmed that he would miss both the PGA Championship and the Ryder Cup—a huge loss for the United States, as Johnson had gone 3-0 in Medinah, posting one of just three American victories on that disastrous Sunday.

I was in the media center in Akron on Thursday when news of his "leave of absence" came down, and witnessed firsthand the instant roar that went up around the room. Personally, I was totally stumped at the reaction—the laughter, the shouting, and most of all, the sense that everybody in the room knew what the hell was going on except me.

Which turned out to be true. Normally, journalists would greet this kind of news with puzzlement and a collective attempt to dig for the truth. This time, no further investigation was necessary. I finally worked up the courage to admit my complete ignorance—what was happening?

A writer in my aisle turned to face me, placed one finger on the right side of his nose, and inhaled mightily through his left nostril.

"No shit?"

No shit—Johnson, they told me, had almost certainly failed a drug test for cocaine, and this wasn't the first time. He had taken a three-month break in early 2012, and the excuse then was that he'd hurt his back lifting a Jet Ski. In media circles, I learned, it was widely known that the story was nonsense—he had tested positive for cocaine, and had been hit with a suspension by the PGA Tour.

All of which leads to an obvious question: How could he lie about a Jet Ski injury when he'd been suspended?

The answer to that question gets to the heart of the PGA Tour's cloudy substance-abuse policy. In contrast to almost every other professional sports organization, the Tour does not publicize its suspensions. Which means that when they told Dustin Johnson he couldn't play for three months back in 2012, he and his agents were free to make up whatever excuse they wanted—in this case, a back injury caused by a Jet Ski that lasted exactly three months.

Any connected journalist knew the real reason, but my ignorance about what had happened in 2012, before I began covering golf, shows how effective the Tour's policy can be at keeping ugly truths hidden from the public. The only way we learn the truth is when the police or courts get involved—Matt Every, for instance, couldn't deny the nature of his absence after news of his arrest for possession of marijuana became public.

The Tour's lack of transparency extends to on-course fines for swearing or slow play, but there is one exception. Since drug testing began in 2008, the Tour is *supposed* to announce when a player has been suspended for performance-enhancing drugs. That's happened exactly twice, to low-profile journeymen Doug Barron and Bhavik Patel.

This is where the actual language of the Tour's bylaws gets tricky: They have to announce a suspension, but they don't have to announce a positive test that *doesn't* result in a suspension. In other words, if Tiger Woods got caught doping, and commissioner Tim Finchem decided that it would be bad for business if the news went public, there would be no suspension, and we'd never know.

The fact that golfers are contract employees who don't belong to a players' union allows the Tour to set and define their own policy, and there's little doubt that it exists mostly to keep up appearances—you only have to read certain quotes from the people in power to know which way the wind blows.

"Why don't we talk about it or give out the details? One, we don't feel like people really care that much," Tim Finchem said in 2009. "We don't get emails from fans saying, 'Why don't you tell us?' So we don't think there's this hunger for that information. Two, candidly, we don't have that much of it, and we don't want to remind people about it."

When questioned about why the policy existed in 2013, executive vice president of communications Ty Votaw told *Sports Illustrated* that the goal was "to make sure we are seen as being a clean sport."

The common thread here is the need to *seem* a certain way, rather than to actually *be* that way. The Tour buckled to pressure by instituting a testing policy in 2008 because that was best for projecting a clean image, and they keep the details secret because that, too, is best for projecting a clean image. It's a bureaucratic absurdity straight out of Kafka, but there's not a damn thing any journalist can do about it.

Unless, of course, they develop a source inside the Tour and blow the whole thing out of the water. Which is exactly what *Sports Illustrated*'s Michael Bamberger and Mike Walker did on Friday, August 1.

If anyone had any doubts about the nature of Johnson's "leave of absence," they were squashed when Bamberger and Walker's story hit. Not only had the Tour levied a six-month suspension after a failed cocaine test, the source said; the old rumors were true, too. For the first time, a legitimate outlet had reported that Johnson's previous Jet Ski injury was a cover-up, and the three months he missed had been the result of his first cocaine suspension (he had also tested positive for marijuana in 2009).

The story spread, and the Tour was reeling. Still, they had one arrow left in their quiver, and they didn't hesitate to use it. The stated policy is that they don't comment on drug suspensions, but they reversed this stance to issue a brief statement:

"With regard to media reports that Dustin Johnson has been suspended by the PGA Tour, this is to clarify that Mr. Johnson has taken a voluntary leave of absence and is not under a suspension from the PGA Tour."

The Tour's unprecedented statement, issued opportunistically and against policy at a time of crisis, was no more than a bit of deceptive wordplay, and a lame attempt to undermine a larger truth.

Perhaps Johnson wasn't "suspended" in the formal sense of the word, but since the Tour didn't refute the notion that he had failed three drug tests and wouldn't be playing for six months as a result of the last one, Bamberger and Walker's facts stand up. Rather than "suspending" him outright, did the Tour offer Johnson the choice to take a voluntary leave of absence? And was this offer not truly voluntary at all, since he'd be suspended formally if he refused? If it's true, the approach *did* allow him to frame things however he wanted, and to avoid the explicit mention of drugs, which seemed beneficial to both him and the Tour.

Ironically, that veil of secrecy now seems like a dubious benefit for players and agents. Johnson's saga in particular serves as a cautionary tale. Guilty parties will have to think twice in the future, because any anonymous leaks from the Tour's rank-and-file stand to leave them exposed, with their own version of the Jet Ski lie napalming their credibility. And though the Tour did its best to run interference against Bamberger and Walker with their coy statement about the suspension, everyone in the media saw it for what it was: disingenuous semantics that failed to do any real damage to the greater truth of the report.

None of the actual information in *Sports Illustrated* surprised anyone in the media, except me, but this was the first time the news went public. That sparked a furor in Akron—suddenly, it was open season on the Tour's drug policy. Bob Harig at *ESPN.com* and Karen Crouse at *The New York Times* swung the biggest hatchets, and on Friday, Crouse and I had the same idea of talking to Matt Every after his round in Akron. As usual, he offered a nakedly honest take on the whole deal: If he hadn't been exposed in the papers, he too would have made up an excuse for his suspension, because it would have protected his image with both his fans and sponsors. Every had been with Bridgestone at the time of his arrest, and while the company eventually decided to stick with him, they obviously weren't pleased—they could have pulled their money, and that would've made Every poison to other companies as well.

The whole byzantine system seems to have an easy solution: If the Tour doesn't want to hurt anyone's image, including its own, with any drug associations, and if they're going to lie by omission when players test positive, then *why test in the first place?*

As Every pointed out, recreational drugs don't actually *help* anyone on the course, and unless a player becomes an addict, they probably don't hurt very much either. Even if they do, it scarcely matters. The Darwinian nature of golf punishes anyone who struggles, and a heroin addict isn't going to last very long in the top ranks of professional golfers. Practically, there's no great reason to test for recreational drugs beyond the morality of it, and if the Tour really cared about that, they'd have started testing long before 2008. Drugs, as far as I'm aware, were not invented that year.

It's window dressing. The Tour wants everyone to *think* they care about drug use, but the few positive tests reveal that they'll frantically try to hide the connections whenever possible. So why not just dispense with the whole system, test for PEDs, and leave recreational drugs out of it?

Impossible—it would be an unacceptable public relations move, signaling to the conservative base that the Tour doesn't care about illegal drug use. They're not going back, but they're sure as hell not going to cost everyone money by heeding calls for transparency.

And so the strange charade continues.

"I can resist anything except temptation."

—Oscar Wilde

And what about Dustin Johnson? The lanky bomber with the "oily gait of a jungle cat," to quote *Golf Digest*'s Jim Moriarty, was out until February.

At thirty years old, he'd been suspended at an interesting time for his legacy. You don't have to be an expert to see that Johnson is one of the game's best athletes. He's a lithe, six-foot-four natural who can dunk a basketball with ease, and swings with the God-given combination of finesse and power that other golfers would kill to possess for a single weekend. He had the most PGA Tour wins of any golfer age thirty or younger prior to that summer, when Rory McIlroy overtook him, and he's long been seen as a superstar-in-waiting. He's the first player since Tiger to win a tournament for seven straight seasons coming out of college, and from 2008 to 2013, he was a moneymaking machine, never finishing outside the top fifteen in the FedEx Cup race. In 2014, he even stayed in the top thirty despite missing the final two months of the season.

By golf's high standards, though, there's a sense that something's missing in his career résumé, and that something is a major. In twenty-three starts, Johnson has put up seven top-tens, including a second at the 2011 British Open and his nearest miss of all—the 2010 PGA Championship.

Over and over, you hear people close to him express the same sentiment. "If he ever puts his mind to it, he's going to be the best player in the world." Okay, but when will that be?

Hand in hand with the lack of major wins comes the widespread perception that he's little more than a dumb jock in a sport that demands cunning and intelligence of its great champions. His interviews are aggressively dull, he barely seems to register when someone is talking to him, and he has the kind of dead eyes and flat affect that make people think there's not much going on under the hood.

I spent an hour with Johnson and his younger brother, Austin—A.J. to everyone else, and Dustin's caddie since late 2013—at the Colonial pro-am in Fort Worth. What struck me most in the hour we spent together was how even-keeled Johnson looked at every moment. There's a sense that nothing can get to him, and whether that's because he's not very bright, or because he's chosen to keep himself behind a sort of wall, is difficult to tell.

There were times, I admit, when he baffled me. At one point, standing on a tee box, one of his pro-am partners approached to ask for an autograph.

"Is this kosher?" the man asked, holding out a yellow flag that was full of other signatures. Johnson barely acknowledged the newcomer as he signed the flag in an empty space.

"There you go," he said.

"Will you just write 'To Steve'?" the man asked, pointing to the signature.

Johnson agreed, or at least seemed to. Slowly—Johnson does everything with the same languorous pace, as if he's never been hurried or worried in his entire life—he took the flag and wrote "All the best" above his name.

The man looked again, and hesitated when he realized that the name "Steve" still did not appear anywhere in the signature. He gave it one more shot.

"Do you mind signing it 'To Steve'?" he asked again.

Johnson slowly looked back. He peered at the flag again, still impossibly calm but a little perplexed, and spotted something.

"Well, they already got their name here," he said, pointing to the upper-left corner, where another player had written "To Steve" above his own signature.

The man looked up, trying to determine if this was some kind of joke. When Johnson just stared back at him with those emotionless eyes, he broke quickly—you don't argue with a pro golfer, even if you've paid ten thousand dollars and made what must have seemed like a very simple request.

"Yeah," the man said. "That's awesome." And he walked away.

For the most part, though, Johnson was fun and friendly with his pro-am partners, despite the fact that this wasn't his favorite activity of the week. He read putts, he chewed and spit tobacco, and he swore when he hit bad shots—"I blocked the *shit* out of it!"—just like they were bar buddies playing an afternoon nine at the local muni course.

His brother, A.J., was equally uninhibited. When Johnson's trainer came by for a hole, I told him I'd read about him online.

A.J. eyed the trainer. "I read about you in the bathroom stall," he deadpanned.

When Dustin hired his brother in late 2013, he joked with the AP that he hadn't seen A.J.'s résumé and "probably wouldn't have believed it anyway." But now, when they weren't giving each other shit, Dustin tried to crack the whip.

"What's the yardage, A.J.?" he asked on a long par 4, as his brother rested in the shade of a nearby pecan tree. A.J. fumbled for his book and scrambled over as Johnson's tone grew sharper. "What's the yardage, A.J.? *How much, A.J.?!*"

He made his point, and then it was back to the old banter. I had to wonder what his management team thought about this relationship. Personally, I found it very entertaining, but even before the suspension came down, Johnson didn't seem like the kind of person who was suited to be the more serious side of a partnership. Still, they won together in China, and he posted solid results in 2014—maybe the brotherly dynamic worked.

In some ways, the Johnsons had a normal athletic childhood. Growing up in Columbia, South Carolina, they loved being outdoors and spending summer days on friends' boats on Lake Murray. Dustin started playing golf at the Mid Carolina Club, where his dad, Scott, was the pro. When I asked what their mother Kandee did, Dustin had no idea, and A.J. had to explain that she investigated worker's compensation claims for the state. Watching his parents, Dustin realized early on that he hated school and never wanted a job that would keep him cooped up inside.

"I could have made straight As no problem," he told me. "But I didn't want to. I didn't want to put forth the effort. I was always really smart with test-taking. I'd make As on every test, but as far as doing homework? Ain't no chance. Ain't *no* chance."

The Johnsons had a great athletic pedigree—his maternal grandfather got drafted by the Lakers, though he never played a game, and his dad was a star football player in high school. What they *didn't* have was money. Johnson became good at earning his own cash, which usually meant hustling grown men at the club. He also worked every possible job at the course—cart boy, maintenance crew, club grill, catering, pro shop—you name it. It gave him a little bit of money and free balls at the driving range, which was critical to his development as a player. I told him I'd been on a golf maintenance crew in high school, too, weed-whacking all day for entire summers—hard, hot, miserable work.

"Fuck yeah, it is," he said. "I'd pull the carts out in the morning, go play a little bit, wash the carts, and then I'd go out and fuckin' weedeat. I might sneak a six-pack of beer out of the cooler and I'd weedeat with a few coldies."

After work, he'd play in "dogfight" matches around the area, hustling for a few extra dollars and honing his competitive instincts.

For fun, he and Austin would go out to a nearby rock quarry and jump from a ledge eighty feet above water's surface. Once, A.J. managed to fall in sideways, and Dustin had to dive in to fish him out.

Things began to fall apart for Johnson in his early teens, when Scott and Kandee divorced and Scott lost his job at the Mid Carolina

Club. Johnson began to skip class—"It was like pulling teeth to get me to go," he said—and got kicked off the golf team as a result.

Six months after he turned sixteen, things got really dark. Writing for *Golf Digest* in 2009, Jim Moriarty detailed a harrowing experience Johnson endured when Steve Gillian, the older brother of Johnson's friend Clint, put together a gang of boys to rob a local house. The details of the heist are available online in the court docket for the South Carolina judicial department, and they make for rough reading. Johnson had previously pawned stolen watches for Gillian, but this would be a new level of crime. It went off, and among the items the group stole was a .38 revolver.

When they met Gillian at a gas station afterward, he yelled at them for not stealing anything more valuable. Gillian then asked Johnson to buy bullets for the gun, which Johnson did, under duress, at a Walmart. The next night, Gillian attacked a group of high school kids in their house for evicting his friend from their party. He broke one's nose with a headbutt, and assaulted several others. When confronted by his friend Jason Ward—"quit picking on these little high school kids"—he became enraged, and Ward had to punch him and pin him to the ground in order to protect himself. When he finally let his friend up, they left the house together. Later that night, Gillian used the gun Johnson had helped rob, and the bullets from Walmart, to shoot and kill Ward.

Along with his anger, part of Gillian's motivation was to gain "street cred" for his music career by killing someone. He was given life without parole, his appeal was denied at both the court of appeals and state Supreme Court level, and he's in prison today. Johnson's punishment was relatively light. He only had to pay for the items he'd stolen, and agree to testify—which, it turned out, wasn't necessary. In 2009, he was granted a full pardon on the burglary charge.

He finished high school, but needed to take time off to get extra credits at Midlands Technical College while he stayed with his grandmother. After a year, he decided to join Coastal Carolina and head coach Allen Terrell at a time when most colleges were looking askance at Johnson because of his past. Terrell was a "hard-ass," Johnson told me, but exactly the kind he needed.

At Coastal Carolina, he flourished, and when he turned pro he secured his card Q-School almost immediately. Late in his rookie year, at the Turning Stone Resort Championship—a defunct tournament played on land owned by the Oneida Indian Nation in central New York—he was alarmed to find that he kept shanking balls on the range. He hit five in a row that nearly clipped the other golfers, and he had to move to the other side of the range to avoid hurting somebody.

Despite the rough beginning, and another shank in the actual tournament, he trailed Robert Allenby by just a single shot when he reached the 12th hole on Sunday.

"I'm like, *huh*," said Johnson. "Here we go, boys! I woke up real quick, because shit, I didn't even think I was in it."

By the 17th, still facing a one-shot deficit, Johnson bombed a drive down the long par 4 and stuck a wedge to six feet. He made birdie to tie Allenby, and had so much adrenaline pumping—"I was so jacked up"—that he hit what he thinks may have been the farthest drive of his life on the par-5 18th. He flew the green on the approach, but an excellent chip left him an eight-footer for birdie. Allenby missed from twelve feet, and Johnson sank the putt to win his first career PGA Tour event.

From there, he never looked back, winning at Pebble Beach the next season and starting his long streak of finishing inside the FedEx Cup top fifteen. At the 2010 U.S. Open, he led Graeme McDowell by three shots on the final day. With the pressure mounting, he rushed everything. Every shot, every putt, and even the way he walked between holes, was *fast*. Fast is not Johnson's style, and he ended up shooting 82 as McDowell won the tournament.

In August, he used that experience to slow himself down at the PGA Championship, where he entered the final hole on Sunday with a one-shot lead before he infamously grounded his club, took a penalty, and lost his chance to at least make a playoff.

• • •

"You know, if I had to do it all over again, I'd probably hit a 3-wood off the last tee instead of driver," he said of the 18th hole. "I was hitting it easy and kinda just dinked it off the heel, and it was windy so it sliced up on the hill and down the right."

As far as he knew, it wasn't a backbreaker. He hit out of the slightly sandy trampled-down area that had been covered a moment before by gallery—surely the first time the fans were ever allowed to watch the event from a "bunker"—got on the green, and gave himself a medium-length par putt to win the tournament.

He missed, which is lucky for the PGA of America, since he would have begun celebrating his first major championship. Instead, he swallowed his disappointment, made bogey, and prepared for a playoff. It wasn't until he showed up at the scoring trailer that the officials told him what had happened.

"I was mad for about thirty minutes," he told me. "At the end of the day, it's just a game, I earn a good living doing it, so I mean, what is there to get really mad about?"

With most players I'd scoff at this notion, but with Johnson, I think I believe it. He has a strange ability to shake off the unfortunate events of his life, which I saw firsthand when I asked him about the shooting incident, and how it had changed his life.

"Shit, I don't know," he said. He seemed genuinely fascinated to remember an event that, for most people, would be impossible to forget. "I haven't really thought about it in a long time. It was more just about hanging out with the wrong people. Everybody makes mistakes and, you know, I've made a lot of them, but I've always been really good about learning from them and not doing them again."

On that point, many people would beg to differ. There's a quote in Moriarty's story from a South Carolina judge who bought into that redemption angle. "Of all those people that I've sentenced, I think he's a shining example of what can be done," the judge said. "Honestly, this is a great story, how he's turned his life around."

That story was published in February 2009. We now know that Johnson failed a drug test later that year, and was also arrested for DUI. Video emerged from the arrest, and Johnson can be seen stumbling in the dark as he tries to walk a narrow line in front of a cop with a flashlight. The two failed tests for cocaine use followed, along with two suspensions (or quasi-suspensions, to play semantics). If nothing else, Johnson is a shining example of why we should always be cautious before proclaiming a person cured of his rocky beginnings.

"The past is never dead," wrote William Faulkner. "It's not even past." That wisdom applies to many golfers, not just Johnson, but he in particular seems to have difficulty escaping his own nature.

As far as his future, there will be skeptics, and there will also be those who gravitate toward the latest iteration of his redemption song. All we really know is that there's a murky cloud around Johnson, and it's impossible to predict how his story will play out over the next decade. His agents, the PGA Tour, and Johnson himself have created a dissembling fog, and for now, we can only guess at the future of a man trying not to drown in the curse of his own potential.

20

AKRON, OHIO

*What Do You Do with a Problem Called Sergio?; Jason Dufner
Chucks His Putter; Rory-Sergio II: The Bridgestone Duel*

> *"This isn't the same Sergio who considered quitting the game or
> shook his angry fist at the golf gods. He's content with himself,
> content with his life and, as a happy by-product, content with
> his golf game . . . You haven't needed to listen to his words lately
> to understand that. That happiness has been written all over
> his face lately, his buoyant smile flashing brighter than it has
> in years."*
>
> —Jason Sobel, *GolfChannel.com*

On Friday, as if determined to prove that his newfound peace
could produce tangible results on the course, Sergio caught fire
on the greens at the WGC-Bridgestone Invitational in Akron, needing
just one putt on eleven straight holes, birdieing his last seven, and tying
a Firestone Country Club course record with a 61. It was a virtuoso
performance, and the kind that proved he could play on the same foot-
ing with the best in the world.

He followed it up with a 67 on Saturday, and his cumulative -14
meant that he would take a three-shot lead into the final round. And

while winning a World Golf Championship isn't quite like winning a major, with seventy-six of the world's best players assembled, it was the next best thing. Sergio's game had never been better, and he did seem legitimately more content. That week, rumors persisted that he'd recently proposed to his girlfriend, Katharina Boehm, and one outlet reported that she confirmed the engagement. Happy at home and happy at golf, he had the chance to win a big event and erase some of the bad memories reaching back through the years.

There were two problems. First, he was only three-for-eleven at closing out fifty-four-hole leads in his career. The second was even more troubling—the man giving chase, who would be playing alongside him on Sunday, was Rory McIlroy. And Rory McIlroy, if he won, would supplant Adam Scott as the number 1 player in the world.

"I am the way I am. And for good and for worse, what you see is what you get. So the same way that my personality helps me a lot, sometimes it hurts me."

—SERGIO GARCIA

At the Players Championship, a friend with the PGA Tour tipped me off that Sergio Garcia was making a brief appearance at a clinic for kids on the other side of the course, near the sponsors' tents. Show up, he said, and maybe you can get some one-on-one time.

So I showed up, and there he was, in his scruffy glory: dressed head-to-toe in black, joking around with the kids, and offering a few tips. When he finished, and his agents corralled him for the drive back to the locker room, my Tour confederate contrived to get me a seat on the back of his four-seater cart, relegating his pretty German girlfriend to an auxiliary ride.

As it turned out, these few minutes would be the only private moments I'd share with Sergio, a character who struck me then—and does now—as both very complex and very simple, but never anywhere in between.

On that brief ride, I tried to make small talk. What's more fun, I asked, a clinic for kids or a press conference? A clinic for kids. Is it hot on a day like this, wearing all black? Yes, a little. An awkward silence descended on us then—I wanted to ask him the big questions, but as he checked his phone and gave off a vague air of distraction, the moment didn't seem right.

But it had to be, didn't it? So, as the people along our path screamed out his name as we motored by, and he nodded back, I wondered aloud if his celebrity ever became a burden.

"I never looked at it like that," he said. "It's wonderful to be great at golf, and I'm happy for that, but in the end I'm the same as you or anyone else."

A safe answer, and a banal one.

"I didn't mean it that way," I said, "but whether the constant attention—

"But that's what *I* mean," he interrupted. "Look, if I said I couldn't go to a restaurant because the people will know me or bother me, I'm putting myself above them. And if you stay away from people because you're afraid of that, or you don't act natural, they'll just be worse when they see you, because you've kept yourself hidden from them. If you're around, and they know you, it makes it easier on you. If you stay apart all the time, it separates you from them and will make your life more difficult."

So, I thought, Sergio has surprised me. Again.

But I couldn't delude myself—Sergio's honesty had not *always* served him well, because his honesty is an emotional kind, predicated on visceral reactions to his feelings of the moment.

As he has often remarked, he's invariably true to himself. The only problem is that Sergio's *self* varies rapidly from day to day, as it does for anyone who is governed more by emotion than cold logic. In reacting, they forget the more stable truths that govern their lives—that there are times when it's best to stifle certain impulses and stay quiet. When they lose control, the result can haunt them long after cooler heads prevail.

Sergio never learned to be quiet, and the thoughts he verbalizes under pressure don't always represent his inner beliefs—they only stand for a fleeting emotion. The words live on nevertheless, chiseled into the permanent record, a standard by which he can forever be judged.

Unfortunately for Sergio, he plays like he thinks. In a game that rewards patience and an even disposition, he fluctuates rapidly between emotional extremes, capable of great brilliance and, inevitably, huge letdowns. Unlike his countryman José Maria Olazabal, he can't flip a switch and become durable when victory is close at hand, and unlike Seve Ballesteros, he can't channel his passion into a great weapon under pressure. Instead, he's subject to its caprice—a prisoner, rather than a master, of his own mind.

It's been like that since the beginning. The way Sergio conducts himself under stress, both on and off the course, has overshadowed the true, thoughtful self that he embodies in quieter times.

Our Sergio—the one for public consumption—is an idiot savant, and you can always count on him to play the fool.

The career of Sergio Garcia is inextricable from that of Tiger Woods; it has been since the moment he burst onto the scene in 1999, during the final round of the PGA Championship. Garcia, then just nineteen and in his first year as a professional, had boldly engaged Tiger Woods in a dramatic back nine duel at Medinah, and was in position to pull off a stunning upset. At one point, after sinking a birdie on the 13th, he stared pointedly at Tiger in the group behind—a ballsy challenge to the best player in the world.

By the 16th hole, Sergio trailed by just a shot, but he ran into trouble off the tee when his ball settled against the base of a red oak tree, with barely enough space to even *consider,* much less execute, a swing. Rather than lay up, he took a crack with his 6-iron, flailing wildly as he twisted his head. He somehow made a clean strike, and as the ball flew up the fairway, Sergio gave chase, sprinting up the hill for a better view as it rolled onto the green. The gallery erupted, and Sergio patted his heart with a wry smile as he reveled in the cheers.

It was the same boyish enthusiasm that earned him the nickname

"El Niño," and he held the crowd in his back pocket. Tiger held on to win the tournament by a stroke, but it didn't seem to matter—finally, a true rival for golf's superstar had emerged.

There may have been warning signs that the young Spaniard was erratic—he had sobbed in his mother's arms after missing the cut at the British Open in '99, and snapped at reporters who brought it up at Medinah—but those could be explained as growing pains. His courage that Sunday proved that greatness lay in his future.

To be fair, the man has had his moments. He's won eight times on the PGA Tour, including the 2008 Players Championship, and eleven times in Europe. He's been a solid force in the Ryder Cup, amassing an 18-9-5 record, and he almost never loses in the pairs sessions. Aside from a few dips, he's spent the better part of the last fifteen years in the top twenty of the World Golf Rankings, and he's climbed as high as number 2. By those measures, he belongs in any discussion of the very best golfers of his generation.

Then why, when we think of Sergio, do our minds summon images of disappointment, and emotional letdown, and public humiliation? Why has the goodwill from Medinah vanished entirely, and why is he now the butt of a thousand jokes? When did the crowds stop loving him, and when did his great promise fade?

Again, we turn to Tiger. In 2000, a day after he'd won the WGC-NEC Invitational in dominant fashion, he met Sergio in the "Battle of Bighorn." Unless you're a very obsessive golf fan, you've probably never heard of this event, and with good reason—it was a glorified TV spectacle, treated derisively by almost everybody connected to the game, and played under the umbrella of ABC's short-lived "Monday Night Golf." Tiger came in suffering from flulike symptoms, and gave the impression that he'd rather be anywhere else.

Sergio, on the other hand, was spoiling for a fight. Twenty years old at the time, the Spaniard caught fire on the back nine and became animated over the final holes. When he won the match, 1-up, he "celebrated as if he had won the California lottery," to quote *SI*'s Michael Bamberger. It was a bizarre reaction under the circumstances, and it rubbed his opponent the wrong way.

Not that Tiger was about to complain—he had his own way of settling the score.

Sergio had challenged the greatest golfer in the world, and now he faced the difficult task of backing it up in tournaments that actually counted. In Tiger's pathologically competitive prime, though, nobody could stand up to him—not Phil Mickelson, not David Duval, and certainly not Sergio Garcia. Without knowing it, the young star carved a target on his own back that day, and it was a target that Tiger never missed. In the seven times they've been grouped together on a weekend since that fateful night, Tiger has shot the better round all seven times. Even more remarkably, *he's won all seven tournaments.*

A player like Woods has a little Michael Jordan in him. He loves—maybe even needs—an enemy, and the sight of Sergio challenging him with that impish smile at Medinah, and pumping his fist after a meaningless win at Bighorn, gave him a rival to crush. And crush him he did, with relish.

Then there was the 2006 Open Championship at Hoylake, when Tiger went out in the final group along with Sergio, who was dressed all in yellow. Tiger won and reportedly texted friends: "I just bludgeoned Tweety Bird."

—*Golf.com,* 2013

Even without Tiger, Sergio struggled under pressure. The second-place finish at the PGA in '99 was the first of 19 top-ten finishes at major championships in the next fifteen years. He won zero of those tournaments, and even though he excelled in Ryder Cup pairs, his singles record is a less impressive 3-4. Left to his own devices on the game's biggest stages, Sergio plays like a man who can't trust himself.

Some of the losses were more dramatic than others. At the 2007 British Open, he came into Sunday leading Steve Stricker by three

shots, and everyone else by six. The collapse that day was slow and agonizing, and on the 18th hole, Sergio still had an eight-foot par putt to
win the Claret Jug. He missed, and after he lost in a four-hole playoff
to Padraig Harrington, he suggested that the dark forces of fate were
aligned against him.

"I'm playing against a lot of guys out there," he said. "More than
the field."

At the PGA Championship in 2008, he held a Sunday lead as late
as the 16th hole before dumping his approach in the water and allowing Harrington to catch him yet again.

More often, the nerves sabotaged him well before the closing holes.
There's an uncomfortable feeling in the air when Sergio gets close at a
major; a sort of anxiety that reflects the energy he emits. There are jit-
ters in the way he moves, and acts, and at these moments, trouble seems
to lurk around every corner. Subconsciously, he's looking for a way to
screw things up so he can escape the awful strain. After the collapse,
he'll just shrug—perhaps believing in his heart that he's merely been
unlucky again—and either complain about his bad fortune, or pretend
that he's not in pain.

The saddest of these moments came at the 2012 Masters, when a
poor third round took him out of contention, and he moaned to Spanish reporters that he would forever have to settle for second-best. "I'm
not good enough," he said. "I don't have the thing I need to have." It
was almost worse the next year at Augusta, after an opening round 66
gave him an early lead, when he bleakly remarked, "Let's enjoy it while
it lasts." Like a self-fulfilling prophecy, it didn't.

That was only the latest in a series of self-pitying reactions from
Garcia, who had proved that he could play the martyr with the best of
them. His defeatist attitude manifested itself in strange decisions, like
the time he climbed a tree to play a shot from the branches at Bay Hill,
only to hurt his shoulder on the swing and his hamstring on the jump
down, forcing him to withdraw later in the round. At majors, he'll take
enormous risks, but not with Phil Mickelson's wild idealism; instead, it
seems as though he's yielding to an impulse that he *knows* is destruc-

tive, but ties in closely with his poisonous pessimism—"I might as well go for it, because I'm going to lose anyway."

That attitude plays directly into Sergio's penchant for quixotic choices, which always seem to strike when the stakes are highest. In the heat of battle, it's impossible for him to behave with any normalcy, which can result in brilliant episodes like the shot at Medinah, or, more often, total meltdowns. I think I understand Sergio's critical problem—his attitude is poorly suited to golf, which punishes failure far more than it rewards success. In this sport, a transcendent moment might gain you a stroke, but a bad mistake can ruin your entire tournament. A risk that ends badly will undermine three or four successes and sabotage hours of hard work.

There's an underlying truism to the spectacle and drama of most tournaments: The winner is the one who screws up the least. Sergio's brain is built wrongly for these circumstances—he may finish with the most dramatic successes, but he'll never make the fewest errors.

"Basically what this boils down to is yet another triumph for Woods over Garcia, and yet another self-inflicted wound for the talented yet seemingly fatally-flawed Spaniard, who has spent his career tilting at windmills, demons of his own creation."

—MONTE BURKE, *Forbes.com*

When you look at it from Sergio's angle, the reality of the relationship, spanning the years, must feel deeply unfair. While he suffered from depression and a collapse of his golf game after being dumped by Greg Norman's daughter, Tiger cheated on his wife with at least eleven women. Where Sergio is funny and engaging and kind to his fans, Tiger remains aloof and cold. Where Sergio lives and dies for Europe at the Ryder Cup, Tiger treats it as a chore. While Sergio is well-liked by his fellow players, Tiger is disliked by many, and merely tolerated by some—good for the game, but an unfriendly egomaniac.

And still, fans love Tiger for winning, and hate Sergio for whining. Even after Tiger's fall from grace, he retained a magnetic energy that drew people in. "Winning takes care of everything," went Nike's Lazarus-themed television spot that accompanied Tiger's comeback, and galling as that sentiment might be, it held a lot of cynical truth. The attraction remained.

Meanwhile, those same fans soured on Sergio. They sensed the absence of courage, they heard his self-pitying sound bites, and they witnessed the total lack of accountability. It's possible to respect a repeat loser who falls with dignity, but someone who can't look his failure in the eye deserves only scorn. And it was this scorn, coupled with the constant losing, that became Sergio's burden. You could see where an obsession with Tiger, and all he represented, might begin.

Tiger barely had to break a sweat to set him off. Just keep winning, and nudge him with a subtle word here and there. The whole thing even seemed to amuse him. Maybe Sergio knew it, and maybe that explains the PR disaster that followed.

At the European Tour Players' Awards Dinner in late May, the Golf Channel's Steve Sands approached Sergio and asked jokingly if he planned to have Tiger over for dinner when the two met again at the U.S. Open.

"We will have him round every night," Garcia said. "We will serve fried chicken."

In 1997, Fuzzy Zoeller speculated to reporters at Augusta that Tiger might serve fried chicken and collard greens at the champions dinner the following year, and called him a "boy" in the process. It was a pretty cut-and-dried case of condescending racism. The reaction was swift and severe—Zoeller lost his sponsorship with Kmart and Dunlop, and he hasn't been heard from since.

The reaction to Garcia's words was no less sudden, and he held an emergency press conference to address the situation. He began by apologizing to his fans, to Tiger, to his European colleagues, etc. He had very few options in the ensuing days. He left a handwritten note in Tiger's locker, and did his best to look contrite at every stop. He was abused by fans at home and abroad, but he took his medicine with a stoic silence.

Finally, the chapter was closed. Unlike the Zoeller incident, most people understood that Sergio was, at heart, harmless—it's hard to imagine a secret racist streak, but it's very easy to imagine his hatred for Tiger careening out of control in a bad moment. And though the fried chicken incident will be a stain on his image, it was never going to bury him. All it really proved—as if we needed more evidence—is that Sergio is golf's most fascinating example of a man with a talent for getting caught up a tree.

In 2014, he had rediscovered his self-belief, and Tiger had disappeared from the scene. But in a cruel irony, Sergio found himself right back in his role of second fiddle at the British Open. He settled into a familiar position, playing bridesmaid to another iconic champion with a ruthless ability to destroy his enemies. Sergio and Rory liked each other well enough, but on the course, McIlroy was unmistakably the new Tiger. And without skipping a beat, the thirty-four-year-old Spaniard stepped down to the lower rung—doomed, it seemed, to always be looking up.

First things first—the week of the WGC-Bridgestone, I was staying in a room out in the hinterlands of Ohio, somewhere between Akron and Cleveland, next to a large pond full of frogs that came out at night to torment me with their belching. In a room across the house, a nice Canadian man named Dave had come to this same house with his wife, all the way from the hinterlands of Ontario, for the same purpose—golf. We exchanged stories nightly, and on Saturday, he told me that he had been particularly surprised to see Jason Dufner give his putter away to a child in the middle of his round. A Scotty Cameron, no less!

I asked him to tell me the story once more, and tuned my ears for any deviations. Like a good witness, he repeated each detail verbatim. The Canadian wasn't cracking, and I had to admit that certain aspects checked out—Dufner had an impulsive streak, especially when he was frustrated, and he couldn't putt to save his life. I'd followed him at the PGA Championship the year before, and it remains one of the most remarkable major victories I've ever seen for the simple fact that he had almost no confidence on the greens. He hit beautiful drives and pin-point irons, then stood shaking over three-foot birdie putts, of which he made about half. Somehow, this formula saw him through

"I just like Duf," Keegan Bradley had said earlier in the week. "He makes me laugh. He's a weird guy. But he's also one of the best players out here, so I enjoy playing golf with him. Everything he does is good, and I watch everything until he gets on the green. . . . But I look away when he's got the putter in his hands."

No subject is out of bounds between the two, and they pick on each other relentlessly, to the point that it sometimes goes too far and leaves one of them seething. Bradley particularly enjoys making fun of Dufner about the PGA Championship he lost in 2011, giving Bradley his first and only major title. It struck me as a rather sensitive topic, and I asked him whether he had at least waited a respectable period before firing the first volley.

"Yeah, it was probably a year and a half later," he said, "and then it all broke loose. But he's brutal on me. There have been times that have been touchy. But I love it. It's tough, but you gotta take it."

He went on to further insult Dufner's putting, and I remembered this conversation as I listened to my Canadian friend. What did we know about Dufner? Weird guy, can't putt, a bit impulsive. Dave from Ontario was making sense. But did he *really* give his putter away?

The next day, before the leaders had even teed off, Dufner finished his awful tournament with a 77, plummeting to +14 for the week. He eluded me at the flash area, but on a desperate sortie to the locker room, I found him waiting for his food and sinking miserably, inch by inch, into a leather chair. He had the definite look of a man who did not want to be approached by a journalist.

"Hello, Jason," I said, sitting beside him. I knew to avoid pleasant-ries. "I heard a story that you gave your putter away to a kid yesterday. I wanted to make sure it was true."

"Yup." He kept his eyes straight ahead.

"Was that on number twelve?" I asked.

"Ten."

So, eight holes with no putter.

"What did you putt with?"

"Three-wood."

It turned out the kid had followed him the rest of the round, still holding the putter.

"Anything else I should know?" I asked, feeling very much like I'd overstayed my welcome.

For the first time, he looked at me. "No."

That wasn't the only bit of novelty in Akron—and thank God for that, because Akron is a town that needs all the novelty it can get.

Early on in the week, after an errant shot, Bubba had shouted, "I just can't *focus!*" at poor Ted Scott. Steven Bowditch told an Aussie reporter that the WGCs were his favorite events, since you still won money even if you shot 80 four straight times. When I walked by Jonas Blixt outside the clubhouse as he signed autographs, and jokingly asked if he could sign my reporter's notepad, he gave me that inscrutable Swedish grin and said, "I'd like to sign your chest." A woman on the ninth green told Rory that she loved him like her own child. Graham DeLaet threw a bag-kicking tantrum on Friday when he missed a series of short putts. A fan gave David Feherty a loud "you da man!" as he walked past, and without cracking a smile, Feherty responded, "I'm a woman." Jason Day withdrew with vertigo-like "dizziness" after Friday's round, probably the result of cortisone shots for his thumb combining with anti-inflammatories he was taking for a throat issue—the perfect culmination of a sabotaged year. And on Saturday, Tiger yelled at a cameraman who had gotten too close: "Can you guys give me some *fucking space?*"

That all led to the main event, on Sunday, when Tiger hurt his back on the second hole and could only gut it out until the ninth tee, at which point the pain won and he withdrew. A golf cart carried him to his car, and as hordes of journalists sprinted out from the media center, he limped over, grimacing the whole way. We surrounded him in a semicircle, like curious children gazing at a zoo creature, as he took off his Nike spikes, moaned a little for the video cameras, and disappeared behind the tinted windows of an SUV.

As I left the locker room on Sunday after tracking down Dufner, I saw something strange at a table in the dining area—Rory and Sergio, along with a smattering of agents and caddies, were eating lunch together before the final round. I knew the two were pals, but it still felt strange to see either of them consorting with the enemy in the moments before battle.

Rory kept a resolute poker face, smiling when necessary, laughing politely at jokes, but mostly just surveying every face with his usual pregame silence. Sergio, on the other hand, was a motormouth, full of nervous chatter and the kind of loud laughter you hear from people who are trying very hard to broadcast that *they are having a good time*. If he sounded transparent to me, I could only guess that Rory felt it, too.

When they made it out to the range, it was the same scene—Rory off on his own, with his caddie, J.P., and his dad, Gerry, intense and isolated. David Feherty made the rounds, stopping briefly to chat with Rory before moving on to Marc Leishman. His story must have been very funny, because it soon roped in Sergio and Justin Rose. I missed most of the main details, but got close enough to hear the punch line. Turning to his side, Feherty took a dramatic pause, squatted low to the ground, and delivered the kicker:

"He shit all *over* himself!"

Sergio and Rose doubled over laughing, Leishman just grinned and blushed, and Feherty shook his head. "Those were the days," he said, and was off.

Sergio, though, couldn't stay quiet for long. He walked over to Adam Scott for a quick chat about room service, then approached a cameraman to ask how he felt in the hot weather. "When you're as cool as me, you don't get hot," the man said.

"Ah, good answer! Good answer!" Sergio raved.

A peal of thunder rang in the sky, but the black clouds passed, and after Sergio wandered past the table with all the different balls in their color-coded bags, it was time to make the walk to the first tee.

The brick clock tower of the clubhouse loomed behind Rory and Sergio, and the crowds lined the bleachers and walkways and club-house paths. Watching the scene, I believed completely that Rory would win. But even great players have bad rounds, and maybe today was Sergio's moment to exorcise a demon or two.

Starting three back, Rory knew he had to come out and tie Sergio as soon as humanly possible in order to change the tone. The quicker he could force Sergio to grind, the quicker he could beat him with su-perior pressure play down the stretch.

Rory took driver on the short, uphill par 4, blistering it 315 yards into the left rough, while Sergio laid up. With 129 yards remaining, Sergio's approach was very mediocre, leaving thirty feet to the pin. Rory, with just seventy-eight yards, decided to take dead aim and hope an overhanging tree didn't get in his way. It did—the ball clipped the leaves on the way to the green—but the impediment only helped. The shot landed three feet from the green, and after Sergio hit his lag close, Rory made birdie.

Already, he'd chipped one shot off the lead, and I couldn't help but wonder if he hit the leaves on *purpose,* knowing exactly how they'd af-fect the ball. It was a stupid theory, and a wrong one, but Rory's game was making people like me think some very strange thoughts.

On the second, a par 5, another bomb by Rory sailed true—carving the middle path through a gauntlet of spruce, pine, oaks, maples, and sweetgums—and landed 311 yards down the fairway. He reached the green with a 5-iron from there, and two-putted for birdie. Sergio caught his second shot from the fairway a bit fat—"Is it fair to say that if he hit any farther behind it, he'd have to add it to *yesterday's* score?" Feherty asked another journalist, as he marched by. A decent pitch got him to within six feet, he hit his birdie putt tentatively, and watched the ball run past the hole. Two strokes gone.

Rory's drive on the third hole, a 442-yard par 4, was his best yet, struck pure and hard, traveling 331 yards, nothing but fairway. Forty yards behind him, Sergio found the left rough, where the ball struck a fan's hand and knocked her diamond ring into the thick grass. A search party commenced, and the jewel was finally recovered—which is more than you could say for Sergio, who failed to land his approach on the green.

Rory was better again—he lofted a perfect second shot over the small pond guarding the green, leaving himself nine feet for birdie. On the way to the green, a fan turned to his friend, pointed at Sergio, and said, "He's the definition of anti-clutch."

Sergio, now in full flailing mode, chipped his third shot to six feet, and watched as Rory canned his birdie. Three shots gone, and he had to hole a tricky par putt just to stay *tied* for the lead. When he missed, he stared in disbelief at a spot on the green and tapped in for bogey. In disgust, he tossed the ball to a standard bearer.

Four shots gone. With three birdies in three holes, the WGC-Bridgestone had a new leader: Rory McIlroy.

I could go on—fifteen holes still remained—but why bother? At that moment, everybody knew the tournament was over. At the start of the day, most of us thought Rory would be too much for poor Sergio to handle, even with a three-shot lead. If anything, we had underestimated how quickly they'd switch places. The cushion had vanished in the space of three holes, and despite his new mind-set and satisfying romantic life, Sergio was still Sergio.

It reminded me of the press conferences at the 2012 Ryder Cup, when American players and captains insisted that Brandt Snedeker, despite his penchant for collapsing in big moments, had a fierce competitive streak. That may have been true, for all we knew, but when it came time to step up on the 18th hole against Rory and Graeme McDowell in the very first match on Friday, he put his tee shot forty yards into the rough, and the Americans lost. Then, on Sunday, he fell 5&3 to Paul Lawrie as the Euros stormed back for a dramatic win.

Lesson learned: Being a winner takes more than simply *wanting* to win. If hope defined a player's career, everybody would be Rory McIlroy.

For all his talent, Sergio has something that keeps him down. Pigs will fly, and hell will freeze, before he beats Rory McIlroy head-to-head in the final round of an important tournament—at least without a tub full of anxiety pills to pacify his restless brain.

Rory was kind in the aftermath. He allowed himself just a muted fist pump on the 18th green, where he tapped in for a 66 and a two-stroke win, and he hugged Sergio. The man in second tried to take it in stride, as he always does, muting his sorrow and noting that the "spin of the greens" had changed after the rain, which apparently left him discombobulated.

In the media room, Tour officials took the two miniature Spanish flags they had prepared and placed them under a potted plant. In their place, they set up the Northern Irish flags next to the colorful trophy, framing the place where the new world number 1 would soon take his seat.

On Saturday night, Rory allowed himself to imagine what it would be like to reach that plateau. He stopped his dreaming before he got too far—"Sergio is still three ahead of me going into tomorrow"—but you couldn't help thinking that he knew exactly what would happen on Sunday.

When the dream came true, he dispensed with the false modesty. Somebody asked how many wins he thought he could snag before the season ended, and he began counting on his fingers—calculating how many tournaments remained. A few of us laughed, but it didn't seem the least bit arrogant or presumptuous. We believed him.

After the formal Q&A session had ended, as he signed the flags and boxes and hats and even a fathead emblazoned with his face, I sidled up to ask the important question: What movie had he watched the night before? What could possibly follow *Jackass Number Two*, which had seen him through Saturday night at Hoylake?

"Last night. What was it last night . . . I was flipping through channels, there was a bit of . . ."

He stared at the ceiling. When he looked down, he was smiling.

"Kick-Ass 2."

21

GREENSBORO, NORTH CAROLINA

Intolerable Cruelty at the Wyndham

Try this dilemma: You have a forty-eight-foot putt on the 18th green of a golf tournament. If you make it, you enter a playoff and have a chance to win your first PGA Tour event since 2010, snag a two-year exemption, and land in next year's Masters. But there's a catch—if you three-putt for bogey, you lose your Tour card and have to take your chances at the Web.com Tour finals series, where you'll be battling more than 130 hungry, desperate golfers over four weeks for just twenty-five spots. So, do you take the big risk? Or do you hit a nice lag and keep your card?

If you're Heath Slocum at the Wyndham Championship, there's only one answer: Go for the win. And, in this case, you run the birdie putt six feet past, miss the comebacker for par, and walk around the scoring tent in a wide-eyed daze, trying to explain your inexplicable trauma to a half-dozen television cameras while you fall deeper into shock.

"Everything just piled up on top of me," he said, his eyes moving from face to face, searching for answers that weren't there.

The PGA Tour will dish out its fair share of cruelty throughout the season, but it saves its sharpest sting for last. There is very little glory to be had in Greensboro, North Carolina—the season-ending Wyndham Championship is a minor event, skipped by many of the Tour's best players—but there is plenty of pain. It may look like a fun affair on the surface—the venue includes tropical-themed party tents, live bands, sand sculptures, and, for some reason, fake snow at the base of its sidewalk cedar trees—but the glossy veneer can't disguise the underlying anxiety.

Out on the course, the golfers are engaged in a desperate survival act. They're not fighting for trophies or exemptions or millions of dollars, but merely to keep their jobs. Failure here means relegation, down to the minor leagues of the Web.com or worse. It's their last chance to avoid golfing purgatory—a place from which some players, with time and luck, will fight their way back to the top.

And some won't.

Nicholas Thompson, fresh off a final-round 69 that moved him to even par for the tournament, already had a sense that Robert Allenby was the man to catch if he wanted to make the first event of the FedEx Cup playoffs. From there, anything was possible. A good finish at the Barclays in New Jersey would get him into the Deutsche Bank Championship in Massachusettes, and then the BMW in Colorado, and—who knows?— maybe even the season-ending Tour Championship with its huge purse and prestigious field. It may have sounded like pure fantasy, but similar stories had happened before. He just had to sneak into that first event. But without a top 125 finish in the FedEx Cup points list, the only place to go was home.

Outside the scoring trailer at Sedgefield Country Club, in the oppressive Carolina humidity, he sat beside the PGA Tour's Tom Alter and stared at the two computers resting on a black tablecloth. He knew his position was tenuous—he entered the week ranked 123rd in the FedEx Cup points standings, but a mediocre showing here had relegated him to the bubble. By Sunday morning, with just one round left in the PGA Tour's regular season, he was one of two golfers who had played himself out of the projected top 125. The other was Allenby, and

though Thompson finished early on Sunday, with hours of drama yet
to unfold, he identified the Aussie as his critical target.

In fact, Allenby would enjoy the most interesting day of any golfer
in the field, bouncing above and below the cut line with seismographic
unpredictability. His FedEx Cup fate careened like a roulette ball, diz-
zily spinning into red, and black, and red, and black, for the eight
hours it took the event to finish. These stomach-churning vicissitudes
would have been fascinating under ordinary circumstances, but one
fact made them especially so: Allenby wasn't even playing. He had
missed the cut on Friday, and now sat somewhere far away and private
where a trusted friend probably hovered nearby with a stiff drink and a
sack of smelling salts.

"What I *want* you to tell me," Thompson said to Alter, his irritation
just beginning to show, "is where I have to finish to catch Allenby."

Alter, the VP of Communications for the PGA Tour and the man
who agreed to let me shadow him on the harshest day of golf's calendar, soon arrived at the answer: 68th place.

Alter is in a very delicate and unenviable position on a day like
Sunday. Any idiot can deliver good news, but it takes a practiced hand
to convey misery and heartbreak, and that was the exact nature of Alter's mission on Sunday. Over and over, he had to pronounce death
sentences of all kinds, with only a very occasional bit of happiness
mixed in.

Luckily, the Tour chose well—Alter had a terrific bedside manner.
He was precise, too. Using several computer simulations, and his reser-
voir of experience, he had a very solid idea of which figures the players
would have to reach by day's end to meet certain milestones. For a top-
125 finish on the money list and the chance to retain full Tour status,
he told me on Sunday morning, you'd probably need around $712,000.
For top 125 on the FedEx points list, and a berth in the playoffs, he
estimated that the cutoff would come somewhere near 450 points. As
it happened, the 125th place finisher on the money list earned $713,337,
and the points cutoff came in at 438.

Nicholas Thompson, knowing he needed to jump up to 68th,
peered at the computer. Behind him, leaning over a blue Wyndham

barrier and frantically waving a baseball hat, a raving little autograph hound called out to his playing partner.

"Mr. Malinari!" he screamed, at Peter Malnati. The same kid would later refer to Jeff Overton as "Everton" and address Brooks Koepka with what sounded like a bastardized version of Kansas's state capital: "Kopeka." And he wasn't even the most notable of the urchins; down the line ten feet, a boy wearing a "Got Jesus?" T-shirt asked every player, for reasons that remain unclear to me, to sign his white coffee mug.

If Thompson was fazed by the circus, he didn't show it. "Am I back to T-69 now?" he asked, finding the name "Thompson" on the computer in that spot. The hope faded almost as fast as it appeared—a case of mistaken identity.

"Oh, that's *Michael* Thompson. Fuck."

When he located his actual name farther down at T-73, he pronounced himself dead and walked away.

Even without a place in the Barclays, Thompson had a nice safety net—his position on the money list was secure, and he'd retain his card in 2015 since the tour offers amnesty to the top 125 on money and FedEx lists alike. But safety nets and silver linings were in short supply Sunday. Everywhere you looked, it was a landscape of suffering and devastation.

J. J. Henry, too far back on the money list and needing to make the cut on FedEx Cup points alone, had an eagle attempt on the 15th hole to go from 130th position to 124th. He made birdie, which got him up to 126th with three holes to play. On the difficult uphill par-4 18th, needing one last three, he placed his approach in the greenside bunker, made bogey, and lost his status.

Brad Fritsch, the Canadian who started the week hopelessly stuck in 163rd place, proceeded to defy the odds by playing his way into Sunday's final group. He still had a chance to earn limited Tour status by finishing in the top 150, and after a decent start to his round, all he needed was a birdie on one of the final six holes. His best chance came on the 15th, but he failed to convert a five-foot putt. When he couldn't reach the 18th green with his second shot, he had doomed himself to 151st place and a trip to the Web.com Finals.

Everyone in Greensboro was playing for something. Even at the top, a player like Patrick Reed hoped to safeguard his spot in the Tour Championship, with its super-elite field of thirty golfers, against the vagaries of what might happen in the first three playoff events. A step below him, others strove to lock up berths at the BMW Championship (seventy players) or the Deutsche Bank (one hundred). Next came the FedEx Cup bubblers, like Thompson and Allenby, hovering around 125, but with a puncher's chance to regain status at the Web.com Tour Finals as long as they finished inside the top two hundred.

Such luxuries were denied Kevin Foley, the twenty-seven-year-old Penn State alum who earned one of the last spots from the Web.com Finals last year but who had trouble even *entering* PGA Tour tournaments in 2014. Once he finally got to play, he couldn't seem to make a cut, and the negative energy mounted. He came into Greensboro fresh off six straight missed cuts, saddled with an ugly FedEx Cup rank of 208th. In order to even have a shot at the Web.com Finals series—a fate most others were trying to avoid—he'd need to find some of the old magic and crack the top two hundred.

He made the cut, and when he birdied 15 and 16 on Sunday, it looked as though he'd broken through. It didn't even matter that he missed a four-foot par putt on 18, we thought—it was irrelevant, he'd done enough. The computers confirmed that he'd reached number 200 on the nose, knocking David Duval into the wilderness below, and we were pretty sure that nobody could catch him. His mother had come to see him play, and was waiting even now beyond the blue barriers. Failure-by-gut-punch would be a rotten way to end the weekend.

But wait. There *was* one more golfer on the course. . . .

There *was* Doug LaBelle II. But he was below Foley and already on No. 15. To pass him, he'd have to play his last four holes at two-under. Even Murphy's Law couldn't be that cruel, because position number 201 is a brutal scene. It means you head straight to the second stage of Web.com Q-School, and even if you fight your way through that, your reward is to face all the losers of the Web.com Finals in the last stage. One stumble in that whole process, and it's a fast track to the small time—sad little tours named after sad little strip-mall restaurants. Or, hell of hells, a desk job . . .

LaBelle birdied 15. He birdied 16 to pass Foley. He made par on 17. He found the fairway and green on 18, and two-putted for par. And those of us who expected a sympathetic finish stood around with our mouths agape. Foley had fallen to 201.

What about Jason Allred, comeback kid of the year, who blazed a trail out of golf obscurity in February when he battled Bubba Watson at the Northern Trust Open to earn a third place finish and more money—$388,600—than he had won in his entire career?

His third child, Lucy Hope, was now six months old, and her life had coincided with her father's rejuvenated golf career. He hadn't had a Tour card since 2008, but he was closer than ever after a year of fighting for tournament spots through Monday qualifying and sponsor exemptions. In that time, he had also become a minor media darling—with his gracious attitude and relentless kindness, everybody liked him.

Since Los Angeles, events had not been easy to come by for Allred, but he capitalized when he could—fifteenth at the Memorial, sixth at the Barracuda Championship—to come close to gaining full status for 2015. He came out firing in Greensboro, shooting 69-66-67 over the first three days. He needed to make about $100,000, which meant posting a final round of 68 or better.

But this wasn't a day for happy endings. The Oregon native began his round knowing exactly how much was at stake, and in golf, that knowledge isn't always helpful. He played tense, and the end came early—on the 8th hole, he hit two shots out of bounds, taking an unthinkable quadruple-bogey. He lost all the momentum he'd built up over three days—hell, over a season—and even an optimistic guy like Allred knew his chances were over. When he walked to the scoring trailer two hours later, all he could do was hug his wife, Kimberly, and fight back the tears.

• • •

Camillo Villegas is the kind of person who, according to Florida coach Buddy Alexander, numbers his socks so he can match them up when they come out of the washing machine. He emerged from the chaos to win the Wyndham Championship for his first Tour victory in four years. As the devastation continued, though, nobody really noticed— his happiness was obscured by all the dark clouds.

Amid the awful vacillations and gratuitous heartbreak, victims stacked up left and right. Among them was Nicholas Thompson, who fell to 126th and would not be making the trip to the Barclays. Nor would Slocum, and nor would Martin Laird, who needed birdie on 18 and, like so many others, found the sand instead.

Traveling in their stead, safe in 125th place after surviving the day of agony, was Robert Allenby. Call it a triumph for the cynics—the big win belonged to the man who wasn't there.

22

LOUISVILLE, KENTUCKY

*The PGA Championship; The Great Schism and a Crisis of Identity;
Valhalla's Bad Rap; The New King*

> *"I've had a great run of golf and played well over the past few
> months. I said at the start of the year that golf was looking for
> someone to put their hand up and sort of become one of the
> dominant players in the game. I felt like I had the ability to
> do that."*
>
> —RORY McILROY

The moment that defined Rory McIlroy, for me, came in the sweltering Kentucky heat at Valhalla Golf Club, in the final round of the PGA Championship. The brutal, unyielding sun seemed to thicken the blood of every golfer on the course, and the pace of play on the front nine moved from lethargic to glacial. McIlroy began the day with a two-stroke lead, but before long, Phil Mickelson and Rickie Fowler had erased the deficit from a group ahead.

By the sixth hole, Rory and Phil were tied at -12, and Fowler, fresh off a three-birdie run, led them both at -13. For Fowler, this was the first time—literally the first full hole—that he had ever led a major on Sunday.

An early weather delay had forced the PGA of America to condense the later tee times, and things got so slow in the early afternoon that multiple groups began to stack up on the tee boxes. That was the case on the sixth, when Rory arrived to find Mickelson and Fowler still waiting to hit their first shots on the long par 4.

Bernd Wiesberger, Rory's playing partner, walked over to the two golfers and made polite conversation. It's what you'd expect—despite the pressure, social decorum dictates that you exchange pleasantries, and pretend it's just an ordinary round on an ordinary day. J. P. Fitzgerald, Rory's caddie, did the same. Phil and Rickie gazed down the fairway and held a halting conversation—something about golf courses they'd played—and Phil mindlessly juggled a ball, tap, tap, tapping it with the face of his hybrid.

As they waited, a strange kind of energy took over the scene, and it emanated from the man who *wasn't* talking. Ten feet away, Rory McIlroy sat on a bench, seething and motionless, hard eyes fixed on empty space. It was hard not to notice that he hadn't offered any greeting to his fellow golfers—not a wave, not a tilt of his head, not so much as a spare look in their direction. He simply sat down and glared.

His silence affected Phil and Rickie. They flashed a glance or two at the bench where Rory sat, and they looked flustered—caught off balance by the fact that he hadn't said hello. Once it became clear that there would be no words exchanged, they paced the tee box, stared ahead, and tried to ignore the best player in the world. The cold shoulder from McIlroy presented them with two options—approach him and blow the thing wide open, or pretend as though it wasn't happening. They chose the latter.

Their small pantomime grew into a full performance as Rory's fixed gaze went unbroken. They knew to look upset would show weakness, so they feigned indifference. All the while, they must have been cursing the delays—they longed for the freedom of the fairway, away from this tension, while Rory could have stayed comfortably in that one spot, you sensed, for hours.

It was such a small moment, but I couldn't forget it. In the days after the tournament ended, I tried to analyze what was happening on that tee box. Was Rory's silence just a result of frustration after a slow start? Was he simply behaving like he does on the range, staying inside a small bubble, free of friends, agents, and writers, to shut out any distractions? Was there an element of purposeful intimidation?

It didn't matter which theory was correct, or if the truth is a blend of them all. What mattered was that Rory himself—the imperturbable force with the bloodless, roaming eyes—seemed totally at ease. It was a feat of competitive psychology, whether he meant it or not. He was at peace with himself, social niceties be damned.

That, I realized, was the gift of total confidence—a liberating freedom from self-doubt, even while your enemies fight off their own demons and blindly reach for greatness. Rory had the ruthless intelligence of the gangster—the ability to reveal the neuroses in those around him, and subconsciously exacerbate and exploit them. His presence dominated the tee box, and he never had to utter a single word. Everyone else—including two of the world's best players—reacted to *him*.

I had never seen anything like it. That's the Rory that stayed in my head long after the season had ended. Forget the thoughtful philosopher he became in the media room, or the fresh-faced icon who elicited screams of adoration from the gallery, or the grinning rogue that made racy headlines off the golf course. That day in Valhalla, on the sixth tee box, the essential Rory emerged—Rory the alpha dog. The man who owns the moment.

————————

Q. There are a lot of young guys this year who are winning that grew up watching you play, idolizing you and being inspired by you, and now here they are competing with you. I'm curious what that feels like, if that's an odd feeling in any way or if it's just flattering or what?

PHIL MICKELSON: Just makes me feel old, that's all (laughter). You know, when somebody says, yeah, I used to watch you on TV when I was six, how do you respond to that? Great. (Laughter).

It was fireworks and drama right from the start in Louisville, where if you were a journalist who didn't want to be left behind, you had better hit the ground running. This was "glory's last shot," as the PGA Championship once called itself—the fourth and final major of the year. It also happens to be the only major with a serious, ongoing identity crisis.

It all stems from the Great Schism of 1968, a dramatic chapter in golf history when more than two hundred active touring professionals, spearheaded by Jack Nicklaus and a few others, made a move to break away from the PGA of America and form a separate organization. For years, their frustration had mounted, owing in large part to the PGA's habit of funneling the growing amounts of television money away from the players who had earned it. The turning point came when Arnold Palmer finally joined the rebellion and funding was secured—with possible assistance from Las Vegas mafia figures, according to a *Vice Sports* article that referenced FBI memos—and by 1975, the "PGA Tour" name had been adopted.

That left the PGA of America as the parent organization of the country's vast network of club professionals, rather than its touring pros.[14] There were, however, two notable exceptions. The PGA of America kept the PGA Championship, a valuable commodity as a major, and they also held on to a modest match play event called the Ryder Cup, which featured American golfers beating the hell out of a sorry group of Brits every two years.

The schism didn't kill the PGA Championship, or strip it of major status, but it did spark the identity crisis that has dogged it ever since. Each of the other three majors has forged an important niche in the golf world—the U.S. Open is America's championship, the British Open functions as the crown event for all of Europe, and the Masters has managed to drape itself in so much prestige that it somehow eclipsed them all. But what is the PGA Championship? Before 1968, it was the players' major, but that changed when it lost the all-important

---

[14] Although, as chronicled in Adam Schupak's excellent *Deane Beman: Golf's Driving Force,* they didn't become completely separate entities until the early nineties.

ingredient—the players themselves. In a move that must have irked their former masters, the PGA Tour even founded an event called The Tournament Players Championship.

Where did that leave the PGA Championship? As a sort of historical leftover—a vestigial tail, so to speak, and one that had to fight for recognition as time went on. In the early PGA Tour days, Commissioner Deane Beman even had ambitions of turning the Players Championship into the fourth major, and there's no doubt which event he thought it might replace.

Even today, the tournament typically registers the lowest television ratings of the three American majors, and a 2012 *Sports Illustrated* survey of Tour pros revealed that if they had their choice of winning any major, only two percent would choose the PGA Championship. Hence taglines like "Glory's Last Shot," which was changed at the PGA Tour's request in 2013, since they felt it diminished the FedEx Cup playoffs, or the 2014 official program, which featured the words, "This is Major"—almost as if golf fans needed the reminder.

That kind of insecurity didn't bode well for 2014, a year that had already been historically poor for television ratings across the board. The numbers told a sorry tale—with no Tiger Woods, the Masters gave CBS its lowest ratings since 1957 (with ESPN faring even worse in the early rounds), the British Open on ESPN tied its second-lowest Sunday ratings since 1981, and the U.S. Open yielded an all-time low in final round ratings as Martin Kaymer strolled to a drama-free victory.

The PGA of America *did* have one ace up its sleeve—Valhalla Golf Club, which it had purchased by increments between 1993 and 2000. The course had hosted two previous PGA Championships and the 2008 Ryder Cup, and always seemed to produce the kind of dramatic golf that exceeded its reputation as a very basic track. This is where Mark Brooks beat Kentucky native Kenny Perry in a playoff in '96, and where Tiger Woods survived the greatest duel of his golf career against the unheralded Bob May, sinking a birdie putt on 18 to force a three-hole playoff, which he won by a stroke. It's also the sight of America's only triumph in the past fifteen years at the Ryder Cup—that unremarkable match play event the PGA of America kept in its back pocket after the schism, and which blossomed with time into one of the sport's greatest showcases.

As it turned out, Valhalla would deliver again in 2014, with a final round so spectacular that it reversed the ratings trends of a tough season and drew the PGA Championship's best audience in five years.

The fun began long before Thursday's first round. For starters, you had Bubba making a fool of himself at the long-drive competition and finally turning the media establishment wholeheartedly against him. That was just the start of a long week that saw him swear freely on the course, complain about the weather, and try to dodge anyone holding a pen or tape recorder once he realized it had all gone horribly wrong.

Then there was Tiger, who surprised us all by stumbling onto the grounds on Wednesday and announcing his intention to actually *play*. We had assumed that his back wouldn't heal in time, but here he was, and he was still talking about making the Ryder Cup team—which, as he told Tom Watson, he wanted to do "in the worst way."

The only problem was that the mere idea of Tiger coming within a mile of Team USA was outrageous. Barring an outright win at Valhalla, he had done nothing to prove that he deserved a captain's pick, but it was just another example of his fanatical self-belief. The same zealotry that had carried him to fourteen major titles was now making it impossible for him to see things realistically, or to admit that maybe he should slow down and stay home for a few months.

On the European side, McGinley would be dealing from a stacked deck. I watched him have a long conversation with Victor Dubuisson during the Frenchman's practice round—something I thought was impossible—and in between his existential shrugs, Victor even smiled once or twice. I had the passing thought that maybe I'd underestimated McGinley, a so-so player in his day and, on the face of it, a strange choice for captain.

When Victor left, I watched in astonishment as he actually signed a few autographs along the ropes.

"Parlez-vous français?!" screamed one of the fans, drawing a glare

from Dubuisson and laughs from the crowd. The Kentuckians began shouting nonsensical phrases at him the way someone might bark at a dog just to see its reaction.

"Sacre bleu!"

"Comment allez-vous!"

In the end, the galleries at Valhalla turned out to be the best, most rambunctious spectators of the season. The noise and passion beat anything we saw all year, and they deserved the Sunday finish they got.

At the same time, it wasn't a delicate or subtle group of people. On Saturday, I made the mistake of accidentally wearing a Duke University hat, forgetting that I was in the heart of Kentucky Wildcat country, where basketball reigned supreme and Duke was a hated enemy. I won't recount my adventures that afternoon, except to say that "Duke cocksucker" was probably the nicest thing I was called. Somewhere around the turn that day, I stuffed the hat in my pocket.

"Out here in the heat and humidity and bluegrass, Valhalla is gangly, hard to love and still trying to grow up and find personal acceptance.

Could that happen this week? Well, it's going to be a struggle. Let's just say that the chances of Valhalla earning respect this week are about as good as the Kentucky Derby switching from horses to lawn mowers."

—THOMAS BONK, *LA Times,*
before the 2000 PGA Championship

The Old Norse word "Valhöll" means "hall of the slain," and in their mythology, Valhalla is where warriors go after death, to assemble under the god Odin and prepare for an apocalyptic battle called Ragnarök. My advice would be to wipe that image completely from your mind, because it's ill-suited to the Southern gothic course bearing its name just east of Louisville—a repurposed plot of undulant land in the Ohio River Valley. This Valhalla sits close to the site of several Civil War skirmishes, where in 1862, Confederates came within ten miles of capturing Louisville and the entire state of Kentucky before being driven back in October.

The slow, brown waters of Floyds Fork, a tributary of the Salt River, carve a sinuous path through the course. With the sycamores and birches growing out from the shore, the whole scene gives off a primordial vibe. The front nine is mostly low river plains, with the back nine rising to higher ground, lined with silver maples and oaks and hickories. It culminates in the 18th hole, an uphill par 5 that runs alongside Brush Run Creek, where a stone-terraced pond attracts wayward drives on the right.

Now might be a good time to mention the heat. The climate in this part of the country is called "humid subtropical," and that tells you just about everything you need to know. An occasional breeze blows from the east, but I emphasize the word *occasional*—for the most part, the heat is trapped in the valley, and when temperatures rise into the nineties and higher in late summer, it's absolutely hellish. That's especially true when it's wet—in most parts of the country, rain will break a humid spell, but in Kentucky, it only makes things worse. On Sunday, in the muggy afternoon heat following a rain delay, Igor Guryashkin of Louisville's *Voice-Tribune* put it best as he surveyed the gallery, thousands strong, sweating in bourgeois agony.

"It's an upper-middle-class Vietnam," he murmured.

Players and writers are not overly kind to the course—it plays too easy, some believe, while others call features like the island green on no. 13 gimmicky, and say it lacks character. Personally, sweltering conditions aside, I loved it—the bluegrass roughs, the dense vegetation, and the deep umber of the river waters made it look totally unique. There were ancient undercurrents here, and walking the course felt like stepping into national folklore. Kentucky's Valhalla didn't feel very Norse, but I wasn't surprised that it always delivered dramatic endings, as if adding chapters to a distinctly American mythology.

.   .   .

On Thursday at the PGA Championship, the year's three major winners set out together in the featured group. Golf can rarely be counted on to deliver the *ideal* Sunday duel—how many times did Tiger and Phil battle it out down the stretch at a major, or Jack and Arnie?—so this threesome is typically as good as it gets. If nothing else, it provides a unique competitive theater for the year's biggest stars, even if lasts just two days. I was particularly excited this year, because the combination of Rory McIlroy, Martin Kaymer, and Bubba Watson presented a confluence of strong personalities, and there was no predicting how they'd mix.

Unfortunately, it didn't amount to much of anything but a showcase for the man from Northern Ireland. The opening days at Valhalla belonged to Rory, and reaffirmed what we'd learned in the past month—nobody compared.

On Thursday, he had already reached -3 by the turn—and many of us were already christening him the winner—when he made two rare unforced errors. A double-bogey on the 10th and a missed par putt on 11 undid all the good work of the front nine, and sent him falling back to even for the day. He threw the putter at his bag after 11, and marched to the next tee knowing he'd just ruined his hot start. I wondered if we'd finally see him wallow, or let discouragement hinder the rest of his round.

But this was Rory in 2014, and I should have known better. He shook off the malaise and made four straight birdies, sinking putts from everywhere, to roar back to -4 by the 15th hole. On 16 and 17, he had two more birdie tries, and reacted with astonishment when he missed the putts. So did everyone else—he was rolling it so perfectly on the greens that every miss felt like an anomaly. On 18, still very much in the zone, he reached the green in two and missed his eagle putt by inches. When he tapped in for birdie, he had played his last seven holes in 5-under—a spectacular finishing flurry.

He started modestly on Friday, but on the front nine, he was keeping up with Bubba off the tee, and occasionally outdriving him. With the veins on his forearms bulging and sweat pouring off his brow, Rory blasted drive after drive with the same power—and greater consistency—than the longest driver in the game. It's no wonder that Kaymer admitted to a bit of intimidation; even Bubba, off in his own world, must have noticed.

The course in general was built for long drivers that week, and the damp conditions meant that short hitters like Graeme McDowell wouldn't get the kind of roll-out that helped bridge the distance gap on dry, hard courses.

"I'm just banging my head against the wall out there," McDowell would say later. "It's impossible for me to compete unless I'm hitting 3-hybrid to ten feet all day long, which I'm not going to do. Watching the coverage this afternoon was depressing. Seeing Rory hit 9-iron to 17; it's like, you know, I hit 3-iron in the morning."

Rory finished with an eagle on 18, and had established a one-shot lead over Jason Day and Furyk, both at -8. Rickie Fowler lurked just a shot behind, trying to become only the third player in history to finish top-five in all four majors in one calendar year. Phil Mickelson was at -6, making one of his few real appearances near the top of *any* leaderboard in 2014, major or otherwise. Tiger, to nobody's surprise, missed the cut.

In the final group on Saturday, Rory and Day played even for the front nine, allowing the rest of the field to catch up. When Day yanked a ball left of the creek on the second, David Feherty managed to find it in the high grass. It enabled Day to walk barefoot across the creek and play out to the green for a par save, while locals grimaced and prayed he wouldn't trip over a copperhead snake.

On nos. 10 and 15, Day succumbed to the same reversals that had disheartened Kaymer—he got closer on his approach, and watched Rory knock in a longer birdie putt just before missing his own. After 15, they were tied at 2-under for the day, but Rory was ready with his patented great finish. A fifteen-footer for birdie on the 16th brought him to -12, and after a good shot from the bunker on 18, he stood in front of a wall of photographers and sunk his seven-foot birdie putt to finish at -13, one shot clear of the Austrian Bernd Wiesberger. Fowler and Mickelson had closed well behind them, and would play in Sunday's second-to-last group.

For Fowler, it would mark his fourth straight shot at a come-from-behind win in a major, and his most realistic chance yet. In order to break through, he'd have to prove that he could withstand Rory's inevitable closing sprint, and put together some late fireworks of his own.

Phil was no stranger to the pressure of major championships, but he had admitted after the first round that his disappointing year—which included zero top tens, to that point—had dulled his instincts, and made him more prone to nerves. His season had undoubtedly suffered because of an FBI investigation that threatened to implicate him in an insider trading scandal, together with a Las Vegas gambling maven and a billionaire investor. Mickelson was cleared of the original charges in June, though the *New York Post* reported in late August that investigations into a related matter continued. They also noted that Mickelson had been stopped by FBI agents at several points during the season, including once at the Memorial in June. The stress had a deleterious effect on his game, and he was only now recovering his form.

He'd have to come out scorching on Sunday if he wanted to make up three shots on Rory. Starting in the late spring, questions about age had been landing on older players like Phil, Tiger, and Furyk. This would be a chance to strike a blow for the old guys, and to drive a stake into the youth movement in the season's final major.

———————

"You know, it's beginning to look a little Tigeresque I suppose. I said to the boys at The Open, I didn't think we were going to see the new Tiger era, as in someone creating their own kind of Tigeresque era just yet. . . . I'm not eating my words, but I'm certainly starting to chew on them."

—GRAEME McDOWELL,
Sunday, as the leaders took the course

Rain soaked Valhalla on Sunday morning, and casual water built up all over the fairways and greens, making early conditions very difficult. The PGA of America let the early wave play as long as they could—sacrificial lambs, in a way, in the fight to ensure that the players who mattered would beat the sunset—but finally, just before one p.m., they had to call the golfers off the course. These are nightmare situations for any major; the battle for TV ratings is tough enough on its own, but a Monday morning finish is the ultimate kiss of death.

When play resumed two hours later, the action slowed to a crawl. Worse, the walkways around the course had turned into mud pits, which meant many of the 46,000 fans in attendance would slip and fall. The only bright side for Valhalla was the new irrigation system, which worked beautifully to drain the worst of the standing water and get the course into playable shape by 2:40. Without it, a Monday finish would have been inevitable. But with Rory and Wiesberger set to finally tee off at 4:19, there was still a faint prayer of finishing.

On the range beforehand, the sun returned with a vengeance, and the combination of torrid heat and post-rain humidity can't accurately be described with words like sultry, sticky, sweltering, or stuffy. It got to the point that we looked forward to the passing of the television blimp, and praised it like a merciful god when it blotted out the sun.

Butch Harmon stood with Rickie, then moved on to Phil. For reasons I still can't understand, Phil was wearing black from head-to-toe, including pinstripe pants that made him look like he was on the way to a mob conference in the Catskills. Rory, as usual, isolated himself from the rest. The cameramen chased them as they moved from the range to the putting green, beneath the clubhouse's giant Omega clock tower. I followed Phil and Rickie to the first tee, where one fan got a huge laugh by shouting, "Light it up, little man!" at Fowler. Another encouraged Phil with a cry of "Today's your day! Rory's gonna choke!"

On the first hole, a short dogleg left, Phil got off to a hot start by draining his birdie, and setting the thousands of spectators afire. There was no question about who the fan favorite would be—even one of the grim policemen broke character and applauded, his thick mustache twitching in pleasure.

Rickie hit his drive into the creek on the second. That must have made the designers happy, because they had moved the green a good twenty yards left to bring this water into play. He took the penalty and scrambled for bogey, but on the third, a long 205-yard par 3, he flew his approach over the muddy waters of Floyds Fork and stuck it on the soft green three feet from the pin. Phil got close, too, ten feet away, and both rolled in their birdie putts.

The fourth hole is a short par 4 that takes an extreme bend to the left, and players aim for the right side of the fairway, setting up an open approach to the center of the green, safe from the bunkers. That's exactly where Rickie ended up, and it gave him a mere seventy-six yards to the hole. A nifty wedge left six feet for birdie, and he hit it again. When news came from behind that Rory had three-putted the third green, it meant that five players were now tied at -12, including Phil, Rickie, Wiesberger, and Henrik Stenson.

The wet heat stifled, but it wasn't affecting Fowler, who continued to shine on no. 5 with another perfect 305-yard drive. He went flag-hunting on his approach, and left it just in the fringe. After Phil got out of trouble from the rough, Rickie stood over his nineteen-foot chip, struck it with just the right touch, and watched as it dropped in the hole.

The moment it fell, he took the first major Sunday lead of his life. He and Phil pounded fists, clearly enjoying every minute of their excellent front nine, and the fans roared their approval.

Rory made par as they waited on the sixth tee, still a shot behind Fowler. He stalked up to join them on the tee box, and that's when the strange scene played out that stuck in my head long after the tournament was over—Rory, in a mad, semi-hypnotic state, sitting by himself, mouth open, staring with a malevolent silence.

Fans and marshals lined the hillside behind the seventh green, holding binoculars and quiet signs. They threw their hands up in agony as Phil's eagle putt refused to take the last break and drop, groaning in concert. He made birdie, though, and so did Rickie, who managed to put backspin on his shot out of the bunker despite a tricky lie, and holed his putt from six feet. That kept him one shot ahead of both Phil and Henrik Stenson, who had also birdied the seventh.

Behind them, Rory took command of the pairing from Wiesberger, who had bogeyed the sixth and wouldn't make a single birdie all day on a very "gettable" course. Unlike Phil and Rickie, who were creating energy for each other, Rory was in the midst of a lonely chase. A bogey on six dropped him back to -11, three shots off the lead, but he recovered with an up-and-down from just beyond Rickie's bunker on seven for birdie. When Stenson buried a twenty-six-footer on nine and Mickelson followed with a ten-footer on the same hole, he now trailed three players by two shots each.

As the back nine began, it looked like Rory's immortal aura had faded. Stenson and Mickelson failed to birdie the difficult par-5 10th, but Fowler did not, sinking a twenty-eight-foot putt to grab solo command of the lead at -15 with just eight holes to play. Rory watched Fowler's putt fall from the 10th fairway, where he stood over his 303-yard drive, and the roar of the fans told him that he trailed his American rival by three shots. He couldn't wait much longer to make a move. He had already lost five strokes to Fowler, who was absolutely scorching, and even if he *could* catch him, Mickelson and Stenson had surged ahead as well.

With 281 yards remaining to the hole, he faced a hard choice. Nobody in the entire field had hit the green in two shots all day—not even Bubba Watson. Rory still had bad memories from Thursday, when he'd attempted a similar shot with a 3-wood and hit it out of bounds, leading to the double bogey that killed his hot start. If Fowler hadn't just made his long birdie putt, Rory likely would have laid up.

That was no longer possible, so he pulled out the 3-wood again. His aim was to hit a "high, hard draw" as he explained later, letting the ball curve its way from right to left and settle onto the green. The minute he struck it, though, his mouth twisted up in distaste—the ball came out low and left, nothing like he'd planned. He saw it drift, and wondered if he was bound for another out-of-bounds penalty, which would bury him for good. Strangely, though, the ball began to fade, cutting back to the right and staying within the confines of the fairway. Rory marched ahead, watching intently as the ball hit a hard patch of turf and skipped onto the green. It didn't stop rolling until it had come to rest seven feet from the cup.

It was by far the best shot of the tournament, and the most important shot Rory had hit all year. The fact that it was completely lucky made no difference to the men he was chasing—all they knew, from the roar of the gallery, was that Rory had done something amazing on the 10th. When he holed the eagle putt, he caught Mickelson and Stenson in one fell swoop, and served notice to Fowler that he was just one shot away, hot on his trail.

Phil and Rickie's front nine momentum came to a screeching halt with that 3-wood, and the tone of the entire tournament changed. Now all the missed opportunities—Stenson's eight-foot miss on the 11th when a birdie would have given him the outright lead, or Phil's errant twelve-footer for birdie on the 10th—looked less like minor mistakes and more like fatal errors. There was no longer any comfort to be found in Valhalla—every chance they didn't convert could be the one that buried them. The best player in the world was on the chase, and everybody knew he would close fast.

The challenge facing Rickie and Phil now was to continue putting out positive energy for each other, and keep the birdie streak alive on the back nine, when the pressure would feel quite different. In a strange way, they had to stay locked in a team effort against Rory—if it turned into a battle of lone wolves, there was little doubt who would win.

Rory's eagle had transformed him into a predator, and facing the same tee shot on the 11th, he didn't bother avoiding the bunker, choosing instead to go straight over it with a 6-iron. The result was brilliant, but he narrowly missed his thirteen-foot birdie attempt, granting his competitors a reprieve. The 12th hole, with its downhill approach, nearly brought Phil down on its own. He made a mess of it, and was forced to pitch his third shot twenty-eight feet past the hole. From there, facing a sure bogey, he drained the long putt and punched his fist in relief. Rickie found trouble, too, but a good chip set him up for a short par putt. Ahead of them, Stenson birdied 13 after an excellent approach to the island green, and tied the lead.

Before Rickie and Phil could get to the 13th tee, Rory, high on a hill above them, stuck his approach on 12 to eight feet. Again, it seemed like the moment when he would catch them, and again, surprisingly, he missed his short birdie and settled for par. Another hole, another reprieve, but Rory was clearly dialed in, and it was only a matter of time before he converted. Phil and Rickie, on the other hand, had begun to scramble after their daylong birdie fest. Rory stole the initiative, and if Phil and Rickie didn't take it back quickly, they were doomed.

When writers denounce Valhalla, they inevitably mention the 13th hole, a short par 4 with an island green that many see as a pointless novelty. Unlike Sawgrass, the hole here is so short that players can take a safe iron off the tee and leave themselves with any distance they want—usually somewhere from 90 to 105 yards—into the pin. It looks nice, with a circular wall of stacked stone rising from the water and framing the green, but as a professional golf hole, it doesn't make much sense. On Sunday, the PGA of America tried to heighten the difficulty by placing the flag on the far right of the green, just a few feet from the water.

Phil attacked from the fairway, eyes now shining with their lunatic fervor, and stuck his wedge to twelve feet. Rickie, on the other hand, hit a mediocre shot that left him thirty-two feet, and he never had the right line on the birdie putt. Phil, with a chance for the outright lead, hit his worst putt of the day—a total misread—and ahead on the 14th, Stenson fell back to -14 with a bogey.

Their missteps gave Rory his third chance to equal the leaders, and this time he didn't waste it. With ninety-two yards to the green, he ignored the water and flew his sand wedge directly at the pin. It stopped two feet away, and he dropped the birdie with a fist pump and a twirl of the putter. The three were now deadlocked at -15 with five holes to play. On paper, Phil and Rickie still had the better Sunday, but for

Rory, it felt like a clean slate. He had the momentum, and more importantly, they were fighting on his turf—the closing stretch.

Fowler did him a favor on the 14th hole, a tricky par 3, when he hit a bad push off the tee. The ball flew toward the gallery and landed in the mud below the hole. He took his relief and hit a nice flop shot up onto the green, but couldn't sink his 18-footer for par. Far back on the green, you could see Rory's silhouette in the sun—he looked impatient—and after Phil made his three, Rory hit a similar tee shot, failing to catch the ridge and relegating him to a two-putt for par.

The designers had made an alteration to the 15th green, replacing a collection area just over Brush Run Creek with a greenside bunker, and the change had the desired effect, forcing all three to hit their approach far past the front right pin location. Rory came the closest, just eighteen feet away, but none could sink their birdie putts, and they moved on to 16, Phil and Rory tied at -15, Rickie one behind.

The 16th hole is one of the hardest on the course—a brutally long 516-yard par 4 with a narrow fairway and a gradual incline. The skies had grown dark over Valhalla, and the easy banter between Phil and Rickie had vanished over the past three holes. Like it or not, they were now on their own against Rory. Rickie in particular was struggling, having lost his ability to hit close approaches. Facing a difficult tee shot, he hit another bad push, sending the ball over the trees and the creek on the right side of the hole and into the rough on the 15th fairway. To get to his ball, he had to circle behind the 15th green, where Rory and Wiesberger were making their putts. Again, Rory didn't acknowledge him.

As luck would have it, Rickie had a small window, and could still access the green with a high draw over the trees. He and his caddie, Joe Skovron, walked back and forth on a scouting mission, and in the meantime, Phil hit his second shot into the left rough, still twenty yards from the hole. As Rickie waited for Skovron to return, Rory took the unprecedented step of hitting his drive. If it had gone right, it could have landed by Rickie, or even hit him, but it was dead straight—a 331-yard beauty that split the fairway. It was as though he wanted to emphasize the symbolism of the moment—he was nipping at their heels, now quite literally.

Rickie realized there was no choice, and opted to go for the green. The shot that followed might have been his most impressive of the day—a near-perfect soaring draw over the trees that hit the front of the green and rolled off the edge. From there, he struck a hundred-foot lag putt, and made the short comebacker for par. Phil was in trouble of his own, and nearly got out of it in spectacular fashion when his pitch from the rough caught the lip of the hole. Instead of falling, it ran past, and the almost-birdie had turned into a ten-foot par putt. His line couldn't have been better, but his speed was tentative, and the ball stopped three inches from the hole. A chorus of groans resounded from the fans on the hillside, stacked on top of one another.

The run was over. Back in the fairway, Rory McIlroy had regained the solo lead.

It was now past eight p.m., and the players were engaged in a second battle against darkness. Rory missed a twenty-two-foot birdie attempt that might have closed out the tournament on 16, but neither Phil nor Rickie could capitalize on 17. Once again, Rickie left himself a long two-putt, and Phil needed a brilliant pitch from the rough to save par. Behind them, Rory put his tee shot into a bunker on the left side of the fairway, but it traveled 318 yards before it got there, and gave him a good look at the green. He took out his 9-iron, sent the ball into the dark sky, and twirled the club as he watched it fall. It settled eleven feet away, and now he had his chance to secure a two-shot lead.

The putt was a curler, and he started the ball well outside the hole. As it traced its way back, the result felt inevitable—the putt would fall, and the lone wolf would walk to the final hole leading by two, ready to close out an astounding summer. And that's just what happened.

Rory's biggest concern now was finishing the round—it was almost eight thirty as he hustled up to the 18th tee box, where Phil and Rickie had just hit their tee shots. He knew that as long as he and Wiesberger hit their drives, the PGA of America had to give them the option of finishing the hole. The problem was they'd have to wait for the others to clear the fairway, and in that time—who knew?—the horn might blow to stop play. Rory had been ravenous throughout the back nine, and the last thing he wanted to do was lose his momentum and let that killer instinct seep away overnight. On TV, the CBS announcers were arguing that he should call it a day and avoid all the risks that darkness entails, but Rory had a one-track mind, and delaying the finish wasn't on his agenda.

He found Fowler as he began to walk off the tee box.

"We want to hit now," he said, after a short preamble.

Grantland's Bryan Curtis, on the scene—I was a few steps behind at the tee—described the look on Fowler's face at that point as "confused and semi-cowed."

"Want me to tell Phil and them?" Fowler asked, looking down the fairway where Mickelson had walked away.

A rumble of thunder echoed in the sky as Fowler left. He caught up with Phil, and along with two officials they agreed to let the players tee off. In his haste, Rory's drive flew right—dangerously close to the creek running along the side of the hole. From the tee, the sky was too dark to follow its path, but David Feherty received word over his headset and conveyed the message to Rory—safe. The ball stopped just a few feet from the red hazard line—only the soft turf had slowed the ball before the water. Rory's rush to finish now looked like a huge risk, and one that might cost him the title he had seemed to win on 17.

Storm clouds gathered, and rain began to fall as the sunset shone with pinks and blues over the clubhouse. Rory looked on impatiently as Wiesberger hit, and then sped down after his ball. He waited as Phil and Rickie made their approaches—both of them under the impression that Rory would at least par, and they needed to make eagle. Rickie reached the green, ending up fifty feet from the hole, while Phil came up just short, landing in the fairway twenty-five yards away.

They began the uphill walk out of the valley and up to the green, and behind them, Rory shot out his arms out in surprised protest.

"Can we play up?" he shouted, but they continued up the slope. He appealed to the officials then, and the eventual verdict reached Phil and Rickie—Rory would be allowed to play. As Wiesberger hit his approach, Phil had an animated discussion with the official—it was normal to allow the players behind to tee off, as a courtesy, but hitting up to the green at the same time? There was no reason for it, and Phil was practically fuming. He wanted a chance to perhaps make eagle, or birdie, and apply pressure to Rory's approach shot.

After the round, he and Rickie would put a good face on the controversy—the most they'd say was that they weren't expecting the approach shots, and that it probably wouldn't have made a difference—but privately, Phil was furious.

The irony of the whole situation was that Rory was so intent on finishing that he was making a mess of a rather easy hole. He hit his approach into the tricky front bunker, and Phil nearly holed his eagle pitch from off the green—an incredible run that came inches away from putting true pressure on the leader. He tapped in for birdie instead, and Rickie couldn't even manage that—in the near-complete darkness, he missed an eight-footer to stay tied with Phil.

They walked off the green, still upset at how the last hole had played out, and only the final pair remained. Just like at the British, Rory's last test was to get the ball out of the bunker and two-putt. Unlike Hoylake, though, he had to leave his bunker shot below the hole in order to avoid a disastrous mistake. He hit out to thirty-four feet, which was not the easiest two-putt under the circumstances. As flashbulbs lit up the darkness, and the wind and rain whipped the flags above the scoreboard, he struck his birdie attempt and watched it roll, and roll, and roll. When it stopped, it rested ten inches from the cup.

He had to mark the ball to wait for Wiesberger to finish, and while he did, he took in the scene, from gallery to green. His eyes then were something to behold—lit up with raw energy as he breathed hard in the twilight, looking as though he might levitate over the grass.

In a moment, he would tap in and become the third-youngest player, after Jack and Tiger, to win four majors. It would cement his status as the sport's new superstar, and give him primacy over all his peers. For now, though, all you could see was the fierce animal instinct as he surveyed his turf—the battlefield on which he had fought and scrapped, refusing to concede a blessed inch.

Fowler stood glum in the flash area after the round, answering a series of feeble questions from the press.

"This is the first one that really hurts," he said, and you could tell he meant it.

"How good is Rory?" asked a voice from the scrum.

"Yeah, he's good," said Rickie, too drained to even be upset at the question. His voice nearly broke as he continued to answer the questions, and he seemed to be on the verge of tears.

Amy Mickelson gave Rickie's sister, Taylor, a pep talk—"That's a heartbreaker, but my *gosh,* this year!"—and David Feherty found Rory's dad, Gerry, beneath the clubhouse awning to congratulate him.

Finally, after fulfilling his press obligations, Rickie disappeared into the locker room with Sam MacNaughton, who had shielded him from redundant questions and placated a jabbering woman who asked Rickie for his autograph during a television interview. The two of them vanished past the cops guarding the door, and I'd bet anything that when they were finally alone, Rickie broke.

Rory, on the other hand, could have stayed all night. He had dominated his opponents by sheer will, clawing back strokes after a bad start, all the way to another emphatic finish. Watching him on the course, you saw a force of nature, but on the podium, he was funny and insightful and eminently human. After his press conference, I caught him just before he drove off in a golf cart. At that moment, I wanted to know what he had watched on Saturday night, following the *Jackass Number Two* and *Kick-Ass 2* screenings that had seen him through Hoylake and Akron. The answer this time was *Suits,* a USA Network law drama—as far as I could tell, his only disappointing answer of the day.

He sped away then—bound for wherever heroes go after Valhalla—

and the Sunday we'd been waiting for all season long drew to an end. For one year, at least, the PGA Championship could put aside its identity crisis and stake its claim as the year's best major. The fervent galleries, the striking course, and the delirious Sunday sprint set up the dramatic finale, where a twenty-five-year-old stormed the castle gates and took his place on the sport's vacated throne.

SEPTEMBER

A Final Push

23

EAST LAKE, GEORGIA

The FedEx Cup Playoffs: The Rise of Billy Horschel;
Rory and Billy at the Tour Championship

"Matt Every just used to abuse poor little ol' Billy Horschel when Billy was a freshman. Billy loved to talk, and sometimes his mouth runs faster than his brain, and when he got into any sort of debate with Matt, it was kind of like candy from a baby. Some of those conversations were absolutely comical to watch. They'd argue about anything . . . it just didn't matter. Matt could get him rolling in the wrong direction, to the point that Billy would sometimes take both sides of an argument."
—Florida coach BUDDY ALEXANDER

On the 18th hole at the Deutsche Bank Championship, trailing Chris Kirk by a single shot in the second of the four FedEx Cup playoff events, Billy Horschel bombed his drive 318 yards down the right side of the fairway. From there, he watched Kirk miss his birdie putt, and turned to his caddie Micah Fugitt.

"I'm going to hit this on the green, I'm going to make eagle, and we're going to win the tournament," he said.

He took dead aim with his 6-iron from 211 yards away. Deep

down, he understood that this shot gave him not only a chance to win, but to make the Ryder Cup team as a captain's pick—unlike the reserved Kirk, he had exactly the kind of energy that Watson coveted. The ball was below his feet, but on an uphill lie relative to the hole. Before he hit, Horschel reminded himself "stay in the golf shot"—not to rise too soon and risk pushing it right.

It was a sound piece of strategy, but as it turned out, he overcompensated and caught the ball fat. Horschel immediately knew it was his worst shot of the day—a total chunk. It landed with a dull thud in the thick native area guarding the front of the green. He took the penalty drop, made bogey, and finished in a three-way tie for second.

Horschel had always struggled with his anger, and after conquering his rage for most of 2013, it had started to creep back over the summer. I'd watched him violently kick a trash can in Greensboro, and when he came into the scoring room after his chunked 6-iron and heard from Tom Alter that he had dropped in the FedEx Cup standings, he let out an anguished scream and punched his own hand.

Horschel's rage is the kind that looks very frightening up close, and Alter briefly wondered if he might punch a wall and break his hand.

He didn't—he collected himself in time to talk to reporters, and all he could say was that standing over the 6-iron, he had believed.

If you had to use one word to describe Billy Horschel, you'd start with "excitable." The twenty-eight-year-old plays with a raw, unfiltered energy, and his emotions are always on naked display. Sometimes, that entails thundering war cries and violent fist pumps. Other times, it comes in the form of intense, self-directed anger. Horschel's rage comes on fast, and when it hits, you sense that he's not entirely in control of himself. But these episodes pass as quickly as they arrive. Where an emotional player like Sergio Garcia might have trouble separating his self-image from what happens on the golf course, Horschel bounces back in an instant, reverting to his natural state—he can't stay in one place for very long, so why should his emotions be any different?

There's something innocent about Horschel—he has the body of a great athlete, but the open face of a curious child. He moves in fits and starts, fascinated by everything, chattering like a bird, and there's no pretense to his personality. He's the kind of person who hangs out with the caddies more than the other players, for the simple fact that they feel like his kind of people.

He's also one of the Tour's quintessential restless wanderers. He has trouble staying calm when the pace of play is slow, and his natural temperament is designed for sports that involve running and jumping—he snowboards in the off-season, potential injuries be damned, and when we spoke, he lamented the lack of a flag football league on Tour.

This hyperactive style makes him unique in golf, and it's why Buddy Alexander's story about him and Every is so funny. They're perfect foils, and you can imagine how it played out—Every with his sly, cynical intelligence, quietly prodding Horschel as the younger player bounced wildly from idea to idea, barely keeping track of his own thoughts as the senior led him around in circles. And you can picture Horschel returning with renewed energy the next day, unfazed and undeterred, convinced that this time he was armed with the logical ammunition he needed to win.

Horschel, above all, is relentless and irrepressible, and it's why the chunked 6-iron at the Deutsche Bank didn't bother him for long, even though he called his shot and looked like a bit of a fool.

"Maybe it's just the way I look at life," he told me at the Tour Championship in Atlanta. "I didn't think of it as that bad. I get over things easily and move on from it, and I think that's why I was able to bounce back sooner than some other guys."

He had put it behind him so thoroughly that it came as a shock when he logged on to his Twitter account to find that legions of so-called "fans" were piling on, calling him a choker and berating his game. It never occurred to him to think of it that way, and he hadn't expected the onslaught. This just redoubled his determination—he knew he was playing well, and now he could stick it right in their eye by winning the next event.

At the third playoff event, the BMW Championship in Colorado,

Horschel launched himself into the lead with a Saturday 63. On Sunday, he sealed himself off from the field, and finally relaxed on the 18th fairway—at which point he realized that he really, really needed to use the bathroom. And so, on national TV, he began sprinting toward the Porta-Potty. He made it in time, and emerged to win by two strokes. The win shot him up to number 2 on the FedEx Cup list, and gave him a good chance to win the ten-million-dollar FedEx Cup prize at the Tour Championship.

"I'm not going to go ahead and guarantee a victory right now," he had told reporters in Colorado, looking ahead to Atlanta, "but I will say that I'm probably going to play very well, and I will have a chance to win on Sunday."

————————

"I think I'm very old school in the way I was raised. I think it's the right way. I would say that any child should be raised the way I was. Maybe if there's anything they could change, it's that the parents had a few extra dollars around where it wasn't so tight sometimes."
                                              —BILLY HORSCHEL

Horschel was born in Grant, Florida, an old fishing village on the Indian River Lagoon, just two miles from the barrier islands that separate Florida from the Atlantic Ocean. It's a small town—less than four thousand people—and the local claim to fame is an annual seafood festival.

"I guess you'd say it's in the woods," Horschel told me. "It's about twenty minutes to civilization, and all our friends lived that far away from me. So it wasn't like they could just ride their bikes to my house."

Billy Horschel Sr. was a carpenter's son who had played a year of football at Carson-Newman College in Tennessee before quitting and making his way into construction. Two of his brothers had played D-1 football, at Cincinnati and Miami, and he was good enough at rugby to earn a contract offer from a team in England before hurting his knee. He worked in drywall and stucco, mostly, and he built his own house in

Grant along with his two brothers, who owned roofing businesses. He and his wife, Kathy, had two boys together—Billy and Brian.

Neither parent had a college education, and depending on the state of the construction industry, money could be tight in the Horschel home. Kathy worked in the purchasing department at several different companies, but the minute she started to move up at one, they'd go under and she'd have to start over. They were forced to take out a second mortgage on their home, and they racked up credit card debt to stay afloat.

Billy remained unaware of the family's troubles in his younger years, when he'd spend happy days on their two and a half acres of land, playing just about every sport in existence, with one exception.

"We didn't play soccer," he said, "because my dad just couldn't stand to watch it."

Everything else was fair game: football, basketball, baseball, tennis, bowling, and even golf. As a three-year-old, Billy would follow his father outside to hit balls in the backyard, and he and Brian, then little more than a baby, would use their father's clubs to hack in the grass. He begged his dad to let him play on a real course, and they struck a deal—if he could hit a ball from the backyard over a creek about a hundred yards away, then he could play with the big boys. Billy practiced by himself for weeks while his dad was at work, and one day, at age five, he finally managed it. The only problem was that his father was at work, and so he waited in the driveway for two hours, ecstatic, waiting to tell him the good news.

Billy Horschel Sr. was a tough man, and not just about golf—he and Kathy took an old-school approach to raising their children.

"They were very strict, and they would discipline us," Horschel said. "We didn't get away with anything. We never got grounded, or got things taken away, like our phone or TV. We never had that. We did something wrong, we paid the price . . . my dad spanked us with a belt once or twice."

He can still remember the time he talked back to his mother, and caught her hand when she reached out to slap him. He thought it was a clever move, but then she uttered the words that scared him more than any other: "Wait until your dad gets home."

At the same time, his parents were loving, and his father only pushed Billy in sports as much as he wanted to be pushed. As the boy grew up and showed immense talent at baseball and golf, his parents did their best to make sure he could play in local tournaments and travel as much as money would allow.

At school, Billy smothered his natural exuberance at first, ashamed of a speech impediment that the other kids would mock. When he said the letter "r," it sounded like a "w," and a word like "railroad" became "wailwoad." From kindergarten through sixth grade, he would routinely get pulled out of class to work with a speech therapist. Despite this impediment, he couldn't stay bashful for long, and was soon one of the most outgoing kids in school. Then, in sixth grade, a new school opened up closer to his home, and he inherited a whole new peer group. When he got pulled out of class for speech therapy, the new kids began to mock and tease him. The abuse was too much for Billy.

"I just went home one day and said, 'Mom, I can't do this anymore,'" he told me. "I said, 'you know what? This is the way I talk, and I can't fix it. It's me, and it makes me a little bit different, but I can't stand doing this again.'"

Kathy gave in, and Billy quit the speech classes. You can still hear the impediment today when Horschel talks, especially when he gets excited. You have to listen closely, though, and it's subtle enough that many people, meeting him for the first time, just assume he's from Boston.

At this point in our talk, I remembered Keegan Bradley, and how he still remembered the names and faces of everybody who had wronged him throughout his life. I wonder if Horschel was the same, so I asked him if he ever thought back to the kids who mocked him.

"No, no, no, no," he said emphatically, demonstrating the difference between the two young golfers. "It was more or less good fun, because I was a pretty good sport about it. I never got in a fight, never got in trouble. I was just tired of listening to it."

By the time he hit high school, he had a tough choice to make between baseball and golf, but a broken elbow made the decision a lot easier.

"I'm highly competitive," he said, "and I couldn't stand playing baseball and football and all these other sports where you have a kid just lollygag and they don't care as much. And all these parents are saying, 'It's supposed to be fun.' And I said, 'there's no fun! It's fun when you win!' "

In some ways, golf was the game for which the energetic Horschel seemed least suited. Nevertheless, he began to improve rapidly, and his commitment turned serious.

Partying was not on the agenda, and it wasn't allowed anyway—his parents enforced a strict ten p.m. curfew. While other high schoolers were out drinking and socializing, Billy read a book and drifted off to sleep. He worked at a golf course in the summer, and on weekends during the school year, his parents dropped him off to practice at six thirty in the morning, and he'd stay until sunset. He developed perfectionist tendencies in those days—the kind that both help and hurt. As his game improved, so did his capacity for anger when things went wrong. Like most Tour golfers, he became his own fiercest critic.

Florida had always been Horschel's dream school, and Buddy Alexander made the trip to see him play at the U.S. Junior Amateur when he was seventeen. They chatted on the range, and Alexander walked with him for a couple of holes, but in a field of 156 players, Horschel beat only two of them. He failed to qualify for the match play rounds.

As with Every, the coach had no expectation that Horschel would become anything more than an average college golfer, and he only offered him an "itty bitty" scholarship. It created a tough decision for the family, because Horschel's parents were just climbing out of debt, and four years at Florida would put a strain on their finances. In the end, they decided the education was worth the risk, and Billy was off to Gainesville.

"Going there is probably one of the biggest reasons I'm on Tour today," Horschel said, "and that reason would be Buddy Alexander, the best golf coach I think that's ever been in the history of golf coaches."

Just like Every, he made incredible strides his freshman year, and in the spring, he won the West Regional in Arizona and finished tied for tenth at the NCAA Championships. He went on to win SEC Player of the Year as a sophomore, and had racked up three first-team All-America honors by the time he graduated.

The most memorable event of his amateur career came at the 2007 Walker Cup. There, on Saturday afternoon, he met Rory McIlroy, who was playing in one of the last amateur events of his life. It was a tight match throughout, and Rory lost 1-down on the 18th hole when he missed a three-foot putt. Horschel had behaved with his usual exuberance, and it did not sit well with Rory, who later told *Golf Digest*'s John Huggan that Horschel's antics had infuriated him:

> "For example, he had hit a bunker shot at the 14th in our morning foursome. It was a great shot and finished inches from the cup. But he came running down the hill hollering at the top of his voice. He was so loud and so obnoxious."

Horschel, on the other hand, thought he was just having fun.

"I drew the hometown favorite boy," he told reporters after his match. "The boy that everybody was rooting for. I had the big crowds and that was fine with me. . . . I could hear that they were cheering for Rory, and once in awhile I would get a little joke in there and say, 'Come on, Billy!' "

The next afternoon, they met again. This time, Rory purposefully played slow in order to antagonize Horschel. It was a sound strategy—if your enemy can be enraged, provoke him. Along those lines, Rory also gave him the silent treatment. For anyone paying attention, it was a sneak preview of the psychological mastery Rory would show later in his career as he climbed to number 1. He gained his revenge, beating Horschel 4&2, and neither knew the match would have echoes later in their careers.

"It was great to win," McIlroy told the *Irish Golf Desk*'s Brian Keogh at the time. "Especially against him. I don't really have much time for him to be honest . . . he wasn't a nice guy to be around."

Horschel turned pro in 2009, and at the 2011 McGladrey Classic, he started the final round one shot off the lead. He shot 75 that day, and became so angry on the course that family and friends took him to task afterward—an intervention that left him feeling humiliated at his own behavior. Even worse, he bombed at Q-School, meaning he would only have conditional status for 2012. It took time, but he regained his confidence. A fourth-place finish at that year's Q-School—his third successful showing in four tries—put him back on the Tour, and now he was ready for the big leagues.

In January of that season, the Australian golfer Matt Jones enlisted Stephanie Wei, a journalist, in a prank. Because Horschel had been forced to go to Q-School so often, certain fans and reporters mistook him for a rookie every time he returned to Tour. It had been happening since 2010, and it was happening again in 2013. Horschel was sick of explaining himself, so Jones's plan was simple—Wei would approach and ask if she could pick Horschel's brain about life on Tour as a rookie. When Wei asked the question, Horschel bit his tongue, turned his head to the side, and tried to control his annoyance. Just as he was about to snap at Wei, Jones broke out laughing.

Lucky for Horschel, his anonymity was coming to an end. At the Zurich Classic that April, he began the rainy final round two shots behind Lucas Glover, and proceeded to tear the course apart. By the 18th hole, Glover had faded, and he led D. A. Points by a shot. After hitting his drive in the left rough, he heard a sound nobody with any momentum wants to hear—the weather horn. For a player with Horschel's nervous energy, it seemed like the worst possible outcome. He sat inside the clubhouse with Matt Every and Chris DiMarco, two of his good friends, and waited it out. When they returned to the course, he laid up on the par-5, hit a wedge into twenty-seven feet, and watched as Points left himself five feet for birdie.

For Horschel, it meant one thing—if he didn't hole his twenty-seven-footer, he was probably bound for a playoff. The putt was a right-to-left twister, breaking away from the water, and Horschel made a run at it. "Get there! *Get there!*" shouted CBS's Nick Faldo, and it did—Horschel had won his first event, and he let out a primal yell before holding his head in disbelief.

He went on to make $3.5 million that year, part of which he used to take care of his family as repayment for their sacrifices. He continued working with his sports psychologist to control his temper and frustration on the course, but toward the middle of 2014, he slipped into old habits—watching the Golf Channel too much, staring at leaderboards, and overwhelming himself with information. For an ADD personality like Horschel, too much data can be distracting, and he grew frustrated on the course in ways that reminded him of 2012. When he missed the cut at the Barclays, the first FedEx Cup event of the season, he went home and told his wife, Brittany, that he wished the year would simply end—2014 felt like a waste, and he needed a fresh start.

Then he came to the Deutsche Bank, where his coach, Todd Anderson, made a few adjustments to his putting grip. The change was immediate—he won in Colorado, and with the field reduced to twenty-nine players for the final event of the season, he had the ten-million-dollar top prize in his sights. To reach the loftiest heights of his young career, though, he'd have to go through his old Walker Cup adversary—Rory McIlroy.

Of the players who made the year-end event, the game's young stars were heavily represented, and the sport's generational change was made manifest. Gone were Tiger Woods and Phil Mickelson, and in their place came the standard bearers for the new wave—Jordan Spieth, Rickie Fowler, Rory McIlroy, Jason Day, Hideki Matsuyama, Russell Henley, Morgan Hoffmann, Patrick Reed, Billy Horschel, Brendon Todd, and Chris Kirk. They were joined by a group of slightly older players trying to take over the game as the legends faded, including Adam Scott, Justin Rose, Bubba Watson, Hunter Mahan, Sergio Garcia, and Martin

Kaymer. In all, only six golfers in the field were older than thirty-five, and fourteen of them—nearly half—were still under thirty.

The FedEx Cup is a creature of momentum, though, and in the end, the players who wound up in Sunday's final group were those who had been on the best form for the past month—Rory McIlroy and Billy Horschel. The course on Sunday was playing a bit too difficult for anyone to make a big move, and it became increasingly clear that the big money would go to one of the two golfers in the final pair.

Horschel showed up on the first tee wearing a pair of bright, pastel-plaid pants, and asked Tim Finchem, the Tour commissioner, if he liked them. Finchem nodded, but Horschel wouldn't let him off the hook: "So you won't make me change, then?"

Rory showed up next, with J. P. Fitzgerald in tow looking weary and put-upon, but it was the golfer, not the caddie, who was worn out. While Horschel birdied twice on the front nine, Rory made a mess of the par-3 sixth, hitting his tee shot into the water and taking a costly double-bogey. He finished the front half with an errant tee shot, and walking to the 10th tee, he was now at -7, trailing Horschel by four shots.

Rory had the same determined look I saw at Valhalla, but there was something else, too—something almost resigned. It was a subtle difference, but the truth was that losing the FedEx Cup was *acceptable* in a way that losing the major wasn't. After falling to Chris Kirk at the Deutsche Bank, it felt like he had run out of steam. Kaymer had shown after Pinehurst that there's only so much stress one player can withstand before the brain shuts down, and Rory had lost at least some of his sharpness.

He still had a chance for a two-shot swing when Horschel got stuck in the right rough on 10 and made bogey. Instead, he missed the twenty-foot birdie putt and the three-footer coming back, suffering another bogey. When he failed to get up-and-down from the right rough on the 11th, falling to -5, reality had set in: His chance was over.

By then, Horschel was walking with purpose, spurred on by cries of "Go Gators!" and his own constant anxiety. He hit an eight-foot par

putt on 13, and on the par-5 15th, he got up and down from a greenside
bunker for another birdie. Jim Furyk had reached -10 with a birdie on
15, and Horschel now led by just a shot. When he found trouble on the
16th, he began giving full speeches to himself—"Come on, Billy, make
a better swing than that. . . . You don't want to hit left and left's better
than right!"—and McIlroy patted him on the back as they walked
down the fairway. It was a gesture of both encouragement and concession, and a sign that the Walker Cup animosity was ancient history,
replaced now by mutual respect.

On the 16th green, Horschel left himself a thirty-one-footer for
par. Staring from beneath his white Ping hat, Horschel's eyes looked
almost delirious with focus. He thought back to the long putt at the
Zurich that gave him his first win, and standing over the ball, he saw
the line perfectly. He didn't even bother calling in Micah Fugitt for a
read. He just gave it a run—too much of a run, maybe, and Fugitt worried that it might roll ten feet past—but it caught the right edge of the
hole and dropped. Horschel unleashed a fist-pumping flurry worthy of
Zurich, and the crowd erupted.

He had saved his one-shot lead with two holes to play, and as it
turned out, the veil of stress was about to fall. Furyk, as he does so
often in the most critical moments, hit a loose approach from 178 yards
on 17, and couldn't make his twelve-footer for par. Horschel had a
birdie attempt to shut the door, and he gave the crowd a bit of Kabuki
theater by throwing his leg out and shouting, "Come *on*!" when he
missed. Standing on the 18th tee box moments later, Horschel watched
as Furyk made another bogey. He sunk to -8 and a tie with Rory McIlroy, who, even in his weakened state, had made his trademark late
sprint with three birdies on the final four holes.

Horschel simply needed to land his last tee shot on the green. When
the ball fell safely, he breathed a sigh of relief—he had just become a
very, very rich man.

Since childhood, Horschel had exprienced dreams that were more like
premonitions—visions of future events that eventually came true. Once,

at age ten, he dreamed of being hit in the head with a baseball bat, and when it happened in real life, the adults who rushed to his side heard him say, "I saw this coming." Later, in college, he dreamed of the exact spot where he would later marry his wife in Plantation, Florida.

On the walk to the 18th green, Horschel told his caddie, Micah, about a dream he'd had earlier that season, in December or January—one in which he won the FedEx Cup. This dream was fainter than the others. He knew he had held the trophy in the fog of his fantasy, but beyond that, everything was less distinct.

When he woke up, he didn't know what to make of it—was it real? Did it mean he'd win *this* year, or just sometime in the future?—and he confided only in his wife. As the difficult year went along, he told himself to forget the dream, because it clearly wasn't going to happen.

He thought of that dream again on Sunday morning, and despite his usual nerves, there was an underlying calm that helped him through the round. With his mother and father in the gallery, and Brittany at home bearing his first child—a daughter named Skylar Lillian who would arrive two days later—he reveled in the moment. When he made the winning par, he couldn't help himself—the proud Florida alum gave an emphatic gator chomp to the crowd, who booed accordingly.

The ten million dollars meant he could take care of the parents who had given him so much, and the trophy meant that his dreams were still real. He saw it all coming together, and when he showed up in the press area a few minutes later, you could tell he'd been crying.

24

WENTWORTH, ENGLAND, AND NEW YORK, NEW YORK

The Captain's Picks

At the Deutsche Bank outside Boston—the second event of the FedEx Cup playoffs—the collective mind was on the Ryder Cup captain's picks, scheduled for the following Tuesday. It would be the first strategic act for McGinley and Watson, and our first real hint at their leadership styles.

For the Europeans, the automatic picks wouldn't be set in stone until Sunday evening, but already speculation swirled. Paul McGinley would almost certainly pick Ian Poulter, for one. If Scotland's Stephen Gallacher played well in Italy but failed to make the team, McGinley might be forced to pick him or risk losing the goodwill of the Scots. That left just one pick, and two very successful Ryder Cup veterans to choose between—Lee Westwood and Luke Donald.

The nine American spots had already been clinched after the PGA Championship. Watson had been traveling with the Tour all year, doing his best to give evasive answers about his captain's picks, and he kept the act up in Louisville. When asked about Tiger, he left the possibility open, while dropping a few subtle of hints that it might not be the *greatest* idea.

"If he's playing well and he's in good health, I'll pick him," Watson said. "Obviously he's not in great health right now and he hasn't played very well. So the question is, will I pick him? Well, I can't tell until things happen in the next three or four weeks."

Can't tell, indeed . . . except to say that he's hurt and he stinks.

Elsewhere, his options had narrowed. Dustin Johnson was out on suspension, and Jason Dufner had to quit during the opening round in Louisville due to the chronic pain from bulging discs at c4 and c5. Even his cocktail of medicine—anti-inflammatories and the steroid Medrol Dosepak—didn't help. "It's just pointless," he told the AP, before leaving the course.

Dufner dropped to 10th on the points list, with Phil Mickelson and Zach Johnson leapfrogging him, and it didn't take a genius to understand that Watson would have to leave him at home.

Tiger's story took a bit longer to play out. He missed the cut at Valhalla, as almost everyone predicted, but even though he didn't make the FedEx Cup playoffs and wouldn't have a chance to play a competitive round before the Ryder Cup, he still maintained that he wanted to be part of the team.

Watson said little, as though he were giving *Tiger* the chance to remove himself from consideration, rather than having to deliver the bad news himself. Finally, two days later, Tiger did exactly that. In a statement, he announced regretfully that his health wouldn't permit him to make the trip. We'll never know if Watson ever gave him an ultimatum— "You're not making the team, so decide for yourself how that information gets out"—but practically, the effect was the same. For whatever it's worth, Watson later revealed that he was the one to call Tiger when he supposedly "withdrew," and not the other way around.

The Dufner and Tiger sagas were just the latest evidence that Watson would be fighting at a disadvantage against Paul McGinley and the Europeans. He couldn't afford to screw up the captain's picks, and he'd be watching the action at the Deutsche Bank closely. Conventional wisdom said that Keegan Bradley had a great chance, after playing so well with Phil Mickelson in 2012. Nobody played the political game as well as Bradley—he and Watson had grown friendly—and he was practically a lock. Beyond that, the other two picks were up in the air—Hunter Mahan had an inside track after he won with a Sunday back nine surge at the Barclays, but anyone from Brendon Todd to Chris Kirk to Webb Simpson to Harris English to Ryan Palmer still seemed to have a shot.

It was Chris Kirk who would eventually triumph in Massachusetts, and in surprising fashion—by beating Rory McIlroy, the world's best player, after 36 grueling holes in the same pairing. On the eve of the picks, his win seemed like the most compelling argument imaginable.

But Kirk was stubborn, and he refused to admit that the Ryder Cup mattered to him at all. During his post-round interview, he'd only say, "I'm planning on seeing Georgia play Tennessee that weekend." He made vague comments about how it would be a "bonus" if he made the team, but none of it sounded very convincing. I pressed the issue when I saw him by the flash area, but he wouldn't budge.

"I don't know," he said. "Maybe it'd be a better story if I was like Keegan, and was freaking out about it and really, really excited and going nuts. But I'm just not."

Kirk and Watson had played a practice round together at the British Open, and when Kirk struggled on the front nine—he still had jet lag from his flight—Watson got on his back a little, and they ended up winning. Whether Kirk appreciated the pep talks is doubtful—he's a self-motivator, and not the kind of person who searches for mentors. Even agreeing to play with Watson as a sort of audition probably rubbed him the wrong way, and the two hadn't spoken since.

Making matters worse, Watson had an ego, and he wanted players who would be excited to play for *him*. He saw himself as a general— tough but inspiring, harsh but well-loved. He appreciated players who would flatter the John Wayne aspect of his self-image. Unfortunately, Kirk was a natural-born mercenary who adamantly refused to move even an inch toward Watson, much less beg. The ring was extended, but Kirk wouldn't kiss it.

"I think, as a human being, I have empathy and an understanding of people and hopefully I can bring that to the captaincy.

When the debate about who should get the captaincy was going on, people were saying: 'We need a big name, a Major winner, who has achieved a lot in the game.' And I wanted to scream. I mean, show me the correlation between being a great player and a great captain. And not just in golf, but in any sport? There is none."

—PAUL McGINLEY, in the *Irish Independent,*
two weeks before the Ryder Cup

On Tuesday, September 2, in a twelve p.m. ceremony at the Wentworth Club in Surrey, England, Paul McGinley sat behind a simple podium and spoke for exactly one minute before he announced his three captain's picks in quick succession: Stephen Gallacher, Ian Poulter, Lee Westwood.

The first two names were expected. Westwood—one of the great European Ryder Cup players of all time but in the waning stages of his career at age forty-one—was the surprise. In late 2012, when McGinley was the presumptive favorite for the captain's position, his chief opponent was Darren Clarke, another Northern Irishman and a good friend. McGinley had even pulled out of the 2006 PGA Championship when Clarke's wife died, in order to attend the funeral. McGinley was viewed as the natural choice for captain in 2014, and Clarke wrote him a letter saying he wasn't interested in the job.

That vow didn't last long. Clarke changed his mind after the 2012 Ryder Cup, and became a candidate for a short period before withdrawing and declaring his support for Colin Montgomerie, stating that he didn't believe McGinley had the appropriate stature to stand opposite Tom Watson. McGinley had never won a major and had only played in three Ryder Cups, Clarke's argument went, and it would put Europe at a disadvantage. *This* move, more than his original candidacy, torpedoed the friendship between McGinley and Clarke, and it also did significant damage to McGinley's chances.

Montgomerie's cause gained momentum, and seemed on the verge of spilling over into success. At that critical moment, Rory McIlory came out publicly in favor of McGinley. His emphatic support prompted a series of endorsements from Luke Donald, Justin Rose, and Ian Poulter.

"I didn't think the right thing to do was react to that," Rory said of the near mutiny against McGinley. "The Ryder Cup is won on the golf course, not on stages where speeches are made."

Rory, with his hard intelligence, knew that picking a new captain would show fear, and if he wasn't already motivated enough to support his countryman, this confirmed it—why run scared from the Americans?

McGinley won the job, but before the final vote, Lee Westwood went public with his *own* support—for Darren Clarke.

When the time came to make captain's picks, and the third and final choice came down to Luke Donald and Lee Westwood, it seemed like a no-brainer—McGinley would reward loyalty by picking Donald.

He didn't. Westwood was pleasantly stunned, and Donald was upset, but McGinley had a plan. And that plan didn't hinge on holding grudges, or letting his judgment be clouded by ego and pride. The reason behind the move wouldn't be revealed until the Cup began, but for now, it was an interesting indication of what we could expect from a McGinley captaincy.

That same night, the Golf Channel ran a half-hour Ryder Cup special to announce Tom Watson's picks. The legendary American sat on a large stage framed by American flag imagery, his face caked with television makeup, and stumbled his way through thirty agonizing minutes. Unlike the straightforward European picks, this looked like low-rent reality television, with the three announcements spaced out across the program's half hour in order to build suspense. Julius Mason did a fine job hosting, but Watson couldn't seem to focus as he introduced and justified his three picks: Keegan Bradley, Hunter Mahan, and Webb Simpson.

The first two picks needed no real explanation, but with Webb Simpson, things got a bit tricky. Not only had Simpson failed to win in the 2014 calendar year; his form wasn't even particularly strong, and he had missed the cut in three of four majors. By choosing him, Watson was also leaving Chris Kirk at home—the man who had just outdueled Europe's best player.

"I kind of had a revelation this morning," Watson explained on-stage. "I just took a look at last time the Ryder Cup was played . . . and I was cleaning up all these stats and folders and things like that this morning, and the last one out there was the results from the 2012 Ryder Cup. And I looked down there and I see Webb Simpson. 5&4. Webb Simpson. 5&4. And I said, that's gotta be the guy. Webb Simpson is my next pick."

It was a nice story, even if it was derived from a very shortsighted look at Simpson's 2012 performance. He had indeed teamed with Bubba Watson for two runaway wins at Medinah, but he had also lost a pairs match with Bubba to Poulter and Rose, and then lost his singles match to Poulter on Sunday, for a 2-2 overall record.

The semantics didn't matter, because the truth was that Watson *hadn't* made his decision based on some folder he found on a desk. That was a convenient explanation, but it wasn't the real engine behind his decision. The "revelation" he spoke of *had* come that morning, but it had come, we later learned, from a series of text messages with Webb Simpson himself.

As Simpson would tell the media at Gleneagles, he had been tossing and turning in a Denver hotel in the predawn hours on Tuesday. He was there to play in the BMW Championship, and the captain's picks would be announced that night. He got the sense that his chances were slim, he said, and decided to send Watson a text. The content was simple: He acknowledged that Watson was facing a tough decision, but said he *really* wanted to play on the team and represent America.

He received a quick reply—it was about four a.m. Denver time, but five a.m. in Kansas City where Watson deliberated—saying simply, "this is a tough decision, Webb." A half hour later, Watson actually called and put the question to him: Why should he put Simpson on the team? A bit groggy, Simpson trotted out the same arguments—he had "passion" for the Ryder Cup, and wanted redemption for Medinah. By the end of that phone call, according to the Golf Channel's Jason Sobel, Watson told him he had made the team.

The way he presented it at the Ryder Cup, this was a feel-good story—Watson was swayed by Simpson's fighting spirit, and filled his vacant twelfth spot in good conscience. In fact, things were not so cut-and-dried—Watson had actually made a *different* captain's pick prior to speaking with Simpson. Sobel became the first to report that information later that day, and most of us assumed the pick had been Chris Kirk, with some guessing Billy Horschel, who had finished second at the Deutsche Bank but only made his FedEx Cup run after the picks.

We were all wrong. *Golf Week*'s Alex Miceli finally broke the real story—after the Deutsche Bank ended, Watson had indeed decided on his three picks, but the third was neither Kirk nor Horschel. It was Bill Haas, who had finished ninth that weekend. Miceli's scoop was strange news by almost any reckoning—Haas had put together a consistent year, and never missed a cut, but he hadn't won a tournament, or made any real impact in the majors. His only top-five finish came at the Wyndham, which most of the best players skipped. In addition, he was far down the Ryder Cup standings, in twenty-eighth place, well below anybody else who had been seriously considered. Tom Watson had never mentioned him in a pre–Ryder Cup press conference, and as far as I could tell, nobody else had either. Haas was the ultimate dark horse—a five-time career winner on Tour and a steady veteran, but not exactly an inspiring choice.

One of the few players to mention him at all, interestingly enough, was Webb Simpson. He brought up Haas at the Ryder Cup press conference when he told the story of his conversation with Watson. When he spoke with Watson that fateful morning, he mentioned Haas (along with Kirk and Horschel) as a strong alternative. He was one of the only people who thought to include Haas, and it makes little sense—unless he already knew that Haas had been picked.

Which brings us to the piece of information that turns Simpson's story a bit sour. As Miceli reported, Watson had called several of his automatic selections on Monday night to let them know the three players he would pick. By the time the golfers hit the range on Tuesday morning, word was out—he had chosen Bradley, Mahan, and Haas. They didn't know that Simpson had swayed him in a different direction in the predawn hours Tuesday morning, but—this is the critical point—it's hard to imagine that Simpson didn't know about Watson's picks *before* he ever sent the first text on Tuesday morning. He had too many friends on the team, many of whom had received word from Watson himself about the impending captain's picks, not to have heard. If word was out on Monday night, as we now know it was, Simpson would be in the loop.

If Simpson truly mentioned just three names in his talks with Watson—Kirk, Horschel, and Haas—and he already knew the picks, it means that at least in a subtle way, he was targeting Haas. Otherwise, why not bring up Keegan Bradley and Hunter Mahan as part of Watson's "tough decision"? Simpson is smart, though—he would have known that Bradley and Mahan were safe, and that if he could finagle his way onto the team, it would be at the expense of Bill Haas, the vulnerable third pick.

It gets more damning. In his press conference, Simpson even let it slip that Keegan Bradley and Hunter Mahan had *already received* their congratulatory phone call from the captain by the time he sent his fateful texts, and that he learned of their inclusion on Monday night, before he ever contacted Watson. The one lingering doubt is whether he also knew that Haas had been selected, but with the way word traveled between the players—and the variety of sources in Simpson's immediate network—it seems ludicrous to think he was in the dark.

Reasonable people can disagree about Simpson's last-ditch plea—golf is a competitive game, and if he sensed Watson wavering on the third pick, who's to say he was wrong to advocate for himself, even at the expense of Haas? It casts a ruthless light on the whole spectacle, but what Simpson did wasn't illegal, and golf, in the end, is just a game—any rule he broke was an unwritten one.

The real issue here was Watson himself. By leaking his three picks before he had solidified them, he created the embarrassing spectacle at Denver, where a large group of players wrongly believed Bill Haas was on the team—including Haas himself, probably. When Watson allowed himself to be overruled by Simpson, a player in objectively worse form than Haas, the farce was set in motion. Somehow, America's leader managed to turn the simple task of making three captain's picks into an embarrassing comedy of errors.

McGinley's picks told us something important about how he planned to lead Team Europe, but it would be some time before the truth emerged about Watson's maneuvers. Winning in Scotland was always going to be difficult against a loaded European side, and it would take a strong, levelheaded captain to help the Americans pull off the upset. Unbeknownst to us, as Webb Simpson sat in front of the Golf Channel cameras and rambled on about "redemption," Watson had already given the first indication that he might not be the man for the job.

25

ANTIBES, FRANCE

The Real Dubuisson

"Mr. Ryan, I will take the time to answer your questions, with sincerity and in great details. Some truths will not please him, but as a father, I want truth to be known once and for all."
—ALBAN DUBUISSON, Victor's father

To Paul McGinley, the emergence of Victor Dubuisson as a match play star in Arizona must have seemed like an incredible bonus—another weapon to throw at the depleted Americans in Scotland. At the same time, he realized that the Frenchman's personality made him a challenge—how do you deal with this guy? How do you incorporate him into the team and make sure he's a positive presence? As he came closer to automatically qualifying for the team, the onus fell on McGinley to solve the Dubuisson mystery. Coincidentally, I was trying to do the same thing.

Late in 2014, I expressed my frustration to a French journalist after hitting a brick wall on the story of Dubuisson's past. The burgeoning star who had won his first tournament in Turkey the previous fall—and made himself famous in America with his heroic shots at the Accenture Match Play Championship—remained a complete enigma to the entire American journalistic establishment. His past was shrouded in mystery; his personality was an unbroken code.

Sometimes, the secrecy led to incredible feats of misinformation. The UK's *Daily Mail,* for one, reported in May that Dubuisson lived in Honduras—a fascinating detail, I thought, since it made absolutely no sense. Why would a golfer who plays primarily in Europe take up residence in Central America?

I puzzled on that one for a few minutes, and finally the truth clicked—the journalist had heard a French person say the word "Andorra"—the tiny country in the Pyrenees where Dubuisson *actually* lives, in order to escape France's punitive tax rate—and his ears picked up "Honduras." Undeterred, they ran the same factoid in September—still convinced, months later, that Dubuisson flew back and forth between his European tournaments and the small nation in the Caribbean.

It's the kind of mix-up that makes you laugh, but it's also symbolic of the whole Dubuisson debacle. Digging for information on him is like playing the children's game of telephone, where each new fact is incurably distorted from its point of origin—a point that is, itself, difficult to identify with any accuracy.

After expressing my frustrations to the French journalist, he simply shrugged—*c'est la vie*—and told me that perhaps I should look up the golfer's father on Facebook. I grumbled at this advice, thinking it was merely a shot-in-the-dark suggestion that would only lead to more silence, along with the added obstacle of a language barrier. Plus, hadn't Dubuisson claimed that he *had* no family?

When I returned from the Ryder Cup, I thought back to that conversation, and decided to venture online and see what I could find. As it turns out, Dubuisson comes from a tremendously athletic family. His uncle, Hervé Dubuisson, is considered one of the greatest professional basketball players in French history—the "Kobe Bryant of France." There are articles that feature him alongside Tony Parker, the French point guard who became a star with the San Antonio Spurs, and Parker is considered the Hervé Dubuisson of his generation. Dubuisson holds the French record with 254 games played for Team France. He also owns the record for most career points—3,821—and the most points in a single game—51 against Greece in 1985. He won multiple scoring titles and a few championships in France's top professional league, and for two of those years, he played alongside his brother Alban—Victor's father.

When I sent Alban a friend request on Facebook, I expected to encounter someone trained in the family's secret arts. To my surprise, he proved very willing to talk about his son. This willingness preceded our connection—he had written extensively about him on Facebook already. The messages showed a father who was equal parts proud of what Victor had accomplished, hopeful for his future, and bitter at the turn their own relationship had taken. In a story that instantly reminded me of Patrick Reed and his parents, Victor and his father had not spoken a word to each other in four years.

A typical example of Alban's posts:

> "I am proud of his success, but when he says he didn't have a family, it's absurd!!! It makes me want to puke to read all this bullshit. Without his grandfather, his mother and myself, he would never be at the level he is at today and he would have never had his dream come true. It's pathetic!! My Facebook friends who followed his rise will be able to testify to it, I hope, but that's life and I wish him the greatest of success. He is and will always be in my heart."

I reached out to Alban, and we began corresponding over email. With the help of a translator—a native Parisian—I began to piece together the story of Victor Dubuisson.

What I discovered was that even very basic details of his accepted biography are wrong. In every story written about him at home and abroad, for instance, his birthplace is listed as Cannes. In truth, he was born on April 22, 1990, at the Clinique St. Georges in Nice, and though his family moved several times, they never once lived in Cannes. Victor only moved there himself after he turned pro, and was apparently content to tell any journalist who asked that he had been born and raised in the city.

Alban had played at the top level of French professional basketball for two years, winning a title playing with his brother for Le Mans, but he wasn't good enough to stay. He went on to toil in the minor leagues for a team on the French Riviera, but when he met his future wife, Cathy, they decided to start a laundry business. Alban quit basketball, business boomed, and the family was prospering by the time Victor, their first child, was born.

The Dubuissons lived in Antibes then, another town on the Mediterranean, and when Victor was six, thinking that he might follow in the family tradition, Alban and his wife Cathy registered him for basketball. The boy hated it. He also hated tennis, soccer, track and field, and judo—not to mention school. They began to believe their son simply wasn't meant to play sports.

His maternal grandfather, Leon, was a golfer, and one night when Cathy's parents were babysitting, Leon began playing with his grandson on a small putting mat. It's impossible to say why the activity intrigued the boy, now eight years old, but soon he was begging his "Papé" to take him to a real course. Leon obliged, picking Victor up from school one day and buying him a short 7-iron. They drove to the practice green at a course in nearby Biot, where they chipped and putted. By the time they drove home, Victor was in love.

This origin story also conflicts with another popular Dubuisson myth—that he was first seduced by golf when he watched Tiger Woods win the 1997 Masters. Alban was not a golfer or a fan, and if it's true that Victor was first introduced to the game by his grandfather at age eight, that would have been at least a year after Tiger's first green jacket. Here again, we may be running up against Victor's tendency to exaggerate to the press.

Leon, incidentally, is another casualty of Victor's code of silence to his family.

"Without his grandpa, what would he do today?" Alban asked rhetorically, in one of his mournful Facebook posts. "Is it that difficult to say thank you and have some recognition for his grandpa. For Victor, apparently it is!!!! All I have to say today is that today, his grandpa and all the people who guided him over the years are happy for his success, even though he doesn't deserve our respect. He is forever in our hearts, our little Victor in shorts who we knew and made us dream."

At the time, Alban was thrilled to see that Victor, who could be a moody child, had something that made him happy. He and Cathy supported their son's new passion, and Victor showed immediate talent—no surprise, considering his genes. Alban took up golf so he could spend time with his son, but soon Victor was beating him every time.

Nothing could deter Victor from his obsession, and Alban signed him up for weekend tournaments against kids three or four years older than him—another echo of the Patrick Reed saga. Alban sensed this was the best way to help his son become competitive, and though the boy got thrashed initially, he believes the difficulty made Victor tough. Alban took his inspiration from a Tiger Woods biography that discussed Earl's past as a Marine, and he admits that he could be hard on his son.

Victor was a perfectionist, and had a habit of throwing clubs, or banging them on the ground, and Alban tried to tell him that he needed to accept bad shots and stay positive. They'd have long talks about his attitude, but no matter what, Victor had trouble handling the reality of error on the course. It took years before he was able to keep his cool during a round, and even today, he retains those perfectionistic tendencies. According to Alban, these talks represented the extent of his "tough love."

Contrary to media reports—a familiar refrain, at this point— Victor did not quit school at age ten, and reports to that effect always made Alban laugh. Education is mandatory in France until age sixteen, but Victor did make use of a French Department of Education program called CNED—the National Centre for Distance Education—so that he could be homeschooled using online materials for the last years of his education.

The family moved a few miles inland to Opio, and during holidays, his mother would drive him to a golf course called "Golf de la Grande Bastide," where he would have friendly competitions with the caddies, and play thirty-six holes every day. The course allowed him to play as much as he wanted for a flat fee, which saved the family money, and allowed Victor to avoid the "boring" driving range. He explained to his father that playing on the course put him in "make-believe situations," where he could pretend he was in a real tournament. Even today, he often trains by playing against three friends, using two balls per hole, and taking the worst of his two scores against the best of their three.

When Victor was twelve, he and his father played at the Grand Bastide in the winter, under difficult conditions. As they made the turn after the front nine, Alban asked his son for his score. Victor told him: 3-under.

"I thought he was joking," Alban wrote, "but no. He ended up shooting 8-under and beating the course's record. And it happened to be the Christmas Cup so the conditions were not favorable."

In Opio, realizing his son's extraordinary talent, Alban brought Victor to a swing coach named Stephane Damiano. They worked together until Victor was thirteen years old, when he began working with Stephane's uncle, Roger Damiano, one of the region's most famous instructors. Both were tremendously impressed with Victor's short game, and the way he thought his way around the course with a sort of quiet, ruthless intelligence.

They also learned that Victor had a deep and abiding mistrust of authority, along with a propensity to simply skip appointments without any notice. They had to fight for his trust, and forgive him when he flaked out—a double standard that all of Victor's future coaches would encounter. Stephane Damiano, despite becoming one of his staunchest supporters, told *Le Monde* that with Victor, "You need to be able to wipe the slate clean."

Victor can come across as selfish in these stories, but eventually, a more complex truth emerges—he's self-centered, sure, but not malicious. It simply doesn't occur to him that life could be lived another way. It's almost as though there's a barrier between Victor's brain and the world of social niceties—until he can be convinced, he sees nothing but bad intentions in other people, and therefore sees no reason to extend his own good faith. It smacks faintly of paranoia, and any goodwill he establishes with others tends to be tenuous at best.

As he reached his teens, Victor was already recognized as one of the brightest young talents in France. He had begun training with the *Pôle France Élite* at age twelve—a group of the country's top young golfers sponsored by the French Golf Federation. It didn't go well. According to Alban, Victor acted "pig-headedly" and refused to adhere to their training methods unless they came from his specific coach. He would miss practices, ignore advice, and generally thumb his nose at anyone who tried to order him around. He would disappear for weeks without any explanation, and soon his friends came up with a new term for the vanishing act: "Do a Dubush." Finally, the exasperated Federation cut off his funding for certain trips in 2006, though they continued to let him travel with the national team, which Victor had joined at age fifteen.

In his late teens, Dubuisson worked with another coach, Dominique Larretche, who told *Le Figaro* that his pupil was like a "Ferrari." Still, life was not easy. "It was difficult to coach him," Larretche said. "When things don't go well, Victor tends to not tolerate any form of authority . . . at the end of our collaborations, there are things I didn't accept."

Another coach, Benoît Ducoulombier, told the *Journal du Golf* that when he first tried to help Dubuisson with his putting, "he ran away and treated me as if I were a terrorist." It took a year before Victor would give it another go, and the coach learned that it was better to let the golfer lead. If he made the mistake of taking any initiative, Victor would become tremendously uncomfortable and flee.

Despite these testy relationships, the boy prospered, and the honors came fast—French amateur champion, U18 European champion, Junior Ryder Cup, European amateur champion, and the number 1 amateur ranking in the world.

When he turned professional, he came down with a case of "golden staph," a bacterial infection that slowed him down for nearly two years.

He pressed on, kept his European Tour card despite playing sick, and fought his way to Antalya, Turkey, where in the fall of 2013, his whole life changed with his first victory on the European tour.

———————

> *"And who pays? Daddy does. Today, the Federation is taking credit for Victor's success!!! Rubbish. Victor, he adored me until he turned professional and earned a good living for himself. His dough, he can stuff it wherever he wants, surrounded by all these arrivistes [social climbers] and hypocrites . . . Victor, just a little respect and recognition for the people who accompanied and guided you when you were starting out."*
>
> —ALBAN, on Facebook

When Victor decides to cut ties, he really means it. A report in *Le Monde* indicated that he hasn't spoken with his uncle Hervé, the basketball star, for more than eight years due to an "irreversible rift between Hervé and Victor's mother," and he once told a French journalist that his uncle was responsible for "breaking up his family."

He didn't elaborate, but that was just the start of his retreat from the family. Four years later, his father and mother went through an ugly divorce, and Victor has yet to forgive or forget.

"A painful breakup between his mom and I happened," Alban told me. "It really disturbed Victor, who is a sensitive boy, and that is why he hasn't spoken to me in four years."

And of course, that may not be the entire story between father and son. Here again, we come to a point of ignorance regarding their relationship in Victor's formative years. Perhaps the divorce was the sum of Victor's anger, or maybe it was only the final straw. Clues are few and far between, and our only real hint comes from Victor's claim that he has no family, and, perhaps, from another post I found on Alban's Facebook. According to him, the last words that passed between the two came almost five years ago, in a text message from Victor.

"You broke my balls during my entire amateur career," he wrote. The two haven't spoken since.

―――――――

"The golfer agrees to meet with journalists about as often as a French victory in a Grand Slam tournament happens. In any case, as soon as a microphone gets close to him, the young man becomes a cactus himself: elusive."

—*Le Monde,* October 2014

Victor Dubuisson's second-greatest talent, after his golf, comes in holding a grudge. This goes beyond his family, and extends to anyone he perceives as a threat. He holds a particular animosity toward France, and French media.

The first sign of this antipathy came in a February 2011 story in *L'Équipe,* written by Phillippe Chassepot, in which Victor was quoted as saying, "When I see the shitty reputation I'm given and the unbearable mentality of my country, I really don't want to play for France."

In a 2013 interview with *Le Figaro,* Victor expounded on the topic. He liked the other French players on the European Tour, he said, but as for the country, he didn't feel supported since they always criticized him. For proof, he offered the fact that he had no French sponsors, which meant that they didn't like his image.

It's clear that Victor's distaste for his country runs deeper than a punitive tax system—he doesn't like their journalists either. He told Twitter followers in July that he'd rather stick with English and American media, who understand golf better than the French journalists, and with whom he had a better relationship.

I spoke with François Scimeca at the French Golf Federation, who first met Victor at the French Open when the boy was just fifteen years old. Scimeca has a good relationship with Victor, but he recognizes the pitfalls of dealing with the erratic star.

"He is not very friendly with the media," Scimeca told me. "He doesn't like it. In France, nobody can access him easily, because he wants to play golf, live golf, and have his outside life, and that's it."

As much as Victor's friends and agents and coaches tell him that he has to accept the presence of French media, and that speaking cordially with them is one of the obligations that comes along with the perks, the lesson hasn't stuck. He still avoids journalists at all costs, and he openly detests the *Journal du Golf*, a subsection of the French sports media giant *L'Équipe*.

Benjamin Cadiou, a writer for *Journal du Golf* who has borne the brunt of Victor's fitfulness, entertained a few of my questions at the Ryder Cup. He first met the budding French star in 2007, in an interview organized by the French Golf Federation with the top amateurs. Even then, Dubuisson was shy and reticent.

"Our relationship is complex," he said. "It's very difficult to communicate with that kind of guy. I'm not complaining, but it's tough."

In the beginning, Cadiou said, Victor loved to read the *Journal*, and claimed that he had it all the time in his youth, since it was free and he came from a poor background—another exaggeration from Dubuisson, at least according to his father, who said the family lived comfortably. The semi-cordial relationship continued, with a few minor ups and downs, all the way to 2014. In January, Cadiou spent ninety minutes chatting with Dubuisson at Torrey Pines, and came away thinking they had solidified a good working relationship. The next day, Victor shot a final round 76, and wouldn't even look at Cadiou when he approached him for a quote.

Later in the year, Cadiou did a video interview with Victor, and asked him what he liked to do outside the course. The golfer took out a set of car keys from his pocket, dangled them, and told them this was his main hobby. It seemed like an innocuous moment, but Dubuisson became angry when the footage aired, and it set a pattern for his interactions with the media. He would give a quote without regard for how it sounded, and when it ran, he would accuse the outlet of either distorting his words or using material that was supposed to have been off the record—a dubious assertion, since he doesn't have many private conversations with journalists in the first place.

Cadiou doesn't trust any information he hears about Victor—there's no way to investigate each new rumor, and even if the information came from Victor himself, it's likely to be a half-truth at best.

Finally, fed up with the mistreatment at the hands of France's brightest stars, the writers of the *Journal* broke their long stoic spell at the British Open. Philippe Chassepot penned an article called "Le Malaise Dubuisson," which started out with a bang:

> "Victor Dubuisson is at war against the French press. Since forever. But he seems to have crossed another line this week at the British Open, which is good for no one: neither for him, nor us.
>
> Small recap of an ordinary week with Victor Dubuisson: On Tuesday, we looked for him unsuccessfully. On Wednesday, we followed him at practice holes but we weren't able to catch his eye. On Thursday, after his frustrating +2, he told us "have a good day" and left. Yesterday, the French player was once again about to leave, but Benoît Ducoulombier [Dubuisson's coach] brought him back to his senses and Victor welcomed us with a "Go ahead, ask them, your rubbish questions!"

Chassepot went on to call Dubuisson "the most hypersensitive athlete we have ever met," and to accuse him of "paranoid projections." In one absurd episode, Chassepot wrote, Dubuisson became angry with an Internet user who had called him "a pathetic schmuck" in the comments section of an article, and transferred his anger to the *Journal* itself.[15]

Chassepot pointed out that unlike the British tabloids, which would be only too happy to delve into Dubuisson's dark side—"of which he doesn't lack"—the *Journal* had respected his request for privacy in his personal and family life.

Needless to say, Dubuisson did not respond well to this piece. He immediately cut off all ties with *L'Équipe,* and hasn't spoken with them

---

[15] His current coach, Benoît Ducoulombier, said in January that Victor had been hurt by messages on social media, and that he had encouraged him to quit.

since. A French cameraman told me that Dubuisson was "still a child in his mind," and that it was a "nightmare for us trying to talk to him." It got so bad for journalists like Cadiou at Victor's events that they finally resorted to asking sympathetic foreign journalists for help—ask this question, please, and relay the answers back to us, or we'll have nothing to write. (I rendered this service on more than one occasion.)

"It's finished," said Cadiou, of their relationship with Victor. "Nothing, absolutely nothing since. And we didn't do any mistakes, it's totally wrong. We never use off-the-record words for our article. He's very suspicious, and we will never speak together again."

Q. What do you make of Victor?
LEE WESTWOOD: It's very difficult to know what to make of Victor. He's quite shy. He's quite unpredictable. He's got a lot of flair. He's got tons of game.

Victor is not without his defenders. Even his most frustrated coaches say he can be humble and kind, and that his sour turns are merely the result of a sensitive boy who has trouble knowing how to behave in the intense glare of the spotlight. Benjamin Cadiou thinks that he's very smart, even if it doesn't come across in the academic sense. The Damianos scoff at the idea, bandied about in his early days, that Victor is lazy, and even Larretche, the coach who found him too difficult to stay with in 2010, shed a tear when he won in Turkey.

His father, too, always recovers from the moments of anger to express his love for Victor. The very last message he sent me, before our correspondence ended, felt a little heartbreaking. *"Victor est une belle personne et très attachante, j'aimerai que vous le rencontriez un jour,"* he wrote. *Victor is a beautiful person, and very endearing. I would love for you to meet him one day.*

Well, I *had* met him, and even if I hadn't seen those qualities, the father's affection still moved me. For everyone else, Dubuisson has remained a mystery. Had he actually left school at age ten? Did he live alone, with no parents? Is he crazy?

After dazzling the golf world in Arizona, Victor changed his phone number without letting anyone know, which led to missed texts from a few people, including Paul McGinley. It was nothing new—his reputation for skipping important meetings had continued, and now plagued his sponsors. Supposedly, he even failed to show up for a practice round with his hero Thomas Levet in January, though this bit of information comes from *The Daily Mail,* who are still under the impression that Victor lives in Honduras.

In any case, bonding with Dubuisson—and incorporating him into the team—was always going to be one of McGinley's greatest challenges. But he had a plan. He would enlist Graeme McDowell—a man whose charisma and wit made him a perfect counterpoint to the quiet Frenchman—to play an avuncular role. McDowell's task was to integrate Victor with the rest of the Europeans, assuage his discomfort and nerves, and join him as a partner in the cauldron of Ryder Cup foursomes.

26

AUCHTERARDER, COUNTY OF PERTH, SCOTLAND

The Ryder Cup; An American Course in Scotland; McGinley's Ascension; The Gutting at Gleneagles; A Tale of Two Captains; The Mickelson Rebellion

"Thus it follows that the highest form of warfare is to out-think the enemy . . . the great warriors of old not only won victories, but won them with ease; because their victories were achieved without apparent difficulty, they did not bring them great fame for their wisdom or respect for their courage. Being prepared for all circumstances is what ensures certain victory, for it means you are fighting an enemy who is already beaten."
—SUN TZU, *The Art of War*

The Ryder Cup came to Scotland less than a week after the country's 5.3 million citizens hit the polls to vote on breaking away from the United Kingdom to form an independent country. The UK loyalists took a 55.3 percent majority, but in the apartment windows of Glasgow's beautiful West End—a liberal stronghold, and one of the few cities to vote against the grain—the blue "yes" signs remained, endorsing a bygone dream.

From the city center, hourly shuttles took journalists on the forty-five-mile ride northeast, on the M80 and A9, to the town of Auchterarder and the Centenary Course at Gleneagles. We drove through the lowland swells, past fields the color of dark moss, where stone walls fenced in herds of sheep and cattle. The first No THANKS signs—a polite refusal of the independence movement—appeared as city became countryside, and politics became conservative. The bus labored as we continued north, and soon we were on the very edge of the Scottish Highlands.

We rumbled on through the narrow roads, and for the first time in my limited UK travels, I was experiencing a shade of that old American feeling—the expansive sense that you are *on the road,* heading into the unknown, and that the horizon might be infinite. If England had always felt cramped and claustrophobic to me, this was the wild green yonder I had been missing. The difference was that in contrast to the newness of America, the Scottish frontier came laden with a heavy sense of history.

We drove past the town of Stirling, where William Wallace won his great victory against the English. As the road twisted and climbed toward Gleneagles, we left the motorway and passed through the village of Braco, where cobblestone footbridges spanned lazy creeks, and the main street held small shops and linked cottage homes with gabled roofs. Aside from the satellite dishes poking out from second-floor windows, I felt that a place like this might have looked the same five hundred years ago.

The PGA Centenary Course, on the other hand, has barely been open two decades. In the shadow of the palatial Gleneagles hotel—a massive work of Georgian architecture, made of blaxter sandstone and rough-casted brick—it stands as an opulent fraud. First there's the name, "Centenary," which signifies a one hundredth anniversary and sounds very prestigious. The problem is that when the course opened in 1993, neither Gleneagles nor the PGA of Great Britain and Ireland had attained the century mark. In fact, it was originally called "The Monarch's Course," and only renamed to Centenary in 2001 to honor the PGA anniversary—a bit of a cheat, if you ask me.

There's also the problem of the course's style, which the Gleneagles website makes a valiant effort at tying into the country's long history: "The Gleneagles courses, although not by the sea, resemble the older links golf courses in Scotland in that they are built on sand and gravel."

That's a little like saying my golf game resembles Rory's in the sense that we both use metal clubs. In truth, Gleneagles looks far more like an American course than anything you'd see on linksland. Which doesn't detract from its beauty—framed by farmland and hills that fade from a robust hunter green to clover to dark olive to fallow brown, the rolling valleys would make a pretty postcard. Pershire County is also "Big Tree Country," and pines, beech, oak, yews, and larch lend a certain ancient stature to the scene. There's absolutely nothing wrong with the Centenary, except that it doesn't feel like British golf, and for a competition that travels to Europe only once every four years, there's something just a little *off* about a course that departs so completely from tradition.

So why hold the Cup at Gleneagles, when there are slews of legendary links tracks all over Scotland that would gladly do the job? The answer, as *ESPN*'s Bob Harig reported that week, was money. The European Tour operates the Ryder Cup when it's away from America, and because they're not as financially robust as the PGA Tour, and have to subsidize their own events in the face of less generous sponsors, they milk their marquee event for every penny. *Golfweek* reported that the difference in the European Tour's annual profit between the home Ryder Cup year in 2010 and the non-Cup year in 2011 was over sixteen million pounds—a £14 million profit in '10, and a £2.2 million loss in '11.

The Ryder Cup is how the European Tour survives. Aside from the fee the course pays them, the hosts also have to commit to hosting and providing the purse for a Tour event for a term of around fifteen years following the Cup. All the expenses involved in preparing the course fall on the club, while the profits from gate sales and concessions and merchandise go to the European Tour. It costs a pretty penny, and since the European Tour depends on the revenue for its survival, they will inevitably sell the event to the highest bidder, regardless of history or prestige.

Hence, Gleneagles.

· · ·

The first Ryder Cup was held in 1927, in Massachusetts, and a team from the United States that included Walter Hagen and Gene Sarazen defeated a Great Britain squad by a score of 9.5-2.5. The teams alternated victories for the next six years, at which point the U.S. went on a run of dominance from 1935 to 1983 that produced twenty victories in twenty-two events. The unbroken dynasty made the whole thing a bit of a bore—nobody cared, which is why the PGA Tour never fought very hard to wrench the event from the PGA of America's grasp when the two organizations split.

Things began to change in 1979, when, in an attempt to make the Cup more competitive, the Great Britain & Ireland team was expanded to include all of Europe. The next two events produced two more routs, but in 1983, a European team led by Nick Faldo, Seve Ballesteros, and Bernhard Langer came within a point of doing what no European or British team had ever done—winning on American soil. On Sunday, with two matches remaining on the course, the score was tied at 13-apiece, and Lanny Wadkins played hero by hitting a pinpoint wedge on the 18th to halve his match against José Maria Cañizares. Tom Watson beat Langer in the final match, and the U.S. survived—barely.

It was a shock to the system, and the shock got worse in 1985, when the Europeans broke the long drought and won easily in England. Two years later in Ohio, the Europeans, led by Ballesteros and José Maria Olazabal, jumped out to such a huge two-day lead that even a late Sunday surge by the Americans couldn't close the deficit. For the first time in sixty years of matches, the Europeans had won on American soil.

And just like that, the Ryder Cup turned from an unremarkable exhibition to one of the most tense, exciting weekends in golf. The Europeans shifted the paradigm entirely, and before long the Americans got a taste of their own medicine, losing over and over across the decades. Coming into Gleneagles in 2014, the Euros had nabbed seven victories in the last nine tries, dating back to 1995.[16] Only a miracle comeback at Brookline in '99, and the Valhalla blowout in '08, gave the

---

[16] The September 11 attacks delayed the 2001 Ryder Cup, and now it's held on even years.

U.S. any victories at all, and it had been twenty-one years since they last won on European soil, in 1993, with a younger Tom Watson as captain.

That was the record of success inherited by Paul McGinley. Unlike the Colin Montgomeries of the world, McGinley didn't *look* particularly imposing. His face made you think of a chipmunk's, and his speech had the high, flat, Northern Irish pitch that lacked the poetry native to the south. When he smiled, his teeth loomed large and his eyes popped open, and he had an earnest manner that erased any sense of mystery or power.

But McGinley was smart. He traveled with the players for two full years, scouting his team and envisioning the perfect partnerships. It became clear that it would take something truly shocking to catch this man off guard, but before showing up at Gleneagles, none of us understood the scope of what McGinley had built. What really surprised us, as the details came out, were the obsessive organizational and psychological preparations, all geared toward building a hive mind and creating an atmosphere of relentlessly positive energy. McGinley had considered *everything*.

He spoke all week about a "template" that had been carried out on European Ryder Cup teams dating back to Sam Torrance's win in the 2002 event. (It was no coincidence that Torrance was one of McGinley's vice captains this year.) Early in the week, I joked about the template with colleagues, and most considered it metaphysical hokum. Before long, we'd eat our words.

McGinley's template is notable not for the profundity of its themes—which are as simple as avoiding complacency, having fun, and attacking in waves—but for the comprehensive nature of his setup.

He tailored every aspect of team life to serve the philosophy. This included motivational speeches. On Tuesday night, the players gathered to hear Sir Alex Ferguson, the legendary Manchester United manager who made a career of winning soccer matches at home as a heavy favorite—just as the Europeans would have to do in 2014. McGinley didn't shy away from the "favorite" tag. He felt it was something the team should embrace, and Ferguson's appearance was meant to solidify that mind-set.

This thematic consistency extended to motivational videos, and even to the images that adorned the walls of the team room.

"One particular one comes to mind is right outside our team room," McGinley said on Saturday. "It's a huge big one, probably two meters by three meters. And it's a picture of a European rock in the middle of a raging storm in the ocean. The message underneath is:

'We will be the rock when the storm arrives.'"

McGinley would have prepared obsessively regardless of the situation—it's in his nature—but the urgency was heightened by the fact that the Americans had a deeper motivation. The European comeback at Medinah was an absolutely devastating blow to the Americans, especially after how well Davis Love III had captained his team. While the 10-6 Sunday deficit the Euros overcame was the same as the '99 American victory in Brookline, Massachusetts, this reversal had happened on enemy soil, in front of a hostile crowd. There could be no debate—it was the worst meltdown in Ryder Cup history, and they wanted revenge.

The question on everybody's mind was what sort of captain Tom Watson would make. If the debacle with the captain's picks was an inauspicious beginning, it certainly wasn't a lethal one. In the Monday press conferences, his words indicated that perhaps the same leadership style would carry over into the actual competition, for better or worse.

"I think the captain, he's a person who inspires the team," he said on Monday. "You start off with decisions you think are good for winning points, and they will change. In the heat of the battle, in the heat of the contest."

On the surface, Watson's answer was unremarkable. It was impossible to know at the time that in "the heat of the battle," Watson would isolate himself and make gut decisions that didn't reflect the best interests of the team, or even take their opinions into account. He was not afraid to change his mind at the last moment and obey his instincts, as he had by choosing Webb Simpson, even if they deviated from a set plan. In fact, it almost seemed as though he romanticized the idea—a great leader, he believed, operates as a self-assured maverick. He is a unilateral decision-maker whose motives can't be questioned—bold, decisive, and a little bit secretive. The people below him may be puzzled by the occasional unorthodox decision, but it always worked out because of his razor-sharp intuition. It was a very American idea.

Here was the mind-set that had made him so effective as a player—the total self-belief that brooked no doubt. McGinley, on the other hand, lacked that pedigree, and in the face of his own insecurities, he had planned and planned and planned, connecting with his players when necessary, in order to formulate a comprehensive battle strategy that could be adjusted on the fly when adversity struck. Watson saw no need for this level of involvement. He was the gunslinger and the alpha male, and his moral authority would prevail. That attitude had led him to eight major titles and a brilliant career. Why wouldn't it work in Scotland?

"I said it the very first day I became captain, I don't see myself as a maverick," McGinley said, demonstrating the contrast between the two men. "I see myself as a guy who has been very lucky to ride shotgun on a lot of success, both as a player and vice captain. I've learned a lot from the captains I've played under and been vice captain. This is not a time for me or Europe to have a maverick captain."

———————

"There's nothing quite like the team atmosphere. There's nothing quite like playing for each other in a game which is innately very individual. The game is selfish and we look out for ourselves week-in and week-out, and it's individual achievement, and you live and die by your own achievement. When you come this week and play for each other and play for another 11 teammates, and the bonds that you develop this week, the kind of openness that everyone kind of has . . . We'll do anything for each other this week. It's a very, very special thing to be involved in."

—Graeme McDowell, on Tuesday

The buildup to Friday proved less dramatic than previous Ryder Cups. The only *real* shit-stirring moment came courtesy of Phil Mickelson, who launched an attack on Europe's best player at his press conference on Wednesday.

"Not only are we able to play together," he said, after a question on team chemistry, "we also don't litigate against each other. And that's a real plus, I feel, heading into this week."

Laughter greeted his comment, which was a clear shot at the ongoing lawsuit between Rory McIlroy and Graeme McDowell. The Northern Irish players responded with silence, at least in public, but Ian Poulter wrote in his memoir *No Limits* that Rory found Phil that night at a private ceremony for the players, and hit back with a quip of his own: "At least *I'm* not wanted by the FBI."

Otherwise, chivalry prevailed. The night before the Ryder Cup began, McGinley made a final speech to his players: He knew he had never been on their level, and he trusted them completely. The players left feeling confident and bright, ready for what the morning would bring.

In the cavernous media room at six fifteen a.m. Friday morning, surrounded by empty chairs and a few sleepy journalists, I heard a low rumbling from outside. It sounded like the drone of a distant army, far but monstrous, and it grew louder by the minute. Finally, I could make out a single word, repeated over and over with a chilling, rhythmic insistence:

"EU-ROPE! EU-ROPE! EU-ROPE!"

The European hordes had already arrived—massing on the first tee, chanting, singing, and driving up the energy. In golf, there is nothing like a European Ryder Cup crowd. I had watched a few hundred of them make more noise than tens of thousands of Americans at Medinah, and now they were on their home turf. The soccer tradition overseas differentiates them from their American counterparts—they are organized, they sing, and they're not hampered by self-consciousness. It's a mob mentality—primal, and a bit frightening—and there's simply nothing like it in the States.

The players warmed up on the range in their winter hats, and just after seven, they made their way to the first tee. In the stadium setting, the rowdy voices cascaded down from three sides. The songs came one after another, led by a group of fans in Scottish sweaters sitting just behind the tee. A few brave American fans attempted to start a "U-S-A" chant—the only one they knew—and were quickly shouted down. They went quiet, having learned their lesson, and the Brits quickly launched into a taunting song, a tribute to the U.S. effort at Medinah: "Ten to six, and you still don't win!"

They *did* cheer for Tom Watson, though—a tremendous honor, considering their allegiances. He waved back to them, and may have even received a louder cheer than McGinley, who arrived three minutes later. To the right of the hole, a few yards up the fairway, the Sky Sports team held court in a large TV studio with glass windows. Inside, Colin Montgomerie and Darren Clarke, who had each failed to usurp McGinley as captain, were already on the attack, describing his pairings as a "surprise" and "strange."

Friday morning meant the first four-ball session—all four golfers playing their own ball, and the best individual score on each hole wins—and McGinley sent Henrik Stenson and Justin Rose out to lead the charge. The two had spoken at the BMW Championship in Colorado a few weeks earlier, and mutually decided they would like to play together. Stenson relayed the message to McGinley, who liked this idea even better than his own—unlike Ian Poulter, Rose's traditional partner, both were in top form.

Watson countered with the team of Webb Simpson and Bubba Watson, and Simpson lined up to hit the first drive of the Ryder Cup. You had to wonder if this was some kind of statement—not only had Watson gone with his gut in picking Simpson, but he was going to put him on the front lines against Europe's best. If he was trying to send a message, it worked—Simpson popped his first drive straight into the air. It had to be one of the worst opening shots in Ryder Cup history, and it sent a crystal clear message that the U.S. was well and truly screwed.

Bubba stepped up next, waving the crowd into hysterics, encouraging them to cheer *while* he swung his big pink driver. With the fans in full roar, he launched his drive, and basked in the attention.

This would be the American duo's best moment of the day. Rose and Stenson played steady golf, and that was more than they needed. Put simply, Webb Simpson was a disaster. By the ninth hole, the announcers on the BBC radio stream were roasting him alive, and Bubba wasn't much better. Neither one made a single birdie in the first fourteen holes, and Rose and Stenson cruised to an easy 5&4 victory for the first point of the Ryder Cup. Tom Watson's first two big decisions had backfired in a big way—he wouldn't play Simpson again until the Sunday singles session.

In the second match, Rickie Fowler and Jimmy Walker fell 3-down quickly to Bjorn and Kaymer, but managed to slowly crawl their way back. They still found themselves 2-down on the 16th hole, but Walker stepped up, hitting birdies there and on the 18th to force a halved match.

The bright spot for the Americans came in the third match of the day, when Patrick Reed and Jordan Spieth teamed up against Stephen Gallacher and Europe's Ryder Cup star, Ian Poulter. From the start, things weren't quite right with the Euros. Poulter missed a short par putt on the first hole—a shocking sight—and Reed and Spieth took a 1-up lead. They maintained that edge until the sixth hole, and then turned on the gas. It was the old ham-and-egg act—when Spieth struggled, Reed excelled, and vice versa. They alternated birdies, shouted encouragement to each other, and harnessed every bit of momentum.

The match quickly turned into a surprising rout. Poulter could get nothing going, and Gallacher was stumbling badly in front of the home crowd—for one reason or another, the moment was too big, and his Ryder Cup debut took on the shape of a nightmare. When Reed, looking like Babyface Nelson in his pinstripe pants, sunk another birdie putt on 11, the Americans had rocketed to a 6-up lead with just seven holes to play. From there, it was just a matter of time—the match ended on the 14th hole in a 5&4 victory.

Poulter had struggled all season, and everyone in the American locker room had wanted first crack at him—he was what they called a "big scalp." Spieth and Reed, as Ryder Cup rookies, were excited to have the first chance, and they took advantage with the kind of energy and verve the Americans had been lacking for two decades. It seemed like a foregone conclusion that they'd play again in the afternoon.

In the final match of the morning, the dynamic Medinah duo of Phil and Keegan took on Rory McIlroy and Sergio Garcia. The lead fluctuated back and forth, and a surge by the Europeans on the back nine put them 1-up with three holes to play. For the first time, the Ryder Cup tension had truly arrived—this would be the match that the morning session turned on, and a win by either team would put their side out to an early lead.

The 16th was a par 5, 518 yards, and Bradley hit an excellent approach onto the green. With his teammates looking on from the hillside to the left of the green, he struck the eagle putt and pumped his fist hard, three times, when it fell in the hole. His face at that moment, flushed and anxious, was a picture of Ryder Cup triumph. He slapped five with Reed, Spieth, Bubba, and Webb Simpson, all of whom had come to watch the match. Bradley was in his element—a born teammate at his favorite event.

The teams halved the 17th, leaving them all square heading to 18, another par 5. A series of bad shots relegated the Europeans to par, setting the stage for Mickelson's birdie putt. With Watson watching from behind the green, hands in the pockets of his windbreaker, Mickelson buried the winner. After trailing in three of four matches, the Americans had fought their way back, and held a 2.5-1.5 lead heading into the afternoon.

———————

"I 100 percent assumed we were going back out, and because what Captain Tom said was, 'we'll have our other two afternoon pairings based on how the morning's going.'"

—Jordan Spieth

Au contraire, Mr. Spieth. When he and Reed approached Watson, they were told that they *wouldn't* be playing in the afternoon. Forget the fact that they were young and excited, and had only played fourteen holes—

Watson was going back out with Keegan and Phil, who had played a stressful eighteen-hole match (not to mention Mickelson's arthritis), and the Walker/Fowler combo, who had just gone the distance in a draw.

When he gave the young Americans the news, they acquiesced, for a moment, before Reed changed his mind.

"Well, really, I'm not all right with it," he said.

Once again, Watson had said one thing and done another, and now the players were upset and puzzled. They held their tongues, but their body language told the story—both were angry. Watson hadn't lost the team yet—it was too early, and the Americans were winning— but he was well on his way.

For McGinley, the storm he had prophesied had come early, and now his team needed to fulfill another edict: Attack in waves.

Friday afternoon brought the first "foursomes" session—alternate shot golf, with each team playing one ball per hole. Jamie Donaldson and Lee Westwood led off for the Euros, and they faced Jim Furyk and Matt Kuchar. Rose and Stenson would head out next against Hunter Mahan and Zach Johnson, and Rory and Sergio drew Walker and Fowler in the third match. In the anchor position, Mickelson and Bradley would play their second match against the fresh team of Graeme McDowell and Victor Dubuisson—an ideal match for the Europeans, even if some believed that foursomes was a difficult format for a Ryder Cup rookie's first match. McGinley had addressed his concern by pairing Donaldson and Dubuisson, his rookies, with two hugely successful veterans in Westwood and McDowell.

The drama dissipated early—the European afternoon wave decimated the Americans. Every inch of turf Waton's team had fought for in the morning slipped away in an avalanche of excellence. Donaldson and Westwood made three birdies over the middle of the round, and though Furyk and Kuchar fought back to 1-down with a birdie on 16, a finishing birdie by the Euros on 17 gave them a 2-up win.

Rose and Stenson won their second point of the Cup against Mahan and Johnson in a match of exceptional quality, hitting on five birdies to the Americans' three to win on the 17th hole. In a rare bit of good news, Fowler and Walker played excellent golf against Rory and

Sergio, going 2-up with two holes to play. The Europeans faced a loss on the par-3 17th, when Rory stood over a forty-five-foot putt for birdie. Miss, and the match was likely over. But after a summer full of incredible moments, he delivered one more—the putt rattled home as Walker and Fowler looked on in disbelief and the home crowd roared.

Still, the Americans needed only to halve the final hole to win the match, and their chances looked good when Rory launched his tee shot into the right rough. With a tree in his way, Sergio lined up a 3-wood, knowing he needed to knock it stiff. It was a seemingly impossible shot, but he hit it cleanly from a good lie, and began to pace after the ball as it flew toward the green. "Be good!" he begged, and it was more than good—it was spectacular, coming to rest twenty-five feet from the cup. They two-putted for birdie, won the hole, and stole an incredible half point. It was the second draw for the Fowler/Walker combo, but this one felt more like a loss.

That left McDowell and Dubuisson against the undefeated pairing of Mickelson and Bradley, who had accumulated four wins and zero losses as a team in two Ryder Cups. That streak came to a screeching halt as Dubuisson hit a series of beautiful irons on the front nine to stake the Europeans to a 3-up lead. He even egged the crowd on at one point when the Americans made them putt a four-footer. The hero of the Arizona desert didn't look very much like a rookie at all—he played with a sense of devastating calm. Phil and Keegan fought back valiantly, but the Europeans were relentless, and one last birdie on the 16th sealed a 3&2 win against their fatigued opponents.

The board had been Euro-blue all afternoon, and now the disaster was complete for Watson. The early advantage had disappeared totally, and the Europeans led 5-3 heading into the second day. The media started to hammer the American captain at his press conference, and his answers were defensive and grumpy. He refused to give a concrete explanation as to why he hadn't played Reed and Spieth, and he referred to his gut over and over. He even called Rory's putt on the 17th "Watson-esque" in a shout-out to his glory days—not exactly the self-congratulatory comment the American side wanted to hear at that moment.

He finished by talking about the next morning's pairings, which didn't include Mickelson or Bradley.

"Give them a break in the morning, get their legs back," he said, "and there's a good chance they'll go in the afternoon in some way, shape, or form. They may not go together, but they *will* go in the afternoon."

The Americans came into Saturday with renewed hope, and left staring at a replica of the day before.

In the morning, Rose and Stenson won again in the best match of the Cup, setting a record by going -12 as a team through sixteen holes. Bubba Watson and Matt Kuchar played excellent golf alongside them, but in one stretch, Rose and Stenson birdied ten straight holes between the 7th and 16th. It was a flat-out blitzkrieg, and there was nothing the Americans could do except go down fighting, which they did, 3&2. Collectively, both teams ended at -21 for the round, another record.

That match would be the only American loss of the morning. Furyk and Mahan blew out Donaldson and Westwood, and the young Americans, Spieth and Reed, came out firing yet again, thumping Bjorn and Kaymer 5&3. In the last match, Ian Poulter holed a huge chip on the 15th hole—his first real contribution in two matches—and made a birdie on 16 to square the match. He and McIlroy split the last two holes with Fowler and Walker, who netted their third half-point in three matches.

Once more, the U.S. had won the morning session 2.5 to 1.5, reducing the overall deficit to 6.5-5.5. And once again, Tom Watson was about to undermine their progress with some breathtakingly poor decision-making.

Graeme McDowell and Victor Dubuisson made up the fourth and final European pairing sent out in Saturday afternoon's alternate shot session, but they were the second team to finish. The partnership was more than six months in the making, and McGinley's vision had already paid dividends on Friday. Now, he was asking them to come through again.

Their opponents on Saturday were Jimmy Walker and Rickie Fowler, who had just finished their third eighteen-hole match in a span of about thirty hours. The Centenary course is a difficult one to walk, with endless hills and long distances between holes. Adding to their burden, each of their matches had been an emotional odyssey, ending with no wins. What's more, Watson put them out last, where they were likely to meet the rested McDowell/Dubuisson duo that played in the same position Friday. Once again, McGinley's anchors had a tired, reeling opponent, fattened for the kill.

Despite his assurances from the day before, Watson sat both Bradley and Mickelson all day Saturday—both morning and afternoon. When he delivered the surprising message that they wouldn't be playing in foursomes, Phil made a desperate appeal to his captain. He even tried a text message plea when the first entreaty failed, but this time, Watson wouldn't be swayed. (Apparently, Webb Simpson is a more compelling texter.)

The Europeans were shocked to see one of America's best teams kept on the bench for an entire day. As Poulter later wrote, the Euros' excitement about their own play was matched by their mystification at Watson's decisions, chief among them this strange slight. The only conclusion they could draw was that there was some serious disagreement going on in the U.S. camp, and that idea gave them strength.

More puzzling still, Watson wouldn't even play Bubba Watson, who had made six birdies that morning. His gut told him instead to go with Fowler and Walker, fresh off fifty-four holes of stressful draws.

Unfortunately, Watson's gut had proved to be a seriously unreliable organ. By the third hole of the match, Jimmy Walker was spent. He hit a shot on that hole that, in McDowell's words, was poor even by amateur standards. The Northern Irishman sensed a deep fatigue in his opponents, and he approached Dubuisson with a simple message: "Let's show these guys how energetic we are. Let's show these guys how *up for this* we are."

Dubuisson heeded the advice, and the blitzkrieg was on. By the ninth hole, they were already 5-up on the Americans, who were wilting in the Scottish afternoon. By the 14th hole, it was over.

In that same session, McGinley led with Lee Westwood and Jamie Donaldson. Like McDowell, McGinley saw Westwood as a strong veteran leader, and someone he could pair with a Ryder Cup rookie. Hence his captain's pick, which left Luke Donald off the team. History was his guide; in previous Cups, Westwood had worked the same magic with rookies like Nicolas Colsaerts and Martin Kaymer.

That rookie this time was Donaldson, who had suffered through his own drama to make the team. The Welsh thirty-eight-year-old had narrowly missed making the Ryder Cup team on points when he failed to get up and down on the 18th hole at the PGA Championship in Valhalla. When he saw McGinley in the caddie room after his round, he was distraught. The captain told Donaldson he wanted him to make the team, but that it would be tough to pick a rookie—he needed to earn his way through an automatic pick. Two days later, they spoke on the phone, and McGinley helped him formulate a plan. Donaldson would go to the Czech Republic to play in the European Tour event and try to earn the twenty thousand dollars it would take to make the team. McGinley advised him to play aggressively and without fear, and Donaldson heeded his words. Not only did he make the twenty thousand; he won the tournament.

Now, Westwood and Donaldson would face Zach Johnson and Matt Kuchar, who hadn't played together in any practice rounds in the days leading up to the competition, and were a combined 0-3 up to that point. The Europeans won on the 17th hole.

"Every credit to Paul for having the confidence to send us out again," said Westwood, referencing their loss in the morning four-ball session. "It was a ballsy move."

"We seem to bring out the best in each other in the foursomes," Donaldson said.

Sergio and Rory, fresh off the dramatic halved match Friday afternoon, united again to beat Furyk and Mahan—neither of whom were having the redemptive Ryder Cup they had imagined—for the third victory of the session.

That left Spieth and Reed, the unlikely American stars, trying to hold off the European onslaught and give the Americans a shadow of a prayer.

There are elements a captain can influence, but never completely control. The Europeans were thirty-two strokes better than the Americans over three days, and while pairings and strategy surely influenced that gap, it's possible that no American captain could have overcome McGinley's preparation and his players' excellence.

Then there are other elements, like luck, which are beyond any influence. Spieth and Reed had been the bright spots for Team USA through two days of struggle, but even their momentum faded as the sun began to set. After leading for most of the back nine, a series of missed putts by Patrick Reed reduced their lead to a single hole with just eighteen to play. The killer blow came on the 16th, when Reed stood over a two-foot par putt that would give the Americans a 1-up edge. The crowd gasped as the ball lipped out, and Reed buckled in disbelief. As he walked up the hill to the 17th tee, he ignored the outstretched hands of his teammates as they tried to encourage him. He was a picture of steaming rage, his fists clenched, anger emanating like smoke from his body. He seemed like he might spiral out of control.

Spieth played hero on the 17th, hitting the tee shot on the par-3 to six feet. Reed never had to putt—the Europeans conceded the hole after a poor tee shot—but he did anyway, sinking the birdie for his own reasons. Watson and McGinley looked on, knowing that if Europe halved the match on the last hole, with the final point of the day at stake, it would create an almost insurmountable 10-6 deficit for the Americans heading into Sunday singles.

Reed and Kaymer hit straight drives, but Spieth and Rose put their second shots into a greenside bunker right of the pin. After Spieth's shot, a strange, half-excited groan could be heard from the stands behind the green. Moments later, on the fairway, American vice captain Andy North stood with both hands on his head, looking on in disbelief—the ball had somehow stopped just below the back lip, on a downhill lie in the sand, blocked from a direct strike by the grass jutting over the bunker. Reed was forced to attack it sideways, landing the ball far from the pin. Kaymer, in a more reasonable position, pitched his shot to within five feet. Spieth's putt missed, and after Rose struck his birdie attempt, he turned to his European teammates and raised his putter in triumph. The putt fell.

The fans erupted, and the Americans watched in shock. Rickie Fowler's caddie had arrived at the scene, fresh off their loss to McDowell and Dubuisson. Soon, Miguel Angel Jimenez rode up the center of the fairway on his cart, waving the European flag like a conquering hero—he brought good news from Sergio and Rory, who had just won their match. But Rose was the real star of the moment—he had secured a crucial half-point as dusk hit Scotland on Saturday night.

After darkness fell, Tom Watson came into the media room and spent the next twenty minutes trying to rationalize his decisions while downplaying his own accountability. In the rare moments when he *seemed* to accept a measure of blame—he admitted that a fourth straight match for Fowler and Walker was perhaps not the best idea—he immediately shifted the focus back to the players, implying that Walker had disappointed them all by succumbing to fatigue. One quote in particular displayed Watson at his deflecting best:

"They got a little tired," Watson said. "And that certainly is something that I thought they could handle, and maybe I regret not understanding that they couldn't handle it."

As Watson used his players for a shield, he seemed, just like the day before, insistent on following his instincts. Most of the players didn't seem to understand the logic behind his decisions because, as they noted later, he was reluctant to bring them into the fold.

"You know, you can question my decisions on that," he said. "That's fine. But I was making—I get back to the point, I made the best decisions I possibly could at the time. I was making the decisions with the help of my vice captains and my guts."

Paul McGinley didn't need to rely on his guts. Each time he sent a wave of players out, he was off the course, in constant communication with his vice captains. He plotted his next moves according to information he had obsessively researched before the Cup, and integrated it with new data from the course. Unlike Watson, he knew his players didn't need a cheerleader, and he had a vice captain for each group in case they did (along with a fifth to stay with the four players who weren't playing and organize their movements). His goal was to stay a half-day ahead of the action, and never to be caught unaware.

As he spoke, I thought again about the "template" I had been mocking earlier in the week. It's a fine way to structure a team, but it takes a man with the energy, intelligence, and personal insight to execute it. McGinley was that man and more, a charismatic CEO who has set a standard that future captains may find very difficult to match.

The legacy of this Ryder Cup, I realized, was how it answered the question of whether a captain at a golf event actually mattered: Yes. Emphatically yes. McGinley's hand was behind each of Europe's triumphs, and Watson's shadow darkened every American failure.

Saturday night, McGinley played motivational videos for his team, one of which showed a series of American highlights. The storm might come again, and he reminded them that twice in the last fifteen years, a Ryder Cup team had come back from a 10-6 deficit—the exact score on the board that very moment. It was his last moment of leadership, and a final call to avoid complacency—the final iceberg for the unsinkable European ship.

After the twelve singles matches go out on Sunday, the influence of the captain ebbs to almost nothing. There is no more strategy—good golf is the be-all and end-all. Unrestrained, the Americans finally played with inspiration, and the scoreboard turned a dangerous shade of red. You could feel the anxiety build in the crowd, and for a moment you could allow yourself to believe that the miracle was palpable. At 2:08 p.m., I looked at the scores and realized that if every match ended at that point, the final score would be 14-14—still enough for the Europeans to retain the cup, but on the verge of tilting to an American lead.

Jordan Spieth had led the charge for the Americans in the number 1 singles spot, racing out to a 3-up lead against Graeme McDowell—

just as he had raced out to a lead against Bubba Watson at the Masters and Martin Kaymer at the Players Championship. McGinley had imagined his fellow Northern Irishman in the leadoff spot for years, even before he was announced as a captain, and for a minute it appeared that this would be the rare decision that didn't work out. But McDowell stemmed the tide, avoiding a disastrous 4-down deficit, and starting on the 10th, he began to fight his way back into the match. After making his birdie there, he marched to the 11th with a renewed ferocity, and the first signs of aggravation had appeared on Spieth's face. The American phenom had been brilliant for the entire Ryder Cup, but now he was isolated against a veteran, and he started to resemble the disheartened, sullen golfer from Augusta and Sawgrass.

On 11, framed by the changing leaves behind him, Spieth missed his birdie and gave an angry, petulant look at the hole. When McDowell dropped his own birdie to cut the lead to 1-up, he pumped both fists—the more he had the crowd, the more Spieth would falter, and the fans roared as if they knew it, too. On 12, Spieth missed a six-footer for birdie, and just that quickly, the match was all square.

With six holes remaining, it was time to see what kind of heart Spieth could muster. As it turned out, not much—he spoke harshly to his caddie, Greller, on 13, and by 16, he was back to the old habit of yelling at himself: "Why can't you hit a fairway to save your *life!*" he shouted, with McDowell in earshot. "Cannot hit *one fairway.*" By then, the Northern Irishman had won two more holes to go 2-up, and McGinley swung by to give him a pat on the back and a few words of encouragement.

On 17, after the tee shots, Rory McIlroy joined them, and the three Northern Irishmen walked side-by-side to the green, old conflicts fading away. Graeme hit his par putt, dropped the club, and celebrated his victory. Spieth could only complain to Andy North, and his words were muted by the European cheers. Another big moment had passed him by.

McIlroy could afford to join his countrymen because he had absolutely trounced Rickie Fowler, making birdie on each of the first six holes to go

5-up out of the gate. The idea of a Rory-Rickie rivalry had become popular that season, but Rory had built an enormous psychological advantage, and you had to wonder: Was it a rivalry at all? Even before the match began, it seemed like a bad pairing for the U.S.—strong as each player was, there could be no question who would win. Rory confirmed that suspicion by killing Rickie's spirit within the first hour, and he coasted to a 5&4 win.

The Spieth turnaround destroyed the Americans—for the miracle to happen, that match *had* to go their way. As long as he held on, things looked hopeful, especially with Patrick Reed fighting doggedly against Henrik Stenson in the second match. From the first tee, the European fans had been after him, with one even shouting, "Have you practiced your putting, Patrick?"—a reference to his big miss on 16 the previous afternoon. As the pressure mounted, so did his intensity. When he holed a birdie putt on the seventh, he turned to the crowd and actually *shush*ed them, putting a finger to his mouth and grinning maniacally.

The fans hated and loved it all at once, and the boos rang down around him. Before the match was even over, the British press had dubbed him "the pantomime villain"—another blow to his ongoing attempt to avoid that pesky v-word. But he backed up the gesture, fighting off Stenson with a birdie on 18 to win 1-up and finish the event as America's leading player with 3.5 points to his name—a continuation of his excellent match play record at Augusta State.

Kuchar, Walker, and Mickelson would also register wins on the day, and Webb Simpson, Zach Johnson, and Hunter Mahan would notch half-points. Nevertheless, by three p.m. hope had faded for the Americans, and it was just a matter of guessing who would strike the fatal blow. It turned out to be Jamie Donaldson, whose wedge into the 15th hole stopped on a dime and came to rest a foot from the hole. On a hill in the fairway, the Americans looked on forlornly, sensing the end. Walking up to the green, Keegan Bradley saw the ball, took off his hat, and set off a wild celebration from the home crowd and the men in blue.

· · ·

That evening, on the wrong end of a 16.5-11.5 blowout, Watson was back in the hot seat, in front of the international press, this time with every member of his team beside him. For a while, it looked as though the press conference would be more or less standard—the rookies loved playing at the Ryder Cup, the veterans were disappointed, and the foursomes sessions, which finished 7-1 in favor of the Euros, made all the difference. Somebody asked Phil Mickelson to put his finger on the difference between this loss and the victory at Valhalla.

Mickelson praised Paul Azinger, and spoke about how his pod system had ensured that all the players were invested in the team's success. Each of them could reasonably expect to know when they would play, and with whom. They had a "real game plan" then. And though he never mentioned Watson by name, the contrast in his words spoke volumes. Sensing blood, we asked for more, and the next two questions represented the most intensely awkward and fascinating moments I've ever witnessed at a golf press conference.

> Q. That felt like a pretty brutal destruction of the leadership that's gone on this week.
> PHIL MICKELSON: Oh, I'm sorry you're taking it that way. I'm just talking about what Paul Azinger did to help us play our best. It's certainly—I don't understand why you would take it that way. You asked me what I thought we should do going forward to bring our best golf out and I go back to when we played our best golf and try to replicate that formula.
> Q. That didn't happen this week?
> PHIL MICKELSON: Uh (pausing) no. No, nobody here was in any decision. So, no.

That parenthetical "(pausing)" doesn't begin to tell the story. In that moment, on Mickelson's face, you could see the big decision play out. Was he really going to lead this public mutiny? Would he violate a longstanding code of silence and air his grievances in front of the media? The seconds ticked by, and he stared out at the room, eyes seeming to widen with each passing moment. Finally, he spoke, and the rebellion was on.

Watson wore a strained smile as Phil Mickelson attacked his captaincy from six seats away. When asked, he took the high road and chalked it up to a difference of opinion, but the room was unbearably tense. Next to Mickelson, Hunter Mahan tried to keep from smiling—a shocked sort of grin, amazed that his teammate had said something so inflammatory in such a public arena—while Keegan Bradley covered his face. Jimmy Walker smiled in disbelief at Furyk, who held up a hand as if to warn him from being too demonstrative in such a heavy moment. It became more awkward from there. When I asked for Furyk's opinion, I inadvertently described the exchange between Phil and Watson as a "back-and-forth." That's when Mickelson interjected again.

"I don't think the premise of your question is very well stated," he said. "I don't think that this *has* been back and forth."

Awful silence reigned as the put-down hung in the air and Watson's smile grew tighter. All eyes turned to Furyk.

"Gee, thanks," he said, breaking some of the tension. He then gave a diplomatic answer, finishing with, "If I could put my finger on it, I would have changed this shit a long time ago."

After that showcase, we waited for the Europeans, and all heads turned when we heard the sound of *neigh*ing coming from the door. It burst open a moment later, what I saw next was truly unforgettable: A visibly drunk Jamie Donaldson rode on Thomas Bjorn's back, slapping his ass and shouting while Bjorn trotted ahead and neighed like a horse.

It didn't exactly surprise me. In the celebration immediately following his win over Bradley, Donaldson had stood in the middle of a crowd of reporters, wearing a Welsh flag like a cape, and chugged an entire bottle of Moët & Chandon champagne. Since that moment, he had not been idle, and his teammates followed suit. They came soon after, each wearing the flags of their home countries around their neck.

Most of them were well on the way to being drunk, and they exchanged quips from across the table.

"They always put baby in a corner," said Westwood, eyeing his seat at the very edge. Soon after, Donaldson made an animal noise into the microphone. As Rory spoke—he had become the first player since Tom Watson in 1977 to win two majors and a Ryder Cup in the same year—Westwood popped another bottle of champagne, and Sergio yelled, "Save me a sip!" from across the table. When the questions reached Victor Dubuission, he modestly said, "I think I played well." Rory jumped to his defense.

"You *did* play very well," he said. "No one thinks you played well; you *did* play well."

Earlier that week, Nick Faldo had made waves by saying on live TV that Sergio Garcia had been "useless" at the 2008 Ryder Cup in Valhalla, which he had captained in a losing effort, and Sergio brought the house down when the topic of McGinley's captaincy came up. Westwood mentioned all the previous captains McGinley had taken advice from, including Olazabal and Langer, and Sergio couldn't resist interrupting.

"Do you think he talked to Faldo?" he asked, and that broke the last bit of decorum as his teammates cheered and the press roared. It devolved from there—at one point, the players all sang a song mocking McGinley for wearing a vest—and soon they stumbled out into the night.

———

As we prepared to leave Scotland, I thought back to the end of the day's singles matches, and two vignettes that had struck me as particularly poignant.

The first involved Patrick Reed, who had shushed the fans on the way to beating Stenson. His match over, he looked on with the rest of the Americans, upset when Donaldson hit his Cup-winning wedge. But as the group made their way to the 18th green, something strange happened—he found that the Scots loved him for what he had done, for his audacity and his spirit and, most of all, his success. They shouted his name as he walked past, and reached out to touch him. Slowly, Reed's face turned from a set frown to a reluctant smile, and then to something like real joy. He slapped their hands and acknowledged their cries. Even though he was on a losing team, he strode like a hero for a moment—the pantomime villain turned out to be the favorite American.

Moments later, after Victor Dubuisson and Zach Johnson halved their match to bring the day to a close, I watched the massive European huddle form on the green. The champagne bottles were out, spraying everywhere, and in the middle of it all, I spotted the shy smile of Dubuisson. The other players—especially Rory—brought him in close, hugging him and drenching him with the bubbling alcohol. And even though it was in Victor's nature to be suspicious, to resist this kind of thing, I watched him lower his defenses, if only for a moment. Through the flashbulbs and the shouting, you could see the moment when he surrendered, and the happiness overcame him.

Paul McGinley enjoyed the moment quietly, away from the celebrations. He was destined never to get the credit he deserved, but that was okay— it's not why he wanted the job. To everyone else, this might have looked like an easy European victory, but he knew exactly how hard it had been. Momentum is a capricious force, but each time the Americans threatened to steal the Cup away, he was there, with two years of brilliant preparation at his back—resolved in the face of the barrage.

He had seen it from the start: The storm came, the rock survived.

OCTOBER
AND
EVERYTHING
AFTER

27

SEASONS CHANGE

B ut the Ryder Cup ended, the year turned, and the storms kept coming. Tiger Woods was the rock that golf had invented for itself, and the rock couldn't stand. The currents of change had been set loose, and now they were sweeping over the sport, eroding the monuments that had once seemed so permanent.

Tiger finally returned in February. He commanded the same fear and respect from his peers, but now their deference was based on reputation alone. It didn't last long—his short game abandoned him, and he suffered through a humiliating 82 at the Phoenix Open. The next week, at Torrey Pines, he withdrew during the opening round with another back injury, and announced an "indefinite break."

While his game continued to diminish, his presence loomed larger than ever. The idea that his career might come to a premature end sent waves of anxiety through golf's establishment. What happens to a golden age when the foundation crumbles?

The only answer is change. At home and abroad, the list of winners early in the 2015 season told a story of youth—Rory McIlroy, Martin Kaymer, Jason Day, Patrick Reed, Dustin Johnson, Matt Every, Brooks Koepka. The new wave gathered energy with each victory, and the biggest coup of all came at Augusta National in April. There, Jordan Spieth demonstrated the same extraordinary skill from 2014, but none of the self-defeating impulses. In four dreamlike days, the great white hope matched Tiger's tournament record of -18, fought off Phil Mickelson and Justin Rose on a nervous Sunday, and became a Masters champion at age twenty-one.

With Spieth and McIlroy in the vanguard, the rising stars braced for the brave new world. Professional golf was *their* sport now, even if that sport was still in thrall to the icon who changed it forever.

Spring became summer, and they fought on against the myth and the memory—shadows that would linger long after the man himself had walked away.

ACKNOWLEDGMENTS

For a book like this, it's inevitable that some of those who have helped me along the way will not be thrilled with the finished product. To those, I can only say that I did my best to be honest.

Before anyone else, I have to thank Chris Reimer, Joel Schuchmann, and Tom Alter at the PGA Tour for helping me gain the access I needed to make this book possible, starting at the McGladrey Classic in November 2013—and in Chris's case, much earlier. They continued to be helpful throughout the year, as did so many others with the Tour, including Doug Milne, John Bush, Mark Stevens, Laura Neal, D. J. Piehowski, Sean Martin, Kelly Barnes, and Royce Thompson, as well as Ty Votaw and commissioner Tim Finchem. I hope the minor criticisms I've sprinkled in here or there won't overshadow the immense amount of respect and admiration I have for the Tour, and the efficiency, talent, and professionalism of those who work there.

Elsewhere among golf's governing bodies, I owe a tremendous debt to Una Jones at the PGA of America for all her help over the past two years. I'd also like to thank Julius Mason at the PGA of America, Pete Kowalski and Mary Rung at the USGA, Mike Woodcock and Mary Flanagan at the R&A, Frances Jennings and Gordon Simpson of the European Tour, and Patrick Stiegman and Chad Millman at ESPN, all of whom were extremely helpful in facilitating my access to these wonderful events.

This book would not have been remotely possible without the help of my friends and colleagues in the golf media, a group of whip-smart professionals who are funny and wise, and whom I hold in very high esteem as the best of the best. I have to recognize Doug Ferguson, a pro's pro who was generous with his time and advice far beyond what I deserved, even in my clueless early days. I think of Stephanie Wei the same way, and without her help and knowledge and encouragement, I'd probably still be wandering the driving ranges like a timid wall-flower. John Feinstein belongs with them—he could not have been kinder to someone attempting to accomplish a shadow of what he had done two decades earlier with *A Good Walk Spoiled.* The talented Jim Moriarty helped me both in real life and with his terrific writing, and the same could be said for Alan Shipnuck, Michael Bamberger, and Tim Rosaforte. Jason Sobel was a great resource all year as I learned about life on Tour, and a chance meeting with him at the Edinburgh airport saved me from making a very stupid mistake. Adam Schupak was a good friend and, having written *Dean Beman: Golf's Driving Force,* a solid source of knowledge about the early days of the PGA Tour. Michael Collins, who was always ready with a joke or a good story or a game of Ping-Pong, agreed to speak with me about his fasci-nating life for the book, and would barely let me buy him dinner in return. There are countless others who helped me in large and small ways throughout the year, including Jim McCabe, Alex Miceli, Ben Everill, Bob Harig, Farrell Evans, Stephen Hennessey, Ashley Mayo, Will Gray, Ron Green, Steve Eubanks, François Scimeca, Benjamin Cadiou, Sean Zak, Igor Guryashkin, Bryan Curtis, Tommy Roy, Jeff Szklinski, Teddy Greenstein, Kevin Ryan, Bernie McGuire, Steve El-ling, Curt Sampson, Brian Keogh, Stephen Schramm, Dan Weiderer, Bret Strelow, and Brian Wacker.

Great thanks go to Sam Weinman and everyone at *Golf Digest* for letting me write for them in 2014—it was a huge honor, and on top of that, it was a pleasure to work with you. My gratitude also goes out to Dan Fierman and Bill Simmons at *Grantland,* along with Tommy Craggs, Tim Marchman, and Kevin Draper at *Deadspin.*

To all the golfers and caddies who spoke to me over the course of the year, as well as their families, I offer my thanks. To the agents who helped me along the way, especially David Winkle and Matt Judy, who gave me insight into their side of Tour life, I'm in your debt.

To the college coaches who gave freely of their time—a list that includes Frank Darby, John Fields, Mike McGraw, Josh Gregory, Buddy Alexander, and especially Chris Haack, whose Georgia alums played so well this year that I had to call him over and over, and was pleased to find him just as helpful and interesting each time—you, too, have my thanks.

There are many others to whom I owe a debt of gratitude.

To Stephen Hamblin at the AJGA, a great storyteller with an excellent memory, for sharing his perceptive and hilarious tales of the world's greatest golfers in their younger days.

To Steven Bunn at the College Golf Fellowship, for speaking frankly with me about his faith and his work with Christian golfers.

To Roxane Coche, who was instrumental in helping me translate interviews and articles from French to English, and did so with great speed at a time of urgency.

To Wade Liles and Johnny Thompson, for their insight into the strange and wonderful world of equipment.

To Amy Wilson, president of the PGA Tour Wives Association, for speaking to me about the life of a spouse in the traveling circus.

To Josh Jackson at *Paste Magazine,* for his incredible understanding and patience as the process unfolded. To Nick Purdy and family, for the shelter.

To Byrd Leavell, literary agent extraordinaire who should get all the credit for envisioning this book and manufacturing its existence from thin air. To Mark Tavani at Random House, who nurtured it from a rough draft into the final form you see today, and to Lucy Warburton and Melissa Smith at Aurum Press in the UK for similar services. Will Bennett's late editing services were similarly indispensable.

To everyone who read passages of the book and gave me great advice along the way, including Will Leitch, Andrew Westney, Spike Friedman, Adam Sarson, Chris Solomon, Kyle Porter, Chris Chaney, Robert Stewart, and Spike Friedman, this belongs to you as well.

To David Allen Sibley, for his wonderful guide to trees, and to all the course superintendents and others who helped me identify flora and fauna that I couldn't discern on my own, including Alistair Beggs, Todd Raisch, Roger Meier, Mike Giuffre, Missy Maxson, David Hallford, Don Thornburgh, and Scott Walker.

To Wes Anderson and Stuart Murdoch.

To my wonderful family, including my parents, Tom Ryan and Kathy Fisch; my stepfather, Tom Fisch; my grandparents Harold and Joyce Ryan and Tom and Clare Cowell, Tommy and Carol, Maureen and Jim; and my three siblings—Thomas, Keegan, and Shannon—I thank you for the support.

To my best friend, Brandon Gardner, for a lifetime of inspiration.

Finally, to my wife, Emily—without you, there's nothing.